Mississippi Laws, Lemuel O. Bridewell

The Mississippi Justice of the Peace

A manual of the laws relating to the courts of justices of the peace, and the practice

therein, in the state of Mississippi

Mississippi Laws, Lemuel O. Bridewell

The Mississippi Justice of the Peace
A manual of the laws relating to the courts of justices of the peace, and the practice therein, in the state of Mississippi

ISBN/EAN: 9783337220723

Printed in Europe, USA, Canada, Australia, Japan

Cover: Foto ©Suzi / pixelio.de

More available books at **www.hansebooks.com**

THE MISSISSIPPI

JUSTICE OF THE PEACE.

A MANUAL

OF THE LAWS RELATING TO THE COURTS OF JUSTICES OF THE PEACE, AND
THE PRACTICE THEREIN, IN THE STATE OF MISSISSIPPI, WITH
FORMS AND PRECEDENTS, APPLICABLE TO EVERY CASE,
INTERSPERSED WITH EXPLANATORY NOTES.

TO WHICH IS ADDED CERTAIN

FORMS OF GENERAL USE AMONG BUSINESS MEN

A DIRECTORY OF THE COURTS, ETC., ETC.

BY

L. O. BRIDEWELL,

ATTORNEY AT LAW.

JACKSON, MISS:
CLARION STEAM PRINTING ESTABLISHMENT.

1877.

PREFACE.

The design of the following work is to impart to novices, gentlemen *not* "learned in the law above their fellows," the routine of business required of them, when they assume the responsible and now important office of Justice of the Peace.

Under the present Constitution of the State of Mississippi, the jurisdiction of the Justices of the Peace in civil suits is raised to one hundred and fifty dollars, and in all criminal matters, their jurisdiction is concurrent with that of the Circuit Courts in all cases where the punishment prescribed by the laws does not extend beyond a fine and imprisonment in the county jail. The office is certainly one of great dignity and responsibility, but the persons who frequently rush in glibly to assume and execute these important duties, have little idea of the responsibility and loose sight entirely of the dignity. The main design of the author and compiler of these pages is, to be of some assistance to the unlearned Justice of the Peace by placing the law relating to his jurisdiction before him in compact form, with forms and precedents, covering almost, if not every case, which can come before him.

The extended jurisdiction of the Justice and the power granted by the laws, has made the practice in this Court of importance to attorneys; and the want of an uniform and sufficiently reliable set of forms and precedents, caused in the first instance the preparing of many of those found in this book. They have been used for some years and are now offered in a permanent form, in the hope that, although the profession may not need them, the many Justices of the Peace in this State, unused as they generally are to the forms of law, will find ready at hand everything required of them in properly fulfilling the important duties of their offices.

The law, as found in the Code of 1871 and in the Pamphlet Acts since, so far as it concerns this jurisdiction, and is distinctly applicable to the Justice of the Peace or the practice in his court, is first given in full, arranged under appropriate heads. That from the Code paragraphed and indicated by sections as therein, and that from the later Acts, digested with reference to the page of the pamphlet. The index gives the section of the Code, or the page of the Acts, and the page on which found in this book. The forms are numbered, with the section of the Code applicable indicated, while the index gives both the number and the page. Notes are added to many forms for the guidance and information of the Justice, endeavoring thereby to explain the law and use of the form, so that none, however ignorant of the law generally, can go far wrong. Many sections of the Code are carefully indexed which are not printed in the book; especially is this the case in felonies, wherein the Justice can only sit as a court of inquiry, and in some few other instances, where the matter is not general in this court.

The author assumes nothing to himself for the liquid legality or the trenchant technicality of his forms, always being more anxious to convey the meaning in such terms as could not be mistaken (especially by the Constable), than to risk loss by fancy attempts at Chittyology or finely rounded periods. The very words of the statute, however, will be found to have been faithfully followed in every instance.

The book is, therefore, presented to the Justice of the Peace, with some confidence, as one which will most materialy lighten his labor, facilitate his business, and probably be the means of his avoiding many mistakes—in fact, herein he will find, set out fully, explicitly and in order his whole official duty.

It is presented to the profession as a convenient compendium or compilation of all the law of our State governing in this jurisdiction, with all necessary forms forms ready prepared to suit any case.

It is especially presented to the citizen and to my friends of the Grange, as a book which points out in small compass and at trifling expense about all the law (and the form of its application) they need to meet the largest amount of litigation of the present day in Mississippi; and one that has been so prepared that the law being plainly seen and its application made easier, litigation may be avoided. The object of good laws, is that litigation may be lessened, therefore they should be in every household and read of all.

Trusting that the book may prove useful not only to him who litigates, but to him who strives to avoid litigation, it goes out on its errand.

L. O. BRIDEWELL.

Beauregard. Miss., January 1st, 1877.

TABLE OF CONTENTS.

Table of Contents.

Table of Contents

FORMS.

AS A CIVIL COURT.

§ 1298.] No. 1.—OATH OF OFFICE.

I, A. B., do solemnly swear (or affirm) that I will faithfully support and true allegiance bear the Constitution of the United States, and the State of Mississippi, and obey the laws thereof: that I will well and truly perform and faithfully discharge the duties of the office upon which I am about to enter, and pay over all moneys collected by me, or which may come into my hands by virtue of my office, to the party or parties entitled to receive the same. So help me God!

§ 1298.] No. 2.—OFFICIAL BOND.

State of Mississippi, } ss.
Copiah County. }

Know all men by these presents, that we, A. B., C. D. and E. F., are held and firmly bound unto the State of Mississippi, in the penal sum of two thousand dollars, for which payment well and truly to be made, we bind ourselves, our heirs and legal representatives, jointly and severally, firmly by these presents; signed with our names and sealed with our seals, this ...... day of ......, A. D. 18....

Whereas, the above bound A. B. was duly elected to the office of Justice of the Peace, in said county, on the ...... day of ....; A. D. 18......, for the term of ...... years from the ......day of ......, A. D. 18......: Now, therefore the condition of this obligation is such that if the said A. B. shall well and truly perform the duties of his office, and pay over all moneys collected by him, or which may come into his hands by virtue of his said office, to the party or parties entitled to receive the same, then the above obligation to be void, otherwise to remain in full force and virtue.

.... [SEAL.]
.... [SEAL.]
.... [SEAL.]

No. 3.—OPEN ACCOUNT AND NOTE.

NOTE.—All open accounts, when filed for suit, under our law must be sworn to. See No. 5. If account is contested, defendant must file, before suit, counter affidavit. See No. 6.

COPIAH COUNTY, MISS., Jan. 1, 1876.

John Smith,   To Wm. Jones,   Dr.

1873.

June 6.—To scraping cotton fifteen days, at 75c. per day......$11 25

" 1 day's plowing.. 1 00

                             $12 25

$50.   COPIAH COUNTY, MISS., Jan. 1, 1875.

On or before the first day of June next, 1875, I promise to pay to C. D., or bearer, the sum of fifty dollars, value received, with interest at ten per cent. from date until paid.   A. B.

---

§1305.]   No. 4.—SUMMONS.

THE STATE OF MISSISSIPPI,

To the Sheriff or any Constable of Copiah county, Greeting:

We command you that you summon John Smith to be and appear before the undersigned, Justice of the Peace for said county, at my office therein, on Saturday, the 10th day of January, 1876, then and there to answer the complaint of Wm. Jones, on open account, for twelve dollars and twenty-five cents (or on promissory note for $50) and have you then there this writ.

Witness my hand and seal this 3d day of January, 1876.

JOHN DOE, J. P. [SEAL.]

---

§ 782.]   No. 5.—AFFIDAVIT TO OPEN ACCOUNT.

STATE OF MISSISSIPPI,} ss.
Copiah County. }

This day personally appeared before the undersigned, an acting Justice of the Peace for said county, William Jones, who being by me duly sworn, says the account hereto attached for twelve dollars and twenty-five cents is correct as stated, and that the same is due from the party against whom it is charged, and no part of it has been paid (except what is credited, if any).

WILLIAM JONES.

Sworn to and subscribed this 1st day of January, 1876.

JOHN DOE, J. P. [SEAL.]

---

§782.]
No. 6.—COUNTER AFFIDAVIT OF DEFENDANT.

STATE OF MISSISSIPPI, } ss.
Copiah County. }

This day personally appeared before the undersigned, an acting Justice of the Peace for said county, John Smith, who, being by me duly sworn, says that the account of William Jones, for twelve dollars and twenty-five cents, charged against this affiant, and filed with John Doe, Justice of the Peace for said county, is not correct as stated; in this, that the item for scraping cotton should be charged at 60c. per day, and for only twelve days, and that the item for ploughing should be charged at 75c. per day.

JOHN SMITH.

Sworn to and subscribed this 8th day of January, 1876.

JOHN DOE, J. P. [SEAL.]

NOTE.—In case the defendant has a legal set-off to plaintiff's account, or note, he must file it with the Justice on or before the day of trial, and make affidavit of its correctness. See Secs. 601 to 605, and 1306.

---

§§ 701, 2, 3 and 4.]

No. 7.—RETURN OF OFFICER ON SUMMONS.

"Executed the within process this day upon the defendant in person, by handing to him a true copy thereof.

"THOMAS CATCH, Constable.

"Jan. 4th, 1876."

"Executed this process this day, by handing to the wife of the defendant (*or, to A. B., of the age of sixteen years, being one of defendant's family*), at his usual place of abode in said county, such person being then and there willing to receive the same, a true copy of this process, said defendant not being found in my county, after diligent search. THOMAS CATCH, Constable.

"Jan. 4th, 1876."

"The within named defendant, John Smith, after diligent search, cannot be found in my county, nor could I find, after diligent search, any person of his family, of the age of sixteen years, at his usual place of abode, who was willing to receive a copy of this process. I therefore executed the same this day, by posting a true copy thereof on the door of the defendant's usual place of abode, in my county. THOMAS CATCH, Constable.

"Jan. 4th, 1876."

---

§§ 1313, 761.   No. 8.—SUBPŒNA.

THE STATE OF MISSISSIPPI,

To the Sheriff or any Constable of Copiah county. Greeting:

We command you to summon A. B., C. D., E. F., G. H., I. K. and L. M., if to be found in your county, to be and personally appear before the undersigned Justice of the Peace for said county, at his office therein, on the 10th day of January, 1876, to testify on the part of the plaintiff in a certain cause pending before said Justice, wherein William Jones is plaintiff and John Smith is defendant, and this they shall not omit, under penalty of ten dollars. Herein fail not, and have then there this writ.

JOHN DOE, J. P. [SEAL.]

Issued Jan. 4th, 1876.

NOTE.—In taxing costs, only one witness to each fact can be paid. If any witness, duly summoned, however, fails to appear, the Justice at once enters up against him judgment *nisi* on his docket, as follows:

§ 1313.]
No. 9.—JUDGMENT NISI AGAINST WITNESS.

STATE OF MISSISSIPPI, COPIAH COUNTY, }
vs.
E. F.

· To the Sheriff or any Constable of said county, Greeting:

On this 10th day of January, 1876, E. F., being called out on his subpœna to appear and testify before the undersigned Justice, on the part of the plaintiff, in a certain cause wherein William Jones was plaintiff and Jno. Smith defendant, failed to appear in pursuance of said subpœna; and said court being satisfied that said witness was duly summoned, judgment for the sum of ten dollars is entered against him; You are, therefore, hereby commanded to summon the said E. F. to appear before the undersigned, at his office in said county, on the 24th day of January, 1876, then and there to show cause, if any he has or can, why said judgment shall not be made final. Have you then there this writ.

JOHN DOE, J. P. [SEAL.]

§ 1313.]   No. 10.—ATTACHMENT FOR WITNESS.

STATE OF MISSISSIPPI,
   To the sheriff or any constable of Copiah county, Greeting:

We command you that you attach the person of E. F., and him safely keep, so that you have him before the undersigned Justice of the Peace for said county, at his office therein, on the 24th day of January, 1876, then and there to testify, on the part of the plaintiff, in a certain case pending before said Justice, wherein William Jones is plaintiff and John Smith is defendant. And have you then there this writ.

Witness my hand and seal, this 10th day of January, 1876.

JOHN DOE, J. P. [SEAL.]

§ 1314.]
No. 11.—NOTICE TO TAKE DEPOSITION.

To John Smith, defendant in the case of William Jones against John Smith, pending before John Doe, a Justice of the Peace for Copiah county, Mississippi:

You will take this as notice, that, in pursuance of a commission to me directed by said John Doe, Justice as aforesaid, I, the undersigned Justice of the Peace for the county of Lincoln, in said State, will, on Saturday, the first day of February, 1876, at the hour of eleven o'clock A. M., at my office, in Brookhaven, in said county of Lincoln, proceed to take the deposition of A. B., a witness on the part of the plaintiff, in said case, which, when taken, will be read in evidence on the trial thereof. You can attend and cross examine, if you see proper.

Witness my hand and seal, January 15th, 1876.

E. L. BOWEN. J. P. [SEAL.]

---

§1314.] No. 12—COMMISSION TO TAKE DEPOSITION.

THE STATE OF MISSISSIPPI,

To E. L. Bowen, a Justice of the Peace for Lincoln county, said State, Greeting:

It has been suggested by William Jones, plaintiff in the case of William Jones against John Smith, now pending before me, John Doe, a Justice of the Peace for Copiah county, in said State, that A. B., a witness on the part of the plaintiff, resides without the limits of my county, and is in the said county of Lincoln: These are, therefore, to require you to take the deposition of said witness, if to be found in your county, first giving five days' notice to the defendant, or his attorney of record, of the time and place of taking the same; which deposition, when so taken, you will at once return to the undersigned, Justice as aforesaid, certified under your hand and seal, to be read in evidence on the trial of said case.

Witness my hand and seal this 24th January, 1876.

JOHN DOE, J. P. [SEAL.]

NOTE.—When the Justice receives this commission, he will, after ascertaining that the witness is in his county, at once mail a copy of the foregoing notice to the defendant or to his attorney of record. This commission must be attached to the deposition and returned, as well as the original notice.

---

§§ 1314, 794 to 799.

No. 13—DEPOSITION.

The deposition of A. B., a witness on the part of the plaintiff, in the case of William Jones against John Smith, now pending in the county of Copiah, Mississippi:

In pursuance of the foregoing and annexed commission to me directed, I. E. L. Bowen, a Justice of the Peace for the county of Lincoln, Mississippi, after having given to the defendant, John Smith, five days' notice of the time and place of taking this deposition (as per original notice herewith returned), caused the said witness to come before me at my office, in the town of Brookhaven, in said county of Lincoln, at the hour of eleven o'clock A. M., on the first day of February, 1876, which said witness, after having been duly sworn, testified as follows:

(*Here write down fully what the witness says. After which, conclude as follows:*)

All of which foregoing testimony I caused to be reduced to writing, and said witness, after having the same read over to him, signed the same in my presence, at the place and on the day mentioned in the caption; all of which I hereby certify under my hand and seal, this 1st day of February, 1876.

E. L. BOWEN, J. P. [SEAL.]

No. 14.—OATH OF WITNESS.

You do solemnly swear that the testimony you shall give in the case now in hearing, wherein .... is plaintiff and............. is defendant, shall be the truth, the whole truth, and nothing but the truth. So help you God.

---

§§ 1326, 1328.

No. 15—VENIRE FACIAS, OR SUMMONING THE JURY.

THE STATE OF MISSISSIPPI,

To the sheriff or any constable of Copiah county, Greeting:

You are hereby commanded to summon twelve good and lawful men of your county to be and appear before the undersigned Justice of the Peace for said county, at his office therein, instanter (*or, on the 10th day of July*, 1876), then and there to serve as jurors, in certain cases pending before said Justice. And have you then there this writ, with the names of the jurors summoned endorsed thereon.

Witness my hand and seal this ...... day of ...., 1876.

JOHN DOE, J. P. [SEAL.]

NOTE.—If any juror fails to appear, he is subject to the same fine, and like proceedings can be had, as against defaulting witness. See Form No. 9, and Sec. 1329.

No. 16.—AFFIDAVIT FOR CONTINUANCE.

STATE of MISSISSIPPI,}   In Justices' Court
    Copiah County,   }   for District No. 2, Jan. 10th, 1876.

Personally appeared before the undersigned, an acting Justice of the Peace for said county, John Smith, defendant in the case of William Jones vs. John Smith, now pending before the undersigned, and made oath that, owing to the absence of A. B., a material witness in his behalf, who has heretofore been subpœnaed in this case, he cannot safely go to trial; that he expects to prove by said witness that at the time of hiring said Jones by affiant, he was present, and it was distinctly understood that affiant would only give 60 cents per day for scraping cotton, and 75 cents per day for ploughing; that affiant expects to have said witness or his deposition before the court at the next term thereof; that this affidavit for continuance is not made for delay, nor to vex or harrass the plaintiff, and that affiant knows of no other person by whom he can prove the same facts; therefore affiant asks a continuance of said case until the next term of said court.   JOHN SMITH.

Sworn to and subscribed this .... day of ...., 1876.

               JOHN DOE, J. P. [SEAL.]

§537.]   No. 17.—SUBPŒNA DUCES TECUM.

STATE OF MISSISSIPPI,

     To the sheriff or any constable of Copiah county, Greeting:

We command you to summon A. B., if to be found in your county, that all business and excuses being laid aside, he be and personally appear before the undersigned, a Justice of the Peace for said county, at his office therein, on the 10th day of January, 1876, at 11 o'clock A. M., to give evidence in a certain case now pending before said Justice, between William Jones, plaintiff, and John Smith, defendant, on the part of the plaintiff; and further to command the said A. B. to bring with him, and then and there produce in evidence, a certain agreement in writing (*or, as the case may be, describing the paper or book*); and herein fail not under the penalty of the law. Have you then there this writ.

Witness my hand and seal this 5th day of January, 1876.

               JOHN DOE, J. P. [SEAL.]

No. 18.—OATH TO ANSWER QUESTIONS.

You do solemnly swear that you will true and correct answers make to such questions as shall be propounded to you by or under the direction of the court. So help you God.

No. 19.—OATH OF JURORS.

You and each of you do solemnly swear that you will well and truly try the issue joined between William Jones, plaintiff, and John Smith, defendant, and a true verdict give, according to the evidence. So help you God.

No. 20.—VERDICT OF A JURY.

We, the jury, find for the plaintiff, and assess his damages at .... dollars.

No. 21.—JUDGMENT ON JURY VERDICT.

This day come the parties in proper person (*or, by their attorneys, or both*), and the writ of *venire facias* heretofore issued being duly returned, come the following good and lawful men of Copiah county, to-wit: A. B., C. D., E. F., G. H., J. K., L. M., N. O., P. Q., R. S., T. U., V. W. and I. X., who, being accepted by the parties, were duly sworn and impaneled; and after hearing the testimony of the witnesses, and all the evidence in the case, retired in charge of a constable, and after consideration, returned into court the following verdict: We, the jury, find, for the plaintiff, and assess his damages at .... dollars. It is therefore considered by the court that the said plaintiff do recover of and from the said defendant, as well the sum of .... dollars, with legal interest from this date till paid, as also his costs and charges by him in this behalf expended, to be taxed, and that execution issue herein.

Jan. 24th, 1876. JOHN DOE, J. P. [SEAL.]

No. 22.—JUDGMENT OF JUSTICE.

This day come the parties in their own proper person, and the testimony of the witnesses and all the evidence in the case, and the argument of counsel, having been heard and duly considered, it is thereupon ordered and adjudged by the court that the plaintiff, William Jones, do have and recover of and from the defendant John Smith, the sum of .... dollars, with legal interest from this date, as also his costs and charges by him in this behalf expended, to be taxed, and that execution issue herein.

Jan. 24th, 1876. JOHN DOE, J. P. [SEAL.]

NOTE.—If there be a jury, the Justice must enter and sign the judgment in his docket at once; if the case be tried without jury, the justice may take a few days for consideration. But the better practice is to decide and enter judgment at once. To make the judgment a lien upon all the property of the defendant, it must be enrolled in the Circuit Clerk's office at once.

---

§ 1332.] ### No. 23.—AFFIDAVIT FOR APPEAL.

STATE OF MISSISSIPPI,⎫ ss.
Copiah County. ⎭

This day personally came and appeared before the undersigned Justice of the Peace for said county, John Smith, and prays an appeal from the judgment of said Justice, in the case of William Jones against John Smith, rendered by said Justice on the 24th day of January, 1876; and said Smith makes further oath that he prays said appeal not for purposes of delay, nor to vex and harrass or oppress his adversary, but that justice may be done in the premises. JOHN SMITH.

Sworn to and subscribed this 29th day of Jan., 1876.

JOHN DOE, J. P. [SEAL.]

---

§ 1332.] ### No. 24—APPEAL BOND.

STATE OF MISSISSIPPI,⎫ ss.
Copiah County. ⎭

Know all men by these presents, that we, John Smith, Samuel Tucker and Luke Rankin, are held and firmly bound unto William Jones in the penal sum of two hundred dollars, for payment of which well and truly to be made, we bind ourselves, our heirs and legal representatives, jointly and severally, firmly by these presents.

signed with our names and sealed with our seals, this 29th day of January, 1876.

The condition of, the above obligation is such, that, whereas, the above-named William Jones, on the 24th day of January, 1876, before John Doe, a Justice of the Peace for said county, recovered a judgment against the above bound John Smith, for the sum of .... dollars, with interest and costs ; and, whereas, the said Smith hath prayed an appeal to the next term of the Circuit Court for said county, and made the affidavit pursuant to the statute in this behalf ; Now, therefore, if the said John Smith shall well and truly pay and satisfy such judgment as the Circuit Court aforesaid may render against him in the premises, then this obligation to be void, otherwise to remain in full force and effect.

JOHN SMITH, [SEAL.]
SAMUEL TUCKER, [SEAL.]
LUKE RANKIN, [SEAL.]

I approve this bond and security. Jan. 29th, 1876.

JOHN DOE, J. P.

NOTE.—The foregoing affidavit and bond must be given within five days, or the party will have to resort to petition and writ of certiorari to open up his case—which see below. I desire especially to call the attention of Justices to the fact that too many defective bonds are taken. Straw bonds are now and have been in this State the bane of litigation. Be rigid in your examination of all sureties. The form of their justification is given below, which must be annexed to or endorsed on all bonds.

No. 25.—AFFIDAVIT OF JUSTIFICATION OF SURETIES ON BOND.

STATE OF MISSISSIPPI,
  Copiah County. } ss.

Personally appeared before me, the undersigned, a Justice of the Peace for said county, Samuel Tucker and Luke Rankin, who, being by me duly sworn, on their several oaths depose and say, that they are worth over and above their legal exemptions and liabilities, in visible property subject to execution, the sum of two hundred dollars : that is to say, the said Tucker one hundred dollars, and the said Luke Rankin one hundred dollars.

SAMUEL TUCKER,
LUKE RANKIN.

Sworn to and subscribed this 29th day of January, 1876.

JOHN DOE, J. P. [SEAL]

---

§ 1336.]   No. 26.—PETITION FOR CERTIORARI.

To the Hon. Uriah Millsaps, Judge of the 5th Judicial District of the State of Mississippi:

Your petitioner, John Smith, would respectfully show unto your Honor, that on or about the 10th day of January, 1876, one William

Jones commenced a suit against your petitioner, before John Doe, a Justice of the Peace for the county of Copiah and said State, on an open account for the sum of .... dollars; that afterwards, on or about the 29th day of January, 1876, the said Justice rendered judgment against your petitioner for .... dollars, &c., &c.

Your petitioner, therefore, alleges that injustice has been done him on the trial of said cause, the judgment being illegal, unjust and oppressive ; wherefore your petitioner prays your Honor for the writ of certiorari and supersedeas, directed to said John Doe, Justice of the Peace as aforesaid, returnable at the next regular term of the Circuit Court of said county, in order that justice may be done in the premises. And as in duty bound will ever pray, &c.

JOHN SMITH.

Sworn to and subscribed this 15th day of February, before me.
[SEAL.]   JAS. L. ARD, Clerk.

NOTE—On this petition the Judge endorses his fiat to the Clerk, who issues the writ, upon the petitioner's entering into bond in the sum of two hundred dollars, conditioned as in appeal bond. See Sec. 1334, on appeals.

---

§ 1333.]   No. 27.—TRANSCRIPT OF RECORD.

In making up the record of the proceedings in any case before a Justice on an appeal or in pursuance of a writ of certiorari, commence with

1st, The account, note or other writing upon which suit was begun.

2d, The summons or writ.

3d, Subpœnas.

4th. Affidavits for continuance, motions, &c., &c.

5th. Any other papers filed in the case, as summons for garnishees and their answers, &c., &c.

6th. A copy of your entries on the docket, and the judgment of the court in full; let your judgment be against defendant before against garnishees.

7th. A copy of all costs accrued in your court, including this transcript.

8th. The original affidavit for appeal and the bond.

9th. Your certificate.

Attach these papers together in the order stated, by eyelets or thread. Be particular in this, as a correct return of record is indicative of a justice worthy to hold his place. I give the certificate below:

I hereby certify that the foregoing and attached papers are all the original papers in the case of A. B. vs. C. D., tried before me, and that the above and foregoing is a full, true and perfect record of the proceedings had in said case, including the judgment rendered by me, with the original affidavit for appeal and bond.

Dated the .... day of ...., 1876.

JOHN DOE, J. P. [SEAL.]

No. 28.—AFFIDAVIT FOR GARNISHMENT.

STATE OF MISSISSIPPI, } ss.
Copiah County. }

Personally appeared before me, the undersigned Justice of the Peace for said county, William Jones, plaintiff in a judgment rendered by the undersigned, on the 24th day of January, 1876, against John Smith, for .... dollars, with interest and costs, and made oath that he does not believe that said defendant has in his possession visible property, upon which a levy can be made, sufficient to satisfy said judgment, and said plaintiff suggests that Henry Washington and Solomon Bruce, of said county, are indebted to said defendant, or have effects of said defendant in their hands or possession. WILLIAM JONES.

Sworn to and subscribed this 29th day of January, 1876.

JOHN DOE, J. P. [SEAL.]

No. 29—WRIT OF GARNISHMENT.

STATE OF MISSISSIPPI, } ss.
Copiah County. }

To the sheriff or any constable of said county, Greeting:

Whereas, William Jones, plaintiff in a certain judgment rendered by the undersigned Justice of the Peace for said county, against John Smith, for .... dollars, with interest and costs, hath suggested that Henry Washington and Solomon Bruce are indebted to the said defendant in said judgment, or have effects of said defendant in their possession, and hath also made oath that he does not believe that said defendant hath in his possession visible property, upon which a levy can be made, sufficient to satisfy said judgment:

We, therefore, command you to summon the said Henry Washington and Solomon Bruce to be and appear before the undersigned Justice, at his office in said county, on the 24th day of January, 1876, to answer on oath, whether they are indebted to the said defendant, and in what sum, and what effects of said defendant they have in their hands or possession, or had at the time of serving this summons; and whether they know of any other persons indebted to said defendant, or who may have any of the effects of said defendant in their hands or possession; and have you then there this writ.

Witness my hand and seal this 10th day of Jan., 1876.

JOHN DOE, J. P. [SEAL.]

NOTE.—The best mode for answer of garnishee is in writing, and in the nature of an affidavit. The following form will do, altering to suit the facts, in all cases and in all courts. It can be forwarded to the Justice.

§ 874.]   No. 30.—ANSWER OF GARNISHEE.

STATE OF MISSISSIPPI, }   In Justice Doe's Court,
Copiah County.   } ss.   Dist. No. 2. January Term, 1876.

This day personally appeared Henry Washington, summoned as garnishee in the case of William Jones against John Smith, who, being by me, the undersigned, a Justice of the Peace for said county, duly sworn, on his oath, answering says: That at the date of the service of the summons of garnishment herein, he was not indebted in any sum to John Smith, the defendant aforesaid (*or, that he was indebted, and the sum*); that he has in his possession one bay mare, the property of said defendant, which was delivered to him for the purpose of making a crop on defendant's land for the year 1876; that he knows of no one indebted to the said defendant in any sum; that he has been informed and believes that Solomon Bruce, now resident on the farm of defendant, has in his possession a certain black mule, which is the property of the defendant; that he knows of no other persons who have in their hands or possession any property or effects of the defendant; and having herein fully answered, prays to be discharged, with his reasonable costs.

HENRY WASHINGTON.

Sworn to and subscribed before me, this 24th day of January, 1876.   JOHN DOE, J. P. [SEAL.]

NOTE.—This or any answer of garnishee can be by the plaintiff traversed, by statement in writing or by affidavit, setting up the facts wherein the garnishee has evaded the summons. An issue can be made up, a jury summoned, and the correctness of the answer of garnishee at once decided. See Sec. 1445.

———

§§ 1317, 838.]   No. 31.—EXECUTION.

STATE OF MISSISSIPPI,
To the sheriff or any constable of Copiah county:

We command you that of the goods and chattels, lands and tenements of John Smith you cause to be made the sum of fifteen dollars and .... cents, which sum was lately, before the undersigned, one of the Justices of the Peace for said county, recovered against said John Smith, with interest on said sum at the rate of six per cent. per annum from the .... day of .... 1876, until paid; also, ... dollars and .... cents, costs of suit; and that you have the said sums of money before the undersigned, at his office in said county, to render to the plaintiff in said suit, on the .... day of ...., 1876. Have you then there this writ, with your proceedings thereon endorsed.

Witness my hand and seal this .... day of ...., 1876.

JOHN DOE, J. P. [SEAL.|

(BILL OF COSTS.—*See Fees of Officers.*)

JUSTICE'S FEES.

Issuing summons or warrant.................Summoning ..... garnishees...................
Entering suit................................Taking examination of ...... garnishees..

Issuing ...... subpœnas ...... names.........Issuing execution.......... ....
Affidavit to account..........................Issuing vendi. exponas........................
Counter-affidavit........................ ....Affidavit and appeal bond.......................
Venire facias ....Transcript of record and certificate......
Swearing jury...........................Issuing attachment, bond and affidavit..
Swearing ...... witnesses...........................Issuing replevin, bond and affidavit;......
Affidavit for continuance..........................Iss'ng distress war'nt, bond and " ......
Commission to take deposition.............Recognizance ....
Proceedings to judgment.............Mittimus..........................
Entering judgment...........................Jury fee...........................
Affidavit for garnishee...........................witnesses ....

CONSTABLE'S FEES.

Serving summons or warrant..............Summoning inquest.......................
Serving an attachment..............Conveying criminal to jail, ...miles....
Summoning ...... witnesses.. ....Attending trial......................
Executing mittimus...........................Summoning jury.......................
Taking ...... bonds.......................... ....Jury trial, attendance......... ....
Levying execution and making money...Summoning ...... garnishees..................

A true bill of costs.   JOHN DOE, J. P. [SEAL.]

No. 32.—RETURN ON EXECUTION.

Executed the within writ by levying on and taking into my possession one bay mare, the property of the defendant, John Smith. This ...... day of ...., 1876.

THOMAS CATCH. Constable.

No property of the defendant, John Smith, found in my county. Jan. 29th, 1876.   THOMAS CATCH, Constable.

---

§§ 844, 845.]   No. 33.—BOND OF INDEMNITY.

STATE OF MISSISSIPPI, COPIAH COUNTY. } ss.

Know all men by these presents, that we, William Jones and George Shannon are held and firmly bound unto Thomas Catch, his heirs, assigns or legal representatives, in the penal sum of seventy-five dollars (*the penalty should be sufficient to cover value of property seized, and a margin for costs*), for which payment well and truly to be made, we bind ourselves and legal representatives, jointly and severally, firmly by these presents. Signed with our names and sealed with our seals, this ...... day of January, 1876.

The condition of the above obligation is such, that, whereas, an execution issued by John Doe, a Justice of the Peace for said county, on the ...... day of ...., 1876, in favor of William Jones and against John Smith, for .... dollars, judgment, with interest and costs, was, by Thomas Catch, a constable of said county, levied upon a certain bay mare, valued at fifty dollars, as the property of said defendant; but doubts having arisen whether the right to said bay mare is in the said defendant or not (*or, the said mare is liable to seizure by reason of exemption*); Now, therefore, if the above bound obligors will indemnify and save harmless the said Thomas Catch against all damages which he may sustain in consequence of the seizure or sale of the mare aforesaid, on which said execution has been levied, and, moreover, will pay and satisfy to any person claiming title to said mare (*or, the defendant*) all damages which said person (*or defendant*) may sustain in consequence of such seizure or sale, then this obligation to be void, otherwise to remain in full force and effect.

WILLIAM JONES,   [SEAL.]
GEORGE SHANNON, [SEAL.]

---

§ 851.]
No. 34.—FRAUDULENT CONVEYANCE—AFFIDAVIT.

STATE OF MISSISSIPPI, COPIAH COUNTY. } ss.

This day, William Jones, plaintiff in a judgment rendered by the undersigned Justice of the Peace for said county, on the .... day of January, 1876, against John Smith for .... dollars and interest and costs, came before the undersigned and being by me duly sworn, deposes and says, that the execution issued by virtue of the judgment aforesaid has been returned *nulla bona*; that he has reasons to believe, and does believe, and hereby suggests to the court that the said defendant hath property, but hath fraudulently conveyed the same for the purpose of defrauding his creditors, or to avoid the payment of the execution in this behalf, to-wit: three yoke of oxen and one wagon, now in the hands and possession of John Crawford in said county (*or any other property whatever that may have been disposed of or conveyed in fraud of his creditors.*)

WILLIAM JONES.

Sworn to and subscribed, this ...... day of ......, 1876.

JOHN DOE, J. P. [SEAL.]

---

§ 851.]
No. 35.—FRAUDULENT CONVEYANCE—SUMMONS.

STATE OF MISSISSIPPI.

To the Sheriff or any Constable of Copiah County. Greeting:

Whereas, William Jones, plaintiff in a certain judgment rendered by the undersigned Justice of the Peace for said county, against John Smith for ...... dollars, with interest and costs, the execution issued by virtue of said judgment being returned *nulla bona*, hath suggested that John Crawford, of said county, hath in his hands and possession certain property of the defendant, to-wit: three yoke of oxen and one wagon, and hath also made oath that he has reasons to believe, and does verily believe, that said defendant hath fraudulently conveyed the same to said Crawford for the purpose of defrauding his creditors, or to avoid the payment of the execution in this behalf:

Therefore, we command you to summon the said John Crawford to be and personally appear before the Justice of the Peace aforesaid, at his office in said county, on the ...... day of .... 1876, then and there to answer unto the complaint and affidavit of said plaintiff, that issue may be made up in this behalf: and have you then there this writ.

Witness my hand and seal, this ...... day of ...., 1876.

JOHN DOE, J. P. [SEAL.]

NOTE.—For manner of stay of execution before a Justice of the Peace, see Secs. 1343 and 1344.

NOTE.—Lands and tenements can be levied on by execution and attachment issuing by a Justice of the Peace, but the officer making the levy must endorse the fact upon the execution and return it to the Justice: after which the full duty of the Justice in the premises is set forth in Sec. 1319, which see.

---

§ 1338, 858.]

No. 36.—CLAIMANT'S ISSUE—AFFIDAVIT.

STATE OF MISSISSIPPI, COPIAH COUNTY. } ss.

Personally appeared before the undersigned Justice of the Peace for said county, William Ragland, who made oath that a certain bay mare, levied on as the property of John Smith by Thomas Catch, a constable of said county, by virtue of an execution issued by the Justice aforesaid, on the ...... day of January, 1876, and returnable before said Justice on the ...... day of January, 1876, upon a judgment rendered by said Justice against said John Smith and in favor of William Jones, for the sum of ...... dollars, with legal interest from date of rendition till paid, as also costs of suit, is not the property of said defendant, but the property of this affiant, the right and title being in him; that this claim is not propounded for fraudulent purposes or delay, and that affiant desires to replevy said property and have his claim thereto tried.

WILLIAM RAGLAND.

Sworn to and subscribed this ...... day of ...., 1876.

JOHN DOE, J. P. [SEAL.]

NOTE.—It is a matter of option with the claimant to give bond, and replevy and take the property seized or not. If he does not do so, the property will remain with the officer, to abide the issue; and the execution is stayed until its determination, for an amount equal to the value of the property in issue. See Secs. 1338, 859.

---

§ 858.]

No. 37.—CLAIMANT'S BOND.

STATE OF MISSISSIPPI, COPIAH COUNTY. } ss.

Know all men by these presents, that we, William Ragland and Henry Whitfield, are held and firmly bound unto William Jones, his heirs, assigns or legal representatives, in the penal sum of one hundred dollars (*double value of property*), for which payment well and truly to be made, we bind ourselves, our heirs and legal representatives, jointly and severally, firmly by these presents. Signed

with our names and sealed with our seals, this ...... day of ....,
1876.

The condition of the above obligation is such, that whereas, a
judgment was rendered by John Doe, a Justice of the Peace for
said county, on the ...... day of ...., 1876, against John Smith
and in favor of William Jones, for the sum of .... dollars, with
interest and costs, upon which execution duly issued and was levied
upon a certain bay mare, as the property of said defendant, valued
at fifty dollars; and, whereas, William Ragland has made oath that
said mare is his property, and not the property of said defendant,
and that he desires to replevy said property and have his said claim
tried; Now, therefore, if the said William Ragland shall prosecute
his said claim with effect, or in case he fail therein, shall pay to the
said William Jones, plaintiff in execution, all such damages as may
be awarded against him, in case his claim shall not be sustained, or
shall appear to have been made for fraudulent purposes or for delay,
and will well and truly deliver the said mare to the sheriff or other
officer, if the claim thereto should be determined against him, the
said claimant, then this obligation to be void, otherwise to remain
in full force and effect.

WILLIAM RAGLAND, [SEAL.]
HENRY WHITFIELD, [SEAL.]

---

§861.]
No. 38.—JUDGMENT IN CLAIMANT'S ISSUE.

William Jones, plaintiff in execution,⎫
        vs.   ⎬ February 10th, 1876.
William Ragland, claimant,   ⎪
Henry Whitfield, surety.   ⎭

Whereas, execution was issued by John Doe, a Justice of the Peace
for said county, on the ...... day of January, 1876, upon a judgment
rendered by said Justice on the ...... day of January, 1876, in favor
of William Jones against John Smith, for the sum of .... dollars,
with legal interest and costs, which execution was levied upon a
certain bay mare as the property of John Smith, the defendant in
said judgment, which said mare is now here claimed by the said
William Ragland as his property; and the said Ragland having
heretofore made oath and given bond in pursuance of the statute
in this behalf, it is ordered by the court that an issue for the trial
of the right of property, between the said plaintiff in execution and
the said William Ragland, be made up.   Whereupon a writ of venire
facias was issued, returnable instanter, which being duly returned,
come the following good and lawful men of said county, to-wit:
(*here insert the twelve names*) who being accepted by the parties to
the issue, were sworn and impaneled.   The said jury, after hearing
the testimony and all the evidence in the case, and the argument of
counsel, upon their oath do say: We, the jury, find for the plaintiff
in execution, and assess the value of the mare at fifty dollars; and
we further find that the claim of the defendant, William Ragland,

was made for fraudulent purposes, or for purposes of delay. It is therefore ordered, considered and adjudged by the court, that the said plaintiff in execution do have and recover of and from the said defendant, claimant as aforesaid, and of and from his aforesaid surety, the bay mare levied on as aforesaid, if to be had, and if not to be had, then to have and recover against the said defendant and his said surety the sum of fifty dollars, the value of said mare as assessed by the jury aforesaid, with legal interest from this date till paid, and also ten per centum damages on the assessed value aforesaid, with his costs in this behalf expended; for all which execution may issue.

February ......, 1876.   JOHN DOE, J. P. [SEAL.]

NOTE.—If the jury find for the claimant, the court shall discharge him from his bond, and give judgment of costs against the plaintiff in execution, if he was present and contesting. The execution in the above judgment is the same as in detinue, which see *post.*

§§ 281, 1345.]   No. 39.—CONSTABLE'S SALE.

William Jones   Execution for $.........
      vs.   Costs for....... ....
John Smith.

                                        $.........

By virtue of the above stated execution to me directed by John Doe, a Justice of the Peace for the county of Copiah and State of Mississippi, I will, on Saturday, the 25th day of February, 1876, at the depot in the town of Beauregard, within legal hours, expose to sale, at public outcry, to the highest bidder for cash, all the right, interest and claim the defendant, John Smith, has in and to a certain bay mare, which has been levied on as the property of the said defendant, and will be sold to satisfy the above stated case and all costs.   THOMAS CATCH, Constable.

February 10th, 1876.

§ 1346.]   No. 40.—VENDITIONI EXPONAS.

STATE OF MISSISSIPPI,
    To the sheriff or any constable of Copiah county:

We command you, that you expose to sale those goods and chattels, lands and tenements, of ...., to-wit: (*here insert what is to be sold*), which, according to our command, you have taken, and which remain in your hands unsold, as you have certified to the undersigned, to satisfy the sum of .... dollars and .... cents, with interest at the rate of ...... per cent. per annum from the .... day of ...., 187..., until paid, as also the sum of .... dollars and .... cents, for costs and charges by said plaintiff in this behalf expended, whereof .... defendant herein has been convicted, as appears to us of record; and that you have said moneys before the undersigned to render to the plaintiff herein, on the .... day

2

of ...., 1876, for his damages and costs aforesaid; and have
you then there this writ with your proceedings thereon endorsed.

Witness my hand and seal this .... day of ...., 1876.

............, J. P. [SEAL.]

BILL OF COSTS.—(*See Fees of Officers.*)

JUSTICE'S FEES.

Issuing summons or warrant................Summons for ...... garnishees...............
Entering suit......................................Taking examination of ...... garnishees.
Issuing ...... subpœnas, ... names,........Issuing execution......................................
Affidavit to account..........................Issuing vendi exponas.......................
Counter-affidavit...............................Affidavit and appeal bond...................
Venire fac as....................................Transcript of record and certificate......
Swearing jury...................................Issuing attachment, bond and affidavit..
Swearing ...... witnesses....................Issuing replevin, bond and affidavit......
Affidavit for continuance....................Iss'ng distress war'nt, bond and affidavit.
Commission to take deposition..............Recognizance......................................
Proceedings to judgment....................Mittimus..
Entering judgment.............................Jury fee..
Affidavit for garnishees...................... Witnesses..

CONSTABLE'S FEES.

Serving summons or warrant................Summoning Inquest..............................
Serving an attachment......................Conveying criminal to jail ...... miles....
Summoning ...... witnesses.................Attending trial......................................
Executing mittimus...........................Summoning jury....................................
Taking ...... bonds............................Jury trial, attendance..........................
Levying execution and making money..Summoning ...... garnishees...................

A true bill of costs. ...., J. P. [SEAL.]

NOTE.—All executions or vendis must contain, written on the side or attached thereto, a bill of all costs in the case under the hand of the Justice,
and the sheriff or constable shall not execute unless the costs are so distinctly set down. A copy of the same must be handed the party against
whom the execution is levied. See, on this point, pamphlet Acts of 1875.
page 137, and especially Secs. 3, 7, 8 and 9. Every Justice should have printed
with full spaces, blank executions, as well as every other form that can be
so used.

----

§§ 1421, 1422.]

No. 41.—REMEDY BY ATTACHMENT—AFFIDAVIT.

STATE OF MISSISSIPPI, COPIAH COUNTY } ss.

Personally appeared before the undersigned Justice of the Peace
for said county, Mark Loving, who, being by me duly sworn, makes
oath that Edward Reynolds is justly indebted to him in the sum of
sixty-five dollars, on open account, and that although often requested so to do, the said Reynolds wholly neglects and refuses to
pay; and that the said Reynolds "has property or rights in action
which he conceals and unjustly refuses to apply to the payment of
his debts" (*or any other of the several grounds set forth in section
1420, connected together, when more than one of them is used, by the
conjunction* AND, *and not by* OR. *As many of them can be used as
will truthfully apply*): wherefore affiant prays the issuance of the

writ of attachment against the estate of said Reynolds, real and personal.   MARK LOVING.

Sworn to and subscribed this 10th day of May, 1876.

B. F. JONES, J. P. [SEAL.]

---

§ 1425.]   No. 42.—BOND.

STATE OF MISSISSIPPI, COPIAH COUNTY. } ss.

Know all men by these presents, that we, Mark Loving, principal, and Andrew Lusk, surety, are held and firmly bound unto Edward Reynolds in the sum of one hundred and thirty dollars, for which payment well and truly to be made we bind ourselves, our heirs and legal representatives, jointly and severally, firmly by these presents. Signed with our hands and sealed with our seals, this 10th day of May, 1876.

The condition of the above obligation is such that, whereas, the above bound Mark Loving hath, on the day of the date hereof, prayed an attachment, at the suit of himself, against the estate of the above named Edward Reynolds, for the sum of sixty-five dollars, and hath obtained the same, returnable before B. F. Jones, a Justice of the Peace in and for said county, at his office therein, on the 20th day of May, 1876;

Now if the said plaintiff in said attachment shall well and truly pay and satisfy to the said defendant all such damages as he shall sustain, by reason of the wrongful suing out of the said attachment, and shall pay all costs which may be awarded against the said plaintiff in said suit, then the above obligation to be void, otherwise to remain in full force and effect.   MARK LOVING, [SEAL.]

A. LUSK,   [SEAL.]

I approve the foregoing bond, this 10th day of May, 1876.

B. F. JONES, J. P. [SEAL.]

---

§ 1429.]   No. 43.—THE WRIT.

THE STATE OF MISSISSIPPI,

To the sheriff or any constable of Copiah county, Greeting:

Whereas, Mark Loving hath this day complained by affidavit before me, the undersigned Justice of the Peace for said county, that Edward Reynolds is justly indebted to the said Mark Loving in the sum of sixty-five dollars, due by open account, and oath having been also made before me that the said Edward Reynolds has property or rights in action which he conceals, and unjustly refuses to apply to the payment of his debts, and bond, with security, having been given to me, pursuant to the statute, you are therefore hereby commanded to forthwith attach the estate, real and personal, of the aforesaid Edward Reynolds, in your county, to the full value of said demand, and the probable cost of this proceeding, and that you safely keep the property so attached or levied upon in your hands, unless replevied according to law, so as to compel the aforesaid Edward Reynolds to appear before me, B. F. Jones, a Justice of the

Peace for said county, at my office therein, on the 20th day of May, 1876, to answer unto the complaint of the aforesaid Mark Loving, and that you summon the said defendant, if to be found in your county, to be and appear before the Justice of the Peace aforesaid, on the day named, then and there to answer accordingly; and have you then there this writ, with your proceedings thereon endorsed.

Witness my hand and seal, this 10th day of May, 1876.

B. F. JONES, J. P. [SEAL.]

NOTE.—Garnishment in attachment cases issue at the commencement of the action, and if the creditor suggests any person indebted to, or who has property of defendant, the Justice will add the following command to the writ, after the word "accordingly:"

§ 1430.]   No. 44.—SUMMONS OF GARNISHEE.

And whereas, it being suggested that Peter Bowles is indebted to said defendant, or hath property of said defendant in his hands, and whereas, it being further suggested that Charles A. Hamilton knows of persons so indebted to said defendant, or who have effects or property of the said defendant in their hands, you are hereby further commanded to summon the said Peter Bowles and the said Charles A. Hamilton to be and appear before said Justice, at the time and place aforesaid, to answer, under oath, in writing, whether they are indebted, as aforesaid, and to what amount, or have property of said defendant in their hands, or know of any other persons so indebted or who may have property or effects of said defendant in their hands or possession.

NOTE.—In case the plaintiff desires, after the issuance of the writ of attachment, to garnishee other persons, the Justice may issue *alias* writs. See Sec. 1432.

§§ 1434, 5 and 6.]
No. 45.—OFFICER'S RETURN.

I executed the within writ by going upon the land of Edward Reynolds, the defendant, and then and there declaring that, at the suit of Mark Loving, plaintiff, I attached the southeast quarter of the northwest quarter of section ten, in township nine of range eight east, as the property of said defendant, and delivering to said defendant, in person, a true copy of this writ.

I executed the within writ by going to the store-house of Daniel & Co., in the town of Beauregard in said county, and, in the presence of the clerks and agents therein, declared that, at the suit of Mark Loving, plaintiff, I levied upon and attached the stock, share or interest of Edward Reynolds, defendant, in said store-house and business, and delivered to said defendant, in person, a true copy of the within writ.

I executed the within writ by levying the same upon and taking into my possession one black horse-mule and one single horse spring wagon as the property of the defendant, and delivered to said defendant, in person, a true copy of this writ.

NOTE.—If the property attached is replevied in the hands of the officer, by the defendant or other person in whose hands the property was found before the return of the writ, the officer will add that fact to his return and state that he replevied the property, &c. See Secs. 1435 and 1440. The property can be replevied after the return of the writ and before judgment.

Before serving a writ of attachment, or after, the officer may demand of plaintiff a bond of indemnity. See Sec. 1438.

---

§ 1439.]
No. 46.—REPLEVIN BOND—TO HOLD PROPERTY SUBJECT TO JUDGMENT.

THE STATE OF MISSISSIPPI, COPIAH COUNTY. } ss.

Know all men by these presents that we, Edward Reynolds and Samuel Adams, are held and firmly bound unto Mark Loving, his heirs and assigns, in the penal sum of (*double the value of the property attached*), for which payment well and truly to be made, we bind ourselves, our heirs and legal representatives, jointly and severally, firmly by these presents; signed with our hands, and sealed with our seals this 15th day of May, 1876.

The condition of the above obligation is such, that whereas, on the 10th day of May, 1876, an attachment was issued by B. F. Jones, a Justice of the Peace for said county, against the estate, real and personal, of Edward Reynolds, for the recovery of a debt of sixty-five dollars, alleged to be due from said Reynolds to said Loving, which said attachment is returnable before said Justice, at his office in said county, on the 20th day of May, 1876; and whereas, Thomas H. Wheeler, constable for said county, hath levied said attachment upon one black horse-mule and one spring wagon, valued at *'true value*) dollars, as the property of said Reynolds; and whereas, the said Reynolds desires to replevy the same: Now, therefore, if the said above bound Edward Reynolds shall have said mule and wagon forthcoming to answer and abide the judgment of said Justice (*or the court*) in this suit, or in default thereof, shall pay and satisfy the said judgment to the extent of the value of said property in case of recovery by said Loving, then this obligation to be void, otherwise to remain in full force and effect.

EDWARD REYNOLDS, [SEAL.]
SAMUEL ADAMS, [SEAL.]

I approve and accept the foregoing bond, and redeliver the property, this 15th of May, 1876.

THOMAS H. WHEELER, Constable.

---

§ 1440.]
No. 47.—REPLEVIN BOND TO DISCHARGE ATTACHMENT.

THE STATE OF MISSISSIPPI, COPIAH COUNTY. } ss.

Know all men by these presents, that we, Edward Reynolds and Samuel Adams, are held and firmly bound unto Mark Loving, his heirs and assigns, in the penal sum of one hundred and thirty dollars (*being double the amount claimed*), for which payment well and truly to be made, we bind ourselves, our heirs and legal representatives, jointly and severally, firmly by these presents, signed with our hands and sealed with our seals, this 15th day of May, 1876.

The condition of the above obligation is such, that whereas, an attachment was issued by B. F. Jones, a Justice of the Peace for said county, against the estate of the above bound Edward Reynolds, for the recovery of a debt of sixty-five dollars alleged to be due from said Reynolds to said Mark Loving, which said attachment is returnable before said Justice, at his office in said county, on the 20th day of May, 1876; and whereas, Thomas H. Wheeler, constable for said county, hath levied said attachment upon a certain black horse-mule and a one horse spring wagon, as the property of said defendant; and whereas, the said defendant desires to replevy the said property and to discharge the attachment; Now, therefore, if the said Edward Reynolds shall pay and satisfy any judgment which may be recovered by the plaintiff in said attachment suit, with all costs, then this obligation to be void, otherwise to remain in full force and effect. EDWARD REYNOLDS, [SEAL.]

SAMUEL ADAMS, [SEAL.]

NOTE.—Any garnishee in whose hands property of defendant is found, may replevy the same by giving forthcoming bond, as No. —. If the plaintiff is not satisfied with any such bond taken by the officer, he has his remedy. See Sec. 1441. The two following forms will be applicable in such cases:

---

§ 1441.]
No. 48.—PETITION OF PLAINTIFF IN ATTACHMENT, ATTACKING THE REPLEVIN BOND.

MARK LOVING }
vs. } Attachment.
EDWARD REYNOLDS. }

In the Justice court of B. F. Jones, for the county of Copiah, Miss., May 18th, 1876.

In the matter of the replevin bond of said defendant, approved by Thomas H. Wheeler, constable.

To B. F. Jones, Justice of the Peace for said county:

Your petitioner, the said plaintiff in the suit aforesaid, would respectfully represent unto your Honor that he is dissatisfied with the bond and security given by the said defendant, replevying the property herein attached, and taken and approved by said constable, and charges that the same is wholly insufficient for the protection of the rights and interest of your petitioner in the premises; in this, that the surety on said bond, Samuel Adams, was not justified as to his solvency, &c., (*or set forth all the facts as in the replevy bond— but this is sufficient*): wherefore, your petitioner prays that Thomas H. Wheeler, constable as aforesaid, may be cited, according to the statute in this behalf, to appear before your Honor and show cause, if he can, why the said bond or the security shall not be adjudged insufficient; and your petitioner will ever pray, &c.

MARK LOVING.

---

§ 1441.] No. 49.—CITATION TO CONSTABLE.

To Thomas H. Wheeler, constable for the county of Copiah, and State of Mississippi:

Whereas, in the matter of the replevy bond given by Edward Reynolds, with Samuel Adams as surety, and taken and approved by you, in the attachment suit by Mark Loving against the said Edward Reynolds, now pending before the undersigned, a Justice of the Peace for said county, the said Mark Loving, plaintiff, conceiving himself aggrieved thereby, has prayed for and obtained citation against you; now, these are to command and cite you to be and appear before the undersigned Justice of the Peace for said county, at his office therein, on the 24th day of May, 1876, and show cause, if you can, why the said bond, or the security, shall not be adjudged insufficient under the penalty of the law in this behalf.

Witness my hand and seal this 18th day of May, 1876.

B. F. JONES, J. P. [SEAL.]

---

§ 1455.) No. 50.—AFFIDAVIT—DEBT NOT DUE.

STATE OF MISSISSIPPI, COPIAH COUNTY. } ss.

Personally appeared before the undersigned Justice of the Peace for said county, Mark Loving, who, being by me duly sworn, makes oath that Edward Reynolds, on the 1st day of July, 1876, will be indebted to him in the sum of one hundred and twenty-five dollars, as evidenced by his promissory note to be due on the date aforesaid, with interest at ten per cent. from maturity; and that he, the said Loving, has just cause to suspect, and verily believes, that the said Reynolds will remove himself or his effects out of the State before the said debt will become payable, with intent to hinder, delay or defraud his creditors (*or that said Reynolds hath removed, with like intent, leaving property in this State*); wherefore this affiant prays the issuance of the writ of attachment against the estate of said Edward Reynolds, real and personal.

MARK LOVING.

Sworn to and subscribed this 10th day of May, 1876.

B. F. JONES, J. P. (SEAL.)

NOTE.—Before the writ issues the plaintiff must give bond as in other attachments, and the defendant may reply as before. In case of garnishees, judgment is stayed until the debt falls due. The property attached, after judgment, will be sold on a credit to the maturity of the claim, the purchaser giving bond, payable to plaintiff, for full amount of judgment, interest and costs. If property brings more than the demand and costs of plaintiff, the officer must take bond for the residue, payable to defendant, from the purchaser.

---

§ 1455.] No. 51.—BOND OF PURCHASER.

STATE OF MISSISSIPPI, COPIAH COUNTY. } ss.

Know all men by these presents, that we, Elias Rowan and Adam Crane are held and firmly bound unto Edward Reynolds, and to his legal representatives, in the penal sum of one hundred and thirty-seven dollars and fifty cents, which payment well and truly to be made we bind ourselves, our heirs and legal representatives, jointly and severally, firmly by these presents, signed with our hands and sealed with our seals, this 10th day of June, 1876.

The condition of the above obligation is such, that whereas, at an execution sale, on a judgment against Edward Reynolds, in an attachment case, rendered on the 20th day of May, 1876, by B. F. Jones, a Justice of the Peace for said county, in favor of Mark Loving, for the sum of one hundred and twenty dollars, for a debt not due, but to fall due on the 1st day of July, 1876, and twelve dollars and fifty cents, costs of suit; and whereas, the above bound Elias Rowan became the purchaser, at said sale, of a black-horse mule for the sum of one hundred and thirty-seven dollars and fifty cents, payable on the said 1st day of July, 1876, the same being sufficient to pay and satisfy said judgment and costs of suit; Now, therefore, if the said Elias Rowan shall fully pay and satisfy the debt aforesaid, at the maturity thereof, and the costs aforesaid, then this obligation to be void, otherwise to remain in full virtue, and have the force and effect of a judgment of a court of record, pursuant to the statute in that behalf.

ELIAS ROWAN, [SEAL.]
ADAM CRANE, [SEAL.]

NOTE.—Claimant's issue in attachment is governed by the same rules as the claim of third party under execution. See Secs. 1456 and 1457.

NOTE.—The grounds stated in the affidavit for attachment may be controverted. See Secs. 1459 to 1464.

---

§ 1459.)   No. 52.—PLEA IN ABATEMENT.

Mark Loving   }
   vs. } Attachment. }   Before B. F. Jones, Justice,
Edward Reynolds.   }   May 20th, 1876.

This day comes the defendant in the above stated case, and files this his plea in abatement, and for plea in this behalf says that he has not, as plaintiff charges, property or rights in action which he conceals, and unjustly refuses to apply to the payment of his debts; and of this he puts himself upon the country.

EDWARD REYNOLDS.

Sworn to and subscribed before me, this 20th day of May, 1876.

B. F. JONES, J. P. (SEAL.)

---

§ 1462.)   No. 53.—NOTICE TO PLAINTIFF.

Mark Loving   )
   vs. } Attachment.)   Before B. F. Jones, Justice,
Edward Reynolds.   )   May 20th, 1876.

To Mark Loving, defendant in the above stated case, or to ...., ..., his attorney of record:

You will take this as notice that I will, upon the trial of this issue, insist and offer in evidence the following, as special damages to me in this case, to-wit: lawyer's fee, ten dollars; traveling expenses and hotel bills, twenty-five dollars; special injury to my business in detention and loss of credit, one hundred dollars.

EDWARD REYNOLDS,
By A. B., his Attorney.

NOTE.—When a plea in abatement is filed, this issue must be first tried. If the defendant gains, the whole attachment is at an end; if he loses, the Justice then proceeds to try the attachment on its merits.

---

§ 1467 and 8

No. 54.—PERISHABLE GOODS. OATH AND CERTIFICATE OF HOUSEHOLDERS.

STATE OF MISSISSIPPI, COPIAH COUNTY. } ss.

This day, I, Thomas H. Wheeler, constable for said county, summoned before me Edward Cotton, John Cason and Elbert Dunbar, householders of said county, who being by me first duly sworn to examine the goods and chattels presented to them, seized by me under and by virtue of a writ of attachment, and believed to be in danger of immediate waste and decay, do, under their oaths, say: We, the undersigned, do hereby certify that having fully and carefully examined the goods this day exhibited to us by Thomas H. Wheeler, constable, find the same to be perishable and in danger of immediate waste and decay.

EDWARD COTTON,
JOHN CASON,
ELBERT DUNBAR.

Sworn to and subscribed this 15th day of May, 1876.

THOMAS H. WHEELER, CONSTABLE.

---

§ 1472.)   No. 55.—AFFIDAVIT—NON-RESIDENT.

STATE OF MISSISSIPPI, COPIAH COUNTY. } ss.

Personally appeared before the undersigned, a Justice of the Peace for said county, Mark Loving, who being by me duly sworn, made oath that Edward Reynolds, against whose estate a writ of attachment was issued, and certain property seized by virtue thereof, has not been found and summoned to answer to said attachment: that said affiant has been informed, and verily believes the fact to be, that said Reynolds is not within the State; but that said Reynolds is now supposed to be at Frost Station, a postoffice in the State of Tennessee (*if the place is unknown, say, "and affiant hath no information of the place of residence of the said Reynolds."*)

MARK LOVING.

Sworn to and subscribed this 15th day of May, 1876.

B. F. JONES, J. P. (SEAL.)

NOTE.—If the defendant is attached as a non-resident, this affidavit must be filed when attachment issues; and then only state that defendant is in a certain State, and the place, if you know, as above. Publication must be made by notices posted in three public places. See Sec. 1473, and Acts 1876, p. 78.

§ 1473.)   No. 56.—ATTACHMENT NOTICE.

(To be published.)

STATE OF MISSISSIPPI, COPIAH COUNTY. } ss.

Mark Loving,   }
     vs. } Attachment for $125. }
Edward Reynolds.   }

An attachment having been issued in the above stated case against the estate of said Edward Reynolds, at the suit of said plaintiff, returnable before B. F. Jones, a Justice of the Peace, holding his court at Beauregard, in said county, on the 20th day of May, 1876.

Now, the said defendant is hereby cited to be and appear before said Justice, at Beauregard, in said county, on the 22d day of June, 1876, and plead to the case; in default of which appearance judgment by default shall be rendered against him, and the property sold and the effects applied to the payment of plaintiff's claim.

Witness my hand and seal this 20th day of May, 1876.

B. F. JONES, J. P. (SEAL.)

NOTE.—This notice must be published four times in some paper in the county, and a copy must be mailed, postage paid, to the defendant, by the Justice, if the postoffice is known. The Justice makes affidavit of that fact as follows: See Sec. 1475.

---

§ 1475.)   No. 57.—AFFIDAVIT OF JUSTICE.

STATE OF MISSISSIPPI, COPIAH COUNTY. } ss.

Personally appeared before the undersigned, a Justice of the Peace for said county, (*or clerk or judge, &c.,*) B. F. Jones, a Justice of the Peace, who, being by me duly sworn, made oath that, on the 20th day of May, 1876, at the town of Beauregard, in said county, he mailed, postage paid, to Edward Reynolds, at Frost Station, Tennessee, a published (*or written*) notice of the pendency of an attachment against him at the suit of Mark Loving, in pursuance of the statute in that behalf.

B. F. JONES, J. P.

Sworn to and subscribed this 25th day of May, 1876.

JOSIAH HESTER, J. P. (SEAL.)

NOTE.—If the defendant does not appear, the Justice will enter up judgment by default on proof of publication only. If published in a paper, the affidavit of the printer; if posted, on the affidavit of the constable or plaintiff who stuck up the notices, and copy of notice filed with the papers in the case.

---

§ 1477.)   No. 58.—PROOF OF PUBLICATION.

STATE OF MISSISSIPPI, COPIAH COUNTY. } ss.

Personally appeared before the undersigned, a Justice of the Peace for said county, D. W. Jones, publisher of a newspaper printed and published in said county, in the town of Hazlehurst, called the Copiah Herald, who, being by me duly sworn, made oath that the publication of a certain notice, a true copy of which is hereto attached, has been made in said paper for four consecutive weeks, to-wit:

Vol. 3, No. 20, dated May 15th, 1876.
Vol. 3, No. 21, dated May 22d, 1876.
Vol. 3, No. 22, dated May 29th, 1876.
Vol. 3, No. 23, dated June 5th, 1876.

And I hereby certify that the several numbers of the newspapers containing the notice hereto attached, have been before me exhibited and examined, and I find the publication thereof to have been correctly made and as stated. D. W. JONES.

Sworn to and subscribed this 10th day of June, 1876.

A. LOWE, J. P. (SEAL.)

NOTE.—On this proof Judgment will be entered by default and the property attached ordered sold; but must not be so sold without the giving of the following bond by plaintiff, before execution.

§ 1479.)

No. 59.—BOND IN JUDGMENT BY DEFAULT.

STATE OF MISSISSIPPI, COPIAH COUNTY. } ss.

Know all men by these presents, that we, Mark Loving and Andrew Lusk, are held and firmly bound unto Edward Reynolds, and to his legal representatives, in the penal sum of three hundred dollars, for which payment well and truly to be made, we bind ourselves, our heirs and legal representatives, jointly and severally, firmly by these presents, signed with our names and sealed with our seals, this 22d day of June, 1876.

The condition of the above obligation is such, that whereas, the above bound Mark Loving, on the 22d day of June, 1876, obtained a judgment by default upon proof of publication only, against the said Edward Reynolds, before B. F. Jones, a Justice of the Peace for said county, in a certain attachment suit against the estate of the said Reynolds, for the sum of one hundred and twenty-five dollars, as also costs of suit; and whereas, execution has been issued thereon, and levied upon a certain black horse-mule and spring wagon, the property of said Reynolds; and whereas, Thomas H. Wheeler, constable for said county, is about to sell said mule and wagon, and as the law requires, that before the making of such sale the plaintiff shall give bond; Now, therefore, if the said defendant, Edward Reynolds, shall, within a year and a day next following the execution hereof, come into court and disprove or avoid the debt recovered by the plaintiff against him, and thereupon the said plaintiff, Mark Loving, shall restore to the said defendant the money he may have received toward the satisfaction of his demand, or so much thereof as shall be disproved or avoided, then this obligation to be void, otherwise to remain in full force and effect.

MARK LOVING, (SEAL.)
A. LUSK, (SEAL.)

Bond and security approved, this 22d day of June, 1876.

B. F. JONES, J. P. (SEAL.)

NOTE.—If the plaintiff, in cases of judgment on proof of publication only, does not come forward and give the foregoing bond, it is the duty of the officer holding the property to notify him in writing to do so. See sec. 1480.

REMEDY BY REPLEVIN.

§§ 1528-9.)　　　No. 60.—AFFIDAVIT.

STATE OF MISSISSIPPI, CLAIBORNE COUNTY. } ss.

Personally appeared before the undersigned, a Justice of the Peace for said county, Edward Stiles, who being by me duly sworn, made oath that Benjamin F. Booth wrongfully took and detains (*or wrongfully detains*) from him the possession of a certain sorrel mare mule, called Kate, of the value of one hundred and twenty dollars; that this affiant is legally entitled to the immediate possession of the same, and affiant's right of action in the premises has accrued within one year.　　　　　　　　　　　EDWARD STILES.

Sworn to and subscribed, this 10th day of July, 1876.

　　　　　　　　　GEO. PAGE, J. P. (SEAL.)

§ 1530, 1531.)　　　No. 61.—WRIT.

THE STATE OF MISSISSIPPI,

To the sheriff or any constable of Claiborne county, Greeting: We command you to take into your possession and custody a certain sorrel mare mule, called Kate, now in the possession of Benjamin F. Booth, and unlawfully detained by him from the possession of Edward Stiles, as we have been informed by the affidavit of said Stiles, filed with us this 10th day of July, 1876; and that you deliver the said mule to said Stiles, plaintiff, upon his entering into bond according to the statute in this behalf, with sufficient security, in double the value of said property, to be ascertained by you, conditioned according to law, unless the said Booth, defendant, shall enter into bond, with sufficient security, in like penalty, payable to said plaintiff, within two days from the seizure of said property, conditioned according to law.

You are further commanded to summon the said Booth, to be and appear before the undersigned, Justice of the Peace for said county, at his office therein, on the 20th day of July, 1876, then and there to answer to this action of replevin. To the damages of said plaintiff one hundred and fifty dollars.

Witness my hand and seal, this 10th day of July, 1876.

　　　　　　　　　GEO. PAGE, J. P. (SEAL.)

§§ 1530, 1531.　　　No. 62.—BOND.

STATE OF MISSISSIPPI, CLAIBORNE COUNTY, } ss.

Know all men by these presents, that we, Edward Stiles and William Morris, are held and firmly bound unto Benjamin F. Booth, his assigns and legal representatives, in the penal sum of two hundred and forty dollars, for which payment well and truly to be made, we bind ourselves, our heirs and legal representatives, jointly and severally, firmly by these presents, signed with our hands and sealed with our seals, this 14th day of July, 1876.

The condition of the above obligation is such, that whereas, the said Edward Stiles, plaintiff, hath, on the 10th day of July, 1876, prayed a writ of replevin, at the suit of himself, against certain property in the possession of Benjamin F. Booth, defendant, to-wit: one sorrel mare mule, called Kate, and hath obtained the same, returnable before George Page, a Justice of the Peace for said county, at his office therein, on the 20th day of July, 1876; and whereas, Columbus Hall, constable for said county, hath seized and taken into his custody said mule, and valued the same at one hundred and twenty dollars; Now, therefore, if said plaintiff shall prosecute the said writ with effect, or in default of which, without delay make return of the said mule to the said defendant, if return thereof be adjudged, and pay the said defendant such damages as he may sustain by the wrongful suing out of said writ, and also such costs as may be awarded against him, and save harmless the said constable for replevying the said mule, then this obligation to be void, otherwise to remain in full force and effect.

EDWARD STILES, (SEAL.)
WILLIAM MORRIS, (SEAL.)

---

§ 1531.)　　No. 63.—DEFENDANT'S BOND.

NOTE.—If the defendant gives bond within the two days after seizure, it will be as plaintiff's bond, but concluding as follows:

Now, therefore, if said defendant shall have said mule forthcoming to satisfy the judgment of the court, then this obligation to be void, otherwise to remain in full force and effect.

NOTE.—In trials of writs of attachment and replevin, it is always safe, and the best practice, to have a jury. For the entering up of judgment and issuing execution, examine carefully sections 1533, 1534 and 1535. There is a constitutional question whether replevin is within the jurisdiction of a Justice of the Peace.

UNLAWFUL ENTRY AND DETAINER.

§ 1583.　　No. 64.—COMPLAINT.

STATE OF MISSISSIPPI, CLAIBORNE COUNTY. } ss.

James S. Mason, of the said county, complains that Sidneyham Hawkins unlawfully withholds from him the possession of a certain tenement, being the east half of the south-east quarter of section four in township twelve of range three east, containing by estimation eighty acres of land, with the appurtenances, lying and being in the county aforesaid, whereof he prays restitution of the possession.

JAMES S. MASON, Plaintiff.

STATE OF MISSISSIPPI, CLAIBORNE COUNTY. } To-wit:

This day the above named James S. Mason made oath before me, a Justice of the Peace for said county, that he verily believes the allegations of the above complaint to be correct and true.

Given under my hand, this 10th day of December, 1876.

T. J. SMITH, J. P.

NOTE.—The foregoing is the proper form in case a tenant, or other person, refuses to deliver possession; or in case of merchants or others holding deeds of trust and mortgages on land, and the party in possession refusing to deliver, outside of towns or cities. The following will do for corporations:

§ 1583.) COMPLAINT NO. 2.

STATE OF MISSISSIPPI, CORPORATION OF PORT GIBSON. } To-wit:

James Selman, of the said corporation, complains that John Byrd hath unlawfully turned him out of possession (*or unlawfully withholds from him the possession*) of a certain tenement, to-wit: being a frame house on lot one in square six, containing, by estimation, one-quarter of an acre of land, with the appurtenances, lying and being on Cherry street in the corporation aforesaid, whereof he prays restitution of the possession.

JAMES SELMAN, Plaintiff.

STATE OF MISSISSIPPI, CORPORATION OF PORT GIBSON. } To-wit:

This day the above named James Selman made oath before me, a Justice of the Peace for said corporation, that he verily believes the allegations of the above complaint to be correct and true.

Given under my hand this 10th day of November, 1876.

T. J. SMITH, J. P. (SEAL.)

---

§ 1584.) No. 66.—WARRANT.

STATE OF MISSISSIPPI, COUNTY OF CLAIBORNE. } To-wit:

To the sheriff or any constable of said county, greeting:

Whereas, James S. Mason hath made complaint, on oath, before me, a Justice of the Peace for said county, that Sydneham Hawkins unlawfully, and against his consent, holds him out of possession of a certain tenement and eighty acres of land, with its appurtenances described in said complaint, lying and being in said county, and hath prayed restitution of the possession thereof; these are, therefore, in the name of the State of Mississippi, to require you to summon the said Sydneham Hawkins to appear at my office, in the town of Port Gibson, in said county, on the 20th day of December, 1876, before the Justices of the county aforesaid, to answer to the complaint aforesaid, and, also, require you to give notice of this warrant to two other Justices of the Peace for the said county, and to request their attendance at the time and place aforesaid; and have then there this warrant.

Witness my hand and seal this 10th day of December, 1876.

T. J. SMITH, J. P. (SEAL.)

NOTE.—Change the warrant to suit the allegations of the complaint.

§§ 1585, 1586.) No. 67. RETURN OF OFFICER.

Executed the within writ by delivering to Sydneham Hawkins, in person, a true copy thereof; and, also, true copies of the same, in person, each, to William Hutchinson and Spooner Forbes, Justices of the Peace for said county.

B. THOMAS BLAND, Sheriff.

---

§§ 1590, 1591.) No. 68.—JUDGMENT—No. 1.

This day came the parties in person, and by their attorneys, and the testimony being submitted and all the evidence in the case heard and duly considered, it is, by the court, ordered, adjudged and decreed that James S. Mason, plaintiff, do have and recover of and from Sydneham Hawkins, defendant, the possession of the tenement, in said plaintiff's complaint described, with full costs in this behalf expended; and the writ of *habere facias possessionem* is hereby awarded. And it is further considered by the court and adjudged that the said plaintiff do have and recover of and from said defendant the sum of twenty five dollars, compensation for the use and occupation of said tenement, for which execution may issue.

Adjudged this 20th day of December, 1876.

T. J. SMITH, J. P.

---

§ 1592.) No. 69.—JUDGMENT—No. 2.

This day came the parties in said action, in person, and by attorneys, and the testimony and all the evidence in the case heard, it is, by the court, considered that the complaint, filed by the plaintiff herein, be dismissed, and that the said defendant recover of said plaintiff full costs in this behalf; for which execution may issue.

Adjudged this 20th day of December, 1876.

T. J. SMITH, J. P.

---

§ 1591.) No. 70.—WRIT OF POSSESSION.

STATE OF MISSISSIPPI, CLAIBORNE COUNTY. } ss.

To the sheriff or any constable of said county, greeting:

Whereas, Sydneham Hawkins, unlawfully withholds from the possession of James S. Mason (*or, if a tenant wrongfully holds over from his landlord, or, if plaintiff has been unlawfully turned out of possession, say so,*) certain premises, to-wit: the east half of the southeast quarter of section four in township twelve of range three east, containing eighty acres of land, by estimation, with the appurtenances, lying and being in said county, as appears to us by the record of the undersigned Justice of the Peace for said county; we, therefore, command you to remove the said Hawkins from the aforesaid premises, as well as all other persons who may be wrongfully therein or thereon, and to put the said James S. Mason in full and complete possession thereof; and that of the goods and chattels of said defendant you cause to be made the sum of .... dollars, cost of this suit, so that you have the same with this writ, with your proceedings thereon endorsed, before me.

Witness my hand and seal this 26th day of December, 1876.

T. J. SMITH. J. P. (SEAL.)

---

§ 1595.) No. 71.—APPEAL BOND.

STATE OF MISSISSIPPI, CLAIBORNE COUNTY, } ss.

Know all men by these presents that we, Sydneham Hawkins and Mack D. Sims, our heirs and legal representatives, are held and firmly bound unto James S. Mason, his heirs and legal representatives, in the penal sum of two hundred and fifty dollars, (*being double the amount compensation or rent obtained, beside the penalty required in other cases,*) for which payment, well and truly to be made, we bind ourselves, our heirs and legal representatives, jointly and severally, firmly by these presents; signed with our names and sealed with our seals this 26th day of December, 1876.

The condition of the above obligation is such that, whereas, on the 10th day of December, 1876, a claim was filed against the above bound, Sydneham Hawkins, by James S. Mason, alleging that said Hawkins unlawfully withheld from the possession of said Mason certain premises therein described; and, whereas on the 20th day of December, 1876, a writ of possession was issued ousting from said premises the said Hawkins, as, also, judgment for costs and the sum of twenty-five dollars compensation for use and occupation of said premises; and, whereas, said Hawkins has prayed an appeal to the next regular term of the circuit court of said county, and made the necessary affidavit to obtain the same; now, therefore, if the said Sydneham Hawkins shall stand and abide by the judgment of the circuit court in this behalf, and shall, also, well and truly pay, satisfy and discharge such sums as may be adjudged against him in the circuit court for arrears of rent or damages, for the use and occupation of the property in controversy, beside costs of suit, then this obligation to be void; otherwise to remain in full force and effect.

SYDNEHAM HAWKINS, (SEAL.)

MACK D. SIMS, (SEAL.)

NOTE.—The appeal does not stop the execution of the writ. This whole proceeding is summary, for the protection of landlords whose tenants hold over against them, and against landlords who unlawfully turn out tenants; for merchants and others who hold deeds of trust against those who will not deliver the lands, after default made, to the trustees, &c. It is very doubtful whether the court established by this statute is constitutional in all its latitude, while I heartily approve these summary remedies. The object of all law should be to avoid litigation; and, if once commenced, to shorten all actions. In this day we want no Jaundice vs. Jaundice.

---

§ 1603.) MECHANIC'S LIEN.

This statute has become not only the protection for large contractors and master builders, but equally so for the simplest laborer upon any character of improvement on any land or lot of ground. And as it is cognizable before a Justice of the Peace to the amount of $150, it is really the laborer's law.

§ 1603.) No. 72—PETITION.

STATE OF MISSISSIPPI, HINDS COUNTY. } ss.

To the Honorable W. L. Smylie, a Justice of the Peace for said county:

Your petitioner, the undersigned, Carl Shaifer, would respectfully show unto your Honor, that on or about the 3d day of March, 1876, one Henry McBride, resident in said county, employed, by verbal contract, your petitioner, to build and erect upon his farm, in said county, on which the said McBride now resides, and more particularly described as the east half of the southeast quarter of section nine, in township eight of range four east, a garden fence (*or a hen house, or pig house, or crib or stable, or any other improvement, or the materials therefor*) of the dimensions and style, to-wit: one hundred and sixty feet front by two hundred and forty feet deep, being the panels on the front, near the public road, east of said residence, ten panels in the rear and fifteen on each side, making, in all, fifty panels of fence, said panels being sixteen feet each; and in consideration of said work and improvement to be done by your petitioner, from materials furnished to hand by said McBride, your petitioner was to receive from said McBride, and he so agreed and promised at the time, the sum of fifty cents per panel, making in all the sum of twenty-five dollars, to be paid on the completion of said fence. And your petitioner would further show that he did said work and erected upon said land said fence, in a substantial and workmanlike manner, according to agreement, completing the same in the time given and agreed upon, but that said McBride failed to pay your petitioner as aforesaid, and still fails and refuses to pay; Wherefore, your petitioner prays the benefit of the Act in relation to lien of mechanics in his behalf, and that the said Henry McBride be summoned to appear before your Honor to answer and defend this action; and that all persons having an interest in the controversy, and all persons claiming liens on the same property, if any there be, by virtue of the statute in this behalf, be made parties to this suit, and be summoned to answer herein.

And your petitioner will ever pray, &c.

CARL SHAIFER, Plaintiff.

Sworn to and subscribed before me, this 3d day of July, 1876.

W. L. SMYLIE, J. P.

———

§ 1609.) No. 73.—BILL OF PARTICULARS.

NOTE.—Unless the contract be in writing, an account stated, or bill of particulars, must be filed with the petition; if a contract in writing exists, then file the contract with the petition.

3

Henry McBride   To Carl Shaifer,   Dr.
March 25th, 1876.

To putting up fifty panels of picket fence, from materials
furnished by you, on your farm in Hinds county, from
March 3d to March 25th, 1876, at 50c. for each panel........$25 00

This was a garden fence, with sawed posts 4x6x7 feet long, put
in the ground two feet deep, with railing nailed to the top and bot-
tom of posts, 1½x3x16 feet long; posts set every eight feet, and
pickets 1x3x5 feet long, nailed to railing at the distance of two.
inches apart, set above a twelve inch baseboard. Material was furnished in the rough; the posts sawed, the holes were dug, posts set
and rammed, baseboard placed, railing sawed to length and nailed
on, pickets sawed to length, sharpened at one end, nailed on, and
the labor performed in the time and at the price stated above.

----

§ 1610.)
No. 74.--SUMMONS IN MECHANIC'S LIEN.

STATE OF MISSISSIPPI,
   To the sheriff or any constable of Hinds county, Greeting:
   We command you to summon Henry McBride (*and any others
interested in the land, or who have liens upon the same property, if
known*) to be and personally appear before the undersigned Justice
of the Peace for said county, at his office therein, on the...... day of
........., 1876, to plead, answer or demur to the petition of Carl
Shaifer, asking for the benefit of an Act for the enforcement of
mechanic's lien, to secure the payment of the sum of twenty-five
dollars, on the following property, whereon work was done and
improvements built, to-wit: the east half of the southeast quarter
of section nine, in township four of range eight east, in said county,
now occupied by said Henry McBride (*and the dwelling thereon, if
the work was done on a dwelling*). Herein fail not, and have you
there this writ.
   Witness my hand and seal, this ...... day of ...., 1876.
                              W. L. SMYLIE, J. P. (SEAL.)

----

§ 1606.)   No. 75.--NOTICE TO OWNER.

NOTE.--If any contractor or builder refuses to pay any one employed by
him to labor or to furnish materials, such person should at once give the
owner notice of the amount due by such contractor or builder, which notice
will be in the nature of a garnishment, and bind what may be due from the
owner to the contractor or builder. If the contractor sues the owner, the
party giving notice must be summoned; and if the party giving notice,
after it, sues the contractor, the owner must be made a party to the suit.

                              BYRAM, Miss., March 20th, 1876.
Henry McBride, Esq.:
   SIR:--You will please to take this as notice, that Carl Shaifer,
under verbal contract (*or contract*) to build and complete for you

on your farm in Hinds county, a certain garden fence, is indebted to me in the sum of eight dollars, which he fails and refuses to pay, for work and labor done on said fence.

Respectfully, CHARLES RAMMER.

---

§§ 1614, 1615. No. 76.—JUDGMENT.

(To be entered on Docket.)

This day come the parties in person (*and by their attorneys*) and the testimony of the witnesses and all the evidence in the case (*and the argument of counsel*) having been heard, it is thereupon considered by the court that the said plaintiff, Carl Shaifer, do have and recover of and from the said defendant, Henry McBride, the sum of $25, and his costs in this behalf expended, for which execution may issue. And it is further considered by the court, that the following described property, situate in said county, to-wit: the east half of the southeast quarter of section nine, in township eight of range four east (*or, the house and lot, fully described, in the town or city upon which work was done, or for which materials were furnished*) be and the same is hereby condemned to be sold, or so much thereof as shall be sufficient to satisfy the judgment in this behalf and all costs, for which a special execution may issue.

---

§§ 1615, 1616.) No. 77.—EXECUTION.

STATE OF MISSISSIPPI,

To the sheriff or any constable of Hinds county:

We command you that of the goods and chattels, lands and tenements of Henry McBride, you cause to be made the sum of twenty-five dollars, which sum was recovered before the undersigned Justice of the Peace for said county, on the ...... day of . ..., 1876, against said McBride, and interest thereon at the rate of ...... per cent. per annum from the ...... day of ...., 1876, in favor of Carl Shaifer, and also .... dollars and .... cents, his costs in this behalf expended, whereof said Henry McBride is convicted, as appears to us of record. And you are hereby further especially commanded to cause to be made the aforesaid sums, recovered as aforesaid, by the seizure and sale of the east half of the southeast quarter of section nine, in township eight of range four east, in said county, or so much thereof as shall be sufficient, to satisfy said judgment and all costs; and that you have said moneys ready to render to said plaintiff, before the undersigned, at his office in said county, on the ...... day of ...., 1876. And then there have this writ, with your proceedings thereon endorsed.

Witness my hand and seal, this ...... day of ...., 1876.

W. L. SMYLIE, J. P. (SEAL.)

(BILL OF COSTS.—*See Fees of Officers.*)

JUSTICE'S FEES.

Issuing summons or warrant.............	Summoning ..... garnishees.............
Entering suit.............................	Taking examination of ...... garnishees..
Issuing ...... subpenas ...... names.........	Issuing execution............................
Affidavit to account.....................	Issuing vendi. exponas.................
Counter-affidavit........................	Affidavit and appeal bond.............
Venire facias............................	Transcript of record and certificate.....
Swearing jury...........................	Issuing attachment, bond and affidavit..
Swearing ...... witnesses...............	Issuing replevin, bond and affidavit......
Affidavit for continuance...............	Iss'ng distress war'nt, bond and " ....a
Commission to take deposition.........	Recognizance............................
Proceedings to judgment...............	Mittimus.................................
Entering judgment.......................	Jury fee.............................
Affidavit for garnishee.................	witnesses ....

CONSTABLE'S FEES.

Serving summons or warrant.............	Summoning inquest...................
Serving an attachment..................	Conveying criminal to jail, ...miles....
Summoning ...... witnesses..............	Attending trial......................
Executing mittimus.....................	Summoning jury......................
Taking ...... bonds.....................	Jury trial, attendance...............
Levying execution and making money...	Summoning ...... garnishees...........

A true bill of costs.   W. L. SMYLIE, J. P. [SEAL.]

LANDLORD AND TENANT.

§ 1620.)   No. 78.—AFFIDAVIT—RENT DUE.

STATE OF MISSISSIPPI, COPIAH COUNTY. } ss.

Personally appeared before the undersigned Justice of the Peace for said county, D. W. McRae, who states on oath that Charles Cook is indebted to him in the sum of seventy-five dollars, for rent due and in arrear, on certain leased premises, situate in said county, and described as follows, to-wit: the east half of the southeast quarter of section nineteen, in township two of range one west (*or, the farm known as the Holly Farm; or, the frame house in the town of Crystal Springs, on .... street, described on plat of said town, as lot 4, in square 10. Locate fully.*); therefore affiant prays an attachment against the goods and chattels of said tenant.

                                        D. W. McRAE.

Sworn to and subscribed this 10th day of January, 1876.

                              A. B. LOWE, J. P. (SEAL.)

---

§ 1622.)   No. 79.—AFFIDAVIT—RENT NOT DUE.

STATE OF MISSISSIPPI, COPIAH COUNTY. } ss.

Personally appeared before the undersigned Justice of the Peace for said county, D. W. McRae, who states on oath that Charles Cook is justly indebted to him in the sum of seventy-five dollars, for rent of certain leased premises, situate in said county, known as the Oak Grove place, and being a part of the southwest quarter of section nineteen, in township two of range one west, the same to be due and payable on the first day of January, 1877; and this affiant further makes oath that he has just cause to suspect, and does verily believe, that his said tenant will remove his effects from said leased premises to some other place, within or without said county, before the expiration of his term, or before the rent will fall due, so that no distress for rent can be made; wherefore affiant prays an attachment to distrain sufficient goods and chattels on said premises to satisfy said rent. D. W. McRae.

Sworn to and subscribed this 20th day of November, 1876.

A. B. Lowe, J. P. (seal.)

---

§ 1623.)
No. 80.—AFFIDAVIT WHEN EFFECTS HAVE BEEN REMOVED.

Note.—If tenant removes effects without paying rent, landlord within thirty days has his remedy by attachment, and can seize the goods wherever found.

State of Mississippi, Copiah County. } ss.

Personally appeared before the undersigned Justice of the Peace for said county, D. W. McRae, who states on oath that Charles Cook is justly indebted to him in the sum of one hundred dollars, to be due and payable on the 20th day of December, 1876, for the rent of certain leased premises for said year, described as follows: lot numbered six in square or block numbered ten in the town of Hazlehurst, in said county, with the tenements and appurtenances thereunto belonging; and that said tenant has actually removed his effects from said leased premises before the rent has become due, so that there is not sufficient property, liable to distress, left on said premises, and that said removal has taken place within the last thirty days; wherefore affiant prays an attachment, &c.

D. W. McRae.

Sworn to and subscribed this 10th day of December, 1876.

A. B. Lowe, J. P. (seal.)

---

§ 1620.) ### No. 81.—BOND.

State of Mississippi, Copiah County. } ss.

Know all men by these presents, that we, D. W. McRae and L. B. Harris, are held and firmly bound unto Charles Cook in the sum of two hundred dollars, for which payment well and truly to be made, we bind ourselves and our legal representatives, jointly and severally, firmly by these presents, signed with our names and sealed with our seals, this 18th day of December, 1876.

The condition of this obligation is such that, whereas, the above bound D. W. McRae hath on the day of the date hereof prayed an attachment, at the suit of himself, to distrain the goods and chattels of the above named Charles Cook, to the amount of one hundred dollars, for rent alleged to be due for certain leased premises set forth therein; and whereas, said McRae has also made affidavit that said tenant has actually removed his effects from said leased premises before the rent has become due, so that there is not sufficient property, liable to distress, left on said premises, and that said removal has taken place within the last thirty days (*or, that he has just cause to suspect, and does verily believe, that said tenant will remove his effects from said leased premises to some other place, within or without said county, before the expiration of his term, or before the rent will fall due, so that no distress for rent can be made*), and hath obtained the same returnable before A. B. Lowe, a Justice of the Peace for said county, at his office therein, on the 20th day of December, 1876.

Now, if the said plaintiff in said attachment shall well and truly pay and satisfy to the said tenant, defendant, all such damages as he shall sustain by reason of the wrongful suing out of said attachment, and shall also pay all costs which may be awarded against the said plaintiff in said suit, then the above obligation to be void, otherwise to remain in full force and effect.

D. W. McRae,   (SEAL.)
L. B. Harris,   (SEAL.)

---

§ 1620.)   No. 82.—WARRANT.

STATE OF MISSISSIPPI.

To the sheriff or any constable of Copiah county, Greeting:

Whereas, D. W. McRae hath complained on oath, before the undersigned Justice of the Peace for said county, that Charles Cook is justly indebted to him in the sum of seventy-five dollars, for rent alleged to be due and in arrear on certain leased premises, situate in said county, to-wit: the east half of the southeast quarter of section nineteen, in township two of range one west;

Or, 2d, is justly indebted to him in the sum of seventy-five dollars, for rent of certain leased premises, situate in said county, known as the Oak Grove place, and being a part of the southwest quarter of section nineteen, in township 2 of range one west, and that affiant has just cause to suspect, and does verily believe, that his said tenant will remove his effects from said leased premises to some other place within or without said county, before the expiration of his term, or before the rent will fall due, so that no distress for rent can be made;

Or, 3d, is justly indebted to him in the sum of one hundred dollars, to be due and payable on the 20th day of December, 1876, for certain leased premises for said year, to-wit: lot numbered six in square or block numbered ten, in the town of Hazlehurst, in said county, and that said tenant has actually removed his effects from said leased premises, before the rent has become due, so that there is not sufficient property, liable to distress, left on said premises, and that said removal has taken place within the last thirty days;

And whereas, the said D. W. McRae hath given bond and security as required by law: We, therefore, command you to attach and distrain the goods and chattels of the said Charles Cook, liable to distress (*if 3d cause, say, " wherever they may be found*), to an amount sufficient to satisfy the rent due and in arrear (*or, to be due*) as aforesaid, and all costs. And having given notice, according to law, to said tenant, you shall forthwith advertise the property distrained, for sale, in not less than ten days after such notice, on said premises, or at some other convenient public place. And if the said Cook, or claimant of the goods distrained, shall not, before the time appointed for the sale, replevy the same, by giving bond and security, to be approved by you, you shall sell the said goods to the highest bidder, for cash, at public outery, and shall, out of the proceeds of the sale, pay all costs, and to the plaintiff the amount due him for rent, with interest (*or, if 2d cause, " deducting interest for the time until the rent shall become payable*"); and make return of this writ to the undersigned, at his office, in said county, on the ...... day of ...., 1877.

Witness my hand and seal, this ...... day of ...., 1876.

A. B. Lowe, (seal.)

Note.—The distress warrant is not served on the tenant, but levied at once on property of his subject to distress or seizure. The following notice, however, to make the seizure legal, must be served on the tenant:

---

§ 1621.　　　No. 83.—NOTICE TO TENANT.

Copiah County, Miss., Dec. 10th, 1876.

Mr. Charles Cook :

Sir—You will take notice that at the suit of D. W. McRae against you, for the sum of seventy five dollars, rent alleged to be due and in arrear, by you to him (*or, to be due*), and by virtue of a warrant issued by A. B. Lowe, Justice of the Peace for said county, I have this day distrained and taken into my possession one bay mare, as your property; which will be sold by me to satisfy said debt and costs, at public outery, for cash, to the highest bidder, at .... on the 21st day of December, unless replevied according to law.

Respectfully,　　　Albert Welch, Constable.

Note.—The tenant can replevy the property in two ways: 1st, by giving a bond in double the amount of rent claimed, with security, to pay the rent and interest and costs, at the end of three months; or by giving bond and security in double the amount of rent claimed, to try the legality of the distress. If any other claims the property seized, he files his affidavit and gives bond, and the issue is tried.

---

§ 1621.)

No. 84.—REPLEVY BOND TO PAY RENT.

State of Mississippi, Copiah County, } ss.

Know all men by these presents, that we, Charles Cook and Moses Curtis are held and firmly bound unto D. W. McRae, and to his legal representatives, in the sum of one hundred and fifty dollars, for which payment well and truly to be made, we bind ourselves and our legal representatives, jointly and severally, firmly by these presents, signed with our names and sealed with our seals, this 15th day of December, 1876.

The condition of the above obligation is such, that whereas, property of the above bound Charles Cook, by virtue of an attachment sued out by D. W. McRae, has been distrained to satisfy the claim of said McRae for rent, and also for costs of this proceeding, amounting in all to eighty-two dollars; and upon the execution of these presents, said property has been restored to said Cook:

Now, if the said Cook shall make payment of the rent claimed, with lawful interest for the same, and all costs, at the end of three months after making such distress, then this obligation to be void, otherwise to remain in full force and effect.

CHARLES COOK, (SEAL.)
MOSES CURTIS, (SEAL.)

I approve the foregoing bond and security, this 15th day of December, 1876.   ALBERT WELCH, Constable.

----

§ 1630.)   No. 85.—REPLEVY BOND BY TENANT.

STATE OF MISSISSIPPI, COPIAH COUNTY. } ss.

Know all men by these presents, that we, Charles Cook and H. C. Vance, are held and firmly bound unto D. W. McRae, and to his legal representatives, in the sum of two hundred dollars, for which payment well and truly to be made, we bind ourselves and our legal representatives, jointly and severally, firmly by these presents, signed with our hands and sealed with our seals, this 15th day of December, 1876.

The condition of the above obligation is such that, whereas, a certain bay mare, the property of the above bound Charles Cook, has been distrained, by virtue of an attachment issued by A. B. Lowe, a Justice of the Peace for said county, at the suit of D. W. McRae, to satisfy the claim of said McRae for rent alleged to be due and in arrear; and, whereas, said Cook desires to replevy said mare, in order to try the legality of said attachment, and hath obtained a writ of replevin upon the execution of these presents, returnable before said Justice, at his office, in said county, on the 23d day of December, 1876; Now, therefore, if the said Charles Cook shall perform and satisfy the judgment of the court in this replevin suit, in case he shall be cast therein, then this obligation shall be void, otherwise to remain in full force and effect.

CHARLES COOK, (SEAL.)
H. C. VANCE, (SEAL.)

I approve the foregoing bond and security, this 15th day of December, 1876.   A. B. LOWE, J. P. (SEAL.)

§ 1630.)
No. 86.--WRIT OF REPLEVIN FAVOR OF TENANT.

STATE OF MISSISSIPPI,

To the sheriff or any constable of Copiah county, Greeting:

Whereas, a certain bay mare has been distrained by virtue of an attachment issued at the suit of D. W. McRae, against the goods and chattels of Charles Cook, for the sum of one hundred dollars rent alleged to be due and in arrear, which said mare the said defendant desires to replevy, in order to try the legality of said attachment; and having given bond in this behalf, as directed by law; we command you to take said mare and deliver and restore the same to said defendant, and to summon said McRae to be and appear before the undersigned Justice of the Peace of said county, at his office therein, on the 23d day of December, 1876, then and there to answer the complaint of defendant in the premises. And have then there this writ.

Witness my hand and seal this 15th day of December, 1876.

A. B. LOWE, J. P. (SEAL.)

---

§ 1631.)   No. 87.--CLAIMANT'S AFFIDAVIT.

STATE OF MISSISSIPPI, COPIAH COUNTY. }ss.

Personally appeared before the undersigned, a Justice of the Peace for said county, W. M. Haley, who states on oath that a certain bay mare distrained as the property of Charles Cook, by virtue of an attachment issued by A. B. Lowe, Justice of the Peace for said county, at the suit of D. McRae, for the recovery of rent alleged to be due and in arrear (*or, to be due on the ..... day of ....*), is the property of this affiant, and not the property of the tenant, said Charles Cook, nor held in trust for the use of said tenant in any manner whatsoever, and that said mare, in his opinion, is not liable to such distress. Wherefore, affiant prays in this behalf the writ of replevin, that the right of property may be tried

W. M. HALEY.

Sworn to and subscribed, this 15th day of December, 1876.

A. B. LOWE, J. P. (SEAL.)

---

§ 1631.)   No. 88.--BOND BY CLAIMANT.

Know all men by these presents, that we, W. M. Haley and Andrew Mangold, are held and firmly bound unto D. W. McRae, &c., (*as in No. 85, only penalty double value of property distrained*).

The condition of this obligation is such that, whereas, a certain bay mare, valued at .... dollars, has been distrained as the property of Charles Cook, by virtue of an attachment issued by A. B. Lowe, a Justice of the Peace for said county, at the suit of D. W. McRae, to satisfy a claim for rent alleged to be due and in arrear; and whereas, the above bound W. M. Haley makes claim to said mare, and has filed his affidavit in this behalf, according to law, and prayed a writ of replevin upon the execution of these presents, returnable before said Justice, at his office, in said county, on the 23d day of December, 1876; Now, therefore, if the said W. M. Haley, in case he be cast in said replevin suit, shall perform and satisfy the judgment of the court, then this obligation to be void, otherwise remain in full force and effect.

W. M. HALEY,   (SEAL.)
ANDREW MANGOLD, (SEAL.)

No. 87.—WRIT OF REPLEVIN FAVOR CLAIMANT.

STATE OF MISSISSIPPI,

To the sheriff or any constable of Copiah county, Greeting:

Whereas, a certain bay mare has been distrained, by virtue of an attachment issued at the suit of D. W. McRae against the goods and chattels of Charles Cook, for the sum of one hundred dollars, rent alleged to be due and in arrear, which said mare, valued at .... dollars, is claimed by affidavit filed before us, by W. M. Haley as his property, and not the property of said tenant Cook, and bond and security having been given as directed by law, in this behalf; we command you to take said mare and deliver the same to said Haley, and to summon said McRae to be and appear before the undersigned Justice of the Peace for said county, at his office therein, on the 23d day of December, 1876, then and there to answer the claim of said Haley in the premises. And have you then there this writ.

Witness my hand and seal, this 15th day of December, 1876.

A. B. LOWE, J. P. (SEAL.)

§ 1640.)
No. 90.—NOTICE TO DETERMINE TENANCY.

NOTE.—Tenants from year to year must have two months notice; half yearly or quarterly tenants, one month's notice; and by the month, one week's notice in writing.

HAZLEHURST, Miss., Oct. 28th, 1875.

Mr. Charles Cook :

SIR--You will take notice that your tenancy of the house and lot now occupied by you in this town, rented of me by the year, will be determined and ended on the first day of January, 1876, on which date I shall require of you possession of the same.

Respectfully,   D. W. McRAE.

§ 1647.)
No. 91.—NOTICE TO TERMINATE TENANCY AT WILL OR SUFFERANCE.

BEAUREGARD, Miss., Feb. 25th, 1876.

Mr. William Hampton :

SIR--You will take this as notice that the rent due me for the house now occupied by you, in this town, amounting to fifty dollars, for the months of September, October, November and December, of 1875, and the months of January and February, 1876, though often demanded, has not been paid, and unless paid by the 1st day of March proximo, you are hereby required to deliver to me the possession of said house and lot on that day. In default of which, I shall proceed as authorized by law in the premises.

   Respectfully.   CHARLES A. HARRIS.

---

§ 1648.)

No. 92.—LANDLORD OR AGENT'S AFFIDAVIT TO REMOVE TENANT AT WILL.

STATE OF MISSISSIPPI, COPIAH COUNTY. } ss.

Personally appeared before the undersigned Justice of the Peace for said county, Charles A. Harris, who makes oath that William Hampton is justly indebted to affiant in the sum of fifty dollars, for the rent of a certain frame house in the town of Beauregard, in said county, described on the plat of said town as lot one in square two; that said house and lot was let to said Hampton on the 1st day of September, 1875, at the rate of eight dollars per month, and said tenant to occupy the same at the will and sufferance of affiant; that the said tenant neglects and refuses to pay said rent, or any part thereof, although often requested so to do, and the necessary notice, according to law, having been given to terminate such tenancy, that said tenant, without permission of affiant, still holds over and will not deliver to affiant possession of said premises. Wherefore, affiant prays that said Hampton may be summoned to show cause why possession of said premises shall not be delivered to affiant.

          CHARLES A. HARRIS.

Sworn to and subscribed this 1st day of March, 1876.

        B. F. JONES, J. P. (SEAL.)

NOTE.—If the cause of removal is only for refusal to pay rent, after three days' notice, change affidavit to suit.

---

§ 1646.]

No. 93.—LANDLORD OR AGENT'S AFFIDAVIT TO REMOVE TENANT HOLDING OVER WITHOUT PERMISSION.

STATE OF MISSISSIPPI, COPIAH COUNTY. } ss.

Personally appeared before the undersigned Justice of the Peace for said county, D. W. McRae, who makes oath that Charles Cook, tenant, after the expiration of his term, and without the permission of this affiant, owner and lessor, holds over and refuses to deliver possession of the following described premises, to-wit: a frame house in the town of Hazlehurst, known and designated in the survey of said town as lot six in square ten; that all of the rent due on said premises has been paid (or, *that so much rent is due*);

wherefore affiant prays that said Cook may be summoned to show
cause why possession of said premises should not be delivered to
this affiant.   D. W. McRAE.
Sworn to and subscribed this 1st day of January, 1876.
                                    A. B. LOWE, J. P. [SEAL.]

NOTE.—Tenant, if sufficient grounds exist, can file counter affidavit, denying the facts, and the Justice then causes an issue to be made up and tried.
See Secs. 1652, 1653 and on

§ 1649.]
No. 94.—SUMMONS TO TENANT TO REMOVE OR SHOW
CAUSE.

STATE OF MISSISSIPPI,
     To the sheriff or any constable of Copiah county, Greeting:
     Whereas, by affidavit of D. W. McRae, this day filed before us,
we are informed that Charles Cook, tenant, now in possession of a
certain frame house in the town of Hazlehurst, in said county,
known as lot six in square ten of the survey of said town, without
permission of said McRae, landlord, holds over after the expiration
of his term, and will not deliver to said McRae possession of the
same; we, therefore, command you to require the said Cook, or the
person in possession of the same, or claiming possession thereof,
forthwith to remove from the same, or to be and appear before the
undersigned Justice of the Peace for said county, at his office therein,
on the 5th day of January, 1876, to show cause why possession of
the said premises should not be delivered to said McRae. Herein
fail not; and have then there this writ.
     Witness my hand and seal, this first day of January, 1876.
                                    A. B. LOWE, J. P. (SEAL.)

NOTE.—If the tenant does not forthwith remove, or shows no sufficient
cause, upon summons being duly served, as in Sec. 1650, the Justice issues
his warrant of removal.

§ 1651.]   No. 95.—WARRANT OF REMOVAL.

STATE OF MISSISSIPPI,
     To the sheriff or any constable of Copiah county, Greeting:
     You are hereby commanded forthwith to remove Charles Cook
and all other persons from the frame house and lot in the town of
Hazlehurst, in said county, known and designated in the survey of
said town as lot six in square ten, and to put D. W. McRae in full
and complete possession thereof, and of the goods and chattels of
Charles Cook you cause to be made the costs of this suit. Herein
fail not; and make return of your proceedings in this behalf to the
undersigned.
     Witness my hand and seal, this 5th day of January, 1876.
                                    A. B. LOWE, J. P. [SEAL.]

PROCEEDINGS IN BASTARDY.

NOTE.—This is entirely an *ex parte* proceeding before the Justice, where it must commence. See Sec. 1802. The complaint should always be in writing, signed by the woman. In her subsequent examination, in the presence of the accused, she is not under oath. It is a matter for the careful consideration of the Justice, and he can bind the accused to answer, or discharge him.

§ 1802.] No. 96.--COMPLAINT.

STATE OF MISSISSIPPI, ⎫ Before A. B. Lowe, Justice of the Peace
Copiah County. ⎭ for said county, Nov. 6th, 1876.

Bella Rose, a single woman, complains of Smith Brown that heretofore, to-wit: at the county aforesaid, on or about the ...... day of ...., 1876, and at divers times since, the said Smith Brown had illicit intercourse with complainant, and that she [*is now with child by said Brown, which said child, if born alive, will be a bastard*]; wherefore complainant prays that a warrant issue in this behalf for the arrest forthwith of said Smith Brown, and this complaint be examined into. BELLA ROSE.

NOTE.—If the child be born and alive, and be under one year old, instead of the words in brackets, say "has been delivered of a child, a bastard, now living, whose father is said Smith Brown."

No. 97.—WARRANT.

STATE OF MISSISSIPPI.
To the sheriff or any constable of Copiah county, Greeting:
Whereas, Bella Rose, a single woman, having this day made complaint before the undersigned, a Justice of the Peace for said county, that she is now with child by Smith Brown, which, if born alive, would be a bastard; we, therefore, command you to cause said Smith Brown to be brought before us, at our office in said county, forthwith, that examination may be had touching the charge against him. Herein fail not, and have you then there this writ.
Witness my hand and seal, this ...... day of ...., 1876.
A. B. LOWE, J. P. [SEAL.]

No. 98.—BOND TO ANSWER IN CIRCUIT COURT.

STATE OF MISSISSIPPI, COPIAH COUNTY. ⎬ ss.
Know all men by these presents, that we, Smith Brown and Emanuel Hardy, are held and firmly bound unto Bella Rose in the penal sum of five hundred dollars, for which payment well and truly to be made, we bind ourselves and our legal representatives, jointly and severally, firmly by these presents, signed with our hands and sealed with our seals, this ...... day of ...., 1876.
The condition of this obligation is such that if the above bound Smith Brown shall be and personally appear before the Circuit Court of said county, at the next regular term thereof, to answer the

complaint of Bella Rose, a single woman, on a charge filed before A. B. Lowe, Justice of the Peace for said county, that she is with child by him, said Brown, which, if born alive, would be a bastard; and shall attend said court from day to day, and term to term, until said complaint shall be heard and disposed of; then this obligation to be void, otherwise to remain in full force and effect.

SMITH BROWN, [SEAL.]
EMANUEL HARDY, [SEAL.]

FENCES, PARTITION WALLS, AND TRESPASS BY STOCK.

§ 1909.]
No. 99.—PETITION FOR ORDER TO VIEW FENCE.

To the Hon. A. B. Lowe, Justice of the Peace for the county of Copiah, and State of Mississippi:

Your petitioner, Stephen Ragland, would show that heretofore, to-wit: during the month of February, 1876, desiring to erect a fence on a line which divides his land from the land of Geo. Riley, in said county, running along the south boundary of the northwest quarter of the northwest quarter of section 27, in township 9 of range 8 east, one-quarter mile in length, the land of said Riley being used by him for depasturing cattle and hogs, while the land of your petitioner was intended for garden and horticultural purposes; the said Riley was requested to contribute his proper share of the work and furnish the requisite materials for building said fence, which he refused to do, whereupon your petitioner constructed the whole of said fence, of a proper and suitable kind, and according to law; wherefore he prays the appointment of proper persons to assess the amount which should be contributed by the said Riley, after viewing said fence, for the construction thereof, &c.

STEPHEN RAGLAND.

---

§ 1909.]   No. 100.—ORDER TO VIEW FENCE.

STATE OF MISSISSIPPI,
To Thomas H. Wheeler, W. P. Beacham and Allen Case, householders of the county of Copiah:

Whereas, Stephen Ragland, by petition in writing filed before the undersigned Justice of the Peace for said county, setting forth that he hath constructed a fence on a line which divides his land from the land of George Riley, being one-quarter mile long, on the south boundary of the northwest quarter of the northwest quarter of section 27, in township nine of range 8 east, in said county, to the erection whereof, after being requested to do so, the said Riley refused to contribute his proper share of the work and furnish the requisite materials necessary for said fence, and still refuses, although using and being benefited thereby; and having prayed for an order for the appointment of proper persons to assess the amount which should be contributed by said Riley; Now, therefore, knowing you to be respectable, impartial householders of the neighborhood of the parties hereto, we do appoint you to view the said fence, after giving five days' notice of the time of your meeting for that purpose, to said Riley; and upon such view, after a full hearing of the parties, and the evidence that each may introduce, to determine and assess the amount, if any, to be paid by said Riley to said Ragland, as his proper share of the expenses of constructing said fence; and certify the same under your hands to said Ragland, endorsed upon this writ.

Witness my hand and seal, this 10th day of March, 1876.

A. B. LOWE, J. P., [SEAL.]

---

§§ 1909, 1915.]

No. 101.—CERTIFICATE OF HOUSEHOLDERS.

By virtue of the within (*or foregoing*) order to us directed, we did, on the 16th day of March, after giving to said George Riley five days' notice of the time of meeting for the purpose, a copy of which notice is hereto attached, view the fence therein described, and, after a full hearing of the parties, and evidence introduced by each as to the value of the said fence, and otherwise, do hereby, under our hands, certify that in our judgment, the amount due by George Riley to Stephen Ragland, as his proper share of the expenses of erecting said fence, is eighteen dollars, and we accordingly assess said sum in favor of said Ragland. We certify that said fence is well built, of large, sound, pine rails, being ten rails high, and staked and ridered, and fully one-quarter mile long. Signed this 16th day of March, 1876. THOMAS H. WHEELER,

W. P. BEACHAM,

ALLEN CASE.

---

§§ 1909, 1915.]

No. 102.—NOTICE BY HOUSEHOLDERS OF TIME OF MEETING.

COPIAH COUNTY, MISS., March 10th, 1876.

To George Riley:

You will take notice that the undersigned, appointed upon the application of Stephen Ragland, by A. B. Lowe, a Justice of the Peace for said county, to view a partition fence dividing the land of said Ragland from yours, for the purpose of ascertaining the amount due by you as your share for erecting the same, will, on the 16th day of March, assemble on the premises to make such view, when you can be present, if you see proper, and be heard with your witnesses. Respectfully,

THOMAS H. WHEELER,

W. P. BEACHAM,

ALLEN CASE.

NOTE.—The same proceedings as above are applicable in partition walls, and the forms as set down can be used, except that in the order to view wall the Justice appoints three mechanics, instead of householders.

TRESPASS BY STOCK.

§ 1922.]　　No. 103.—NOTICE OF DETENTION.

Copiah County, Miss., June 10th, 1876.

Mr. Polk Ferguson:

SIR—You are hereby notified that a brown mare mule (*or horse, ox, goat or hog*), belonging to you, and addicted to fence breaking, and found within my cultivated fields (*or pasture, or enclosed grounds*), has been taken and confined in my stables this day; that the same is at your disposal, upon the payment to me of seventy-five cents for each day so kept by me. And injury has accrued to me by this trespass.　　Respectfully,

A. J. LUSK.

§ 1921.]　　No. 104.—NOTICE OF DAMAGE.

Copiah County, Miss., June 10, 1876.

Mr. John Crawford:

SIR—You are hereby notified that six oxen in your charge, and said to belong to you (*or any other stock, number and kind*), did, on the night of the 9th of June, 1876, break into my growing corn field, enclosed by a lawful fence; that the said stock have done me great damage, and that for each ox I demand the payment of three dollars, being eighteen dollars, damage done me by them. I shall demand double damages, as authorized by law.

Respectfully,　　　　　J. M. MOODY.

§ 1921.]

No. 105.—SUIT FOR DAMAGES DONE BY STOCK.

Copiah County, Miss., June 12, 1876.

John Crawford　　　　To J. M. Moody,　　　　Dr.

June 9th, 1876.—To damages done by six oxen, in breaking into my corn field...$18 00

§ 1923.]　　No. 106.—NOTICE TO PLAINTIFF.

Copiah County, Miss., June 15th, 1876.

Mr. J. M. Moody:

SIR—You will take notice that in the suit instituted by you against me, to be heard on the 24th of June, 1876, for damages done your growing crop by my stock, I will controvert by witnesses the sufficiency of your fence.

Respectfully,　　　　　JOHN CRAWFORD.

§1925.] No. 107.—SUIT FOR THROWING DOWN FENCE.

Copiah County, Miss., }
July 8, 1876. }

Albert Martin,   To Harvey Dodds,   Dr.

July 4, 1876. To throwing down fence on my land and enclosing same, in said county, on said day, without my permission, and to my injury...$20 00

---

§1924.]
No. 108. SUIT FOR SHOOTING OR DOGGING STOCK.

Copiah County, Miss., }
October 26, 1876. }

Oct. 15, 1876. Simon Jones,   To Henry Duncan,   Dr.

To shooting (or injuring by beating, cutting, or dogging) one white horse, found within his field, on said day in said county, not being enclosed by a lawful fence, and damaging the same, twenty-five dollars...............................$50 00

NOTE.—The point to inquire into in these suits is, what is a lawful fence? See §§ 1905, 1906, and 1907.

OBSTRUCTION TO WATER COURSES.

§1935.]   No. 109.—COMPLAINT.   •

To H. J. Harris, Esq., Justice of the Peace for Copiah County, State of Mississippi:

The undersigned, a citizen of said county, complains of Samuel Stackhouse that heretofore, to-wit: In the month of October, 1875, he did, not being duly authorized so to do by law as provided by the statute in that behalf, erect an embankment on land adjoining your complainant (and constructed a dam across a stream dividing the land of complainant from his own), whereby, the water not having free course, and being obstructed by said embankment (*or dam*), has been caused to overflow on the land of complainant, to the injury of said land (*and the growing or planted crop thereon.*) Your complainant has informed said Stackhouse thereof, and requested the removal of said embankment (*or opening said dam*), but he failed and refused so to do, and still fails and refuses ; wherefore, your complainant prays that said Samuel Stackhouse may be summoned before you, and such proceedings had in the premises, as shall be according to law.   March 9, 1876.

WILLIS BARNES.

---

§1935.]   No. 110.—SUMMONS.

THE STATE OF MISSISSIPPI,

To the sheriff or any constable of Copiah county. Greeting:

We command you to summon Samuel Stackhouse to be and appear

4

before the undersigned Justice of the Peace for said county, at his office therein, on the 12th day of March, 1876, to hear the complaint of Willis Barnes, filed before the said Justice, on the 9th day of March, 1876, touching his refusal to remove a certain embankment (*or open a dam on a certain water course*), erected by him without authority of law, and to the injury of said complainant, and to do what the law requires in the premises ; and have then and there this writ.

Witness my hand and seal, this 9th day of March, 1876.

H. J. HARRIS, J. P. [SEAL.]

---

§§ 1935, 1936.]   No. 111.—SUMMONS TO HOUSEHOLDERS.

STATE OF MISSISSIPPI,

To the sheriff or any constable of Copiah county, Greeting:

Whereas, Willis Barnes, on the 9th day of March, 1876, filed with the undersigned Justice of the Peace for said county, a complaint against Samuel Stackhouse, for the erection of a certain embankment (*or, a dam across a certain stream*), on lands adjoining his own, in said county, without the authority of law, whereby the lands of complainant were injured by the overflow of the water ; and whereas, the said Stackhouse has heretofore been summoned in this behalf, and there was chosen, according to law, on the return of said summons, by the said Justice and the parties hereto, three respectable, impartial householders of the neighborhood of said parties, to-wit: A. F. Andre, W. C. Wilkerson, and John Thompson, who, after being duly sworn faithfully and impartially to discharge the duties required of them, shall examine the obstructions complained of, and shall, or a majority of them, report, in writing, to the said Justice, whether, in their opinion, such obstructions injure the land of said Barnes, or may prevent him from planting a crop thereon, or will injure the same when planted ; Therefore, we command you to summon said householders to be and appear before said Justice, at his office, in said county, forthwith, that they may be sworn as aforesaid, and proceed to make the examination and report, as by law required, and herein they shall fail not under penalty of twenty dollars; and have you before us, at an early day, this original.

Witness my hand and seal this 12th day of March, 1876.

H. J. HARRIS, J. P. [SEAL.]

---

§1935.]   No. 112.—REPORT OF HOUSEHOLDERS.

STATE OF MISSISSIPPI, }
Copiah County.   } ss.

To H. J. Harris, Esq., Justice of the Peace for said county :

The undersigned, heretofore chosen, required and sworn to examine and report upon certain obstructions complained of by Willis Barnes, as having been erected by Samuel Stackhouse, on lands adjoining the lands of said Barnes, in said county, would respectfully report that they did, on the 13th day of March, 1876, proceed to the land of said Barnes, and make a full examination of said obstructions, and in our opinion, ... acres of the land of said Barnes is materially injured thereby, so much so as to prevent him planting a crop thereon, the land being open tillable land, and suitable for crops of any character, if not overflowed, and that said obstruction caused the overflow thereof; the said Stackhouse being notified of our opinion herein. All of which is respectfully submitted, this 14th day of March, 1876.

A. F. ANDRE,
W. C. WILKERSON,
JOHN THOMPSON.

§1935.] No. 113.—PRECEPT TO SHERIFF OR CONSTABLE.

THE STATE OF MISSISSIPPI,

To the sheriff or any constable of Copiah county, Greeting:

Whereas, A. F. Andre, W. C. Wilkerson, and John Thompson, householders of said county, heretofore chosen and sworn to examine into and report to the undersigned Justice of the Peace for said county, concerning certain obstructions complained of before us, by Willis Barnes, as having been, without warrant of law, erected on lands adjoining lands of said Barnes, by Samuel Stackhouse, whereby injury results to the lands of said Barnes, have filed with us the report of their examination, which sustains the complaint of said Barnes; and whereas, the said Stackhouse being notified of the opinion and report of said householders, and having failed immediately to remove said obstructions: We, therefore, command you, forthwith, to cause such obstruction to be removed, so as to afford free passage for the water: and herein fail not, and make return of this writ, with your proceedings indorsed thereon, to the undersigned.

Witness my hand and seal, this 15th day of March, 1876.

H. J. HARRIS, J. P. [SEAL.]

ARBITRATION AND AWARD.

NOTE.—This is a chapter of our laws which should be more freely used by litigants; it would save to them money and time, and lessen the business of courts. Hundreds of minor matters, vigorously prosecuted in the courts, assume before the end, in costs alone, huge proportions, while submitted to friends and neighbors, as arbitrators, in the commencement, could be settled at once, with insignificant outlay. All the parties have to do in a pending suit in any court, is to consent to submit the matter to two or more arbitrators, and so declare in open court, when a rule for such submission must be entered on the minutes or docket.

§§ 1962 to 1965.]

No. 114.—RULE FOR SUBMISSION.
(To be entered on the Docket.)

This day appeared in open court the parties to this suit, and the court being informed that said parties have consented to have all.

matters in controversy in such suit referred, for decision, to A. B.,. C. D. and E. F., or any two of them, selected by them as arbitrators, a rule of court is therefore hereby entered for such submission to the arbitrators selected pursuant to the application of the parties; the papers filed in the case being given to said arbitrators, and further proceedings herein being suspended. Entered this ...... day of ...., 1876.   HORACE MILLSAPS, J. P.

---

§ 1965.]   No. 115.—AWARD.
(To be entered of record as the judgment of the court.)

The arbitrators, A. B., C. D. and E. F., to whom was submitted the matters in controversy between O. F. and G. H., parties to this suit, by their selection and consent, having taken the statement of the parties and of all witnesses adduced, make and return into court this award, to wit: The said G. H., defendant, to pay to O. F., plaintiff, the sum of forty dollars, in full satisfaction of his claim (*or damages, &c.,*) and one-half the costs accrued to be taxed, and the said plaintiff to pay the other half of the costs. The arbitrators making no charge for services. Made and returned this ...... day of ...., 1876.   A. B.,
                                                  C. D.,
                                                  Arbitrators.

Approved: HORACE MILLSAPS. J. P.

NOTE.—When matters of controversy are pending between parties, before suit brought, they can also be submitted to arbitrators; and should always be so submitted, if the parties can be brought to consent. They will make money by the operation. The following forms will answer:

§ 1967.]   No. 116.—AGREEMENT TO SUBMIT.

This agreement entered into this ...... day of ...., 1876, by and between A. B. and C. D., citizens of the county of Copiah and State of Mississippi, between whom pecuniary differences (*or legal controversies*) exist. witnesseth: that said parties. not desiring to resort to the courts for a settlement of said differences, but desirous of terminating the same without litigation, hereby stipulate that the matters in dispute between them shall be submitted to the decision and award of E. F. and G. H., neighbors and citizens of said county, arbitrators, mutually selected and chosen by them, granting hereby to said arbitrators the power, if it shall in their judgment become necessary, to choose another impartial and disinterested person to act with them; That the award of said arbitrators, when made in writing and signed by them, and attached to this agreement. shall finally decide said differences, and shall be submitted to Horace Millsaps, a Justice of the Peace for District No. 3 of said county (*or to the Circuit Court of said county, if the award will probably be more than* $150), to be entered as a rule of his said court, and then to have the effect of a judgment and be enforced as other judgments of said court; and that the parties hereto bind themselves, each to the other, firmly by these presents, in the penalty of one hundred dollars, to abide by and perform the award, when made, pursuant to the terms hereof, by said arbitrators.

The matters in dispute to be submitted, are agreed to be substantially these; and that evidence, in any way relating thereto, can be fully heard by said arbitrators: A. B. claims the sum of one hundred and twenty-five dollars as due him by C. D., for the sale and delivery to him of a certain bay mare, in the spring of 1875, and that as evidence he holds the promissory note of C. D. for that sum; C. D. does not deny the execution of the note or the purchase, but claims, as set-off, that A. B. sold him the mare as sound in all respects, as only eight years old, and good in harness, when she was fully ten years old, unsound, and only fit for the plow, etc., etc. (*or any matter of difference whatever set forth distinctly.*)

In witness of which, the parties hereto have hereunto set their hands, the day and year first above written, in the presence of witnesses.

S. T., witness.

A. B.
C. D.

---

§1968. No. 117.—AWARD.

(To be attached to agreement, and delivered to party entitled to it.)

This ...... day of ......, 1876, personally came and appeared before the undersigned arbitrators, A. B. and C. D., at the residence of L. M., in Copiah county, and submitted to us the matters of difference between them, pursuant to the agreement hereto attached; and the parties being heard in their own behalf, and all the evidence adduced on both sides, duly considered, the arbitrators do make this award, as a full settlement between the parties, and attach the same to the agreement, as aforesaid, to wit: We find the said mare to have been ten years old at the day of sale, and further find her, by abundant testimony, to have then been, and still is both balky and unreliable in harness, and that, in our opinion, was not worth more than eighty dollars on the day sold; therefore, our decision is, that the said C. D. pay to the said A. B. the sum of eighty dollars, with interest at ten per cent. from the date of the maturity of the note given, and the same, when paid, shall be in full satisfaction thereof, and the said note shall then be returned to said C. D.

Made and awarded, this ...... day of ......, 1876.

E. F.
G. H.
Arbitrators.

Witness:

    S. T.

---

§ 1968.]

No. 117.—AFFIDAVIT OF WITNESS TO AGREEMENT AND AWARD.

STATE OF MISSISSIPPI, } ss.
  Copiah County. }

Personally appeared before the undersigned Justice of the

Peace for said county. S. T., who being by me duly sworn, deposes and says, that he was present and saw A. B. and C. D. sign an agreement to submit all matters of controversy between them to E. F. and G. H., and that he signed the same as witness, on the ...... day of ......, 1876; that he was also present and saw the said E. F. and G. H. sign, publish, and declare their final award and arbitration, in writing, between the said parties, bearing date the ...... day of ......, 1876, and that this deponent set his name as a subscribing witness to the said award, at the time of its execution and publication aforesaid: and that the papers now submitted to him are the agreement and written award aforesaid.

S. T.

Sworn to and subscribed, this ...... day of ......, 1876.

HORACE MILLSAPS, J. P. [SEAL.]

NOTE.—If the party against whom the award is made fails or refuses to pay, the party having the agreement and award files the same in the court mentioned, and after proof of the execution of the agreement and award, will enter up judgment.

§ 1968.   No. 119.—JUDGMENT ON AWARD.

A. B. 〕   On agreement of parties and award
vs. 〕   of arbitrators.
C. D. 〕   Filed the ...... day of ...., 1876.

On reading and examining the articles of agreement made and entered into between said A. B. and C. D., on the ...... day of ...... 1876, in pursuance of the statute in that behalf, wherein E. F. and G. H. were selected and chosen by the parties as arbitrators, to settle all matters of difference between them, and upon due consideration of the award and decision of said arbitrators, attached to said agreement, and the court being satisfied, by affidavit of S. T. filed with said award, and full proof of the execution of said agreement and written award, have caused the same to be filed, and hereby consider, adjudge and order that the said A. B. do have and recover of and from the said C. D. the sum of eighty dollars, with interste from maturity of the note of said C. D., at ten per cent. per annum, hereby declaring said award shall be final, and that both parties are finally concluded by the same, and the judgment herein. For said sum of eighty dollars, interest and costs, execution may issue. Ordered this ...... day of ...., 1876.

HORACE MILLSAPS, J. P.

EXEMPT PROPERTY.

NOTE.—The officer levying an execution or attachment, where there are doubts as to the liability of the property seized, or about to be seized, or a statement made that the property is exempt, should always demand of plaintiff bond of indemnity.

§ 2132.] No. 120.—BOND OF INDEMNITY.
(Same as No. 33.)

---

§ 2134.] No. 121.—DEFENDANT'S REPLEVY BOND.

STATE OF MISSISSIPPI, COPIAH COUNTY. }ss.

Know all men by these presents, that we, James Case and William Cole are held and firmly bound unto John Ford in the sum of two hundred dollars, for which payment well and truly to be made, we bind ourselves and legal representatives, jointly and severally, firmly by these presents, signed with our hands and sealed with our seals, this ...... day of .... 1876.

The condition of this obligation is such that, whereas, an execution issued by Horace Millsaps, a Justice of the Peace for said county, on the ...... day of ...., 1876, in favor of John Ford and against the above bound James Case, for eighty dollars, by virtue of a judgment heretofore obtained before said Justice against said Case, for the said sum, with interest and costs, was, by J. P. Matthews, sheriff of said county, levied upon a certain yoke of oxen and wagon, valued at one hundred dollars, as the property of said Case; and whereas, the said Case claims said property as exempt under the laws in that behalf, and desires to replevy the same that an issue shall be made up, at the return term of said execution, by the court, and said claim tried, and upon the execution and approval of these presents, the said property is restored to said Case; Now, therefore, if the said Case shall have said property forthcoming to abide the event of an issue to be made up and tried as aforesaid, then this obligation to be void, otherwise to remain in full force and effect.   JAMES CASE,
                                                    WILLIAM COLE.

Approved: J. P. MATHEWS, Sheriff.

NOTE.—If land of debtor exceeds 80 acres, or $2,000 in value, and no other property found, it is the duty of the officer holding the execution or attachment, to levy on all the land, and proceed as directed in Secs. 2136 and 2137. This applies as well to towns and cities, as to the country.

---

§ 2136.] No. 122.—OATH OF FREEHOLDERS.

You, and each of you, do solemnly swear, that you will well and truly perform the duties enjoined upon you, in regard to the matters submitted to your consideration, according to Article IV of an Act entitled "An Act in relation to exempt property," of the Revised Code of Mississippi.

§ 2136.] No. 123.—ATTACHMENT BY FREEHOLDERS.

THOMAS POLLOCK,   )   Before Horace Millsaps, Justice of the
       vs.   }   Peace for the County of Copiah, State of
ROBERT BUIE.   )   Mississippi.

The undersigned freeholders of said county, heretofore selected

and sworn according to law, to set off to said defendant a portion
of his land in said county, embracing his dwelling-house and out-
houses, not to exceed eighty acres in quantity, nor two thousand
dollars in value, did, on the ...... day of ......, 1876, proceed to said
land and make due allotment thereof, as follows, to-wit: The quantity
of land owned and occupied by said defendant, as a homestead, we
find to be only eighty acres, to-wit: The east half of the southwest
quarter of section ten, in township nine of range two west, but we
assess the value of the same, including improvements, at two thous-
and five hundred dollars, cash value, and hereby allot and set off to
said defendant the southeast quarter of the southwest quarter, and
ten acres across the southern portion of the northeast quarter of
the southwest quarter, the said allotment embracing the dwelling-
house and out-houses of said defendant.

Made and allotted, this ...... day of ......, 1876, and delivered to
the Sheriff of said county; (*or, if the land exceeds eighty acres, allot
eighty acres, if it does not exceed $2000 in value; or, if only eighty
acres, and not worth, in cash, over $2000, allot the homestead.*)

A. B.,
C. D.,
E F.,
Freeholders.

§ 2138.] No. 124.—~~ATTACHMENT~~ CONTESTED—PLAIN-
TIFF'S AFFIDAVIT.

Allotment.

STATE OF MISSISSIPPI,}
  Copiah County.   } ss.

Personally appeared before the undersigned, Justice of the Peace
for said county, Thomas Pollock, who being by me first duly sworn,
on oath says, that J. P. Matthews, Sheriff of said county, by virtue
of an execution in his hands, duly issued by Horace Millsaps, a
Justice of the Peace for said county, in favor of affiant and against
Robert Buie, on a judgment of said Justice, for the sum of one
hundred and fifty dollars, interest and cost, was levied by said
Sheriff on certain lands of said Buie, which was claimed as exempt
as a homestead, under the laws in that behalf, and that in pursuance
of the statute made and provided, A. B., C. D., and E. F. were
duly selected, as freeholders of said county, to set off to said defendant a portion of said land, embracing the dwelling-house and out-
houses, and not exceeding eighty acres of land, nor two thousand
dollars in value, that said freeholders did, on the ...... day of ......,
1876, make said allotment, giving to said defendant all of said land,
being eighty acres, and assessing the same as not exceeding in value
$2,500 ; that this affiant, plaintiff as aforesaid, verily believes the
allotment made by said freeholders, is not correct (*and that the
land so alloted by them, or some part of it, is liable to sale under his
said execution ;*) wherefore affiant prays a summons may issue for

said defendant, to appear and answer this affidavit, and thereupon an issue be made up in the premises, and tried.

THOMAS POLLOCK.

Sworn to and subscribed, this .... day of ...., 1876.

HORACE MILLSAPS, J. P. [SEAL.]

---

§ 2139.] No. 125.—ALLOTMENT CONTESTED—DEFEND-ANT'S AFFIDAVIT.

[This affidavit is like plaintiff's, changing it to suit, in names, and for that part in brackets, stating distinctly wherein he believes it is not correct.]

---

§ 2142.]

No. 126.—SPECIAL JUDGMENT AGAINST PROPERTY FOR PURCHASE MONEY.

This day come the parties in person and by their attorneys, and the witnesses and all the evidence in the cause heard, and the papers and proofs submitted and examined, the court assesses the damages of plaintiff at $.......... It is therefore considered and adjudged by the court that the said plaintiff do have and recover of and from said defendant the sum of .... dollars, the amount sued for, and costs of suit, to be levied of his goods and chattels, lands and tene-ments, for which execution may issue. And the court further con-siders and adjudges that the certain brown mare mule, now in pos-session of said defendant, for which the said note (*or account*) in this action sued on was given, is, by this judgment, especially and expressly condemned to the satisfaction of the amount due on said note, for which special execution may issue.

NOTE.—The execution also must describe the property purchased, as in the judgment. This whole matter of having only what the law gives, and claiming property as exempt, is most grossly and criminally abused. A closer examination, by diligent and honest officers, would not only assist, in the end, in advancing the morals of the people, but make men more cautious in going into debt, and more prompt in paying what they owe.

PROMISSORY NOTES, ENDORSERS AND PROTESTS.

§ 2228.]

No. 127.—NOTE ASSIGNED BY ENDORSEMENT.

$135 00   JACKSON, MISS., January 1st, 1875.

On or before the 1st day of January, 1876, I promise to pay to H. S. Carter (*or, or order*), the sum of one hundred and thirty-five dollars, value received of him, with interest at the rate of ten per ct. per annum from date.   S. H. HART.

(Endorsed on the back:)

Assigned to G. H. Smith, for value received, this 15th day of October, 1875.   H. S. CARTER.

---

§ 2228.   No. 128.—NOTICE OF ASSIGNMENT.

JACKSON, Miss., Oct. 15th, 1875.

S. H. Hart, Esq.:

DEAR SIR—You will take notice that H. S. Carter has this day assigned to me, for value received, your note to him of date Jan.. 1st, 1875, for one hundred and thirty-five dollars.

G. H. SMITH.

No. 129.—GENERAL ASSIGNMENT, WITH POWER OF ATTORNEY.

(Recorded, it becomes general notice.)

Know all men by these presents, that I, John H. Wilkes, late merchant in the town of Beauregard, Copiah county and State of Mississippi, for value received, have sold, and by these presents do sell, assign and deliver unto Few Ball, all my books of accounts, and each and every account therein entered, now due and owing to me (*or, a judgment, or the full description of anything assigned*), to have and to hold the same unto said Few Ball, his heirs, assigns and legal representatives forever, to and for their only use and behoof, hereby constituting and appointing said Few Ball my true and lawful attorney in my name, place and stead, for the purposes aforesaid, to demand, sue for, attach and recover all such sums which are now due me, as well as all such as may hereafter become due and payable, for or on account of all or any of the book accounts, dues, debts and demands above assigned, hereby giving unto said assignee and attorney full power to do and perform all lawful things in the premises, as fully as I might or could do if personally present, with full power of substitution and revocation, hereby confirming all said assignee and attorney, or his substitute, shall lawfully do or cause to be done in the premises by virtue hereof.

In witness of which, I have hereunto set my hand and seal this ..... day of ...., 1875.

JOHN H. WILKES, [SEAL.]

No. 130.—ASSIGNMENT OF A BOND.

(To be endorsed on the Bond.)

Know all men by these presents, That I, John Smith, in the within obligation named, for and in consideration of the seventy-five dollars, unto me this day paid, by William Jones, the receipt of which I hereby acknowledge, have assigned, transferred, and set over, unto the said Jones, his heirs, assigns, and legal representatives, to and for his and their only use and behoof, the within obligation, which is given and executed by Thomas Watkins and Samuel Nolins, to said Smith, bearing date the ...... day of ...., 1876, to secure the payment of ninety dollars, with lawful interest, as therein fully expressed ; together with all rights, remedies, incidents, and appurtenances, whatsoever, thereunto belonging, or in any wise appertaining, and all my right, title, and interest therein.

In witness of which I have hereunto set my hand and seal, this .... day of ...., 1876.

JOHN SMITH, [SEAL.]

No. 133.—DOMESTIC BILL OF EXCHANGE OR DRAFT.

$125 00.   BEAUREGARD, Miss., Oct. 10, 1874.

At sight (*or*, 30, 60, 90 *days after sight or date,*) for value received, please pay to Samuel Brown, or order, one hundred and twenty-five dollars, on account of,

Yours respectfully,   BENJ. KING.

To J. & T. Green, Jackson, Miss.

SURETIES AND JOINT DEBTORS.

§ 2257.]   No. 132.—NOTICE BY SURETY.

MAGNOLIA, MISS., Nov. 2, 1876.

Mr. W. W. Vaught : Dear Sir—The note held by you for one hundred and ten dollars, signed by A. M. Tendall, and by myself as surety, became due on the first instant, and I hereby notify you to commence and prosecute legal proceedings against said Tendall, principal, for the recovery of said debt.

Respectfully,   J. M. CAUSEY.

NOTE.—The creditor, after the foregoing notice, must commence suit within thirty days, or the surety or endorsee for accommodation, is discharged. On a judgment and execution against principal and surety, for the purpose of making all the money out of principal, surety should file his affidavit ; if he does not do so, the officer makes the money the easiest way, out of either.

---

§ 2261.]   No. 133.—AFFIDAVIT OF SURETY.

STATE OF MISSISSIPPI, } ss.
   Copiah County.   }

Personally appeared before the undersigned Justice of the Peace for said county, E. A. Rowan, who being by me duly sworn, on oath says, that he is only surety on a certain promissory note signed by George Miller and himself, for one hundred dollars, payable to H. Hartlow, upon which note judgment was obtained before John F. Groome, a Justice of said county, and execution issued thereon, on the .... day of ...., 1876 ; wherefore affiant makes this affidavit and files the same with the Sheriff (*or, Constable,*) of said county holding said execution, for his protection in this behalf.

E. A. ROWAN.

Sworn to and subscribed, this .... day of ...., 1876.

JOHN F. GROOME, J. P. [SEAL.]

PUBLIC ROADS.

NOTE.—The laws on the subject of working roads in this State are very full and very good, the difficulty is, they are in no wise enforced. Let the overseers act promptly and vigorously under Secs. 2354, 2355 and 2356. Few delinquents are reported, and those who are, generally escape, because the overseer has not fully complied with the law. Use the following forms, and few will escape.

§ 2354.]

No. 134.—APPOINTMENT TO NOTIFY HANDS.

COPIAH COUNTY, MISS., March 9th, 1876.

Albert Ferguson :

I hereby appoint you to notify and summon the road hands named in the annexed list, belonging to my road, being that part of the Rockport road, beginning at the corporation line of Beauregard on the east, and running five miles, to meet me at the corporation line of said town, on said road, at 8 o'clock, A. M., on the 14th day of March, 1876, with the tools set down with each name, to work on and repair said road for three days, if so long a time shall be found to be necessary. And herein fail not, or become liable to a penalty of ten dollars.

JOHN CRAWFORD, Overseer.

(Attach to this note your list of hands, as follows:)

LIST OF HANDS.

List of road hands owing service on the part of Rockport road, commencing at the corporation of Beauregard, and running east five miles, to be summoned to work on said road, by Albert Ferguson, one of said hands, on the 14th day of March, 1876, and the tools for each to bring with them designated:

Solomon Bruce, chopping ax.
James Buchanan, grubbing hoe.
Jesse Rose, weeding hoe.
Henry Washington, weeding hoe.
John Morgan, one horse and plow.
Elbert Dunbar, weeding hoe.
Thomas Hamilton, weeding hoe.

JOHN CRAWFORD, Overseer.

AFFIDAVIT.

(To be written on or attached to list.)

STATE OF MISSISSIPPI, COPIAH COUNTY. } ss.

Personally appeared before the undersigned Justice of the Peace for said county, Albert Ferguson, named in the foregoing list, and made oath that he personally (*or, by written note left*) notified and warned each and every one named in said list, on the 10th day of March, 1876, designating the tools named for each to bring with him, and the place of meeting.   ALBERT FERGUSON.

Sworn to and subscribed this 14th day of March, 1876.

E. F. MULLINS, J. P.

---

§ 2355.]   No. 135.—OVERSEER'S DELINQUENT LIST.

To E. F. Mullins, Esq., Justice of the Peace for the county of Copiah and State of Mississippi:

The undersigned, road overseer, duly appointed and commissioned by the Board of Supervisors for said county, for that part of the Rockport road commencing at the corporation line of the town of Beauregard, on the east, and continuing five miles, would respectfully report that on the 10th day of March, 1876, he caused the hands allotted to said road to be summoned to work said road, and to meet for that purpose at the corporation line of said town, on the 14th day of March, 1876, a list of those summoned, sworn to by the party making the summons, hereto attached; that on said day and for the two succeeding days, there failed to appear and perform the service required, or to furnish a substitute, or to pay the commutation money, the following persons:

John Morgan, with horse and plow,
Elbert Dunbar.
Thomas Hamilton.

And the foregoing list contains the names of all delinquents.

JOHN CRAWFORD, Overseer.

Sworn to and subscribed this 17th day of March, 1876.

E. F. MULLINS, J. P.

---

§ 2356.]   No. 136.—WARRANT FOR ARREST OF DELIN-
QUENT HANDS.

THE STATE OF MISSISSIPPI,

To the sheriff or any constable of Copiah county, Greeting:

We command you, That you take, forthwith, the bodies of John Morgan, Elbert Dunbar, and Thomas Hamilton, if to be found in your county, and them safely keep, so that you have them before the undersigned Justice of the Peace for said county, at his office therein, on the 18th day of March, 1876, to answer the State of Mississippi on a charge of failing to work on the public roads of said county, after due and formal notice given of the time and place, by the overseer thereto authorized, contrary to the form of the statute in such case made and provided ; and have then there this writ.

Witness my hand and seal this 17th day of March, 1876.

E. F. MULLINS, J. P. [SEAL.]

NOTE.—The delinquent can either pay the fine, upon proof of failure, go to jail one month, or give bond to immediately report to the overseer, and do his portion of work.

---

§ 2356.]   No. 137.—BOND TO PERFORM LABOR.

STATE OF MISSISSIPPI, ⎰
   Copiah County, ⎱ ss.

Know all men by these presents, That we, John Morgan and Wiley J. Tillman, are held and firmly bound unto John Crawford, overseer of part of the Rockport public road, in said county, and to his successors, in the penal sum of one hundred dollars, for which payment well and truly to be made, we bind ourselves and our legal representatives, jointly and severally, firmly, by these presents : signed with our names, and sealed with our seals, this 18th day of March, 1876.

The condition of this obligation is such, That whereas the above bound John Margan having been this day arrested as a delinquent hand on the road aforesaid, by E. F. Mullins, Justice of the Peace for said county, and fined in the sum of six dollars, for three days' delinquency ; and whereas, the said delinquent being discharged from custody by said Justice, upon the execution and approval of these presents ; Now, if the said John Morgan shall immediately report himself to the overseer of said road, or his successor, and perform, under his direction, labor on said road, for the period for which he is delinquent, at such times as said overseer, or his successor, may appoint, and pay the costs of the proceedings against him, this obligation shall be void, otherwise to remain in full force and effect.   JOHN MORGAN,   [SEAL.]

Approved: WILEY J. TILLMAN, [SEAL.]

   E. F. MULLINS, J. P.

NOTE.—It is the duty of the Justice, and he should in no wise omit it, to render judgment on the foregoing bond, against the obligors therein, within thirty days, unless he has been satisfied, by full proof, that the condition has been faithfully performed.

CUTTING TIMBER AND OTHER TRESPASSES.

§ 2473.]

No. 138.—ACCOUNT FOR SUIT IN CUTTING TIMBER.

COPIAH COUNTY, Miss., May 8, 1876.

D. C. Wright,   To A. P. Barry,   Dr.

April 6, 1876. To cutting down (*or, cutting down and taking away, or deadning*) ten pine trees, on my land, in Copiah county, at $5, (*or* $10, *or* $15), for each tree............ ....$50 00

No. 139.—ACCOUNT FOR SUIT FOR TAKING BOAT.

Copiah County, Miss., July 20, 1876.

John Hennington, To C. A. Ray. Dr.

July 4, 1876. To taking away (*or, loosing*) from my landing on Pearl river, in said county, my yawl (*or skiff, or flat,*) without my leave...$20 00

To expenses paid Will. Jenkins in securing and returning yawl, 3 00

$23 00

No. 140.—RAFTSMENS' AFFIDAVIT.

(*To be recorded by Chancery Clerk in "Rafting Record.*)

State of Mississippi, Claiborne County ⎱ ss.

Personally appeared before the undersigned Justice of the Peace for said county, Robert Nally, raftsman, who being by me duly sworn, on oath says, that he is about to engage in cutting and rafting, for sale (*or, for transportation.*) certain cypress and ash timber, on sections seventeen and nineteen, in township thirteen, of range eleven east, in said county, and that the authority by which he acts is, the written permission of John B. Thrasher, who claims said sections as his property. Robert Nally.

Sworn to and subscribed, this 10th day of January, 1876.

Alec. Hutchinson, J. P.

JUSTICE AS CORONER.

No. 141.—SUMMONS FOR JURY.

State of Mississippi, Copiah County. ⎱ ss.

To the sheriff or any constable of said county:

You are required, immediately upon sight hereof, to summon six good and lawful men of said county, to appear before me, Peter Trawick, a Justice of the Peace of said county, at the residence of William Norman, in said county, on the 7th day of June, 1876, at the hour of 4 o'clock in the afternoon of said day, then and there to enquire of, do, and execute all such things as, on behalf of the State, shall be lawfully given them in charge, touching the death of A. B. (*or, a certain person unknown*); and be you then and there, to certify what you shall have done in the premises, and further to do and execute what, in behalf of the State, may then and there be enjoined on you.

Given under my hand and seal, at Rockport, in said county, the 7th day of June, 1876. Peter Trawick, J. P. [seal.]

§ 248.   No. 142.—OATH OF JURORS.

You and each of you do solemnly swear that you will diligently inquire, and true presentment make, on behalf of the State of Mississippi, how or in what manner A. B. (*or, the person unknown*), here lying dead, came to his death, and of such other matters relating to the same, as shall be lawfully required of you, according to the evidence. So help you God!

§ 247.]   No. 143.—OATH OF WITNESSES.

You do solemnly swear that the evidence you shall give to this Inquest, on behalf of the State, touching the death of A. B., shall be the truth, the whole truth, and nothing but the truth.

NOTE.—After the jurors are sworn, the Justice must give them a charge, as contained in section 250, by reading the same to them.

§ 250.]   No. 144.—VERDICT OF JURY.

We, the jury, sitting as an inquest, upon the body of A. B., do find that the said A. B. came to his death by the act of God, in that he died by disease of the heart (*or, in a fit of apoplexy.*)
(Signed by the Jurors.)

Or—

We, the jury, sitting as an inquest, upon the body of A. B., do find that the said A. B. came to his death on the morning of the 7th day of June, 1876, by reason of a gun shot wound in the body of said A. B., made and fired therein by C. D., with a double-barrel shot gun, in the hands of C. D., on the 6th day of June, 1876, in the county of Copiah ; the same being done in a difficulty between the said A. B. and C. D., on the public river road ; we further find that E. F. and G. H. were near by at the time of the shooting, and that J. K. and L. M. were present immediately before and at the death of said A. B.; and we further find the said C. D. guilty of manslaughter (*or, murder, or, that said C. D. acted alone in self-defense, and that the homicide was justifiable.*)
(Signed by Jury.

NOTE.—In case the verdict of the jury should find any one guilty of the death, as principal or accessory, by murder or manslaughter, and not in necessary self-defense, the Justice should at once put the evidence in writing, bind the witnesses to appear before him, or the next Circuit Court, and issue a warrant for the arrest of the parties causing the death, if not already in custody.

AGRICULTURAL LIEN LAW, AND FRAUDULENT REMOVAL OF MORTGAGED PROPERTY.

Acts 1876, page 110.]

No. 145.—AFFIDAVIT FOR WAGES BY CROP LABORER.

STATE OF MISSISSIPPI, COPIAH COUNTY } ss.

Personally appeared before the undersigned Justice of the Peace for said county, Henry Whitfield, who states on oath that Allen Case is justly indebted to him in the sum of sixty dollars, which he refuses to pay, for wages due and unpaid, for work and labor done on the farm of said Case, in said county, whereon said Case resides, in building fences, ploughing land, planting and working a crop of corn, cotton, potatoes and peas, for five months, from the first day of March to the first day of August, 1876, at the rate of twelve dollars per month, for and under contract with said Case; that Samuel House and his wife, Margaret, and Willis Calhoun worked on said farm with affiant during the said year, in cultivating and gathering said crops, and still reside and work thereon, and claim, as your affiant is informed, an interest in said crops; that said Case has gathered, ginned and baled, and has ready for market, two bales of cotton of said crop, on said farm;

Or, has, at Mathews' gin house, a lot of cotton of said crop;

Or, has delivered to Dover & Morris, merchants in the town of Beauregard, said county, one, or two, or three bales of cotton of said crop, sold to them or for shipment;

Or, has in crib so much corn and peas of said crop; or, pumped so many bushels of potatoes of said crop;

Wherefore, your affiant prays the writ of seizure and summons, as by law directed, that said agricultural products may be subjected to his lien thereon, and that justice may be done in the premises.

HENRY WHITFIELD.

Sworn to and subscribed this 10th day of October, 1876.

B. F. JONES, J. P. [SEAL.]

Acts 1876, p. 110.

No. 146.—AFFIDAVIT FOR SHARE OF CROP BY LABORER.

STATE OF MISSISSIPPI, COPIAH COUNTY. }ss.

Personally appeared before the undersigned Justice of the Peace for said county, Lawson Anderson, who states on oath, that on the 15th day of January, 1876, affiant made, with G. W. Mathews, of said county, a verbal contract (*or, written contract, a copy of which is hereto attached*), for the year 1876, to work thirty acres of land of the farm of said Mathews in said county, on which said Mathews now resides (*or, situated, &c.*), the same to be planted in corn and cotton, in equal parts or thereabouts; that said Mathews agreed to furnish affiant house room, team and suitable implements and seed, for preparing the land, cultivating and gathering said crops, as also to feed such team; while affiant, on his part, was to furnish the labor necessary to prepare, cultivate, gather and make the same ready for market, and each party was to have an equal share of all said crops, so raised and gathered; that on said land affiant raised and put into the cribs of said Mathews two hundred and fifty bushels of corn, and has picked and put into cotton houses (*or, gin house*) on said farm, cotton sufficient to make eight bales; that said Mathews has hauled off and sold five bales of cotton raised by affi-

5

ant, and proposes, in the division of said crop, to give affiant only one bale of cotton and fifty bushels of corn, and refuses otherwise to settle with affiant, owing to some pretended set-off against affiant; that all of said corn now remains on said farm, as also as much cotton in the seed as will make three bales; wherefore, affiant prays the writ of seizure and summons, as by law directed, that said agricultural products be subjected to his lien thereon, and that an equitable division of the same be ordered.

LAWSON ANDERSON.

Sworn to and subscribed this 20th day of November, 1876.

HORACE MILLSAPS, J. P. [SEAL.]

Acts 1876, page 111.]

No. 147.—WRIT OF SEIZURE AND SUMMONS FOR WAGES ON CROP.

STATE OF MISSISSIPPI,

To the Sheriff or any Constable of Copiah County:

Whereas, Henry Whitfield has this day filed before the undersigned Justice of the Peace for said county, an affidavit claiming the sum of sixty dollars as wages due and unpaid for work and labor done on the farm of Allen Case, in said county, for five months, from the 1st day of March to the 1st day of August, 1876, at the rate of twelve dollars per month, in building fences, ploughing land, and planting and working a crop of corn, cotton, potatoes and peas, on said farm, and for said Case; and that Samuel House and Margaret, his wife, and Willis Calhoun worked with affiant during said year, on said farm, and believed to be interested in said crops: and, whereas, said Case refuses to pay said affiant the said sum for said wages, and has ready for market, on said farm, two bales of cotton, and has in cribs, on said farm, two hundred bushels of corn, of said crops; Therefore, we command you to seize such agricultural products, or so much thereof as shall be sufficient to pay the complainant's demand, and all costs, and to safely hold the same, so as to have it subject to the further order of said Justice, and that you summon the said Case, or other persons in possession of said products, and the said Samuel House and his wife, Margaret, and Willis Calhoun, if to be found in your county, as defendants hereto, to be and appear before said Justice, on the 15th day of October, 1876, and show cause, if any they have or can, why such products, or so much thereof as shall be sufficient for that purpose, shall not be sold to satisfy the claim aforesaid, and all costs. Herein fail not, and have you then there this writ, with your proceedings thereon endorsed.

Witness my hand and seal this 10th October, 1876.

E. F. MULLINS, J. P. [SEAL.]

Acts 1876, page 111.

No. 148.—WRIT OF SEIZURE AND SUMMONS—SHARE OF CROP.

THE STATE OF MISSISSIPPI,

To the Sheriff or any Constable of Copiah county:

Whereas, Lawson Anderson has this day filed before the undersigned Justice of the Peace for said county, an affidavit claiming four bales of cotton and one hundred and twenty-five bushels of corn, as his share of a certain crop of cotton and corn, raised and gathered by affiant on the farm of G. W. Mathews, in said county, during the year 1876, under and by virtue of a contract with said Mathews; and whereas, we are informed by said affidavit that said Mathews is removing and disposing of said cotton, or some part thereof, and refuses to deliver to affiant his share of the same, or of said corn, and that there remains on said farm two hundred and fifty bushels of corn and seed cotton sufficient to make three bales of cotton; Therefore, we command you to seize the said agricultural products, or so much thereof as shall be sufficient to satisfy complainant's demand, and all costs, and to safely hold the same, so as to have it subject to the further order of said Justice, and to summon the said Mathews, or the persons in possession of said products (*and the person occupying said land and premises, if Mathews does not*), to be and appear before the said Justice, on the 25th day of November, 1876, and show cause, if any they have or can, why such share, or proportionate share, of the said crops as he may be adjudged entitled to shall not be divided, set apart, and delivered to said complainant. Herein fail not, and have you then there this writ, with your proceedings thereon endorsed.

Witness my hand and seal this 25th day of November, 1876.

HORACE MILLSAPS, J. P. [SEAL.]

NOTE.—Upon seizure, the parties may, by mutual consent, settle and compromise all controversy, by paying costs, the same to be endorsed by the officer, on the writ. This can be done in most every instance, and should always be, if the parties can at all agree. The last affidavit and writ for share applies also to the remedy by the landlord, as the first applies for supplies furnished laborer, and can be altered to suit his complaint. If the judgment of the Justice be for complainant, he issues, at once, his writ of possession, for the share determined in the judgment. In case of wages, execution issues and sufficient property sold to pay judgment and costs.

Acts 1876, page 112.]　　No. 149.—WRIT OF POSSESSION.

THE STATE OF MISSISSIPPI,

To the sheriff or any constable of Copiah county:

Whereas, on the 25th day of November, 1876, a judgment was rendered by the undersigned Justice of the Peace for said county, for two bales of cotton and eighty bushels of corn, in favor of Lawson Anderson, as his share of a certain crop raised and gathered by him, during said year, on the farm of, and under contract with, G. W. Mathews, in said county; Now, therefore, these are to command you, without delay, to immediately proceed to divide, set apart, and deliver to the said Lawson Anderson, the said two bales of cotton and eighty bushels of corn, as his proportionate share of said crop, and to redeliver to said Mathews whatever other agricultural products that may have been seized in the premises, upon his payment of all costs in this behalf; and make return to the said Justice, of this writ, at an early day, with your proceedings thereon indorsed. Witness my hand and seal, this 25th day of November, 1876.

HORACE MILLSAPS, J. P. (SEAL.)

NOTE.—Any agricultural products, for which wages are due, or for share thereof, under one law, can be seized in the hands of any one, if found. A merchant who buys, should be satisfied that the products are not subject to the lein of wages or share. When the landlord does not reside on the land, or rents land for share, or furnishes supplies to laborers, these writs are his protection against removal before division. One thing should be particularly noted by the officer, that on judgment for labor, not on crops, nothing is exempt from seizure. The remedies for removal of crops under deed of trust, or mortgage, or lien of law, is justly severe, and should be rigidly enforced. The following forms will answer:

Acts 1876, page 114.]   No. 150.—AFFIDAVIT ON REMOVAL OF PROPERTY—LIEN OF WAGES.

STATE OF MISSISSIPPI, COPIAH COUNTY. } ss.

Personally appeared before the undersigned Justice of the Peace for said county, James Johnson, who states, on oath, that Richard Chrismas, of said county, being justly indebted to affiant in the sum of forty dollars, for wages due and unpaid, for work and labor done on the farm of Calvit Roberts, near Hazlehurst, in said county, under rent to said Chrismas, in plowing, planting, and gathering thereon, during the year 1876, a crop of cotton, corn, peas, and potatoes, did, on the 8th day of November, 1876, without having first fully paid up and satisfied affiant's lein on said crops, pursuant to the statute in that behalf, although being thereto often requested, knowingly remove and sell said agricultural products, without the consent of said affiant, and against the peace and dignity of the State of Mississippi.   JAMES JOHNSON.

Sworn to and subscribed, this 10th day of November, 1876.

A. B. LOWE, J. P. (SEAL.)

Acts 1876, page 114.]

No. 151.—AFFIDAVIT FOR REMOVAL OF PROPERTY— LIEN FOR SHARE.

STATE OF MISSISSIPPI, COPIAH COUNTY. } ss.

Personally appeared before the undersigned Justice of the Peace for said county. J. F. Thompson, who states on oath that he rented to Thomas Wallace for the year 1876, (*or, contracted with T. W. to work for the year* 1876,) forty acres of open land on the farm on which affiant resides, to be cultivated in corn, cotton and sweet potatoes; that affiant was also to furnish sufficient team for the purposes of cultivating said land and feed the same, the said Wallace to do or have done the work and labor necessary in the planting, cultivating, gathering and preparing said crops for market, and for rent and use of same and said team alliant was to be paid one half of said crops so cultivated and gathered, during said year; that said Wallace did, on the 15th day of October, 1876, in violation of the provisions of the statute in that behalf, remove from said farm, and sell and dispose of a portion of said cotton, to-wit: seventy-eight pounds in the seed, to . . . ., merchants, (*or any one else*) in the town of Beauregard, in said county, before any division or distribution of the share or interest therein to alliant, or others, contrary to the contract vesting such share in alliant, and against the peace and dignity of Mississippi.

J. F. Thompson.

Sworn to and subscribed this 17th day of October, 1876.

Ben. F. Jones, J. P. [seal.]

Acts 1874, page 54.]

No. 152.—AFFIDAVIT FOR FRAUDULENT REMOVAL OF MORTGAGED PROPERTY.

State of Mississippi, Copiah County. }

Personally appeared before the undersigned Justice of the Peace for said county, Benjamin F. Martin, who states on oath, that Hampton Tillman did, on the 10th day of February, 1876, execute and deliver to David W. Simmons, in trust for this alliant, a certain deed, filed for record and duly recorded in the Chancery Clerk's office of said county, on the 15th day of February, 1876, in Mortgage Book 3, page 140; that the purpose of said deed was to secure the payment of a certain promissory note of said Tillman of even date with said deed and payable to said alliant, with interest at ten per cent, from date, on the 1st day of November, 1876, for the sum of sixty dollars, and also to secure the payment of advances made and to be made, by said alliant to said Tillman, during said year, to the amount of one hundred dollars, to enable said Tillman to make and gather a crop on the lands in said deed described; that said Tillman, in consideration of the premises aforesaid, granted, bargained and sold unto said Simmons, in trust as aforesaid, all the crops of corn, cotton, peas and potatoes, to be made and gathered by him, or by others for him, on said land, during said year, conditioned, however, that if said Tillman should pay and satisfy the debt in said deed set forth to this alliant, then said deed to be null and void; that said debt has not been paid, (*nor any part thereof*), and that said Tillman not abiding by his covenants, and in violation of the statute in this behalf, did fraudulently remove from said land, secrete, conceal, sell, and dispose of to parties unknown to alliant (*if known, state it, for such parties are liable to arrest*), said mortgaged cotton; or some part thereof, without the consent of said affiant, and againt the peace and dignity of Mississippi.

Benjamin F. Martin.

Sworn to and subscribed this 20th day of October, 1876.

Josiah Hester, J. P. [seal]

Note.—In the writ for the arrest, in the affidavits for removal or sale, repeat the affidavit substantially, and conclude:

"Wherefore, we command you forthwith to arrest the said ...., and bring him before me at my office, in said county, to answer the State of Mississippi, on the above charge, and to do or receive what, according to law, may be considered touching the same; and have then there this writ.

"Witness my hand and seal this ...... day of ...., 1876.

"..................., J. P. [seal.]"

JUSTICE AS NOTARY PUBLIC.

§ 2233, Acts.1872, page 147.]

No. 153.—PROTEST OF DRAFT—NON-ACCEPTANCE.

United States of America, State of Mississippi. } ss.

By this public instrument of protest, Be it known that I, S. D. Ramsey, a Justice of the Peace, and by virtue of my office, Notary Public for the county of Copiah, in said State, on the fourth day of January, 1876, at the request of A. B., holder of the original bill, whereof a true copy is hereto annexed, at the usual place of abode of C. D., presented to him the said bill for acceptance (*or payment*), which he did not accept (*or pay*) : Whefore, I, the said Notary, at the request aforesaid, do protest the said bill, as well against the drawee of said bill as against all others whom it may concern, for all exchange, re-exchange, damages, costs, charges and interest, already incurred, or to be hereafter incurred, for want of acceptance of the same.

This done and protested, in the town of Hazlehurst, in said State.

In testimony of which I have hereunto, on the day and year first above written, set my hand and affixed my notarial seal.

S. D. Ramsey, J. P. [seal.]

No. 154.—PROTEST OF DRAFT OR NOTE FOR NON-PAYMENT.

United States of America, State of Mississippi. } ss.

By this public instrument of protest, Be it known that I, S. D. Ramsey, a Justice of the Peace, and by virtue of my office, Notary Public for the county of Copiah, in said State, on the fourth day of January, 1876, at the request of A. B., holder of the original bill (*or note,*) whereof a true copy is hereto annexed, at the usual place of abode of C. D., presented to him, the acceptor of said bill, (*or maker of said note*), the original bill (*or note*), and demanded payment of the same, which he did not pay: Wherefore, I, the said Notary, at the request aforesaid, do protest the said bill (*or note*), as well against the drawer (*or maker*) of said bill (*or note*) as against all others whom it may concern, for all [exchange, re-exchange, *if a bill*] damages, costs, charges and interest already incurred, or to be hereafter incurred, for want of payment of the same.

This done and protested, in the town of Hazlehurst, in said county.

In testimony of which, I have hereunto, on the day and year first above written, set my hand and affixed my notarial seal.

S. D. RAMSEY, J. P. [SEAL.]

No. 155.—NOTICE OF PROTEST FOR NON-ACCEPTANCE.

HAZLEHURST, MISS., Jan. 4th, 1876.

Mr. C. D :

SIR—You will take this as due notice that your draft for $150, at thirty days from sight, dated December 27th, 1875, drawn on J. & T. Green, of Jackson, Miss., has this day been protested for non-acceptance. Yours, &c., S. D. RAMSEY, J. P.,

and *ex-officio* Notary Public.

No. 156.—NOTICE OF PROTEST FOR NON-PAYMENT— DRAFT.

HAZLEHURST, MISS., Jan. 4th, 1876.

Mr. C. D.:

SIR—You will take this as due notice that your draft for $150, at thirty days sight, dated November 25th, 1875, drawn on and accepted by J. & T. Green, of Jackson, Miss., has this day been protested for non-payment. Yours, &c., S. D. RAMSEY, J. P.,

and *ex-officio* Notary Public.

No. 157.—NOTICE OF PROTEST FOR NON-PAYMENT— NOTE.

HAZLEHURST, MISS., Jan. 4th, 1876.

Mr. C. D.:

SIR—You will take this as due notice that your note for $150, dated November 1st, 1875, payable at the office of Temple S. Coons & Co., New Orleans, La., sixty days after date, and endorsed by E. F. (*if endorsed*), has this day been protested for non-payment.

Yours, &c,, S. D. RAMSEY, J. P.,

and *ex-officio* Notary Public.

NOTE.—To charge the endorser, he must also have notice, at once, of protest. The Notary must give the party entitled his certificate, attached to the protest.

No. 158.—CERTIFICATE OF SERVICE OF NOTICE.

UNITED STATES OF AMERICA, } ss.
   State of Mississippi. }

I, S. D. Ramsey, Justice of the Peace, and by virtue of my office

Notary Public for the county of Copiah, in said State, do hereby certify that on this 4th day of January, 1876, notice of the protest of the before mentioned bill (*or, draft or note*) was served upon C. D., the drawer of said bill (*or, maker of said note, and E. F., the endorser thereon*), by letters, respectively addressed to him (*or them*), at his (*or their*) reputed place of residence, and the post offices nearest thereto, and deposited the same in the post office in the town of Hazlehurst, in said county.

[SEAL.]　　In testimony of which, I have hereto set my hand and attached my notarial seal.

S. D. RAMSEY, J. P.

§ 12, Acts 1876, p. 114.]

No. 159.—ACCOUNT FOR MONEY WAGES FOR LABOR.

.... County.

A. B.　　　　　To C. D.,　　　　　　Dr.

July 20th, 1876.—To ten days labor in scraping cotton on your farm, at $1 per day.....................................$10 00

STATE OF MISSISSIPPI, ... COUNTY. } ss.

Personally appeared before the undersigned, a Justice of the Peace for said county, C. D., who made oath that the foregoing account is just and true as stated, and that the same remains due and unpaid; and that the amount became due by reason of labor performed by affiant, under contract by said A. B., on the farm of said A. B., in said county, during the month of July, 1876.　　　　C. D.

Sworn to and subscribed before me, this ...... day of ......, 1876.

...., J. P.

NOTE.—By an examination of the law referred to, it will be seen that no property whatever is exempt from a judgment and execution, in such cases as the foregoing; the judgment and execution, however, must set forth the fact that the claim was for labor performed.

NOTE —For the following nine forms, I am indebted to the New Clerk's Assistant, by John S. Jenkins, Esq., Counsellor at Law, New York. They are excellent ones, and will be found very useful:

No. 160.—COMPLAINT—ACTION ARISING ON CONTRACT.

In Justice's Court,.................. County.

A. B.　　　　　) 　　Before C. C., J. P.
vs.　　　　　　}
C. D.　　　　　) 　　　　Complaint.

A. B. plaintiff, complains that C. D., defendant, owes and is indebted to him in the sum of one hundred dollars, for goods, wares, and merchandize, sold and delivered to (*or, for work and labor performed for*) the defendant, on the ...... day of ...., 18..., (*or, at various times between the ...... day of ...., 18..., and the ...... day of......, 18...,*) whereupon, the plaintiff demands judgment against the defendant, for the one hundred dollars.　　　　A. B., Plaintiff.

No. 161.—COMPLAINT—INJURING PERSONAL PROPERTY.

In Justice's Court, ... County.

A. B.   Before C. C., J. P.
vs.
C. D.   Complaint.

A. B., plaintiff, complains that C. D., defendant, carelessly and violently ran against the carriage of the plaintiff, with the team and wagon of the defendant, on the ...... day of ......, 18..., and broke and damaged the said carriage to the amount of twenty-five dollars, whereupon, the plaintiff demands judgment against the defendant, for the twenty-five dollars.   A. B., Plaintiff.

No. 162.—COMPLAINT—BREACH OF WARRANTY.

In Justice's Court, ... County.

A. B.   Before C. C., J. P.
vs.
C. D.   Complaint.

A. B., plaintiff, complains that C. D., defendant, sold a horse to the plaintiff, on the ...... day of ......, 18..., for the sum of .... dollars, and warranted the same to be perfectly sound, kind, and true, but the said horse is blind of the right eye, is vicious, and unruly, and not true in harness; whereby, he is injured to the amount of fifty dollars ; whereupon, the plaintiff demands judgment against the defendant, for the fifty dollars.
        A. B., Plaintiff.

No. 163.—COMPLAINT—FRAUD OR DECEIT.

In Justice's Court, ... County.

A. B.   Before C. C., J. P.
vs.
C. D.   Complaint.

A. B., plaintiff, complains that C. D., defendant, sold a horse to the plaintiff, on the ...... day of ...., 18..., for the sum of .... dollars, which said horse, to the knowledge of the defendant, was diseased of the heaves, at the time of the sale, but the defendant did not inform the plaintiff thereof, whereby the said horse is injured to the amount of fifty dollars, and the plaintiff demands judgment against the defendant, for the same.
        A. B. Plaintiff.

No. 164.
COMPLAINT—CONVERSION OF PERSONAL PROPERTY.

In Justice's Court, ... County.

A. B.   Before C. C., J. P.
vs.
C. D.   Complaint.

A. B., plaintiff, complains that, on or about the ...... day of ......,

18..., he was possessed, as of his own property, of a certain gold watch, of the value of one hundred dollars, which afterwards, and on or about the ...... day of ...., 18..., came into the hands and possession of C. D., the defendant, who sold the same and converted the proceeds to his own use ; whereupon, the plaintiff demands judgment against the defendant, for the one hundred dollars.

A. B.,   Plaintiff.

No. 165.—COMPLAINT. — INJURY TO REAL PROPERTY.

In Justice's Court, ... county.

A. B   ⎱   Before C. C., J. P.
vs.   ⎰
C. D.   Complaint.

A. B., plaintiff, complains that on or about the ...... day of ......, 18..., C. D., the defendant (*or, the horses and cattle of C. D., the defendant*), broke and entered the close of the plaintiff, in said county, and tore down and destroyed the grass and the products of the soil there growing; whereby the plaintiff has sustained damage to the amount of fifty dollars, and he demands judgment against the defendant for the same.   A. B., plaintiff.

No. 166.—COMPLAINT BY AN ASSIGNEE.

In Justice's Court, ... county.

A. B.   ⎱   Before C. C., J. P.
vs.   ⎰
C. D.   Complaint.

A. B., plaintiff, complains that C. D., defendant, was indebted to G. H., on the ...... day of ...., 18..., in the sum of one hundred dollars, for medical services rendered to the said defendant previous to that day, which said indebtedness has been duly assigned to the plaintiff; whereupon the plaintiff demands judgment against the defendant for the one hundred dollars.

A. B., plaintiff.

No. 167.—ANSWER OF DEFENDANT.

In Justice's Court, ... county.

A. B.   ⎱   Before C. C., J. P.
vs.   ⎰
C. D.   Answer.

C. D., the defendant, answers to the complaint, that on the ...... day of ...., 18..., he paid the indebtedness mentioned in the complaint;

Or, that the plaintiff did not perform the work and labor for the defendant mentioned in the complaint;

Or, that he did not warrant the horse mentioned in the complaint to be perfectly sound, kind and true.

C. D., defendant.

No. 168.—ANSWER, WITH NOTICE.

In Justice's Court, ... county.

A. B.	)	Before C. C., J. P.
vs.	}	
C. D.	)	Answer.

C. D., the defendant, answers to the complaint that he did not take, and does not detain the property (*or, did not break and enter the close*), mentioned in the complaint, as is therein stated; and he gives notice that he will prove on the trial of this action that the property mentioned in the complaint was taken, and is detained by him, with the consent and permission of the plaintiff;

Or, that he broke and entered the close mentioned in the complaint, in order to remove a quantity of wheat levied on by him as a constable of said county, by virtue of an execution against the plaintiff, issued by E. F., Justice of the Peace of said county, in favor of G. A., and dated on the ...... day of ...., 18....

C. D., defendant.

---

§ 278.]   C O N S T A B L E .

This office, though not generally, by the ambitious, sought after, and generally forced off on some one who does not wish the place, or, who is not capable of filling it, is yet one, not only of importance, but real dignity, and energetic men, with brains, should be sought to take and execute its duties. These duties are extensive, as § 280 fully proves. Let the Constable be prompt in their execution, or fall under the penalties prescribed for their delay or violation. If a Constable fails to execute and return execution, plaintiff, by motion, can recover the amount and damages from Constable and the sureties on his bond, on giving five days' notice of such motion. The Justice also can, on like motion, by the plaintiff, fine the Constable $50 for failing to return execution. For failure, on demand, to pay over money collected, motion of two days' notice, for amount and damages. See fully on these motions and notice, §§ 282, 283 and 284. The two following forms will suit, by change, all the cases:

§ 282.   No. 169.—MOTION AGAINST CONSTABLE.

STATE OF MISSISSIPPI,)	Before B. F. Jones, Justice,
.... County. }	District No. 2.

John Smith	)
vs.	}
Allen Jones.	)

Motion by plaintiff in the above stated cause for a rule against Thomas H. Wheeler, Constable in said county, and the sureties on his official bond, Allen Case and W. C. Loving, for the amount of the judgment therein and interest, costs and damages, for failure to return the execution issued by the said Justice on the .... day of ...., 1876, and delivered to said Constable.

No. 170.—NOTICE TO CONSTABLE.

COPIAH COUNTY, MISSISSIPPI.

Thomas H. Wheeler, Allen Case and W. C. Loving—Gentlemen:

Take notice that on the 10th day of May, 1876, I will call up a motion entered against Thomas H. Wheeler, Constable, and Allen Case and W. C. Loving, as the sureties on his official bond, before his Honor B. F. Jones, Justice for District No. 2, in said county, this fourth day of May, 1876, for failure to execute and return execution delivered to said Constable, in the case of John Smith vs. Allen Jones, in behalf of plaintiff. The amount demanded is the amount of the judgment in said case, with interest, costs and damages as allowed by law.   JOHN SMITH,
                                                                              Plaintiff.

FORMS.

— ⚡ —

AS A CRIMINAL COURT.

The jurisdiction of the Justice criminally is very large and should be vigorously exercised; and this court should always be used by the citizens instead of carrying all the petty offenses before the Grand Jury. This jurisdiction is concurrent in all matters, when the punishment prescribed is only a fine and (or) imprisonment in the county jail. In the statute laws of this State are over one hundred offences, which can be tried before, and finally disposed of, by Justices of the Peace, and it is their duty to make careful examination of these cases, and so become indeed the conservators of the peace and dignity of the State. There are abundant reasons, however, for the indifference of Justices in the matter of the prompt arrest of offenders, in the fact that no provision is made in our Code for their costs, in case of the insolvency of the prisoner, or in his discharge. It is a long oversight in our law-makers, and a well digested law on this subject would not only reflect credit on the Legislature, but advance the morals and peace of the State.

PRACTICE.

§ 1322.]   No. 171.—GENERAL FORM OF AFFIDAVIT.

STATE OF MISSISSIPPI, COPIAH COUNTY. } ss.

Personally appeared before the undersigned Justice of the Peace for said county, Albert Welch, who being by me duly sworn, deposes and says, that in said county, on the ...... day of ...., 1876, one C. D., did ....[*describe the offense, as near as can be, in the words of the law, defining and punishing the offense, and conclude as follows :*] in violation of the statute in that behalf, and against the peace and dignity of Mississippi.

A. W.

Sworn to and subscribed, this ...... day of ...., 1876.

...., J. P. [SEAL.]

---

§ 1322.]   No. 172.—GENERAL FORM OF WARRANT.

STATE OF MISSISSIPPI,

To the Sheriff or any Constable of Copiah county :

Whereas, by the affidavit of A. W., this day filed in the office of the undersigned Justice of the Peace for said county, charging that C. D. did, in said county, on the ...... day of ...., 1876, [*describe the offense in the words of the affidavit,*] Therefore, we command you, That you take the body of said C. D., if to be found in your county, and him safely keep, so that you have him before the said Justice (*or any other Justice,*) at his office in said county, forthwith (*or, on the* ...... *day of* ...., 1876,) to answer the State of Mississippi on said charge, and to do or receive what, according to law, may be adjudged, touching the same. Have you then there this writ.

Witness my hand and seal, this ...... day of ...., 1876.

.. .., J. P. [SEAL.]

----

§1322.]   No. 173.—SUBPŒNA.

STATE OF MISSISSIPPI,

To the Sheriff or any Constable of Copiah County:

We command you to summon A. B., that all business and excuses being laid aside, he be and appear, in his proper person, before the undersigned Justice of the Peace for said county, at his office therein, instanter (*or, on the* ......*day of* ...., 1876,) then and there to testify those things which he knows in a certain matter then and there to be tried, between the State of Mississippi and C. D., on the part of the said State (*or, C. D.,*) hereof failing not, under penalty; and have you then there this writ,

Witness my hand and seal, this ...... day of .... 1876.

...., J. P. (SEAL.)

----

§1323.] No. 174.—JUDGMENT—FINE AND IMPRISONMENT.

(To be entered on Docket.)

Be it remembered, That at a court held by the undersigned Justice of the Peace for the county of Copiah, at his office therein, this day, A. B. was brought before said court, charged on the affidavit of C. D., with having, on the .... day of ...., 1876, in said county (*here state offense ;*) which charge being stated in the warrant issued by me, was distinctly read to the defendant, in open court, to which he plead not guilty; whereupon, such proceedings were had in said court, that the defendant was convicted of the said charge, and the court renders judgment thereon, that the said A. B. be fined in the sum of twenty dollars, [and be imprisoned in the common jail of said county, for thirty days from this date, and that he pay the costs of the suit, to be taxed.]

Witness my hand.   ...., J. P. (SEAL.)

NOTE.—If the judgment is only a fine, instead of the words in brackets, say " and stand committed to the county jail until the payment of said fine and all costs in this behalf." The mittimus following will answer in both instances :

STATE OF MISSISSIPPI,

. 　To the sheriff or any constable of Copiah county:

Whereas, at a court held by the undersigned, one of the Justices of the Peace for said county, this day, at his office therein, A. B. was brought before said court charged, on the affidavit of C. D., with having, on the ...... day of ...., (*here state the offense*), which charge being stated in the warrant by me issued (*or by any other Justice*), was distinctly read to the defendant in open court, to which he plead not guilty; whereupon such proceedings were had in said court, that the defendant was convicted of the charge above specified, and the court having rendered judgment thereon, that the said A. B. (*here state penalty in judgment*); Therefore, in the name of the State of Mississippi, we command you to convey the said A. B. to the common jail of the county aforesaid, the jailor whereof is hereby required to keep him in safe custody, in said jail, until the judgment so rendered be satisfied, or he be discharged by due course of law.

Witness my hand and seal this ...... day of ...., 1876.

...., J. P. [SEAL.]

----

§ 1325.

No. 176.—BOND FOR APPEARANCE—GENERAL FORM.

NOTE.—The constable when he arrests can take bond for the appearance of the accused, if the court will not be held the day of arrest. The Justice can also do so, if a continuance is had. The following form will answer in all such cases, where bonds are taken; the better practice, however, for the sheriff, and especially for the constable, is to bring the accused and his bondsmen before the Justice who issued the warrant, and let him take their recognizance, and enter the same on the docket. Form No. 176, following, is the proper one. These forms will do to appear at Circuit Court, by changing to suit.

STATE OF MISSISSIPPI, COPIAH COUNTY. }ss.

Know all men by these presents, that we, C. D. and ...., are held and firmly bound unto the State of Mississippi, in the penal sum of .... dollars, for which payment well and truly to be made, we bind ourselves, our heirs and legal representatives, jointly and severally, firmly by these presents, signed with our names and sealed with our seals, this ..... day of ...., 187....

The condition of this obligation is such, that if the said C. D. shall be and personally appear before the court of A. B., one of the Justices of the Peace for said county, at his office therein, on the ...... day of ...., 187... (*or, the Circuit Court of said county, at the next regular term thereof, to be held in the town of ...., on the ...... day of ...., 187...*), to answer the State of Mississippi on a charge of (*here set down the charge as set forth in the affidavit or warrant*), in violation of the statute in that behalf, and against the peace and dignity of Mississippi, and shall remain in attendance upon said court from day to day, and from term to term, until regularly discharged by due course of law, then this obligation to be void, otherwise to remain in full force and effect.

.... [SEAL.]

.................,.............. [SEAL.]

.... [SEAL.]

No. 177.—RECOGNIZANCE TO APPEAR—GENERAL FORM.

STATE OF MISSISSIPPI, COPIAH COUNTY. } ss.

This day personally appeared before the undersigned, one of the Justices of the Peace for said county, C. D., E. F and G. H., of said county, and acknowledged themselves to be severally indebted to the State of Mississippi in the penal sum of one thousand dollars; that is to say, the said C. D. in the sum of five hundred dollars; the said E. F. in the sum of two hundred and fifty dollars, and the said G. H. in the sum of two hundred and fifty dollars to be levied of their respective goods and chattels and lands and tenements. And the said E. F. and G. H. being, by me duly sworn, deposed on oath that they were each worth, in visible property, subject to execution and attachment under the laws, and over and above all legal exemptions, liabilities and liens, the sum of two hundred and fifty dollars. This obligation and recognizance, however, to be void and discharged if the said C. D. shall be and personally appear before the court of the said Justice, at his office in said county, on the .... day of ...., 187... (*or circuit court of said county, to be held in the town of* ...., *on the*...... . *day of* ...., 187...) to answer the State of Mississippi on a charge of (*here state the charge*) in violation of the statute in that behalf and against the peace and dignity of Mississippi, and shall remain in attendance upon said court from day to day and from term to term, until regularly discharged by due course of law.

Witness my hand and seal this .... day of ...., 187...

........................, J. P. [SEAL.]

No. 178.—AFFIDAVIT FOR PEACE WARRANT.

STATE OF MISSISSIPPI, COPIAH COUNTY. }

Personally appeared before the undersigned, Justice of the Peace for said county, A. B., who, being by me duly sworn, on oath says that C. D. had threatened to do affiant (*or his property*) as he has been informed, and verily believes, some serious bodily harm (*or hurt and injury, if property is threatened*) and that affiant fears that said threats will be carried into execution, unless said C. D is restrained by law; that this charge is not made through malice, hatred or ill-will, but for the cause aforesaid; therefore, affiant prays the peace against said C. D. that he be lawfully restrained in this behalf.   A. B.

Sword to and subscribed this .... day of ...., 187...

.................., J. P.

No. 179.—RECOGNIZANCE TO KEEP THE PEACE.

STATE OF MISSISSIPPI, COPIAH COUNTY. } ss.

This day personally came before the undersigned Justice of the Peace for said county, C. D., E. F., and G. H., who acknowledged themselves indebted to the State of Mississippi, in the sum of one thousand dollars; that is to say, the said C. D. in the sum of five hundred dollars ; the said E. F. in the sum of two hundred and fifty dollars, and the said G. H. in the sum of two hundred and fifty dollars, to be levied of their goods and chattels, lands and tenements ; and the said E. F. and G. H., being by me duly sworn, on oath state that they are each worth, in visible property, over and above all their legal exemptions, liabilities, and liens, the sum of two hundred and fifty dollars. This obligation and recognizance is upon this condition : If the said C. D. shall abstain and refrain from doing any harm, hurt, or injury to the person or property of A. B., and shall well and faithfully keep the peace toward the people of this State, and particularly toward the said A. B., for and during the twelve months next ensuing (*or, two years,*) then this obligation to be void, otherwise to remain in full force and effect.

Witness my hand and seal, this ...... day of ...., 1876.

..............................., J. P., [SEAL.]

---

§ 2854.]   ### No. 180.—JUDGMENT TO KEEP THE PEACE.

Be it remembered, That this day, C. D. was brought before the undersigned Justice, upon a charge of threatening to do bodily harm to the person of A. B. (*or, to hurt and injure the property of A. B.,*) and I, the said Justice, being satisfied, by due proof adduced in this behalf, that said charge is in all respects true ; the said C. D. is therefore duly convicted thereof ; and it is thereupon adjudged that the said C. D. forthwith enter into recognizance in the sum of one thousand dollars, with security, to keep the peace toward all the people of this State, and especially toward the person and property of the said A. B., and to be of good behavior, for the space of twelve months from this date, and to pay all costs of this proceeding against him ; and in default whereof, the said C. D. to stand committed until such recognizance be executed and costs paid.

Adjudged and ordered, this ...... day of ...., 1876.

.... J. P. (SEAL.)

---

§§ 2831, 2836.]   ### No. 181.—AFFIDAVIT OF VAGRANCY.

STATE OF MISSISSIPPI, COPIAH COUNTY. } ss.

Personally appeared before the undersigned, a Justice of the Peace for said county, A. B., who being by me duly sworn, on oath states that C. D., of said county, has no visible means of support, but, as affiant is informed and verily believes, for the most part, supports himself by gaming ;

Or, who is an able-bodied person, living without labor or employment, and has no visible means of support ;

Or, who has abandoned his wife and family, without just cause, leaving them without support and in danger of becoming a public charge ;

Or, who keeps a house for public gaming ;

Or, who keeps a house of prostitution ;

Or, is a common prostitute, and has no other known employment for her support ;

Or, is an able-bodied person found begging for a livelihood ;)

That affiant, therefore, believes that said C. D. is a vagrant within the meaning of the law, and prays his arrest.   A. B.

Sworn to and subscribed, this ...... day of ...., 1876.

.............................., J. P.

NOTE.—An affidavit is not necessary, if any of the above charges come within the knowledge of the Justice. In such case he should issue his warrant, or himself be prosecuted for neglect of duty, under Section 2889.

No. 182.—WARRANT FOR VAGRANT.

STATE OF MISSISSIPPI,

To the Sheriff or any Constable of Copiah County :

Whereas, A. B., of said county, has this day made oath before the undersigned, one of the Justices of the Peace for said county, that C. D. is an able-bodied person, who lives without labor or employment, and has no visible means of support (*or any other of the charges in the affidavit*) ; you are therefore hereby commanded, in the name of the State of Mississippi, forthwith to arrest the said C. D. and bring him before the said Justice, at my office, in said county, to answer the said charge, and to be dealt with in the premises according to law.

Witness my hand and seal, this ...... day of ...., 187..

.............................., J. P. [SEAL.]

No. 183.—JUDGMENT IN VAGRANCY.

(To be entered on Docket.)

Be it remembered, that C. D. was this day brought before the undersigned Justice, upon the charge of vagrancy, and I, the said Justice, being satisfied by due and personal examination of the said C. D., and the testimony of A. B. and G. H. adduced in this behalf, that said charge and accusation are in all respects true; the said C. D. is therefore duly convicted before me of being a vagrant, within the meaning and intent of the statute in that behalf ; and it is thereupon adjudged and determined that the said C. D., in default of bond, according to law, and the payment of all costs of the proceedings against him, be committed to the county jail of Copiah county, for ten days from this date.

Adjudged this ...... day of ...., 187..

...., J. P. [SEAL.]

---

§§ 2837, 2839.] No. 184.—MITTIMUS FOR VAGRANT.

STATE OF MISSISSIPPI,

To the Sheriff or any Constable of Copiah County:

Whereas, C. D. has been this day convicted before me, one of the Justices of the Peace for said county, as appears of record in my office, of being a vagrant, I have adjuged that the said C. D. be committed as hereinafter expressed, unless he shall enter into bond payable to the State of Mississippi, in the sum of two hundred dollars, with good security, conditioned for his good behavior for twelve months, and the payment of all costs: you are therefore hereby commanded to convey the said C. D. to the jail of said county; the keeper whereof is hereby authorized and required to confine him in safe custody therein for the space of ten days, and until he shall pay the costs of such imprisonment, and all proceedings relative thereto, or until discharged by due course of law, after ten day's notice to the undersigned, of his intended application for such discharge.

Witness my hand and seal, this .... day of ......, 187..

...., J. P. [SEAL.]

No. 185.—AFFIDAVIT FOR SEARCH WARRANT.

STATE OF MISSISSIPPI, COPIAH COUNTY. } ss.

Personally appeared before the undersigned, one of the Justices of the Peace for said county, A. B., who being by me duly sworn, says that certain personal property of said affiant (*or any other person*), to-wit: (*here state the property distinctly*), of the value of ...... dollars, or thereabouts, was stolen and feloniously taken and carried away from his dwelling house (*or premises, or storehouse, &c.*), in said county, on the ...... day of ...., 187...: and this affiant has reason to believe, and does verily believe, that C. D. has stolen and taken and carried away the same as aforesaid, and that said property, or some part thereof, is now deposited or concealed in the dwelling house, or about the premises of said C. D. (*or other person*), in said county; that this suspicion and charge is not made out of malice, hatred and ill-will to said C. D., but is founded on credible testimony; wherefore process is prayed for to search for the same.

A. B.

Sworn to and subscribed this ... day of ......, 1876.

§ 2824.]   No. 186.—SEARCH WARRANT.

STATE OF MISSISSIPPI,

　　To the sheriff or any constable of Copiah county.

Whereas, A. B. has this day made complaint on oath before the undersigned, one of the Justices of the Peace for said county, that certain personal property, &c. (*as in the affidavit*); and that said affiant suspects that C. D., of said county, did steal, take and carry away the same, and that said property, or some part thereof, is now deposited or concealed in the dwelling house or on the premises of ...., in said county; Therefore we command you, that in the day time, with such aid as shall be needful, you do forthwith proceed diligently to search the dwelling house (*or whatever place is particularly described in the affidavit*) of said ...., where said property is suspected to be deposited or concealed, making known to the occupant thereof, if any, your authority for so doing; and if said property, or any part thereof, be found, that you seize and bring the same before me, at my office, without delay, so that lawful action may be had in the premises.

　　Witness my hand and seal, this ...... day of ...., 187....

　　　　　　　　　　......... ...., J. P. [SEAL.]

NOTE.—If the property seized on a search warrant is claimed by other persons, then an issue shall at once be made up and tried before the Justice, if the value of the property is not more than $150. If more than this, claimant must give bond, as in claimant's issue in civil cases, and the Justice sends the whole matter to the Circuit Court.

———

No. 187.—MITTIMUS ON FAILURE TO GIVE BOND OR
　　PAY FINE AND COSTS—GENERAL FORM.

STATE OF MISSISSIPPI,

　　To the sheriff or any constable of ...... county:

Whereas, C. D. has this day been tried before the undersigned, one of the Justices of the Peace for said county, on the charge of (*whatever the charge be in the affidavit, here state in the same words*), and having been duly convicted thereof, upon full proof;

And being fined by said Justice in the sum of twenty-five dollars, with costs of suit, and failing to pay the same;

Or, and being required to enter into recognizance, in the sum of one thousand dollars, with security, to keep the peace towards all the people of this State, and especially towards A. B., and to be of good behavior for the space of twelve months from this date, and to pay the costs of this prosecution, and having failed to execute and pay the same;

Or, and being required to give bond, with good security, in the sum of four thousand dollars, for his appearance at the next term of the Circuit Court of said county, to be held at the court house thereof on the ...... day of ...., 187..., and failing to give the same;

You are, therefore, hereby commanded, in the name of the State of Mississippi, to forthwith convey the said C. D. to the jail of said county, and deliver him to the jailor thereof, who is hereby required to receive him into his custody, and him safely keep in said jail until he shall pay said fine and all costs (*or, until he shall find such security,*) or be discharged by due course of law.

Witness my hand and seal, this ...... day of ...., 1876.

...., J. P., (SEAL.)

NOTE.—If, after commitment, the party or his friends should pay the fine and costs, or find the security, as required, and file with Justice, he should, at once, direct the following warrant to the jailor:

No. 188.—WARRANT TO DISCHARGE PRISONER.

STATE OF MISSISSIPPI, COPIAH COUNTY, } ss.

Horace Millsaps, Esq., one of the Justices of the Peace for said County, to the Sheriff and Jailor of said County, Greeting :

These are to command you, forthwith, to discharge out of your custody, C. D., if detained by you in the jail of said county for no other cause than what is set forth in his warrant of commitment made by the undersigned, on the ...... day of ...., 187.... for failing to pay fine and costs (*or the other causes,*) he having, since his said commitment, paid said fine and all costs (*or, found, before me, the securities required.*)

Witness my hand and seal, this ...... day of ...., 1876.

...., J. P., [SEAL.]

NOTE.—The Mittimus No. 187 will answer in cases of felony, as assault and battery with intent to kill, perjury, bigamy, robbery, grand larceny, manslaughter, &c., &c., when the party is examined and held to bail before a Justice, and fails to find security.

No. 189.—RECOGNIZANCE TO TESTIFY.

NOTE.—Often times malice and other influences induce persons to make affidavits charging serious crimes to others, without having reasonable grounds for so doing. It is the duty of the Justice to compel these affiants and other witnesses, where he has any doubt of failure on their part, to enter into recognizance to appear and testify. In cases of felony examined before him and sent to the Circuit Court, he MUST take the recognizance of all the important witnesses.

STATE OF MISSISSIPPI, COPIAH COUNTY. } ss.

This day, personally appeared before the undersigned Justice of the Peace for said county, A. B. and C. D., who acknowledged themselves indebted to the State of Mississippi in the sum of two hundred dollars : that is to say, the said A. B. in the sum of one hundred dollars, and the said C. D. in the sum of one hundred dollars, to be levied of their respective goods and chattels, lands and tenements : but this recognizance to be void and of none effect if the said A. B. shall personally appear before the undersigned, at his office in said county, on the ...... day of ...., 187..., (*or, Circuit Court of said county, at the court-house thereof, on the ...... day of ...., 187...,*) then and there to testify on the part of the State against ...., charged with [*describe offense,*] and shall not depart therefrom without being legally discharged.

Witness my hand and seal, this ...... day of .... , 18....

.............................., J. P. [SEAL.]

No. 190.—VOLUNTARY CONFESSION OR STATEMENT OF ACCUSED.

NOTE.—When a party has been brought before a Justice, charged with a crime, the Justice should take down in writing the confession or statement of the prisoner, if he has any to make or give. The following will answer in all cases:

STATE OF MISSISSIPPI, ... COUNTY. } ss.

This day, A. B, being brought before the undersigned, one of the Justices of the Peace for said county (*or, came voluntarily before the undersigned, &c., and surrendered himself for examination*) on the charge (*describe the crime or offense*), and he being put on examination, and having first been informed by me that it was his privilege to make or not to make, according to his own free will, any declaration or statement concerning the matter touching the said charge ; that the law neither required nor desired him to make any, but cautioned him not to give the information, or make any confession or declaration in fear of punishment or hope of escape, but only such as on calm reflection and legal advice, he should freely desire to give or make, he thereupon, without any known fear of punishment or hope of favor or escape, did voluntarily declare as follows : (*here write down exactly what the prisoner said in his words*). (Prisoner's Name.)

Written down by me, read over to the prisoner, and subscribed before me by him, this .... day of ......, 187...

...., J. P.

---

§ 2867.]

No. 191.—JUDGMENT OF DISCHARGE ON COMPROMISE.

NOTE.—In all petty misdemeanors, except offences by officers, the party injured and the party arrested, can compromise the matter, by the appearing in open court of party injured and acknowledging satisfaction therefor. The Justices of the Peace should foster and encourage such settlements and friendships, in every legitimate way.

Be it remembered that this day, A. B., being brought before the undersigned Justice, on the charge of assault and battery on the person of C. D. (*or, any other offence less than felony*), that the said C. D. did, then and there, in open court, acknowledge to have received satisfaction for all injury inflicted upon him by the said A. B., and desires that he shall be discharged from custody and the proceedings in this behalf dismissed; and the court being satisfied that the statement of C. D. is true in all respects, it is thereupon adjudged that the said A. B. be discharged and this proceeding dismissed, upon his payment of all costs accrued ; and the costs being thereupon paid in full, it is accordingly so done.

Adjudged and ordered, this .... day of ......, 187.

......................, J. P.

---

§ 1335.] No. 192.—APPEAL BOND IN CRIMINAL CASES.

State of Mississippi, ... County. } ss.

Know all men by these presents, that we, A. B., C. D. and E. F., are held and firmly bound unto the State of Mississippi in the penal sum of five hundred dollars, for which payment, well and truly to be made, we bind ourselves, our heirs and legal representatives, jointly and severally, firmly by these presents; signed with our names and sealed with our seals, this .... day of ......, 187..

The condition of this obligation is such that, whereas, on the .... day of ...., 187..., the above bound, A. B., was tried and convicted before John Doe, one of the Justices of the Peace for said county, on a charge of (*here state the charge*) and was, by said Justice, fined in the sum of fifty dollars and sentenced to imprisonment in the county jail of said county for thirty days; and, whereas, said A. B. has prayed an appeal to the next term of the circuit court of said county: Now, therefore, if the said A. B. shall be and personally appear before the circuit court of said county, at the court house therein, on the .... day of ...., 187..., and remain in attendance thereon from day to day and from term to term, until discharged by due course of law, and shall well and truly pay and satisfy all costs in this behalf, then this obligation to be void, otherwise to remain in full force and effect.

A. B., [SEAL.]
C. D., [SEAL.]
E. F., [SEAL.]

Note.—The Justice should never omit to justify the sureties before receiving bonds. Take no straw bonds—commit to jail if the bond is not good.

---

§ 2792.]

No. 193.—JUDGMENT ON FORFEITED RECOGNIZANCE.

Be it remembered that on the .... day of ...., 187....,
A. B., arrested on a charge of (*here state offense*) was recognized to be and appear before the undersigned Justice for trial, in the sum of fifty dollars for himself and fifty dollars for C. D., his surety,

on this .... day of ...., 187...; but being this day called out on said recognizance, came not, but wholly made default: and C. D., his said surety, being called to bring with him the body of the said A. B. into court, came not, but failed therein. It is, thereupon, considered and adjudged by the court that the State of Mississippi do have and recover of and from the said A. B the sum of fifty dollars, and of and from the said C. D. the sum of fifty dollars, as also the costs in this behalf to be taxed, unless they severally be and appear before the next term of the court of the undersigned Justice and show good cause to the contrary; for which scire facias will issue.

Adjudged this .... day of ...., 187...

...., J. P.

————

§ 2792.]

No. 194.—SCIRE FACIAS ON FORFEITED RECOGNIZANCE.

STATE OF MISSISSIPPI,

To the sheriff or any constable of .... county:

Whereas, before the undersigned, one of the Justices of the Peace for said county, on the .... day of ...., 187..., A. B., who had been recognized to appear before said Justice on said day, to answer unto the State of Mississippi of a charge of (*here state it*) being called, came not, but fails; and C. D., his security, being called to bring the body of the said A. B. into court, came not, but failed therein; whereupon it was ordered by the court that said State recover from said A. B. the sum of fifty dollars, and from said C. D, his surety, the sum of fifty dollars, and the costs in this behalf, unless they severally appear and show good cause to the contrary, at the next term of said Justice's court. You are, therefore, hereby commanded to cite the said defendant and his said surety, to personally appear before the undersigned, at his office in said county, on the .... day of ...., 187..., to show cause, if any they can, why said judgment shall not be made absolute for the amount thereof, and execution thereon; and further to do and perform in the premises what may be right and proper; have then there this writ.

Witness my hand and seal this .... day of ...., 187.

................., J. P.

NOTE.—If the amount of the bond or recognizance exceeds the sum of $150, it is the duty of the Justice, on a forfeiture thereof, to return the recognizance or bond to the Circuit Court, with his certificate of the default attached to the same; and then to issue an alias warrant for the arrest of the defaulter.

————

§ 2874.]

No. 195.—CERTIFICATE OF DEFAULT ON BOND OR RECOGNIZANCE.

STATE OF MISSISSIPPI, ... COUNTY. } ss.

I hereby certify that the bond (*or recognizance*) to which this is-

attached, was entered into on the date therein, and that on the ......
day of .... 187..., the said A. B. being called out on his recognizance (*or bond*), came not, but failed; and that C. D., his security on his recognizance, being called to bring with him the body of the said A. B. into court, came not, but failed therein.

Given under my hand and seal this ...... day of ...., 187.....
...., J. P. [SEAL.]

————

§§ 2515, 2516.]

No. 196.—BRIBERY AT ELECTIONS—COMPLAINT.

STATE OF MISSISSIPPI, ... COUNTY. }ss.

A. B., of said county, being by me, the undersigned Justice of the Peace for said county, duly sworn, says that on the .... day of ...., 187..., C. D. did, at said county, willfully and unlawfully offer (*or give*) to E. F., then and there a legal and qualified elector for said county, five dollars (*or anything else*) as a reward, for the purpose of inducing him, the said E. F., to persuade and procure the electors of said county to vote at the general (*or special*) election held on the ...... day of ...., 187.... for him, the said C. D. (*or for any other*), for the office of ...., against the statute in that behalf, and the peace and dignity of the State of Mississippi.

Or, C. D. did, at said county, willfully and unlawfully procure (*or endeavor to procure*) the vote of E. F. (*or the influence of E. F. over the electors of said county*), at the general (*or special*) election held on the ...... day of ...., 187...., in said county, for himself (*or for any other*) for the office of ...., by threats of violence towards the person of said E. F.;

Or, threats of withdrawing custom or dealing in business or trade, or of enforcing the payment of a debt, &c., or any other threat or injury to be inflicted by said C. D., or by his means.

————

§§ 2598 and on.] ## No. 197.—GAMING—COMPLAINT.

STATE OF MISSISSIPPI, ... COUNTY. }ss.

A. B., of said county, being by me, the undersigned Justice, &c., duly sworn, says that on the ...... day of ......, 187...., at said county, and on divers other days, C. D. did play at a game of cards for money (*or did wager and bet money, or other valuable thing then and there upon a cock-fight, or election then pending*):

Or, C. D. did keep and exhibit a certain gaming table called A. B. C., or E. O., roulette, rowley-powley, rouge et noir, rondo, monte, faro, keno, or any other kind or description, for public play for money, or other valuable thing;

Or, C. D. did publicly (or privately) put up a certain lottery, to be drawn or adventured for;

Or, C. D. did put up a certain prize to be raffled or played for.

Or, C. D. did sell and expose for sale certain lottery tickets (*or prizes, or prize boxes*).

Or, C. D. did keep and exhibit a certain billiard table for public play, without having a license therefor.

---

§ 2531.] No. 198.—DUELS—COMPLAINT.

STATE OF MISSISSIPPI, COPIAH COUNTY. } ss.

A. B., of said county, being by me, the undersigned Justice, &c., duly sworn, says, that on the ... day of ......, 187.., of said county, C. D. did send and cause to be delivered to the said A. B. a written (*or, verbal*) message, purporting and intending to be a challenge to the said A. B. to fight a duel with the said C. D., within said State (*or, without the bounds of said State*); and that E. F. did deliver said message to the said A. B., knowing the same to be a challenge to fight as aforesaid.

Or, C. D. did send and cause to be delivered to E. F. a written (*or verbal*) message, purporting and intending to be a challenge to said E. F. to fight a duel with said C. D., within the bounds of said State (*or, without*); that said message was delivered by G. H., knowing the same to be a challenge to fight as aforesaid, and that the same was accepted by the said E. F., and arrangements are being made by said parties, and others, for said duel, &c.

---

§ 2711.]

No. 199.—DESTROYING BOUNDARY—COMPLAINT.

STATE OF MISSISSIPPI, COPIAH COUNTY. } ss.

A. B., of said county, being by me, the undersigned Justice, &c., duly sworn, says, that on the .... day of ......, 187.., at said county, C. D. did knowingly cut, fell and destroy (*or, cause the same to be done*), a certain pine tree, the same being a boundary one, between the lands of said A. B. and the said C. D. (*or others*), to the wrong and manifest injury of the said A. B. (*or, remove or destroy any other character of land mark, to the wrong of any*).

---

§ 2569.]

No. 200.—OBTAINING MONEY, &c., BY FALSE PRETENCE—
COMPLAINT.

STATE OF MISSISSIPPI, COPIAH COUNTY. } ss.

A. B., of said county, being by me, the undersigned, &c., duly sworn, says, that on the ...... day of .... 187.., at said county, C. D. did designedly, by color of a certain false writing then and there exhibited, with intent to cheat and defraud the said A. B., obtain the signature of said A. B. (*as security*) to a certain promissory note, for the sum of fifty dollars, payable to one E. F., thirty days after date.

Or, C. D. did, designedly and by false pretence, with intent to cheat and defraud the said A B., by representing that he, the said C. D., had then a growing crop of cotton, which would yield at least five bales, in said county, and that the same was wholly unincumbered, and was his property, obtain from said A. B., on a credit, goods and supplies of provisions amounting to the sum of fifty dollars (*or, horse, or mule, or other property*).

§ 2653.] No. 201.—COMPLAINT FOR PETIT LARCENY.

STATE OF MISSISSIPPI, COUNTY OF COPIAH. }ss,

A. B., of said county, being by me, the undersigned Justice of the Peace in and for said county, duly sworn, says, that on the ...... day of ...., 187..., certain personal property of said A. B., to-wit: (*describe it,*) of the value of twenty dollars, was feloniously taken and carried away from his dwelling-house. (*or other place*) in said county ; and that he suspects and verily believes that the same was so taken and carried away by C. D.; wherefore, he prays that the said C. D. may be arrested and the said charge inquired into.

A. B.

Sworn to and subscribed, this ...... day of ......, 1876.

...., J. P. (SEAL.)

NOTE.—Juries are allowed in all criminal cases tried by a Justice, on demand of the defendant. On such demand, let him issue a venirie facias, as in No. —. The following is a form of oath to jurors, in such cases :

No. 202.—OATH OF JURORS IN CRIMINAL CASES.

You and each of you do solemnly swear that you will well and truly try and true deliverance make between the State of Mississippi and the prisoner at the bar, whom you have in charge, and a true verdict give, according to the law and the evidence. So help you God.

REMEDIES AGAINST JUSTICE.

§ 1339.]

No. 203.-COMPLAINT FOR FAILURE TO PAY OVER MONEY.

STATE OF MISSISSIPPI, ... COUNTY. }ss.

This day came before the undersigned, one of the Justices of the Peace for said county, A. B., and makes complaint, on oath, that heretofore, to-wit: on the ...... day of ...., 187..., he recovered before John Doe, a Justice of the Peace for District No. ...., of said county, a judgment for twenty-five dollars, against C. D.; that execution issued thereon, in due course, and was levied on certain personal property, and sold to satisfy said judgment and costs: that due return was made of said moneys to said John Doe, Justice as aforesaid, by the officer making the same ; but although often requested to do so, the said John Doe wholly fails to pay over to complainant the money so collected on said execution, received by him as aforesaid, in his official capacity : wherefore, complainant prays a summons may issue to said John Doe, Justice as aforesaid, commanding him to appear and answer to this complaint.　　A. B.

Sworn to and subscribed before me, this ...... day of ....., 187....

...., J. P., (SEAL.)

NOTE.—On the foregoing, a summons, in the usual form of civil suit, issues, stating therein the cause of action to be a failure to pay over money. A good plan is, always to copy the words of the affidavit or complaint, in all summonses and warrants.

---

§ 1339.]
No. 204.—JUDGMENT AGAINST JUSTICE.

Be it remembered, that this day came A. B., complainant, and John Doe, defendant in said action in person (*and by their attorneys, if so*), and all the evidence being heard (*and the argument of counsel, if any*), it is considered by the court that the complaint of said A. B. is, in all respects, true; thereupon it is ordered and adjudged by the court that the said A. B. do have and recover of and from the said John Doe, the sum of twenty five dollars, with ten per cent. damages on said sum, and costs of suit, without stay of execution. For which execution may issue.　Ordered and adjudged this ...... day of ......, 187.....

...., J. P.

---

§ 2712, Fee bill, § 14.]
No. 205.—AFFIDAVIT FOR EXTORTION AGAINST JUSTICE.

STATE OF MISSISSIPPI, ... COUNTY. } ss.

This day personally came before the undersigned, one of the Justices of the Peace for said county, A. B., who made complaint, on oath, that John Doe, Justice of the Peace for District No. ...., of said county, did, on the ...... day of ...., 187..., knowingly demand, take, collect and receive, under color of his office, and in his official capacity as Justice of the Peace, as aforesaid, the sum of two dollars (*or any sum*), as fees in the case of .... vs. ...., heretofore tried before said Justice, and of record in his office, the same not being authorized by the laws of this State (*nor the fees collected, enumerated in the act establishing fees of certain officers, if so*); wherefore complainant prays the arrest of said John Doe, that he may be tried for extortion.　　A. B.

Sworn to and subscribed this ...... day of ......, 187...

...., J. P.

§ 2889.)

No. 206.—AFFIDAVIT AGAINST JUSTICE OR CONSTABLE FOR FAILURE TO ARREST.

STATE OF MISSISSIPPI, ... COUNTY. } ss.

Personally appeared before the undersigned, one of the Justices of the Peace for said county, A. B., who made complaint, on oath, that John Doe, a Justice of the Peace of District No. ..., of said county (*or constable*), was present at .. ..., on the ...... day of ......, 187..., when one C. D. did violently assault and beat E. F.;

Or, was drunk and using profane language and disturbing the peace in a public place, or any other offense committed or about to be committed;

against the peace and dignity of the State of Mississippi; the offense as aforesaid, although being committed in the view and knowledge of said Justice (*or constable*), the said Justice (*or constable*) has willfully neglected and refused to arrest and return the said C. D.;

Or, the offense as aforesaid being about to be committed, the said Justice (or constable) did willfully absent himself for the purpose of avoiding a knowledge of the same;

Or, the offense as aforesaid having been committed, or about to be committed, the said Justice (or constable) was duly notified thereof, or the danger thereof, but willfully neglected and refused, &c.;

In violation of the statute in that behalf, wherefore affiant prays the arrest of the said John Doe, that this charge may be inquired into. A. B.

Sworn to and subscribed this ...... day of .... , 18...

...., J. P.

NOTE.—It has been too much the case, in this State, that officers have stood by, silent spectators of rows and drunken broils, when offenses not only are in danger of being committed, but are actually committed in their view, and nothing comes of it. Let all good citizens bring such officers to the bar of justice, by filing against them an affidavit to the effect of the foregoing. If an officer leaves, that he may not see and know, he is equally guilty. Let the day be hastened, when offenses shall not be committed in Mississippi, without certain and speedy arrest and punishment.

§ 1599.)

No. 207.—JUDGMENT NISI AGAINST JUSTICE FOR NON-ATTENDANCE IN UNLAWFUL ENTRY AND DETAINER.

Be it remembered, that on the ...... day of .... 187.... A. B. filed before the undersigned Justice, a complaint, on oath, that C. D. had unlawfully turned him out of possession (*or, unlawfully withheld from him the possession*) of certain premises in the county of ...., described in said complaint ; that thereupon, the undersigned issued his warrant, summoning the said C. D. to appear and answer said complaint, on the ...... day of ...., 187..., and also requiring the officer serving said warrant, to give notice to and request the attendance, at the time and place, in said warrant set forth, of E. F. and G. H., two other Justices of the Peace of said county ; but it appearing to the satisfaction of the undersigned, that G. H., one of the Justices aforesaid, was duly notified, and has failed to attend, and no cause shown therefor, it is ordered that a fine of twenty dollars be entered up against said G. H., for the use of said county. And it is further ordered, that scire facias issue in this behalf, commanding said G. H. to appear and show cause why such fine should not be final.

Ordered, this ...... day of ...., 187....

...., J. P.

§1599.]

No. 208.—SCIRE FACIAS FOR DEFAULTING JUSTICE.

STATE OF MISSISSIPPI,

To the sheriff or any constable of .... county:

Whereas, on the .... day of ...., 187..., G. H., a Justice of the Peace for said county, was duly summoned to attend on the undersigned, at his office, for the purpose of holding a court, in a matter under the statute of unlawful entry and detainer, on the ...... day of ...., 187..., came not, but made default ; whereupon, the undersigned entered up a fine of twenty dollars against the said G. H., which shall be final, unless good cause be shown to the contrary.

Therefore, you are hereby commanded to cite the said G. H., Justice of the Peace, as aforesaid, to be and personally appear before the undersigned Justice of the Peace of said county, at his office therein, on the ...... day of ...., 187..., then and there to show good cause, if any he can, why said fine should not be made final, and execution issue thereon. And have you then there this writ.

Witness my hand and seal, this ...... day of ...., 1876.

........................., J. P. (SEAL.)

REMEDIES UNDER THE LICENSE AND LIQUOR LAW.

§ 2692; §2, Acts 1873, p. 97.

No. 209.—SELLING LIQUOR TO MINOR—AFFIDAVIT.

STATE OF MISSISSIPPI, ... COUNTY ⎰ ss.

Personally appeared before the undersigned, one of the Justices of the Peace for said county, A. B., who being by me duly sworn, says on oath that C. D., of said county, did, on the ...... day of ...., 187..., in said county, knowingly sell intoxicating liquors to E. F., a minor under the age of twenty-one years, and not upon the written order of his parents (*or guardian*) or family physician, against the peace and dignity of the State of Mississippi, and contrary to the statute in that behalf. A. B.

Sworn to and subscribed, this ... day of ......, 1876.

...., J. P.

---

§ 2, Acts 1873, p. 97.]

No. 210.—SELLING TO AN INTOXICATED PERSON—AFFIDAVIT.

STATE OF MISSISSIPPI, ... COUNTY. } ss.

Personally appeared before the undersigned, one of the Justices of the Peace for said county, A. B., who being by me duly sworn, says on oath that C D. did, on the ... day of ......, 187..., in said county, sell intoxicating liquors to E. F., who was, at the time of sale, intoxicated, as was well known to said C. D. (*or who was well known to said C. D. as a person in the habit of getting intoxicated*), against the peace and dignity of the State of Mississippi, and the statute in that behalf.

Sworn to and subscribed this ... day of ......, 187...

...., J. P.

---

§ 2459.] No. 211.—PETITION FOR LICENSE.

To the Hon. Board of Supervisors of the county of ......, State of Mississippi:

Or, to the Mayor and Board of Aldermen of the town of ...., county of ... .., State of Mississippi:

The undersigned petitioners would respectfully represent unto your Honorable Board that A. B., who hereby makes application for a license to sell vinous and spirituous liquors in District No. .., in said county, in less quantities than one gallon, at the house in said District, on the public road, situated on the lands of .... (*or, in the town of ......, in said county, in the house on ...... street, known as the .... Saloon*), for the period of one year, is a person of good reputation, and a sober and suitable person to receive such license; and that the signatures hereto are the genuine ones of those signing, or attested in the genuine marks of the petitioners, and represent, as your petitioners verily believe, the majority of the male citizens over twenty-one years of age, residents of the Supervisor's District aforesaid (*or, of said town*); Therefore your petitioners respectfully ask that license be issued to the said C. D.

NAMES.
A. B.,
G. H.

§ 2460—§ 1, Acts 1873, page 97.]

No. 212.—BOND FOR LICENSE.

STATE OF MISSISSIPPI, ... COUNTY, } ss.

Know all men by these presents, That we, C. D., E. F., and G. H., are held and firmly bound unto the people of the State of Mississippi in the penal sum of two thousand dollars, for which payment well and truly to be made, we bind ourselves, our heirs, and legal representatives, jointly and severally, firmly by these presents ; signed with our hands and sealed with our seals, this ...... day of ...., 187....

The condition of the above obligation is such, That whereas, upon petition executed and filed according to law, the Board of Supervisors of the county of ...., said State (*or, the Mayor and Board of Aldermen of the town of* .. .., *in said county,*) did, on the ...... day of ...., 187..., grant and order the issuance of a license to the above bound C. D., to sell vinous and spirituous liquors, in quantities less than one gallon, in District No. ..., of said county, at a certain house on the .... public road, situated on the lands of ...., (*or, in said town, as in the petition,*) for the period of one year from this date ; Now, therefore, if the said C. D. shall, during the continuance of said license, keep a quiet, peaceable, and orderly house, as aforesaid, and will not suffer or permit any riotous or disorderly conduct, or any drunkenness, or any unlawful gaming, in or about the same, or on the premises thereunto belonging, and will, in all things, faithfully observe and keep all the provisions of the statutes in this behalf ; and that said E. F. and G. H., sureties herein, will pay all damages to any person or persons, which may be inflicted upon them, either in person or property, or means of support, by reason of the said C. D., so obtaining a license, selling or giving away intoxicating liquors, then this obligation shall be void, otherwise remain in full force and effect.

C. D., (SEAL.)
E. F., (SEAL.)
G. H.,)SEAL).

---

§ 3, Acts 1873, page 77.]

No. 213.—PLACES TO BE NUISANCES FOR UNLAWFUL SELLING LIQUOR—AFFIDAVIT.

STATE OF MISSISSIPPI, ... COUNTY. } ss.

Personally appeared before the undersigned, one of the Justices of the Peace for said county, A. B., who being by me duly sworn, on oath says that C. D., who keeps a tavern (*or, hotel, eating house, store, restaurant, drug store, grocery store, coffee-house, billiard room, or other place of public resort,*) in said county, sells (*or gives away*) intoxicating liquors, at said tavern, in violation of the Act to provide against the evil resulting from the sale of intoxicating liquors in the State of Mississippi, and against the peace and dignity of the same ; wherefore affiant prays that this charge may be inquired into, and the said tavern dealt with according to law. A. B.

Sworn to and subscribed, this ...... day of ...., 1876.

...., J. P.

NOTE.—The foregoing affidavit can be made as well against him who has a license, as one who has not. It should be certainly filed against all who have no license, and against the licensed saloon keeper who permits drunkenness, riots, or gaming about him, or who, in any other way, violates the law on the subject. If convicted, the house is closed as a nuisance, until new bond, &c.

---

§ 5, Acts 1873, p. 98.]

No. 214.—SUIT BY WIFE, GUARDIAN, CHILD, &c., AGAINST SALOON KEEPER.

STATE OF MISSISSIPPI,⎰ ss.   In Justice .... Court,
.... County. ⎱   July ......, 187...

Mary Rainbow, wife of John Rainbow, of said county, complains of A. B., of said county, in this: That said A. B. is the keeper and owner of a saloon (*or store*), where intoxicating liquors are sold or given away, in said county, and that heretofore, to-wit: on the .... day of .... 187.., the said A. B., either by himself or by his agents or employees, did sell or give to said John Rainbow, the husband of complainant as aforesaid, certain quantities of intoxicating liquors, unknown to complainant, which caused, in whole or in part, the drunkenness and complete intoxication of said John Rainbow; that on the date aforesaid, the said John Rainbow, by reason of the intoxication aforesaid, did violently assault and beat this complainant, and did break the bones of the right arm of complainant (*or, was thrown from his horse and so injured that he remained sick and disabled for many days, being unable to furnish means of support for complainant, or, any other injury caused by the intoxication, as being beat or wounded in a broil or fight with some one or other, or injuring property*), to the great damage and distress of said complainant, to-wit: to the damage of one hundred and fifty dollars ; wherefore she brings this suit, and claims the said sum of one hundred and fifty dollars, and prays that said A. B., as also C. D., owner and lessor of the saloon house (*or, store house*) occupied by said A. B., where said intoxicating liquors were sold or given away, be summoned to appear and answer this complaint.

MARY RAINBOW.

NOTE.—Our laws upon the subject of retailing spirituous liquors, are the best temperance society within my knowledge, if strictly enforced, but while they remain a dead letter on our statute books, they are monuments of our shame. Religious public opinion and the strict and summary enforcement of our laws, before honest officials, must be the means of redeeming the country from the " mocker, strong drink, which biteth like a serpent, and stingeth like an adder."

7

§ 1, Acts 1873, p. 67.]

No. 215.—AFFIDAVIT FOR INFRINGEMENT OF CIVIL RIGHTS.

STATE OF MISSISSIPPI, ... COUNTY. } ss.

Personally appeared before the undersigned, one of the Justices of the Peace for said county, A. B., a citizen of said State, who being by me duly sworn, on his oath says that C. D., the owner or lessee of a public hotel in the town of ...., in said county, known as the .... Hotel, now managed and controlled by the said C. D., for the use and benefit of the public and traveling community, did, on the ...... day of ...., 187..., deny, abridge and infringe, on account of race, color and the previous condition of servitude of the said A. B., his equal and impartial enjoyment of the accommodation, facility, privilege and advantage of said hotel; the said A. B. having respectfully demanded and being abundantly able to pay for the same, as was well known to said C. D.; that the refusal of the said C. D. to grant to said A. B. the equal and impartial accommodation of said hotel as aforesaid, was only for the reason aforesaid and none other, and against the statute in that behalf; wherefore the said A. B. prays that the said C. D. may be arrested and held to answer fully in the premises, and be dealt with as shall be just and according to law.   A. B.

Sworn to and subscribed this ...... day of ...., 187....

...., J. P.

———

ELECTION FRAUDS.

§ 2536 and on.]   No. 216.—AFFIDAVIT.

STATE OF MISSISSIPPI, ... COUNTY } ss.

A. B. being duly sworn by me, the undersigned Justice of the Peace for said county, says that on the ...... day of ...., 187 .., the same day being a general (*or special*) election day in said county and State, for public officers, and at the election precinct in said county called .... precinct, in District No. ... of said county, one C. D. did, by violent action, and intimidation and threats;

Or, by cursing and abusing the inspectors or clerks of said election, or the voters there assembled ;

Or, by the exhibition of deadly weapons, to-wit: a pistol, in a rude, angry and threatening manner;

Or, by attempting to remove the ballot boxes, etc., etc., unlawfully disturb said election ;

Or, did (§ 2537) vote at said election, not being legally qualified;

Or, did vote at said election at said precinct, having voted at ...... precinct in said county, or in .... county, on the same day;

Or, being a resident of District No. ..., in said county, did vote for a member of the Board of Supervisors;

§ 2539.] Or, being an Inspector (*or other officer*,) of said election, at said precinct, did proceed to said election without having the ballot-box locked and secured, in the manner directed by law ;

Or, being an Inspector, &c., did open and read, or consented that .... and .... should open and read ballots given to him to be deposited in the box, at said election, before they were so put into said box, and without the consent of the voters giving the same ;

§ 2540.] Or, being an Inspector, &c., did dispose of and deposit the ballot-box with ...., at the house of .... in a manner not authorized by law, before the votes cast at said election were counted ;

Or, did give the key of the ballot box, he being entrusted therewith, to .... before the votes in said box were counted :

§ 2541.] Or, being an Inspector, &c., and E. F. objected to by a challenger, as a person unqualified to vote, did permit said E. F. to vote without proof of qualification, in the manner directed by law;

Or, did refuse the vote of E. F., after the said E, F. had complied with the requisites prescribed by law, in proving his qualification to vote, the said C. D. knowing him to be so entitled to vote;

Or, did, knowingly, permit E. F., an unqualified person to vote at said election; in violation of the statute in that behalf, and against the peace and dignity of the State of Mississippi.

A. B.

Sworn to and subscribed, this .... day of ...., 187....

...., J. P.

NOTE.—The law of the foregoing will be found in sections 2536, 2537, 2539, 2540, and 2541, and should, at all times, when violated, be enforced most rigidly. Good government results from the purity of elections, and " when the righteous are in authority, the people rejoice; but when the wicked beareth rule, the people mourn."

FORMS AS A COURT OF INQUIRY.

NOTE.—The following few general forms will assist in cases of felony, brought before Justices for examination. In the examination, if the testimony does not warrant the charge, or shows that a lesser offense whereof the Justice is authorized by law to hear and determine, has been committed, he must, nevertheless, discharge the prisoner; but he should arrest him on the lesser charge, or misdemeanor, and proceed to hear and determine the same at once. On a charge for felony, his only duty is to examine the whole case, and hold the prisoner to answer before the circuit court, or to discharge him. His jurisdiction in felonies is only to ascertain if the crime, in his judgment, has been committed—if not, the affidavit falls. He cannot scale the crime and convict, on an affidavit charging a felony, for a lesser offense, although included in the greater.

§ 2628.] No. 217.—COMPLAINT FOR MURDER.

STATE OF MISSISSIPPI, ... COUNTY } ss.

A. B. being duly sworn by me, the undersigned Justice of the Peace for said county, says that on the ...... day of ...., 187...., at the county aforesaid, one C. D. was feloniously, wilfully, and of malice aforethought, killed and murdered : and this deponent has just cause to suspect, and does verily believe and suspect, that the murder aforesaid was committed by E. F.;* wherefore, affiant prays a warrant for the arrest of said E. F., that this charge may be inquired of.   A. B.

Sworn to and subscribed, this ...... day of........., 187....

...., J. P.

No. 218.—ACCESSORY AFTER THE FACT.

[Repeat the above to the *, and add thereto, as follows, to suit the facts:] And that afterward, to wit : on the ...... day of ...., 187..., at the county aforesaid, one G. H., well knowing the said E. F. to have done and committed the said felony, did feloniously and wilfully conceal, aid, comfort, and assist the said E. F., with the intent and in order that the said E. F. might avoid or escape from arrest (*or, trial, or, conviction and punishment*) for the said felony and murder. [Then pray the warrant, and end as in No. 217.]

----

§ 2490.]   No. 219.—COMPLAINT FOR ARSON.

State of Mississippi, ... County } ss.

A. B., of said county, being by me, the undersigned Justice of the Peace for said county, duly sworn, says that on the ..... day of......., 187..., in the night time, at said county, one C. D. did, wilfully and feloniously set fire to and burn (*or either*) the dwelling-house of E. F., there being at the time, the family of said E. F., to-wit: his wife, and daughter (*or, any one else*) residing therein;

Or, in the day time;

Or, the shop, warehouse, out-house, or other building adjoining to or within the curtilage of the dwelling-house of E. F., there being at the time, the family, &c.   A. B.

Sworn to and subscribed, this ...... day of........., 187.....

...., J. P.

----

§ 2672.]   No. 220.—COMPLAINT FOR RAPE.

State of Mississippi, ... County. } ss.

A. B., of said county, being by me, the undersigned Justice, &c., duly sworn, says, that on the ...... day of ...., 187.... at said county, R. H. did carnally and unlawfully know S. T., a female child, under the age of ten years:

Or, did feloniously assault and forcibly ravish, and carnally and unlawfully know, S. T., a female above the age of ten years; or, did administer to S. T., a female above the age of ten years, a glass of wine (*or, other liquid*), containing some substance or liquid, which produced stupor, or imbecility of mind, or weakness of body, and did then and there, without the consent of said S. T., while she was prevented from effectual resistance, by reason of the liquid or substance as aforesaid, feloniously assault the said S. T., and her carnally and unlawfully know; contrary to the statute in that behalf. and against the peace and dignity of Mississippi.

A. B.

Sworn to and subscribed before me, this ...... day of ...... 187..

...................J. P. [SEAL.]

---

§ 2521.] No. 221.—COMPLAINT FOR BURGLARY.

STATE OF MISSISSIPPI, ... COUNTY. }ss.

A. B., of said county, being by me, the undersigned, &c., duly sworn, says, that on the .... day of ...., 187.., at said county, P. R. did feloniously and burglariously break and enter the dwelling house of said A. B., there being at the time in said house the wife and daughter (*or others*) of said A. B., by unlocking the outer door thereof by means of false keys;

Or, picking the lock of the outer door thereof;

Or, by breaking the wall, or outer door, window, or shutter of a window, or the lock or bolt of the outer door thereof, or the fastening of a window, or shutter thereof;

With intent to steal, take and carry away, from said house, divers goods and chattels therein belonging to said A. B. (*or commit any other crime*), contrary to the statute in that behalf, and against the peace and dignity of Mississippi.

A. B.

Sworn to and subscribed before me, this .... day of .... 187.

................., J. P. [SEAL.]

No. 222.—COMPLAINT FOR BRIBERY.

STATE OF MISSISSIPPI, ... COUNTY. }ss.

A. B., of said county, being by me, the undersigned Justice of the Peace in and for said county, duly sworn, says, that on the .... day of ..... 187 .. at said county, C. D. did offer to E. F., the said E. F. being then and there a Justice of the Peace for said county, the sum of ten dollars (*or anything else*), with intent to influence his opinion and judgment, in a certain action at law then pending before said Justice (or, *C. D. being then and there a Justice of the Peace, or other officer*) for said county, did receive of E. F. the sum of ten dollars, for the purpose of and with the intent to influence his opinion and judgment, &c., or, otherwise:

Or, C. D being then and there a juror in attendance on the Circuit (*or other*) Court of said county, did corruptly take (*or receive the promise of*) the sum of ...... dollars (*or anything else*), with intent to influence the verdict of said C. D. in the case of .... vs. ..... then pending in said Court:

Or, offering such award to any juror:

Or, C. D. being then and there an inspector (*clerk or canvasser*) of an election then being held in said county, did receive from E. F. the sum of .... dollars (*or anything*) to influence the voters at said election to vote the .... ticket, or his opinion, judgment and action in relation to said election;

Contrary to the statute in that behalf, and against the peace and dignity of Mississippi.   A. B.

Sworn to and subscribed before me, this .... day of ...., 187...

.... J. P.

---

§ 2667.]   No. 223.—COMPLAINT FOR PERJURY.

STATE OF MISSISSIPPI, ... COUNTY. }

A. B., of said county, being by me, the undersigned, &c., duly sworn, says, that on the .... day of ...., 187 .., at said county, C. D. was presented as a witness in a certain case, then pending before E. F., a Justice of the Peace for said county, (or, *the circuit court of said county*) wherein R. S. was plaintiff and O. P. defendant, on the part of defendant, the said Justice (or *court*) having complete jurisdiction over the said case, and full authority and power to try the same, and to administer oaths to all witnesses sworn upon such trial; the said C. D. was duly sworn by said Justice (or, *by the clerk of said court*); that the testimony he shall give in the case now in hearing, wherein R. S. was plaintiff and O. P., defendant, shall be the truth, the whole truth, and nothing but the truth, so help him God. And the said C. D. being then interrogated, as such witness, whether the said A. B. was present at .... on the .... day of ...., 187..., in said county, which inquiry was material to the issue in the said case, did, wilfully and corruptly, depose and falsely swear that said A. B. was present as aforesaid, when, in truth and fact, the said A. B. was not so present or in said county on said day; wherefore, the said C. D. did, then and there, before the Justice (or *court*) aforesaid, on the day aforesaid, wilfully and corruptly, swear falsely and commit wilful and corrupt perjury, contrary to the statute in that behalf, and against the peace and dignity of Mississippi.

Or, C. D. presented himself at ...... precinct as an elector, a general (or *special*) election being then and there held for public officers, and declaring that he had lost or mislaid his certificate of registration, but, desiring to vote, the following oath was administered to him by the inspector (or *registrars*) holding said election; the said inspectors (*registrars*) having full authority and power, and being required by law to administer such oath, under the circumstances aforesaid (*here set out the oath*), and the same being attached to the ballot offered by the said C. D., was, by said inspectors, (*registrars*) deposited in the ballot-box; the said C. D. having wilfully and corruptly sworn falsely in taking said oath; for, in truth and fact, the said C. D. had, on said day, voted at ...... precinct, in said county, on his registration certificate, which he then had, the same being marked and dated according to law; wherefore, the said C. D. did, then and there, before said inspectors (or *registrars*) aforesaid, on the day aforesaid, wilfully and corruptly swear falsely and commit wilful and corrupt perjury, contrary to the statute in that behalf, and against the peace and dignity of Mississippi.

Sworn to and subscribed this .... day of ...., 187...

, ... J. P.

§ 2710.] No. 224.—COMPLAINT IN MAYHEM.

STATE OF MISSISSIPPI, ... COUNTY. }ss.

A. B., of said county, being by me, the undersigned Justice of the peace for said county, duly sworn, says that on the ...... day of ......, 187..., in said county, C. D., from premeditated design, (*or with intent to kill or commit a felony*) did, unlawfully and feloniously, assault the said A. B.,and did, then and there, bite off the ear of the said A. B. (*or, gouge out the eye, slit or bite off the nose or tongue, &c.,*) against the peace and dignity of Mississippi.

Sworn to and subscribed this .... day of ...., 187...

---

§ 2497.]

No 225.—COMPLAINT IN ASSAULT AND BATTERY WITH INTENT TO KILL.

STATE OF MISSISSIPPI, ... COUNTY. }ss.

A. B , of said county, being by me, the undersigned Justice of the Peace for said county, duly sworn, says that on the ...... day of ......, 187... at said county, E. F. did, willfully and feloniously shoot at him, the said A. B , with a certain gun, then and there loaded and charged with powder and lead, with intent to kill and murder him, the said A. B.;

Or, to maim, ravish, or rob·

Or, with intent t) commit burglary, larceny, or other felony;

Against the peace and dignity of the State of Mississippi ;

Or, did wilfully and feloniously attempt to discharge a certain gun or pistol at the said A. B., loaded and charged with powder and lead, with intent, &c.;

Or, did assault and beat the said A. B. with a certain crow-bar, single-tree, stick, rail, &c., being then and there a deadly weapon, with intent, &c. A. B.

Sworn to and subscribed, this ...... day of ...., 187....

...., J. P.

---

§ 2483.]

No. 226.]—ABDUCTION OF FEMALE OVER FOURTEEN YEARS.

STATE OF MISSISSIPPI, ... COUNTY. }ss.

A. B., of said county, being by me, the undersigned Justice of the Peace for said county, duly sworn, says, that on the ...... day of ......, 187...., at said-county, one C. D. did, unlawfully, against the will of the said A. B., and by force (*or, menace, fraud, deceit, strategem, or duress,* take her, the said A. B., and compel (*or induce*) her to marry (*or, be defiled by*) the said A. B. (*or any other person ;*) or, with intent to marry, &c.; against the peace and dignity of the State of Mississippi. A. B.

Sworn to and subscribed, this ...... day of ...., 187...

.... , J. P.

§ 2529.]

No. 227.—ABDUCTION OF FEMALE UNDER FOURTEEN YEARS.

STATE OF MISSISSIPPI, ... COUNTY. } ss.

A. B., of said county, being by me, the undersigned Justice of the Peace for said county, duly sworn, says that on the ...... day of ......, 187..., at said county, G. H. did, maliciously, willfully, and fraudulently take, lead, carry away (*take, decoy, and entice away*) C. D., a female under the age of fourteen years, from the protection and charge of ...., her father (*or, mother, guardian, &c.*.) without his consent, with intent to detain or conceal said C. D. from the said ...., for the purpose of marrying the said C. D. (*or, for the purpose of prostitution or concubinage on the body of said C. D,*) against the peace and dignity of the State of Mississippi.

                                                                A. B.

Sworn to and subscribed, this ...... day of ...., 187...

                . ..., J. P.

§ 2530.]   No. 228.—COMPLAINT FOR SEDUCTION.

STATE OF MISSISSIPPI. .... COUNTY. } ss.

A. B., of said county, being by me. the undersigned Justice of the Peace for said county, duly sworn, says that on the ...... day of ......, 187..., C. D., at said county, did seduce and have illicit connection with E. F., a female child under the age of sixteen years, the said E. F. being of previous chaste character, against the statute in that behalf, and the peace and dignity of the State of Mississippi.

                                                                A. B.

Sworn to and subscribed, this ...... day of ———, 187...

NOTE.—In the affidavit No. 228, foregoing. the testimony of the female, alone, will not convict. It must be supported by other evidence, either positive or circumstantial, sufficient to convict.

§ 2657.]

No. 229.—COMPLAINT FOR BUYING OR RECEIVING STOLEN GOODS.

STATE OF MISSISSIPPI, ... COUNTY:

A. B., of said county, being by me. the undersigned Justice of the Peace for said county, duly sworn, says that on the ...... day of ...., 187..., at said county, E. F. did buy of (*or receive from*) C. D. a certain lot of cotton in the seed (*or anything else*), he, the said E. F., knowing the same to have been feloniously taken and carried away from him, the said A. B., against the peace and dignity of the State of Mississippi.   A. B.

Sworn to and subscribed this ...... day of ...., 187...

                        ...., J. P.

§ 2652.]

No. 230.—COMPLAINT FOR GRAND LARCENY.

STATE OF MISSISSIPPI, ... COUNTY. } ss.

A. B., of said county, being by me, the undersigned Justice of the Peace for the said county, duly sworn, says that on the ...... day of ...., 187..., at said county, C. D. did feloniously take and carry away the personal property of said A. B., to-wit (*here describe property stolen*), of the value of twenty-five dollars (*or more*) against the peace and dignity of the State of Mississippi.　　A. B.

Sworn to and subscribed this ...... day of ...., 187....

　　　　　　　　　　　　　　　　...... ...., J. P.

---

§ 2505.]　　No. 231.—COMPLAINT IN BIGAMY.

STATE OF MISSISSIPPI, ... COUNTY. } ss.

A. B., of said county, being by me, the undersigned Justice of the Peace for said county, duly sworn, says that on the ...... day of ...., 187...., at said county, E. F., being then a married man (*or woman*), whose wife (*or husband*) was then living, did willfully and feloniously marry and take to wife (*or husband*) one G. H.;

Or, being an unmarried person, did feloniously and knowingly marry the wife (or husband) of C. D.;

Against the peace and dignity of the State of Mississippi.

　　　　　　　　　　　　　　　　　　　A. B.

Sworn to and subscribed this ...... day of ...., 187...

　　　　　　　　　　　　　　　　...... .. .., J. P.

MISCELLANEOUS FORMS.

Note.—The following forms will be useful to country Justices of the Peace, who are frequently called upon to write deeds, prepare contracts, &c. Only such are given as are in common use in this State, under our laws.

No. 232.—BILL OF SALE.

Know all men by these presents, that I, A. B., of the county of ...., and the State of Mississippi, for and in consideration of the sum of .... dollars to me in hand paid by C. D., of the county and State aforesaid, the receipt of which is hereby acknowledged, have bargained and sold, and by these presents do bargain, sell, grant and convey and deliver unto the said C. D. (*or E. F.*), his legal representatives and assigns, one iron gray mare (*or, any other personal property whatever, or growing crop, describing it particularly*), belonging to me and now in my possession, to have and to hold the same unto the said C. D., his legal representatives and assigns forever. And I do, for myself, my heirs and legal representatives, covenant and agree to and with the said C. D., his legal representatives and assigns, to warrant and defend the sale of said property hereby made unto the said C. D., his legal representatives and assigns, against all and every person and persons whomsoever.

In witness whereof, I have hereunto set my hand and seal, this ...... day of ...., 187...   A. B. [SEAL.]

Note.—The gist of a sale of personal property is the delivery of the same and if the above is not acknowledged before a Justice, and recorded, it should be signed in the presence of witnesses, who must be able to testify as to the delivery of the property.

No. 233.—QUIT-CLAIM DEED.

Know all men by these presents, That we, John Doe, of the county of ...., and the State of Mississippi, and Mary Doe, his wife, in consideration of the sum of .... dollars, to us in hand, paid by Richard Roe, of said county and State (*or elsewhere*), the receipt whereof is hereby acknowledged, have bargained and sold and quit-claimed, and by these presents do bargain, sell and quit-claim unto the said Roe and to his heirs and assigns forever, all our and each of our right, title, interest, estate, claim and demand, both at law and in equity, and as well in possession as in expectancy, of, in and to, all that certain piece of land, situate in said county and State (*or elsewhere*), and described as the southeast quarter of section four in township six of range eight east, containing one hundred and sixty acres, more or less, with all and singular the hereditaments and appurtenances thereunto belonging, or in anywise appertaining.

In witness whereof, we have hereunto set our hands and seals, the ...... day of .... 187...

JOHN DOE. [SEAL.]
MARY DOE. [SEAL.]

No. 234.—WARRANTY DEED

This indenture, made this ...... day of ...., 187..., between A. B., of the county of ...., and the State of Mississippi, [*and C. B., his wife*], parties of the first part, and E. F., of said county and State, party of the second part, witnesseth: That said parties of the first part, for and in consideration of the sum of ...... dollars, to them in hand paid by the said party of the second part, at or before the sealing and delivery of these presents, the receipt of which is hereby acknowledged, have granted, bargained and sold, and by these presents do grant, bargain, sell and convey, unto the said party of the second part, and to his heirs and assigns forever, all that certain piece of land, lying and being in said county and State, and described as the southeast quarter of the northeast quarter, and the east half of the southeast quarter, of section twenty-five, in township ten, of range nine, east, containing one hundred and twenty acres, more or less, to have and to hold the same, together with all and singular the tenements, hereditaments and appurtenances thereunto belonging, or in any wise appertaining, unto the said party of the second part, his heirs and assigns forever. And the said A. B. and C. B., for themselves and their heirs and legal representatives, the said premises in the quiet and peaceable possession of the said E. F., his heirs and assigns, against the said parties of the first part, their heirs and legal representatives, and against all and every person whomsoever, lawfully claiming or to claim the same, shall and will warrant, and by these presents forever defend.

In witness whereof, the parties of the first part have hereunto set their hands and seals, the day and year first above written.

A. B. (SEAL.)
C. B. (SEAL.)

No. 235.—WARRANTY DEED, WITH VENDORS' LEIN.

This indenture, made this ...... day of ...., 187..., between A. B. and C. B., his wife, of the county of ...., and the State of Mississippi, parties of the first part, and E. F., of said county and State, party of the second part, witnesseth: That said parties of the first part, for and in consideration of the sum of ...... dollars, paid and to be paid, as follows: that is to say, ... dollars to them in hand, paid at or before the sealing and delivery of these presents. the receipt of which is hereby acknowledged; ...... dollars to be due and payable on or before the ...... day of ...., of 187..., and evidenced by the promissory note of said party of the second part. dated this ...... day of ...., 187..., payable to said party (*or parties*) of the first part, or order, on the date aforesaid, for the said sum of ...... dollars, with interest from maturity (*or date*), at ... per cent per annum; and ...... dollars to be due and payable on or before the ...... day of ...., 187..., and evidenced by the promissory note of the said party of the first part, dated this ...... day of .... 187..., payable to the said party (*or parties*) of the second part, or order, on or before the ...... day of ...., 187..., for said sum of ...... dollars, with interest from maturity (*or date*), at ... per cent. per annum; to secure the payment of which said promissory notes at the several dates thereof, a lein is hereby reserved upon all and singular the land and real estate hereinafter granted and sold in favor of said party (*or parties*) of the first part, their assigns and legal representatives. Now in consideration of the premises, and the payment of said ...... dollars in cash, and the execution and delivery of the two said notes to the said party (*or parties*) of the first part, they have granted, bargained and sold and conveyed, and by these presents, do grant, bargain, sell and convey, unto the said party of the second part, the following described land, lying and being in said county, to-wit: (*here set out the description in full*), to have and to hold the same, together with the appurtenances thereto belonging or in anywise appertaining, unto said party of the second part, and unto his heirs, assigns and legal representatives, in fee simple, forever. And the said party (*or parties*) of the first part. for themselves, their heirs and legal representatives, do hereby covenant and agree unto the said party of the second part and with his heirs and assigns, that they will, and their heirs and legal representatives shall, warrant and forever defend the title of said land against the lawful claims and demands of all persons whomsoever.

In witness whereof, the said parties of the first part have hereunto set their hands and seals, the day and year first above written.

.... [SEAL.]

.... [SEAL.]

No. 236.—DEED OF TRUST TO SECURE NOTE.

This indenture, made this .... day of ...., 18..., between A. B., of .... county, of the first part, C. D. of .... county. of the second part and E. F., of .... county, of the third part, and all of the State of Mississippi. Witnesseth: That, whereas, A. B. is justly indebted to C. D. in the sum of five hundred dollars as evidenced by his certain promissory note of even date herewith (or *of date previous*) due and payable to the said C. D., or order, on or before the .... day of ...., 18..., with interest from date (or *maturity*) at the rate of ten per cent. per annum; and, whereas, the said A. B., party of the first part, is desirous of securing the prompt payment of the money in said note mentioned, with all interest and charges at the maturity of the same, does hereby grant, bargain, sell and convey, for and in consideration of the premises aforesaid, and the further sum of one dollar to him in hand paid by the said E. F., (*hereby appointed and constituted trustee in this behalf,*) party of the third part, the receipt of which is hereby acknowledged, unto the said E. F., trustee, all that certain piece of land lying and being in said county, and described as follows:

(*Let the description be very accurate. If by land numbers, it is sufficient; put down section, township and range.*) Containing .... acres, more or less, to have and to hold the same with all, and singular, the appurtenances thereunto belonging or in anywise appertaining unto the said E. F., party of the third part, and unto his legal representatives and assigns, in fee simple, forever; In trust, however, and for the following purposes, and none other: It is agreed that the said premises shall remain in the undisturbed possession of the said A. B., party of the first part, until the maturity of said note, and that upon the full payment of the same, and all interests and charges by said A. B., or others for him, this deed shall be void and of none effect and so noted by said trustee on the public records; but should the said A. B., party of the first part, or other for him, make default and fail to pay said money, with all interest thereon, and charges for the execution of these presents, according to the tenor and effect of said promissory note, at the maturity thereof, then the said trustee, party of the third part, is hereby authorized, and I it shall be his duty, without further notice to the said A. B., to advertise said land for sale, by giving thirty days' notice of the time, place and terms of sale, with a description of the premises and on what account sold, by posting in three or more public places in said county, written notices thereof; (or, by publishing the same in such newspaper as may be agreed upon,) and at the time and place appointed shall proceed to sell the same at public outcry, for cash, to the highest bidder. From the proceeds of such sale said trustee shall, at once, pay and satisfy said promissory note, with all interest thereon, and the cost and charges of executing this trust, making and executing full warrantee deeds to the purchaser, or purchasers, of said land; and should there remain any balance in the hands of said trustee, he shall, at once, pay all such money over to said A. B., or to his legal representatives. Should the said E. F., trustee, from any cause, be unable to act in the premises, the said C. D., party of the second part, is hereby authorized to appoint a trustee in his place.

In witness whereof, The said party of the first part has hereunto set his hand and seal the day and year first above written.

A. B. [SEAL.]

No. 237.—DEED TRUST ON GROWING CROP TO SECURE ADVANCES.

Note.—In the following, land and personal property may be included, but the form is prepared under Sec. 4 of the Agricultural Lien law of 1873. The parts in brackets, insert or leave out, to suit the case.

This indenture, made this ...... day of ...., 187..., between A. B., of .... county, of the first part, C. D., of .... county, of the second part, and E. F., of .... county, of the third part, all of the State of Mississippi, witnesseth: that whereas, the said A. B. [is justly indebted to the said C. D. in the sum of .... dollars, evidenced, etc. (as in Form No. 236)]: and whereas the said A. B. expects the said C. D. to make advances to him of money, family and plantation supplies [*and merchandise*] during the year 18..... for the purpose of assisting him to cultivate and make a crop in said county during said year; Now, therefore, to secure all said advances (*and the indebtedness aforesaid*), as well as ten per cent. upon the amounts thereof upon settlement, the said A. B., party of the first part, for and in consideration of the premises, as for the further consideration of one dollar to him in hand paid by said E. F., hereby appointed and constituted trustee in this behalf, party of the third part, the receipt of which is hereby acknowledged, does hereby grant, bargain and sell unto the said E. F., trustee, the following property, to-wit:

(*Insert any personal property or real estate, if any be granted, with full description.*) All the crops of cotton, corn, peas and potatoes to be cultivated and raised by the said A. B., or others for him (*or his share thereof*), during said year in said county, to have and to hold the same to him, the said E. F., and to his legal representatives and assigns forever:

In trust, nevertheless, for the following purposes, and none other: if the said A. B., party of the first part, or others for him, shall fully pay and satisfy (*the said indebtedness*) what may be justly due to said C. D. for the advances aforesaid, as well as the ten per cent. upon said amounts, and all costs incurred in this behalf, on or before the 15th day of November, 18..., then this deed to be void and of none effect; but if default is made in said payments, or any of them, the said E. F., trustee, shall at once, without further notice to said A. B., take all said property into his possession, and after giving ten days' notice of the time, place and property to be sold, by written notices posted in three or more public places in said county, shall sell said property, or a sufficient portion thereof, to make said payments, for cash, at public outcry, to the highest bidder, at the time and place appointed. If any balance shall remain after making said payments, the said trustee is hereby required to deliver the same to said A. B., or to his legal representatives. Should the said E. F., from any cause, be unable to execute this trust, then the said C. D. is authorized to appoint a trustee. And if, at any time, the said trustee should have good reason to believe that said property, or any part thereof, is endangered as a security in this behalf, he shall, and is hereby authorized, to seize the same wherever found, and hold till said payments are made, or until said property shall be sold by virtue hereof; but until demanded by the trustee, said property can remain in possession of said A. B.

In witness whereof, the said party of the first part has hereunto set his hand and seal the year and day first above written.

A. B. [SEAL.]

No. 238.—DEED OF TRUST FOR ADVANCES.

NOTE.—The publishers insert the following form, blanks of the same being kept by them in stock, and being extensively used by merchants:

This deed of trust, made this .... day of ... ., A. D., 187.... Witnesseth: That, whereas, ..., part... of the first part ...... indebted to .... in the sum of ...... dollars, on ...., and, whereas, said part... of the first part expect said .... to advance .... money, supplies and merchandise during the year 187...; and, whereas, said part... of the first part... agreed to secure the payment of said sum, as, also, any further amounts that may be advanced as aforesaid and not mentioned herein. That the part... of the first part, in consideration of the premises, as well as for ten dollars to ......, paid by ...., trustee, do.. hereby bargain, sell and convey to said trustee the property, being in ...... county, Mississippi, and described as follows: (here describe property.) The title to which unto said trustee or any successor, warrant... and agree... forever to defend: in trust, however, that if said part... of the first part shall, on or before the ...... day of ......, 187.... pay what may be due said ...., as aforesaid, and all costs incurred on account of this deed, then this deed to be void; but if default is made in said payments, the trustee shall take possession of said property and having given .... days' notice of the time. place and terms of sale, by ...., sell said property or a sufficiency thereof, to make said payments, for cash, at public auction, at ...... And said ...., or his legal representative, can, at any time .... may desire, appoint a trustee in the place of ......, or any succeeding trustee. And should the trustee at any time believe said property, or any part thereof endangered as a security for said payments, he shall take the same into his possession and hold till said payments are made, or till said property is sold as aforesaid; but until demanded by the trustee for either of the purposes as aforesaid, said part.. of first part can hold the same. It is further distinctly understood and agreed between the parties aforesaid, that this deed is made and intended to secure any advances on account of the crop of 187.., made after the .... day of ...., 187.., and not mentioned herein.

In testimony whereof, said ...... ha.. hereto set hand.. and seal.., on the date above written.

........., [L. S.]
........., [L. S.]

No. 239.—DEED OF TRUST FOR RENT.

Whereas, ... ha.. rented from ...., for the year 187.., ... acres of land, being part of...... plantation, situated in the county of ...., Mississippi, and for which ... agree to pay rent as follows : [*Here state the terms fully.*] ..... have also agreed to cultivate said land in a proper manner, and to keep the fences bordering on the same in fit condition to turn stock : ....

And ..... being desirous to secure the prompt payment of said rent, as aforesaid, when the same is due, ... agree and covenant that all the crops of corn, cotton, and other products raised on said land in the year 187..; and also the following other personal property, to-wit: [*Describe property.*] be, and the same is hereby mortgaged, and pledged, and subjected to a lien in favor of said .... for the payment of said rent, and the faithful performance of this contract.

And .... bind .. .. to cultivate, gather, and put into marketable condition, as soon as practicable, enough of the crop of cotton, and to deliver the cotton as fast as baled, to the said...................., to be sold by ...., at ...., the net proceeds to be applied by .... to the full payment of .... indebtedness to ....

Now, if .... should in all things comply with these obligations aforesaid, then this deed to be void; but if .... fail to comply with the conditions thereof, then it is agreed that ...., acting as trustee and agent of both contracting parties herein, is authorized and empowered to seize all the property above enumerated, and to sell the same by public or private sale, at ...., after giving .... days notice in three public places in said county, and to pay the amount due on this contract, and any balance left after satisfying the debt, to be paid over to ....

And the said ...., trustee, is further empowered to employ labor to pick the cotton in case .... fail to do so at the proper time, charging us for the same. [*Insert any other conditions.*]

Given under .... hand... and seal.. . this .... day of.........., 187.....

```
............, [L. S.]
............, [L. S.]
............, [L. S.]
```

No. 240.—DEED OF TRUST FOR RENT AND SUPPLIES.

Whereas, ... has rented from ......, for the year 187..., ... acres of land, being part of ...... plantation, situated in the county of ...., Mississippi, and for which .. agree to pay rent as follows: (*here state the terms fully*); have also agreed to cultivate said land in a proper manner, and to keep the fences bordering on the same in fit condition to turn stock :

And whereas, .. desires to procure, during the year 187., from said ......, advances in money, supplies, etc., for the purpose of cul-

tivating said land, to the amount of .... And .... being
desirous to secure the prompt payment of said rent and advances,
as aforesaid, when the same is due, ... agree and covenant that all
the crops of corn, cotton and other products raised on said land in
the year 187.., and also the following other personal property, to-wit:
(*here describe particularly the personal property*), be, and the same
is hereby mortgaged and pledged, and subjected to a lien in favor of
said ...., for the payment of said rent and advances, and the
faithful performance of this contract.

And .... bind .... to cultivate, gather and put into marketable
condition, as soon as practicable, enough of the crop of cotton, and
to deliver the cotton as fast as baled to the said ... to be sold by
.... at ..., the net proceeds to be applied by ....   to the full
payment of .... indebtedness to ....

Now, if .. . should in all things comply with these obligations
aforesaid, then this deed to be void; but if .... fail to comply with
the conditions thereof, then it is agreed that ...., acting as trustee and agent of both contracting parties herein, is authorized and
empowered to seize all the property above enumerated, and to sell
the same by public or private sale, at ...., after giving .. days'
notice in three public places in said county, and to pay the amount
due on this contract, and any balance left, after satisfying the debt,
to be paid over to .... And the said ...., trustee, is
further empowered to employ labor to pick the cotton in case ....
fail to do so at the proper time, charging us for the same. (*Insert
any other conditions.*)

Given under our hands and seals, this .... day of ....., 187..

          .... [SEAL.]
          .... [SEAL.]
          .... [SEAL.]

No. 241.—BOND FOR TITLE TO REALTY.

Know all men by these Presents:

That we, ..., as principal, and ....,
as his surety, are held and firmly bound to ...., in the
penalty of .... dollars, for which payment well and truly to
be made, we bind ourselves, our heirs, executors, and administrators,
jointly and severally, firmly by these presents; signed with our
names and sealed with our seals, this ...... day of .... A. D. 18...

The condition of this bond is such, that, whereas, said ....
has bargained and sold to said .... certain tracts of
land, (*here describe them*), at and for the sum of five thousand dollars, payable on the ...... day of ...., 18.... Now if the said sum
shall be duly paid, and if thereupon said ...., shall, by
deed, alien and convey to .... the land above described,
with general warranty, then this obligation to be void, otherwise to
remain in full force and virtue. ...., [SEAL.]
                            ...., [SEAL.]
                            ...., [SEAL.]

8

No. 242.—DEED OF GIFT.

STATE OF MISSISSIPPI, ... COUNTY:

Know all men by these Presents:

That I, ..., for and in consideration of the natural love and affection which I have and do bear toward my beloved son, ..., have this day given and granted, and delivered, and by these presents doth give, grant and deliver unto my said son, ... the following property, to-wit: (*here describe the property.*)

To have and to hold the same unto my said son, and to his heirs and assigns forever.

In testimony whereof, I, the said ...., have hereunto set my hand and seal, this the ...... day of ...., A. D. 18....

. ..., [SEAL.]

No. 243.—DEED WITH FULL COVENANTS.

Know all men by these presents, that we, John Jones, and Sarah, his wife, of the town of Greensboro', in the county of Choctaw, for and in consideration of the sum of two hundred dollars, to us in hand now here paid, have granted, bargained, sold, and by these presents do grant, bargain, sell and convey unto James Brown, of the same place, all that certain parcel of land situated in the said town of Greensboro', and described as follows:

Or, which in a deed of conveyance made by Samuel Baker to the said John Jones, dated the 4th day of February, 1860, was described as follows (*here insert boundaries*):

With all the appurtenances, and all the right, title, interest, claim and demand of us, or either of us in the premises; to have and to hold the same, with all the appurtenances, unto the said James Brown and his heirs, in fee simple forever. And we, the said John Jones and Sarah, his wife, for ourselves and our heirs do hereby covenant and agree to and with the said James Brown, and his heirs and assigns, that we are now the owners of the said premises, and are seized of a good and indefeasible estate of inheritance therein, and that we have full right and power to sell and convey the same in fee simple absolute; that the said premises are free and clear of all incumbrances; that the said James Brown, his heirs and assigns, may forever hereafter have, hold, possess and enjoy the same, without any suit, molestation or interruption, by any person whatever, lawfully claiming any right therein; and that we, the said John Jones and wife, and all persons hereafter claiming under us, will, at any time hereafter, at the request and expense of the said James Brown, his heirs and assigns, make all such further assurances for the more effectually conveying of the said premises, with the appurtenances, as may be reasonably required by him or them; and that we, the said John Jones and wife, and our heirs, will warrant and defend the said premises, with the appurtenances, unto the said James Brown, his heirs and assigns forever.

In testimony whereof, we have hereunto set our hands and seals, this 23d day of September, A. D. 1868.

JOHN JONES, [SEAL.]
SARAH JONES, [SEAL.]

———

No. 214.—ADMINISTRATOR'S DEED.

This deed of conveyance, made and entered into this ...... day of ...., A. D., 18..., between ...., administrator of all and singular the goods, chattels and credits which were of ...., deceased, late of county of ...., in the State of Mississippi, of the one part, and ...., of the same county and State, of the other part, witnesseth; that, whereas, at a term of the chancery court of said county, begun and held at the court house thereof, on the ...... Monday in ...., 18..., it was among other things, ordered and decreed that the said party of the first part should sell, on a credit of twelve months from the day of sale, all that certain tract of land situate, lying and being in said county of .... containing about ...... acres of land, more or less, and described as follows, to-wit (*here describe land*). And, whereas, in pursuance of said decretal or order of the court aforesaid, the said party of the first part, as administrator aforesaid, did regularly give notice of the time and place of sale in a newspaper published in the town of ...., in said county and State, called the ...., four weeks successively, commencing on the ...... day of ...., 18.., and ending on the ...... day of ...., 18..., and by posting copies of such notice on the ...... day of ...., 18.., at the following public places in said county, viz: one copy thereof on the door of the court house; one copy on the door of the post office at ...., all in said county; and in accordance with said notice, the said party of the first part did, on the day and year first in these presents written. at the late residence of said ...., deceased, between the hours of 12 o'clock M. and 5 o'clock P. M., offer the said tract of land, with appurtenances, for sale, to the highest bidder; and the said .... then and there bid for the same the sum of .... dollars, which being the highest and best bid therefor, the said premises, with the appurtenances, were struck off to him.

Now this deed witnesseth: that in consideration of the premises, and that the said .... hath executed and delivered his bond, with .... as his joint security, for the payment of the said sum of .... dollars, twelve months after the date of these presents, which, by law, operates as a special mortgage or lien on said tract of land and appurtenances, the said party of the first part has this day bargained, sold, aliened, conveyed and confirmed, and by these presents does bargain, sell, alien, convey and confirm unto the said ...., his heirs and assigns forever, all the above described tract of land, with all the tenements, hereditaments, privileges and appurtenances thereunto belonging or in anywise appertaining, and all the estate, right, title, interest and claim whatsoever, at law or in equity, of him, the said ... ., deceased, his heirs, executors or administrators of, in and to the same.

To have and to hold the above granted, bargained and described premises unto him, the said ...., his heirs and assigns, to his and their only proper use, benefit and behoof, forever, as fully and effectually, to all intents and purposes in the law, as he, the said party of the first part, might, could or ought to sell and convey the same by virtue of the decretal order of the court aforesaid.

In witness whereof, the said party of the first part hath hereunto set his hand and seal the day and year first in these presents above written. ...., [SEAL.]

Administrator.

Signed, sealed and delivered }
 in presence of
....
....

No. 245.—TAX COLLECTOR'S DEED.

I, ..., Tax Collector of .... county, have this day, according to law, sold the following lands, there being no other property found on which to levy and make the taxes due on said land, to wit: [here describe the land], for the taxes assessed to the reputed owner thereof, for the year 18..., when .... became the best bidder, at the sum of ...... dollars. I, therefore, sell and convey said land to the said ...., his heirs and assigns, forever.

Given under my hand and seal, the ......day of........., A. D. 18...

...., Tax Collector.

BILL OF COSTS.—State tax ......; county tax ......; special tax. .....; printer's fees ......; chancery clerk's ......; damages ......; commissions ......; making deed ......; total ....

STATE OF MISSISSIPPI, ... COUNTY:

Personally appeared before me, ..., Clerk of the Chancery Court of said county, ..., Sheriff and Tax Collector of said county, who acknowledged that, as said Tax Collector of said county, he signed, sealed, and delivered the foregoing deed, on the day and year therein mentioned, as his official act and deed.

Given under my hand and seal of office, at ...., this ...... day of ......, A. D. 187...

...., Clerk, [SEAL.]

STATE OF MISSISSIPPI, ... COUNTY:

I, ..., Clerk of the Chancery Court of said county, do hereby certify that the within deed was filed in my office, to be recorded in

Tax Collector's deed book......, page......, of the records of deeds.
Given under my hand and seal of office, at ...., this ...... day
of ...., A. D. 187...

..................., Clerk, [SEAL.]

No. 246.—SHERIFF'S DEED.

This indenture, made and entered into this ...... day of ...., in
the year of our Lord one thousand eighteen hundred and seventy...,
between .... , Sheriff of .... county, Mississippi, of the one
part, and ...., of the other part; Witnesseth, That, whereas,
.... writ... lately issued from the Circuit Court of ...... county,
Mississippi, directed to the Sheriff of .... county, in said State,
at the suit of ...., against the goods and chattels, lands and tenements of ...., which said............ levied on the following lands,
to-wit: [here describe lands], with the appurtenances, as the lands
and tenements of the above named defendant, ..., and the said
Sheriff having given... days previous notice that the above described
...... will be sold at public auction, by virtue of said writ of .... on
the ... day of ......, 18..., between the hours of eleven o'clock, A. M.
and four o'clock, P. M., of said day, at the ......, in said county, did,
at the same time and place, offer said premises for sale, at public
auction, and the said ...., party of the second part, then and there
appeared, and bid for the premises the sum of...... dollars, which said
sum was more than any other person offered or bid for the same;
whereupon, the said ...... were struck off to the said ......, .. being
the highest and best bidder therefor.

Now, this indenture witnesseth, That the said ......, Sheriff aforesaid, for and in consideration of the premises, and of the sum of......
dollars, to him, the said Sheriff, in hand well and truly paid by the
said ...., at and before the sealing and delivery hereof, the receipt
whereof is hereby acknowledged, hath this day bargained, sold,
alienated, and conveyed, and by these presents doth grant, bargain,
sell, alien, and convey unto the said .... heirs and assigns, forever. all and singular, the above described premises, hereditaments,
privileges, and appurtenances thereunto belonging, or in any way
appertaining ; to have and to hold the said premises of the above
named defendant, and all the right, interest, title, or claim, both in
law and in equity, of........., the said ...., with all the privileges
and appurtenances, in or to the same, unto the said ...., heirs
and assigns, forever.

In testimony whereof, the said .... , Sheriff as aforesaid, hath
hereunto set his hand and seal, the day and year above written.

.................., Sheriff of .... county, Miss.

No. 247.—COMMISSIONER'S DEED.

This deed, from ...., Commissioner in Chancery, to
........., of the county of .... and State of Mississippi, made

this ...... day of ...., A. D. 18..., witnesseth: that, whereas, the chancery court of .... county, by its decree of the ...... day of ...., A. D. 18..., in a cause therein between ...., complainant, and ...., defendant, appointed the said .... its commissioner, with power and direction to advertise and sell, as directed, the following: .... And whereas, the said .... pursuantly did duly advertise the same, and the day and place of sale, and on the ...... day of .. .., A. D. 18.... at ...., did expose to sale the lands aforesaid, and at such sale the said .... became the highest, last and best bidder and purchaser of said lands, at and for the sum of .... dollars. Therefore, the said ...., as such commissioner, in consideration of the premises, doth hereby alien and convey to the said .... the lands so purchased by ...., and doth hereby transfer, convey and deliver to .... said lands; to have and to hold the said lands hereby intended to be conveyed, with the appurtenances, to said ...., and heirs and alienees, so by him purchased, in perfect right, free from and against the right, title, claim or demand of the said ...., and ...... heirs and assigns, and all other persons, so far as said ...., as such commissioner, by virtue of the proceedings aforesaid, and the laws of the land can or ought to alien, convey and deliver, but in no other degree. And he hereto puts his name and seal, on the day and year first written.

...., [SEAL.]
Commissioner.

No. 248.—LABOR CONTRACT FOR WAGES.

This agreement between .... of .... county, Mississippi, employer, and ...., laborer; Witnesseth, That said .... hereby hires said laborer as a ......, from this date until ....; and for faithful services to be rendered in said employment, by said laborer, during all that time, the said employer agrees to pay said laborer .... dollars per month, payable at the end of every ...... months; and in addition, the said .... hereby agrees to furnish said laborer, free of charge, during the time of said service, with (*here describe what may be agreed upon*)

And said laborer, in consideration thereof, hereby agrees to render to said employer, or his agent, for and during all of said term, due obedience and faithful service, and well and promptly to perform all work in the line of h... duty, in accordance with the instructions of said employer or his agent, and to bestow due care and attention in all things, upon all property and interests committed to said laborer's charge and keeping, and will faithfully account, or pay for the same, to be deducted out of said laborer's wages, so far as the same will pay; and will discharge, in all things, the duties of a faithful servant. And it is hereby understood, and mutually agreed, that the wages of the said laborer are to cease during such times as said laborer may be absent without leave, each absence not to count less than one day; and said employer, or ...... agent, may, at any time, discharge said laborer for such absence or habitual neglect of duty. Also, that for time lost by sickness, a proportional deduction shall be made in the next succeeding settlement; and the said laborer shall be charged with the actual cost of medical attendance. medicines, and other supplies furnished h... during such period of sickness. And it is further agreed, that the said employer reserves the right to establish such rules and regulations for the government of his plantation or premises, as he may deem proper, not inconsistent with this contract, and the laws of the State of Mississippi.

Given under our hands, in duplicate, this ...... day of .... A. D. 18....

.................., [SEAL.]

Witness: ...., [SEAL.]

....

No. 249—CONTRACT FOR SHARE OF CROP.

STATE OF MISSISSIPPI, ... COUNTY.

This contract and agreement, made and entered into this .... day of ......, 18.., by and between ...., of the first part. and ...., of the second part: Witnesseth, That the said .... has this day employed the said ... ., for the year 18.., (*or, until the crop of said year is gathered and ready for market, at option of employer,*) to labor upon his farm as hereinafter provided; and it is hereby understood and agreed that the said laborer shall be subject to the orders of his employer or superintendent; that he is not to leave the premises without permission first obtained; that he is to labor faithfully on all week days, during such hours as the employer may prescribe, that he will take good and faithful care of all utensils, implements, wagons, horses, mules, and other property in his charge, and be responsible for their loss, and for all damages, except for wear and tear by necessary use.

And it is agreed, That a failure to comply with the conditions of this contract subjects the said .... to be discharged, or charged with loss of time.

It is agreed, by the said ...., that in consideration of the foregoing services, the said laborer shall be entitled to one .... of the crop—(*that is, all the laborers on the plantation shall be entitled to one .... of all the crop they assist in making*)—after deducting from the quantity of corn raised, a proportional share for the necessary feed of teams; and the said .... agrees to furnish the said .... with lodgings, free of charge, and with the following supplies, at cost price: .... per week; and no other supplies to be advanced except at the option of employer.

And it is further understood and agreed, That the said laborer shall pay his own doctor's bills, buy his own clothing, and pay all other expenses, of every description, of himself and those dependant upon him.

And it is further understood, That said .... shall retain a lien on so much of the crop as will pay whatever arrearages may be due him at the end of the season, and the same shall not be moved or sold until said claims are first satisfied.

In testimony whereof, the parties have signed duplicates.

...., [SEAL.]

Witnesses: ...., [SEAL.]

....

....

No. 250.—FORM OF CONTRACT FOR WORK.

These articles of agreement, made and executed this 28th day of December, 1876, between Anthony Warren, of the one part, and Robert Jones, carpenter, of the other part: witnesseth, that the said party of the first part, hath this day employed the said Robert Jones to erect and build for the said Anthony Warren, a dwelling-house, on the premises of the said Anthony Warren, in the county of Washington, in the State of Mississippi, of the following dimensions and specifications, to-wit: (*here insert specifications.*) That said building shall be completed and ready for occupation by the 2d day of March; that on the completion of said building or dwelling-house, the said Anthony Warren is to pay to the said Robert Jones the sum of one thousand dollars, provided said work shall have been done according to said specifications.

In testimony whereof, the parties have signed and sealed this article in duplicate, the day and year first above written.

ANTHONY WARREN, [SEAL.]

ROBERT JONES, [SEAL.]

Attest:

Amos Jackson,}
James Owens. }

No. 251.—FARM LEASE.

This Indenture, made and entered into this ...... day of .... 18..., between ...., landlord, of the first part, and ...., tenant, of the second part, both of the county of ...., and State of Mississippi: Witnesseth, That the said party of the first part, for the consideration hereafter appearing, hath granted, demised, and to farm let, and by these presents doth grant, demise, and to farm let, unto the said party of the second part, his executors, administrators and assigns, the plantation and farm known and styled the ...., in the said county and State, it being the same place on which the said .... now resides. To have and to hold the said plantation, with the appurtenances, unto him the said party of the second part, his executors, administrators and assigns, for and during the term of ...... years from the ...... day of ...., 187...., paying for the same to the said party of the first part, his heirs or assigns, yearly, during the said term aforesaid, the annual rent of ...., the first payment to be on the ...... day of ...., 187..., and the other payments to be made on the ...... day of .... in each and every year thereafter. And in case the said rent is not promptly paid when due, the said .... shall have the power and right to re-enter the premises hereby leased, and enjoy the same, as if this lease had not been made. And the said party of the second part, for himself, his heirs, executors, and administrators, doth covenant and agree to and with the said party of the first part, to well and truly pay the rent according to the terms above expressed, and also to pay all taxes legally assessed against said leased land during the term of lease, and on the last day of the term, or other sooner determination of the estate hereby granted, to deliver up the plantation aforesaid, with the appurtenances, to the said party of the first part, his heirs or assigns. And the said party of the first part covenants and agrees to and with the said party of the second part, that he and the said party of the second part, his executors and administrators, shall quietly enjoy the said premises hereby granted during the term aforesaid, he the party of the second part performing his covenants hereinbefore mentioned.

In witness whereof, the parties have set their hands and seals, the day and year first above written.

...., [SEAL.]

Attest:

...., [SEAL.]

....

....

No. 252.—GENERAL LEASE.

This indenture, made this ...... day of ...., one thousand eight hundred and seventy ......, between ...., of the first part, and ....., of the second part ; witnesseth, that said party of the first part, in consideration of the rents and covenants hereinafter contained, and by said party of the second part, and .... assigns, to be paid and performed, do hereby grant, demise, and lease to the said party of the second part, ..., executors, administrators, and assigns, the premises described as follows : [here describe the premises]; to have and to hold the same, with the appurtenances, unto the said party of the second part, ... executors, administrators, and assigns, from .... , for and during the full term of .... next ensuing, and fully to be completed and ended ; .... yielding and paying therefor, during said term, the ...., payable as follows : ....; *Provided*, however, that if said rent, or any part thereof, shall remain unpaid for .... days after it shall become due, and without demand made therefor; or if said lessee shall assign this lease, or under-let said leased premises, or any part thereof, without the written consent of said lessor, ... heirs or assigns first had; it shall be lawful for said lessor, ... heirs or assigns, into said premises to re-enter, and the same to have again, re-possess, and enjoy, as in .... first and former estate; and thereupon, this lease, and everything therein contained on the said lessor's behalf to be done and performed, shall cease, determine, and be utterly void.

And said lessee, for .... executors, administrators, and assigns, covenants and agrees with said lessor, ... heirs and assigns, as follows, that is to say : that said lessee will pay rents, in manner aforesaid, except said premises shall be destroyed or rendered untenantable by fire or unavoidable accident ; that .... will not do or suffer any waste therein ; that .... will not assign this lease, or under-let said premises without the written consent of said lessor, and that at the end of said term, ... will deliver up said premises in as good order and condition as they now are, or may be put by said lessor, reasonable use and ordinary wear and tear thereof, and damage by fire and unavoidable casualty, excepted.

And said lessor, for .... heirs, executors, administrators, and assigns, covenants with said lessee, ... executors and administrators, that said lessee paying the rents, and observing and keeping the covenants of this lease on .... part to be kept, shall lawfully, peaceably, and quietly hold, occupy and enjoy said premises during said term, without any let, hindrance, ejection or molestation by said lessor, or .... heirs, or any person or persons lawfully claiming under them.

In witness whereof, the said parties hereto have hereunto set their hands and seals, on the day and year first above written.

...., [SEAL.]
...., [SEAL.]

Signed, sealed, and delivered in presence of)
.... (
..................)

STATE OF MISSISSIPPI, ... COUNTY. } ss.

Be it remembered, that on the .... day of ...., in the year of our Lord one thousand eight hundred and seventy-..........., before me, the subscriber, ..., personally came ...., the parties named in the foregoing lease, and acknowledged the signing and sealing thereof to be their voluntary act and deed, for the uses and purposes therein mentioned.

In testimony whereof, I have hereunto subscribed my name, and affixed my (private or official) seal, on the day and year aforesaid.

.... [SEAL.]

No. 253.—LANDLORD'S AGREEMENT OF LEASE.

THE STATE OF MISSISSIPPI, MADISON COUNTY.

This is to certify, that I have, this 25th day of August, 1876, let and rented unto Israel Hopkins, my house and lot, known as No. 37, on Madison street, in the city of Canton, with the appurtenances, and the sole and uninterrupted use thereof, for one year, to commence on the 1st day of October next, at the yearly rent of four hundred dollars, payable quarterly, on the last day of each quarter; rent to cease in case the premises are destroyed by fire or other cause. The said Israel Hopkins is to keep the house and premises in good repair ; but all taxes, assessments, or other charges upon the said premises are assumed by the undersigned.   [*This is to be varied, as the parties may agree.*]

JEREMIAH BROWN, [SEAL.]

No. 254.—TENANT'S AGREEMENT.

THE STATE OF MISSISSIPPI, MADISON COUNTY:

This is to certify that I have hired and taken from Jeremiah Brown, his house and lot, known as No. 37, on Madison street, in the city of Canton, for the term of one year, to commence on the 1st day of October, 1876, at the yearly rent of four hundred dollars, payable quarterly, on the last day of each quarter.   And I do hereby promise to make punctual payment of the rent in the manner aforesaid, except in case the premises become untenantable from fire or any other cause, when the rent is to cease; and do further promise to keep the said premises in good repair, and to quit and surrender the same at the expiration of the term, in as good state and condition as reasonable use and wear thereof will permit, damages by the elements excepted. It being understood that, in consideration of the payment of rent as aforesaid, the said Jeremiah Brown is to pay all taxes, assessments or other charges upon the said premises.

Given under my hand and seal, the 25th day of August, A. D. 1876.   ISRAEL HOPKINS, [SEAL.]

In presence of
J. W. YEARGAIN,
FRANKLIN SMITH.

SECURITY FOR RENT.

In consideration of the letting of the premises above described, and for the sum of one dollar, I do hereby become surety for the punctual payment of the rent, and performance of the covenants in the above written agreement mentioned, to be paid and performed by Israel Hopkins, as therein specified and excepted; and if any default shall be made therein, I do hereby promise and agree to pay unto Jeremiah Brown such sum or sums of money as will be sufficient to make up such deficiency, and fully satisfy the conditions of the said agreement, without requiring any notice of non-payment or proof of demand being made.

Given under my hand and seal, this 25th day of August, A. D. 1876.   H. H. HINES, [SEAL.]

No. 255.—PARTNERSHIP—PLANTING.

Articles of a planting partnership, between ...., of the State of ...., and ...., of ...... county, State of Mississippi, made the ...... day of ...... , 18....

1. The parties have leased from ...., of said county of ......, for ...... years, at and for ...... dollars per year, and as partners under the name of ...... & ......, have given their notes for the payment of the rent. The said ...... has put upon the plantation .... laborers, namely: ......, and the said ...... has put thereon .... laborers, namely: ......, to be worked thereon for the equal benefit of the parties, under the care, control and management of ...., who is to contribute his personal superintendence in planting, raising, securing, consigning and selling the crops of cotton made on said plantation.

2. All necessary expenses incurred in support of the said ..... and his family, and of the hands, and of conducting the plantation are to be borne equally by the parties; provided that the expenses for the support of ...., do not exceed yearly .....

3. .... is to keep an exact account of receipts and expenses; shall use the name of the firm only in consignments, in receipts, for necessary joint expenses, and in correspondence; nor is said .... otherwise to use the same.

4. .... is to cause the said laborers to be well-clad, supported, sheltered, governed and protected, and provided with due medical aid.

5. He is to settle yearly with the said .. ...., and pay him one moiety of the partnership net profits.

6. A portion of the leased plantation may be put in corn, potatoes, etc., for the consumption of family, hands, stock, etc.

And hereto the parties put their names and seals in duplicate.

.............., ⌈L. S.⌉
.............., ⌈L. S.⌉
.............., ⌈L. S.⌉

Witness:
....
....

No. 256.—MERCANTILE PARTNERSHIP.

Articles of Mercantile Partnership, between ...., of the town (*or city*) of ...., in the State of Mississippi, made the .... day of ....

1. The name and style of the firm is ....

2. The partners each contribute as capital, $..........., which is to be invested in such goods, wares and merchandise as the partners may think most saleable, and sold for cash, mainly, except to small amounts, and on short credits to punctual, responsible dealers.

3. Neither of the partners is to become surety, drawer, acceptor, or endorser, in any case whatever, except in, for and affecting the partnership, without the consent of his associate.

4. A settlement shall be had when either party desires; and the firm dissolved at the desire of either.

5. The partnership name is to be used only in respect of the business and affairs of the firm.

Signed in duplicate.

...................., [SEAL.]
...................., [SEAL.]

No. 257.—MERCANTILE PARTNERSHIP.—2.

Articles of copartnership made and concluded this 20th day of August, in the year one thousand eight hundred and sixty-nine, by and between James West, of the first part, and John East, of the second part, both of Jackson, in the county of Hinds, State of Mississippi.

Whereas, it is the intention of the said parties to form a copartnership, for the purpose of carrying on the retail business of dry goods and clothing, for which purpose they have agreed on the following terms and articles of agreement, to the faithful performance of which they mutually bind and engage themselves each to the other, his executors and administrators :

First. The style of the said copartnership shall be "West & East," and it shall continue for the term of two years from the above date, except in case of death of either of the said parties within the said term.

Second. The said West & East are the proprietors of the stock, a schedule of which is contained in proportion of two-thirds to the said West, and one-third to the said East ; and the said parties shall continue to be owners of their joint stock in the same proportions; and in case of any addition being made to the same, by mutual con sent, the said West shall advance two-thirds, and the said East one-third thereof.

Third. All profits which may accrue to the said partnership shall be divided, and all losses happening to the said firm, whether from bad debts, depreciation of goods, or any other cause or accident, and all expenses of the business, shall be borne by the said parties, in the aforesaid proportion of their interest in the said stock.

Fourth. The said East shall devote and give all his time and attention to the business of the said firm as a salesman, and generally to the care and superintendence of the store; and the said West shall devote so much of his time as may be requisite, in advising, overseeing and directing the purchase of dry goods, clothing, and other articles necessary to the said business.

Fifth. All the purchases, sales, transactions, and accounts of the said firm shall be kept in regular books, which shall be always open to the inspection of both parties and their legal representatives respectively. An account of stock shall be taken, and an account between the said parties shall be settled, as often as once in every year, and as much oftener as either party may desire and in writing request.

Sixth. Neither of the said parties shall subscribe any bond, sign or indorse any note of hand, accept, sign, or indorse any draft or bill of exchange, or assume any other liability, verbal or written, either in his own name or in the name of the firm, for the accommodation of any other person or persons whatsoever, without the consent, in writing, of the other party; nor shall either party lend any of the funds of the copartnership without such consent of the other partner.

Seventh. No importation, or large purchase of dry goods, clothing or other things, shall be made, nor any transaction out of the usual course of retail business, shall be undertaken by either of the partners, without previous consultation with, and the approbation of, the other partner.

Eighth. Neither party shall withdraw from the joint stock, at any time, more than his share of the profits of the business then earned, nor shall either party be entitled to interest on his share of the capital; but if, at the expiration of the year, a balance of profits be found due to either partner, he shall be at liberty to withdraw the said balance, or to leave it in the business, provided the other partner consent thereto, and in that case he shall be allowed interest on the said balance.

Ninth. At the expiration of the aforesaid term, or earlier dissolution of this copartnership, if the said parties or their legal representatives cannot agree in the division of the stock then on hand, the whole copartnership effects, except the debts due to the firm, shall be sold at public auction, at which both parties shall be at liberty to bid and purchase, like other individuals, and the proceeds shall be divided, after payments of the debts of the firm, in the proportions aforesaid.

Tenth. For the purpose of securing the performance of the foregoing agreements, it is agreed that either party, in case of any violation of them or either of them, by the other, shall have the right to dissolve this copartnership forthwith, on his becoming informed of such violation.

In witness whereof, we have hereunto set our hands and seals, the day and year first above written.

JAMES WEST, [SEAL.]
JOHN EAST, [SEAL.]

No. 258.—GENERAL RELEASE OF ALL DEMANDS.

Know all men by these presents, that I, E. F., of ...., for and in consideration of the sum of .... dollars to me paid by H. K., of ...., (the receipt whereof I do hereby acknowledge), have remised, released and forever discharged, and I do hereby, for myself, my heirs, executors, administrators, and assigns, remise, release and forever discharge the said H. K., his heirs, executors and administrators, of and from all debts, demands, actions and causes of action which I now have, in law or equity, or which may result from the existing state of things, from any and all contracts, liabilities, doings and omissions, from the beginning of the world to this day.

In testimony whereof, I have hereunto set my hand and seal, this
.... day of ...., 187...

.... [SEAL.]

BONDS OF PUBLIC OFFICERS.

No. 259.

§§ 244, 261, 272, 287; Acts 1876, p. 46.

NOTE.—The following form will answer for Coroners, Rangers, Treasurers, Surveyors, Assessors, Circuit Clerks and Supervisors. The justification of sureties on official bonds is the same for all public officers, which must be endorsed on the bonds, the form of which is given here.

STATE OF MISSISSIPPI, ... COUNTY. } ss.

Know all men by these presents, that we, A. B., C. D., E. F. and G. H., of the county and State aforesaid, are held and firmly bound unto the State of Mississippi, in the penal sum of ...... dollars, for the payment of which well and truly to be made, we, and each of us, bind ourselves, our and each of our heirs, executors and administrators, jointly and severally, and firmly by these presents. Signed with our hands, sealed with our seals, and delivered on this .... day of ...., A. D. 18...

Whereas, the above bounden A. B. was duly elected to the office of .... of said county, on the ..... day of ... ..., A. D. 18.., for the term of ..... years from the .... day of ....., A. D. 18..; wherefore the condition of this obligation is such, that if the said A. B. shall faithfully perform and discharge all the duties of the said office of ...., and all acts and things required by law, or incident to the said office, during his continuance therein, then the above obligation to be void, otherwise to remain in full force and virtue.

.... , [SEAL.]
........., [SEAL.]
........., [SEAL]
........., [SEAL.]

The foregoing bond approved by us this 10th day of December, 1875.

................,
President Board Supervisors.

................,
Clerk.

---

§§ 219, 990, 1298.

No. 260.—BONDS OF PUBLIC OFFICERS.

NOTE.—The following form will answer for Justices of the Peace, Chancery Clerks, Sheriffs and Constables:

STATE OF MISSISSIPPI, ... COUNTY. } ss.

Know all men by these presents, that we, A. B., C. D., E. F., G. H. and I. K., of the county and State aforesaid, are held and firmly bound unto the State of Mississippi in the penal sum of .... dollars, for the payment of which well and truly to be made, we, and each of us, bind ourselves, our and each of our heirs, executors and administrators, jointly and severally, and firmly by these presents. Signed with our hands, sealed with our seals, and delivered on this . ... day of ...., A. D. 18...

Whereas, the above bounden A. B. was duly elected to the office of .... of said county, on the ..... day of ...., A. D. 18.., for the term of ...... years, from the ...... day of ...., A. D 18...; wherefore the condition of this obligation is such, that if the said A. B. shall faithfully perform and discharge all the duties of the said office of ...., and all acts and things required by law, or incident to the said office, during his continuance therein, and pay over immediately, and without delay, to the proper persons, all moneys collected by him, or which may come into his hands by virtue of his said office, then the above obligation to be void, otherwise to remain in full force and virtue.

.... [SEAL.]
.... [SEAL.]
.... [SEAL.]
.... [SEAL.]

The foregoing bond approved by us, this .... day of ...., 18...

....,
President Board Supervisors.
........................,
Clerk.

---

§ 1, Acts 1876, p. 8.

No. 261.—TAX COLLECTOR'S BOND.

Note.—This bond differs from all others in its conditions, and the law should be followed strictly. Presidents of the Boards of Supervisors and Clerks should scrutinize all bonds, not only for the purpose of justifying the sureties, but to see that the bonds are in proper form; and by section 3 of the above Act, the President and Clerk are held criminally to account for the sufficiency of the bond; therefore, if they are satisfied from their own knowledge, or from reliable information, that the surety is not worth the amount sworn to, they should reject the surety. The surety falsely swearing in any particular, although guilty of perjury, does not by his guilty act relieve the President or Clerk, if they had any reason to believe that the oath was false.

State of Mississippi. Hinds County. } ss.

Know all men by these presents, That we, A. B., C. D., E. F. and G. H., of the county and State aforesaid, are held and firmly bound unto the State of Mississippi, in the penal sum of ten thousand dollars, for the payment of which, well and truly to be made, we, and each of us, bind ourselves, our and each of our heirs, executors and administrators, jointly and severally, and firmly by these presents. Signed with our hands, sealed with our seals, and delivered on this first day of January, A. D. 1878.

Whereas, the above bounden A. B. was duly elected to the office of sheriff of said county, on the sixth day of November, A. D. 1877, for the term of two years from the first day of January, A. D. 1878; and whereas said A. B., by virtue of his office of sheriff, is, by law, tax-collector of said county; Now, therefore, the condition of this obligation is such, that if the said A. B. will well, truly and faithfully, collect all the taxes assessed, in said county, and will promptly pay into the State and county treasuries, all money collected by him, and to which said treasuries shall be respectively entitled; and that he will in all things truly and faithfully execute and perform all the duties of tax-collector of his said county, to the best of his skill and ability, so long as he shall continue in office, then the above obligation to be void, otherwise to remain in full force and virtue.

A. B. [SEAL.]
C. D. [SEAL.]
E. F. [SEAL.]
G. H. [SEAL.]

The foregoing bond approved by us, this first day of January, A. D. 1878.

I. J.,
President Board Supervisors.
K. L.,
Clerk.

---

§ 2, Acts 1876, p. 9.]

No. 262.—JUSTIFICATION OF SURETIES ON OFFICIAL BONDS.

NOTE.—The oath of the sureties must be taken before the Chancery Clerk; if no Chancery Clerk, then before the Circuit Clerk; and in counties where both clerkships are filled by the same person, then before the President of the Board of Supervisors, who also approves the bond. The oath of sureties must in all cases be endorsed on the bond—that is, not written on a separate paper and attached. The justification of the sureties must be taken at the office of the Clerk. The contemplation of the law is that the property bound and the bondsmen shall be situated in the county of the officer—whether the bondsmen live there or not, the property must be there situated.

STATE OF MISSISSIPPI, ... COUNTY. } ss.

This day personally came before me, the undersigned Clerk of the Chancery Court (*or Circuit Court, or President of the Board of Supervisors*), in and for county and, State aforesaid, and at my office therein, the sureties on the within and foregoing bond, and whose names are signed thereto, who, being by me first severally and duly sworn, depose and say, that they are collectively worth the sum of (*penalty of bond*) dollars in freehold estate, held and owned in their own right, and situated in said county of ...., over and above all their just debts, legal liabilities, and the amounts of their suretyships on any other official bonds, and over and above all their legal exemptions: that is to say, the said .... the sum of........ dollars; the said .... the sum of ...... dollars; the said ......

9

...... the sum of ...... dollars; and the said .... the sum of ...... dollars; and that said several sums aggregate the full penalty of said bond; and further they say not.

Sworn to and subscribed before me, this .... day of ...., A. D. 18...

...., [SEAL.]
.... Clerk.

No. 263.—MORTGAGE TO SECURE NOTE.

This Indenture, made this ...... day of ...., between A. B., of .... county, of the first part, and C. D., of .... county, of the second part, all of the State of Mississippi; witnesseth, That, whereas, said party of the first part is justly indebted to said party of the second part, in the sum of .... dollars, as evidenced by his certain promissory (*or, two or more certain promissory notes.*) of even date herewith, for the sum of five hundred dollars, payable to said party of the second part, or order. on or before the ...... day of .... , 18...., with interest at the rate of ...... per cent. per annum from maturity (*or, date :*) and being desirous of securing the prompt payment of said note, at maturity, and interest thereon, the said party of the first part, for and in consideration of the premises, and of the further sum of one dollar in hand to him paid by said party of the second part, the receipt of which is hereby acknowledged, has granted, bargained, and sold, and by these presents does grant. bargain, and sell unto said party of the second part, and to his heirs and assigns, all that certain piece of land lying and being in said county, and described as follows: [*describe it*] to have and to hold said bargained premises, together with all and singular the appurtenances thereunto belonging or in anywise appertaining. unto the said party of the second part, his heirs and assigns, in fee simple, forever. And the said party of the first part, for himself, his heirs and legal representatives, covenants and agrees to and with the said party of the second part, his heirs, legal representatives, and assigns, that he will and shall warrant and forever defend the title to the aforesaid premises, against the legal claim or claims of all and every person or persons whomsoever.

This deed is, nevertheless, intended to operate as a mortgage to secure the payment of the amounts aforesaid ; Now, therefore, if the said party of the first part, or others, for him, shall well and truly pay and satisfy said note, at maturity, with interest accrued thereon, then this deed is to be void and of none effect, otherwise to remain in full force and effect.

In witness whereof, said party of the first part has hereunto set his hand and seal, the day and year first above written.

A. B., (SEAL.)

No. 264.—MORTGAGE WITH POWER OF SALE.—SHORT FORM.

This Indenture, made this ...... day of .... , 18...., between A. B., of .... county, of the first part, and C. D., of .... county, of the second part, all of the State of Mississippi; witnesseth, That the said party of the first part, for and in consideration of the sum of .... dollars (*amount of the debt or advance,*) to him in hand paid, hereby grants, bargains, and sells unto the said party of the second part, and to his legal representatives and assigns, forever, all (*if land, describe it, or growing crops, or personal property,*) lying and being in said county, to have and to hold the same, together with the appurtenances thereunto belonging or in anywise appertaining, and all the right, title, interest, claim and demand of said party of the first part in and to the same, unto said party of the second part, his legal representatives and assigns, in fee simple, forever.

This grant is intended as a security for the payment of the sum of .... dollars (amount due said party of the second part, as evidenced by the promissory note, &c., of said party of the first part; or, amount to be advanced by said party of the second part, for the purpose of assisting said party of the first part in cultivating and making a crop for the year 18.... in said county, to be paid on the 15th day of November, 18....] which payments, if duly made, will render this conveyance void ; but if default shall be made in payment of the principal or interest above mentioned, then the said party of the second part, his legal representatives or assigns, are hereby authorized to sell the property above granted, or so much thereof as will be necessary to satisfy the amount then due, with the cost and expenses of executing this deed and said sale.

In witness whereof, the said party of the first part has hereunto set his hand and seal, the day and year first above written.

A. B., [seal.]

————•

No. 265.—POWER OF ATTORNEY.

Know all men by these presents, That I, A. B., of .... county and State of ...., have made, constituted, and appointed, and by these presents do make, constitute, name, and appoint C. D. my true and lawful attorney for me and in my name, place, and stead, to (here insert the thing to be done; to demand and recover debts, to buy or sell, to execute deeds, to sign papers, &c., &c.,) giving and granting unto my said attorney full power and authority to do and perform all and every act and thing whatsoever requisite and necessary to be done in and about the premises, as fully to all intents and purposes, as I might or could do if personally present, with full power of substitution and revocation, hereby ratifying and confirming all that my said attorney, or his substitute, shall lawfully do or cause to be done by virtue hereof.

In witness whereof, I have hereunto set my hand and seal, this ...... day of ...., 18...

A. B., [seal.]

Note.—No deed is perfect until duly acknowledged before a justice, or some other officer authorized, and the transaction should not be considered concluded, or the money paid, before it is acknowledged. After acknowledgement, the deed should be, at the earliest day practicable, filed with the clerk of the chancery court, for record. In the foregoing deeds, if there be a wife, she should always join and sign with her husband. In such case, say: "A. B., and C. D., his wife, of ——— county, parties of the first part." The following forms of acknowledgements, will answer in all cases:

No. 266.—ACKNOWLEDGEMENT BY A MAN, OR SINGLE WOMAN.

STATE OF MISSISSIPPI, ... COUNTY } ss.

This day, personally appeared before the undersigned justice of the peace for said county. A. B., who acknowledged that he (or she) signed, sealed, and delivered the foregoing (or, attached) instrument of writing, on the day and date thereof, for the uses and purposes therein set forth, as and for his (or her) voluntary act and deed.

In witness whereof, I have hereunto set my hand and seal, this ...... day of ...., 18...

.................................., J. P. [SEAL.]

No. 267.—ACKNOWLEDGMENT BY HUSBAND AND WIFE.

STATE OF MISSISSIPPI, ... COUNTY. } ss.

This day, personally appeared before the undersigned justice of the peace for said county, A. B., who acknowledged that he signed, sealed, and delivered the foregoing (or, attached) instrument of writing, on the day and date thereof, for the uses and purposes set forth, as and for his voluntary act and deed. And at the same time also personally appeared C. B., wife of said A. B., who, being by me examined, privately, separate, and apart from her said husband, and the foregoing (or, attached) instrument of writing fully explained to her by me, acknowledged that she signed, sealed, and delivered the same, on the day and date thereof, for the uses and purposes set forth therein, freely, as and for her voluntary act and deed, without any fears, threats, or compulsion of her said husband.

In witness whereof, I have hereunto set my hand and seal, this ...... day of ...., 18...

................................., J. P., [SEAL.]

No. 268.—GENERAL CONTRACT.

Articles of agreement and contract, made this ...... day of ...., between A. B., of the county of ...., and the State of Mississippi, party of the first part, and C. D. (and others, if so,) of the same county and State, party of the second part; witnesseth, That the said party of the first part, for and in consideration of the promises and agreements hereinafter made by the said C. D. hereby covenants and agrees to and with the said party of the second part—

[Here set forth distinctly what A. B. proposes to do, whatever it may be.]

And the said party of the second part, on his part, for and in consideration of the promises and agreements of the said A. B., aforesaid, hereby covenants and agrees to and with the said party of the first part—

[Here write exactly what C. D. is to do.]

(And in case of the failure of the said party of the second part to make, do, or perform any of the covenants on his part hereby made and entered into, this contract shall, at the option of the party of the first part, be forfeited and determined, and the party of the second part shall forfeit all advantages and profits acquired or to be acquired on or by virtue of this contract; and the said party of the first part is hereby authorized to retain what may have been done or paid in this behalf, by said party of the second part, in full satisfaction, and in liquidation of all damages or injury by him sustained.)

[And it is mutually agreed and covenanted, that if it shall happen that said party of the first part, his heirs or legal representatives, shall neglect to do, furnish or perform his or their parts of the covenants and agreements herein contained, that then, and in any such case, the said party of the second part, his heirs and legal representatives, shall not hereby be obliged to make, do or perform his and their covenants herein contained, but shall, at his or their option, be absolutely discharged therefrom.]

[And it is also agreed that said party of the second part shall not, nor will, during the continuance of this contract, cut down any timber or trees, or commit any waste or spoil whatsoever, in or upon the premises, or any part thereof, nor shall or will grant any new leases of the premises, or any part thereof, without the knowledge and consent of said party of the first part, or his heirs or legal representatives.]

And it is mutually agreed that all covenants and agreements herein contained shall extend to and be obligatory upon the heirs, legal representatives and assigns of the respective parties.

In witness whereof, the parties to these presents have hereunto set their hands and seals, the day and year first above written, to two copies of this agreement interchangeably.

A. B. [SEAL.]
C. D. [SEAL.]

Signed and interchanged in the presence of
....

NOTE.—The foregoing contract will answer for most any purpose; the part in brackets to be used or not. The farmer who rents land, or who crops on shares, or who hires farm laborers, can find all he wants in this form, if supplies are not furnished,—and, in fact, under our present labor and agricultural lien laws, the better plan is only to write one copy, have the same acknowledged by the parties, and let the contract be recorded.

No. 269.—CONTRACT TO CULTIVATE LAND ON SHARES.

This agreement, made this ...... day of ...., 187..., between A. B., of .... county, and C. D. (*and others, if so*), of .... county, all of the State of Mississippi, witnesseth: That the said C. D. agrees to break up, properly fit, plant and seasonably cultivate ...... acres of land of the farm of said A. B., in said county, for the purpose of making thereon crops of cotton, corn, peas, potatoes, oats and wheat, during said year; that when said crops, to be planted and sown as aforesaid, shall be in fit condition, he will cut, harvest, gather and pick, and safely house the same in the barns, pens, or ginhouses of the said A. B.; and that he will properly thrash, clean, pump and assist in ginning and baling the same; that one-half of the oat, wheat, potato, and corn seed is to be furnished by the said C. D.: that all the labor and work necessary in the premises is to be performed by the said C. D.; and that the said C. D. will faithfully and honestly deliver one-half of all said products to said A. B., or to his legal representatives or assigns, on or before the 25th day of December of said year, and all of the cotton seed.

A. B., on his part, agrees to furnish the said C. D. sufficient and comfortable house room, plough team, wagons and team necessary, and all farm tools and implements requisite in the premises, as also feed for the plough team.

In witness whereof, the said parties have hereunto set their hands and seals this .... day of ...., 18...

A. B. [SEAL.]
C. D. [SEAL.]

No. 270.—CONTRACT TO CULTIVATE ON SHARES.
(Another form.)

This agreement made this ...... day of ...., 18..., between A B., of .... county, of the first part, and C. D., of .... county, of the second part, all of the State of Mississippi, witnesseth: That the said party of the second part hereby covenants and agrees to work and labor upon the farm of said party of the first part, in said county, for and during the year 18...; that in all matters of preparing, ploughing, planting and cultivating said farm, the said party of the second part is to be under the general direction of said party of the first part, or his duly appointed agent; that a day's labor is to be considered from the rising to the setting of the sun, with reasonable time at noon for food and rest; that the said party of the second part will take good and faithful care of all implements, tools, horses, mules, wagons and other property at any time in his charge or under his control, and shall be responsible for their loss and all damage, except from usual wear and tear, and providential interposition; and shall faithfully labor, at all times, on said farm, during said year, when not prevented by sickness or other unavoidable cause.

In consideration of the foregoing, the said party of the first part agrees and covenants to deliver to said party of the second part, or to his legal representatives, one-half of all cotton, and one-third of all corn, peas and potatoes, and one-fourth of all wheat and oats cultivated, grown and raised, and made ready for market, on said farm during said year, being the product of the labor of said party of the second part. That said party of the first part also agrees at all times to furnish sufficient plough team, wagons and team, and all farm implements and tools requisite, with suitable house room for said party of the second part, and feed for the teams employed. And the said party of the first part, at the request of said party of the second part, agrees, for the purpose of assisting him in the cultivation and making of said crops during said year, to furnish to said party of the second part provisions sufficient to supply himself and family, at cost prices, and retains hereby for the payment of all supplies, and any other payments made for said party of the second part, the special first lien on his share of crops.

And it is mutually agreed, that if the said party of the second part fails to comply with the conditions of this contract, in giving his whole time and attention to the cultivating and raising and preparing said crops for market, or in any other respect, it subjects him to such reasonable damages, to be assessed by three disinterested arbitrators to be selected by the parties thereto, and to be charged for loss of time, at labor rates.

Given under our hands and seals, the day and year first above written.

A. B. [SEAL.]
C. D. [SEAL.]

NOTE.—If a farmer rents land for a money consideration, his best plan is to take a deed of trust on the crop and personal property.

No. 271.—AGREEMENT FOR RAISING MONEY TO BUILD A CHURCH OR OTHER BUILDING.

We, the undersigned, do hereby severally promise and agree to pay or deliver to A. B., C. D. and E. F., the trustees of ...... church, known as ...... church, in .... county, the sums of money, or lumber and materials, set opposite to our respective names, on demand, for the purpose of building a church, or place of worship for the said society, in said county; and we request the said trustees to contract for the building of such church or place of worship, and to build the same, and to apply the sums of money and lumber and material, hereto subscribed, in payment therefor and completion thereof.

Witness our hands this ...... day of ...., 18....

NAMES.	SUBSCRIPTION.
J. H.	$10 00
W. P.	30 00
S. D.	1,000 feet lumber.

No. 272.—MARRIAGE CEREMONY FOR JUSTICE.

NOTE.—I am induced to add the following from the memory of a transaction in my own experience, many years ago, when called upon, in my official capacity, to unite in the bonds of wedlock two willing souls. The feat was performed, but how, I have never exactly known to this day.

[The man standing on the right hand and the woman on the left, the Justice will approach and say:]

We are gathered here in the sight of God, and this company, to join together this man and this woman in holy matrimony. If any one here can show just cause why they may not be lawfully joined together, let them now speak.

[Here let the Justice, joining the right hands of the two, continue:]

A. B., will you have this woman to thy wedded wife, to live together after God's ordinance and the law in the holy estate of matrimony? Will you love her, comfort her, honor, and keep her in sickness and in health, and, forsaking all others, keep only unto her, so long as you both shall live?

[The man will answer, I will.]

C. D., will you have this man to thy wedded husband, to live together after God's ordinance and the law in the holy estate of matrimony? Will you obey him, and serve him, love, honor and keep him in sickness and in health, and, forsaking all others, keep only unto him, so long as you both shall live?

[The woman will answer, I will.]

Forasmuch, therefor, as A. B. and C. D., here standing, have consented together in holy wedlock, and have witnesseth the same before God and this company, by virtue of the authority which I hold in my hand, I pronounce that they are legally man and wife.

[The Justice can, and very appropriately, add:]

May you be, my friends, help-meets of each other, indeed, in all things, but especially the helpers of each other's faith and joy. If you are true Christians, your habitation will not be desolate, but will be the dwelling of holiness, love and peace. May the God of our fathers be your God, and may you live as fellow heirs of life, and at last dwell together in the land where they neither marry nor are given in marriage.

JUSTICE OF THE PEACE.

AS A CIVIL COURT.

[FROM REVISED CODE AND SUBSEQUENT ACTS OF THE LEGISLATURE.]

ELECTION AND QUALIFICATION.

§ 1296. There shall be chosen at the next general election, and biennially thereafter, by the qualified electors of each district, two Justices of the Peace, who shall be commissioned by the Governor, and shall hold their offices for the term of two years, and until their successors are qualified; and in case there be a tie between the two highest voted for, the President of the Board of Supervisors shall immediately determine said election by lot.

§ 1297. The districts in each county, for the election of Justices of the Peace, shall be the same as those laid off for the election of members of the Board of Supervisors, except when otherwise directed by said Board, or by law.

§ 1298. Every person elected a Justice of the Peace shall, before he enters on the duties of the office, take the oath of office, and enter into bond, in the same manner as other county officers, in the penalty of two thousand dollars, conditioned that he will well and truly perform the duties of his office, and pay over all moneys collected by him, or which may come into his hands by virtue of his said office, to the party or parties entitled to receive the same; and and any party interested may proceed on such bond, in a summary way, by motion, in any court having jurisdiction of the same, against the principal and sureties, upon giving ten days' previous notice: *provided*, that the Boards of Supervisors of the respective counties, shall have power to limit the penalty of said bonds, to a sum not less than one thousand dollars.   (Forms 1 and 2)

VACANCIES, CHANGE OF VENUE AND CONTESTED ELECTIONS.

§ 1340. Whenever the office of Justice of the Peace, in any county, is vacant, suit may be brought before any Justice of an adjoining district; and whenever, by reason of interest or other cause, any Justice of the Peace shall be incompetent to sit in any case before him, the same shall be transferred to the nearest Justice of the Peace, free from such objection, in said county, who shall have and determine the same.

§ 1301. When any Justice of the Peace shall remove out of the district for which he was or shall be elected, all his powers as such shall cease and determine, and his office shall become vacant, and the vacancy shall be filled, as provided in other cases.

§ 1299. In case a vacancy shall happen in the office of Justice of the Peace, the Board of Supervisors, or the President thereof in vacation, shall order an election to be held in the proper district, to fill such vacancy, not more than twenty days after the date of such order, and shall appoint three commissioners, residents of the district, to hold the same, and receive and count the votes, any two of whom may act, having first taken an oath to conduct the same fairly and impartially, and to make due return thereof. The said commissioners shall give ten days' notice of the time and place of holding said election, by posting up a notice in three or more public places in the district, and shall hold the same at the regular place of holding elections in such district; and if there be more than one such place, then three commissioners shall be appointed for each precinct; and if there be no such regular place of holding elections in such district, then at such public place therein as may be most convenient. The said commissioners shall make due return of said election, to the President of the Board of Supervisors, who, at the expiration of five days after the receipt thereof, shall certify and transmit the result to the Governor, and shall give a certificate of election to the person having the highest number of votes.

§ 1300. Any person desiring to contest such election shall, within five days after the return thereof as aforesaid, file his petition to the Board of Supervisors, signed by at least ten voters of the district, setting forth the particular causes for which said election should be set aside, and thereupon a special meeting of said Board shall be called, if necessary, and the said Board shall hear the allegations and proofs of the parties, and may set aside the election, or declare the contestant to be duly elected; and, in case the election shall be set aside, they shall immediately order a new election to be held as before: *provided*, the party whose election is contested shall have ten days' notice of the time of trial. And if the said election be confirmed, it shall be certified to the Governor, as aforesaid.

§ 391. Any person desiring to contest the election of any person returned as elected to any office, within any county in this State, may, within twenty days after the election, file a petition before any Justice of the Peace, of such county, setting forth the grounds upon which said election is contested; and the Justice shall, thereupon, issue a summons to the party whose election is contested, returnable instanter, which summons shall be served as in other cases; and the Justice shall cause an issue to be made up and tried by a jury, and the verdict of the jury shall specify the person having the greatest number of legal votes, at such election. If the jury shall find against the person returned as elected, the Justice shall issue a certificate thereof, and the person in whose favor the jury shall find, shall be commissioned by the Governor; and each party shall be allowed ten peremptory challenges; and in case the election of any District Attorney be contested, the petition for that purpose may be filed in any adjacent county, of an adjoining district, and like proceeding shall be had thereon, as in the case of county officers. Either party shall have the right of appeal to the next term of the circuit court, and both parties shall have the same right of challenge, as provided in this section for the proceedings in the Justices' Court.

JURISDICTION CONFERRED ON MAYORS.

An Act to confer upon Mayors of incorporated towns in this State jurisdiction as Justices of the Peace, and for other purposes.

SECTION 1. Be it enacted by the Legislature of the State of Mississippi, That the mayors of all the incorporated towns in this State be, and they are hereby made *ex-officio* justices of the peace, and the marshals or constables of said towns, be, and they are hereby made *ex officio* constables in and for the several counties in this State, in which their respective towns are situated, and said officers, whether heretofore or hereafter elected, shall have, and exercise the jurisdiction, and all the rights, duties, and powers, and be subject to all the liabilities of justices of the peace and constables, respectively; *Provided,* That in towns where the mayors and constables, or marshal, have not been heretofore clothed with the jurisdiction and powers herein conferred upon them, said officers shall, and also, such officers in all towns now possessing the jurisdiction and powers herein conferred, where no bonds have been given, execute bonds to be approved, in the same manner and similar in all respects to those required by law to be given by justices of the peace and constables, and the powers and jurisdiction herein conferred, shall not be exercised until said bonds have been given; *Provided,* That the provisions of this Act shall not apply to cities or towns of five thousand inhabitants or more.

SEC. 2. Be it further enacted, That this Act take effect and be in force from and after its passage.

By limitation, March 29, 1876.

An Act to compel offenders against town or city ordinances, to work out their fines upon the streets, and for other purposes.

SECTION 1. Be it enacted by the Legislature of the State of Mississippi, That the mayor of any incorporated town or city, be and he is hereby authorized and empowered to compel offenders against town or city ordinances, who are unable, or wilfully refuses to pay their fines, to work out the same, upon the streets, or any public works within the town or city in which said offense or offenses were committed; *Provided,* The mayor and selectmen of such incorporated city or town, shall fix the amount to be allowed for each day's work.

SEC. 2. Be it further enacted, That the mayor of any incorporated

CIVIL JURISDICTION.

§ 1302. Justices of the peace shall have jurisdiction of all actions for the recovery of debts or damages. or personal property, where the principal of the debt. the amount of the demand, or the value of the property sought to be recovered, shall not exceed one hundred and fifty dollars.

§ 1303. The jurisdiction of every justice of the peace shall be coextensive with his county. and he may issue any process in matters within his jurisdiction. to be executed in any part of his county, but every freeholder or householder of the county shall be sued in the district in which he resides. if there be a justice acting therein. and qualified to try such suit. or in the district in which the debt was contracted. the liability incurred, or in which the property may be found.

PRACTICE IN CIVIL CASES.

§ 1305. Any one desiring to sue before a justice of the peace shall lodge with him the evidence of debt. statement of account. or other written statement of the cause of action. and thereupon the justice of the peace shall issue a summons for the defendant, returnable to the next term of the court of said justice of the peace. which shall be executed five days before the return day thereof: and any summons issued within five days before its return day. shall be made returnable to the next succeeding term of the court after that to be held within five days. (Forms 3. 4.)

§ 1306. The defendant in any such action shall. on or before the return day of the summons, and before the trial of the case. file with the justice of the peace the evidence of debt. statement of account. or other written statement of the claim which he may desire to set off against the demand of the plaintiff. and in default thereof. he shall not be permitted to use it on the trial.

§ 1307. On the return day of the summons. issued as aforesaid. the justice. before whom the complaint has been made. shall proceed to hear and determine the same, if the parties appear. give judgment by default. if the defendant fail to appear and contest plaintiff's demand, or judgment of non-suit against the plaintiff if he fail to appear and prosecute his claim: to enter judgment in favor of the defendant. where. in cases of mutual debts. or set off, it shall appear that there is a balance due him. for the amount of such balance. and issue execution against the goods and chattels. lands and tenements. of the party against whom judgment is rendered, for the amount of such judgment and costs. or costs alone. as the case may require. returnable to the first term of the court to be held more than twenty days after the rendition of the judgment, and such execution shall continue in force for one year, without being renewed, unless sooner satisfied.

§ 1308. Every justice of the peace shall keep a well-bound book, styled "a docket," in which he shall enter in full the names of the plaintiffs and defendants in any suit brought before him, the nature of the suit or action, and the sum demanded, the time of issuing process, and when returnable, and the return made thereon by the officer, the time of filing the plaintiff's demand, and the defendant's set off, the names of witnesses sworn, the date and amount of the judgment, the execution, when issued and the return thereon, the appeal, when and by whom demanded, and all the proceedings before him had touching the said suit; and he shall make like entries of all proceedings of a criminal nature before him heard and determined; and it shall be the duty of such justice, when required, to grant to either party a certified copy of such proceedings, and of all papers and process relating thereto.

§ 1309. Justices of the peace shall hold regular terms of their courts at such times as they, or either, may appoint, not exceeding two, and not less than one in every month, and at such convenient place in their districts as they, or either, may designate; and they may continue to hold their courts from day to day, so long as business may require, and all process shall be returnable, and all trials shall take place at such regular terms; *provided*, that where the plaintiff or defendant, or both, are non-resident or transient persons, and it shall be shown, by the oath of either party, that a delay of the trial until the regular term would be of material injury to him, it shall be lawful for the justice to have the parties brought before him at any reasonable time, and hear the evidence and give judgment. Such court shall be a court of record, with all the power incident to a court of record, including power to fine, to the extent of fifty dollars, and imprison one day for contempt of court.

§ 1312. The justices of the peace, in their respective districts, may sit together in holding their courts, but any one may hold his court by himself, at any point in his district which he may designate. In case of disagreement between them, as to the decision of a case, the Justice who issued the process shall decide.

§ 1316. When any suit brought before a justice of the peace shall be finally decided on its merits by such justice, it shall be a bar to a recovery for the same cause of action or set-off before any other justice of the peace or other court; and a transcript of the record of such judgment shall be sufficient evidence to bar such second recovery.

§ 1320. In all suits or proceedings against two or more defendants jointly, or jointly and severally, liable, it shall be lawful to bring such suit before any justice of the peace of the district wherein either of the defendants shall reside; and such justice shall have power, and he is hereby authorized, to issue a summons, or other process, to bring in all co-defendants from any other district in the county where the suit is brought, or from any other county in this State; and upon service of process, as required in other cases before justices of the eace, the jus.ice, before whom the suit is pending, shall have full jurisdiction, as to all of the defendants, in as full and ample a manner as in cases where all the defendants reside within the district where suit is brought; and if the process of such co-defendants be not returned executed, it shall be lawful for the plaintiff to dismiss his action as to such co-defendants.

§ 1321. Proceedings in replevin, attachment, and for the enforcement of mechanics' liens, before justices of the peace, shall be, as far as practicable, according to those in the circuit court in like cases.

§ 580. When an open account is sued on, there shall be filed with the declaration, before process issues, an itemized copy of the account sought to be recovered; and if this be not done, plaintiff shall not be permitted to give evidence in support thereof.

§ 782. Any person desiring to institute suit upon any open account in any court of this State having jurisdiction of the amount, may go before any justice of the peace of this State, or any other State, or the United States, authorized by law to administer oaths, and make affidavit to the correctness of such account, and that it is due from the party against whom it is charged; and in any suit upon such an account thus sworn to, the affidavit of the plaintiff, or the party in whose favor the account is stated, or his agent, made as aforesaid, and attached to the account, shall be *prima facie* evidence of the correctness of the account and indebtedness of the defendant against whom the service is charged, and shall entitle the plaintiff to judgment at the trial term of the suit, unless the defendant shall make affidavit and file with his plea that the account is not correct, in which event the affidavit to the account shall not be evidence, except to entitle the plaintiff to judgment for such part of said account as the defendant, by his affidavit, may admit to be due. A general denial in the counter affidavit of the defendant to the correctness of the account sued on, shall be insufficient to put the plaintiff to the proof of the same, but said account shall be treated as proved on the trial, except as to the particular items of indebtedness, the correctness and validity of which are specified and described in the counter affidavit of the defendant; *provided*, That this shall not apply to accounts against decedents and suits against executors or administrators. (Forms 5 and 6.)

§ 601. When a mutual indebtedness shall exist between the plaintiff and defendant, the defendant may plead payment, and may prove and set off against the demand of the plaintiff, any debt, or demand, which he may have against the plaintiff; and if it shall appear that the demand of the defendant equals the demand of the plaintiff, the jury shall find for the defendant, and judgment shall be entered that the plaintiff take nothing by his writ, and shall pay the costs. And if it appear that any part of the sum demanded has been paid, but that the plaintiff's demand exceeds that of the defendant, the amount paid shall be deducted and the plaintiff shall have judgment for the residue of his demand only, with costs of suit. But if it appear to the jury that the plaintiff is overpaid, and is indebted to the defendant, they shall give in their verdict for the defendant for the amount due him, and, thereupon, judgment shall be entered up against the plaintiff, in favor of the defendant for the amount so found, with costs, and execution may issue therefor.

§ 602. Where there shall have been mutual dealings between two or more persons, and one or more of them shall die before an adjustment of such dealings, the lawful demands of such persons against each other, shall be a good payment, or set-off, to the amount thereof, notwithstanding the estate of one or more of such deceased persons shall be insolvent, and only the balance due shall be the debt.

§ 603. In all actions for the recovery of any debt or demand, alleged to be due by the defendant to the plaintiff, it shall be lawful for the defendant to plead payment of the money demanded, at or after the time when the same became due, or at any time before action brought; and under such plea, to prove any payments that have been made, in part or in full of the sum demanded.

§ 604. If the defendant shall plead, or give notice of any set-off, or shall desire to prove any payment, or set-off, under his plea of payment, he shall file with his plea, an account, stating distinctly the nature of the payment or set-off, and the several items thereof, and a copy of any writing intended to be set-off; and on failure to do so, he shall not be entitled to prove, on the trial, such payment or set-off.

§ 605. In actions founded on any sealed instrument, the defendant may, by a special plea, impeach the consideration thereof, in the same manner as if such writing had not been sealed.

§ 621. The court shall have full power and authority to allow all amendments to be made in any pleading, or procedure, at any time before verdict, so as to bring the merits of the controversy between the parties, fairly to trial, and may allow all errors and mistakes, in the name of any party, or in the form of the action, to be corrected; and the court shall require all such amendments to be made on such terms, as to costs and delay, as may seem proper, to prevent surprise or undue advantage. Either party may except to the decision of the court, allowing or refusing amendments, and the same may be assigned for error.

§ 625. If in detinue the verdict shall omit price or value, the court may, at any time, award a writ of inquiry to ascertain the same. If, on an issue concerning several things in one count in detinue, no verdict be found for part of them, it shall not be error, but the plaintiff shall be barred of his title to the things omitted.

§ 627. When, in the record of any judgment or decree of any court of law or equity, there shall be any mistake, miscalculation, or misrecital of any sum of money, quantity of merchandise, or other thing, or of any name, and there shall be among the records of the proceedings in the suit, in which such judgment or decree shall be rendered, any verdict, bond, bill, note, or other writing of the like nature or kind, whereby such judgment or decree may be safely amended, it shall be the duty of the court in which such judgment shall be rendered, and of the Judge thereof, in vacation, to amend such judgment or decree thereby, according to the very truth and justice of the case; *Provided,* The opposite party shall have had reasonable notice of the application for such amendment ; and if the transcript of such judgment or decree, at the time of such amendment, or at any time thereafter, shall be removed to the supreme court, it shall be the duty of that court, upon the inspection of such amended record (to be brought before it by *certiorari,* if need be,) to affirm such judgment, if there be no other error apparent on such record.

§ 628. When any bond, taken by virtue of any process or order, by miscalculation or mistake, shall be conditioned for the payment of a larger sum of money than by law ought to have been required thereby, or where a verdict shall be rendered for more damages than the plaintiff shall have demanded by his suit, and judgment shall be rendered accordingly, it shall be lawful for the plaintiff, at the same or any future term of the court, to release, in open court, any such excess ; or he may, in vacation, release the same, in writing under his hand, and filed among the papers of the cause ; and such release shall cure any error growing out of such excess.

§ 632. No judgment by default shall be entered at the return term, when it shall appear that the process has not been served personally on the defendant.

§ 633. In all applications for a continuance, the party shall set forth in his affidavit the facts which he expects to prove by his absent witness or testimony, that the court may judge of their materiality.

§ 634. In civil suits, each party may challenge peremptorily four of the jurors, and as many more as they can show cause for.

§ 635. Whenever there shall be a deficiency of jurors, the sheriff, or other officer, shall, by order of the court, summon a sufficient number of qualified by-standers, or others, to complete the panel; but in case the sheriff, or other officer, be interested, or related to either of the parties, or not impartial, or for other good cause, the court may appoint any disinterested person to summon and return such by-standers or others. The court may fine, in a sum not exceeding thirty dollars, any person summoned as a talesman, who shall not appear, or who being present when he is called, does not appear in court, or who, after appearance, wilfully withdraws himself during the day.

§ 636. A jury *de mediætate linguæ* may be directed and summoned whenever, in the opinion of the court, it may be necessary.

§ 637. Jurors knowing anything relative to the point in issue, shall disclose the same, on oath or affirmation, in open court.

§ 638. No sheriff or other officer shall converse with a juror, but by order of the court, after the jury have retired from the bar.

§ 639. All papers read in evidence on the trial of any cause, though not under seal, may be carried from the bar by the jury.

§ 640. Interpreters may be sworn, truly to interpret, when necessary; and in criminal cases the court may appoint such interpreter, and allow him a reasonable compensation, not exceeding five dollars per day, payable out of the State treasury.

§ 641. Every plaintiff desiring to suffer a non-suit on trial shall be barred therefrom, unless he do so before the jury retire from the bar.

§ 642. The plaintiff may suffer a non-suit, or dismiss any cause, before the clerk in vacation, on paying all costs that have accrued; and the clerk shall enter on the writ or declaration the disposition made of the same, with the date; and where the plaintiff has received satisfaction of the cause of action, he shall, by himself or his attorney, enter such satisfaction on the writ or declaration, and sign the same: and such entry of satisfaction shall be a bar to any suit brought thereafter for the same cause of action; and where the plaintiff suffers a non-suit, or dismisses his suit, without having received satisfaction, he shall stand in the same situation as though he had never instituted such suit; *provided*, that this section shall not extend to cases in which the defendant has filed or pleaded any set-off or payment, unless by consent of such defendant.

§ 652. All or any of the issues of an action, whether of fact or law, may be referred to one or more referees, not exceeding three, upon the consent of the parties.

§ 655. Referees appointed under this act shall have power to administer oaths, and to issue subpœnas for all witnesses, and to compel their attendance.

§ 658. In an action against a sheriff or other officer, for the recovery of property taken under an execution or attachment, and replevied by the plaintiff in such action, the court may, on application of the defendant, and of the party in whose favor the execution or attachment issued, permit the latter to be substituted as defendant, security for costs being given if required.

§ 659. If the plaintiff in such execution or attachment, be a non resident of the State, the summons may be served on his attorney, and shall have the same effect as if served personally on the party.

§ 660. The defendant in any personal action, except actions for assault and battery, false imprisonment, libel, slander, malicious arrest and prosecution, criminal conversation, or debauching the plaintiff's daughter or servant, may offer with his plea, or in writing afterwards before trial, and pay into court, a sum of money by way of compensation or amends, and may plead that the sum is sufficient to satisfy the plaintiff in respect to the cause of action in the declaration mentioned. If the plaintiff accept the same, judgment shall be entered therefor with costs. If he fails to accept the same, the offer shall be considered withdrawn, and shall not be given in evidence; and if the plaintiff fail to recover more than the sum so offered, he shall pay all the costs accruing after such offer.

§ 661. In all actions in which the right to real estate, or to goods and chattels, is in controversy, the court, or the judge thereof, may make an order for the protection of the property in controversy, from waste, destruction, or removal beyond the juris-

10

diction of the court, upon satisfactory proof being made of the necessity of such order, and may enforce such order by an attachment for contempt.

§ 669. In any case where such persons, as be within age, may have cause of action, their next friend shall be admitted to sue for them, and such next friend shall be liable for the costs.

§ 670. The assignee of any chose in action, may sue for and recover the same, in his own name, if the assignment be in writing; and in case where the assignment is not in writing, and the original payee is dead, and there is no executor or administrator of the estate, suit may be brought in the name of the assignee. In case of a transfer of interest after suit brought, the action shall be continued in the name of the original party, or the court may allow the person to whom the transfer is made, to be substituted in the action. No set-off or other defense existing at the time of, or before, notice of the assignment, shall be prejudiced thereby.

§ 677. When either of the parties to any suit shall die before judgment, the executor or administrator of such deceased party, plaintiff or defendant, shall have full power, in case the cause of action by law survives, to prosecute or defend such suit of action to final judgment, and the court shall render final judgment for or against such executor or administrator, in the same manner as if the original party to the suit or action were in existence; and if such executor or administrator, having been duly served with a *scire facias*, or citation, five days before the meeting of the court, shall neglect or refuse to become a party to the suit, the court may proceed to render judgment against him in the same manner as if such executor had voluntarily made himself a party to the suit; and the executor or administrator, who shall become a party as aforesaid, shall be entitled to a continuance of the cause until next term of the court; and for the purpose of revival under any section of this chapter, the suit shall be considered to have commenced and been depending, from the time of the filing of the declaration, whether the writ was executed before the death of the deceased party or not.

§ 678. If any suit shall be commenced in the name of any person, for the use and benefit of another, the same shall not abate by the death of the nominal plaintiff, but shall progress to final judgment and execution, in like manner as if brought in the name of the person for whose use and benefit such suit was instituted, who shall be liable for the costs of suit, as in other cases; and, in case a party for whose use and benefit a suit shall be brought shall die before final judgment, it shall be lawful for the party representing such deceased person, as executor or administrator, to be entered on the records and papers of such suit in the place of such deceased person.

§ 679. If there be two or more plaintiffs or defendants in any suit, and one or more of them should die, if the cause of action should survive to the surviving plaintiff or plaintiffs, or against the surviving defendant or defendants, the suit shall proceed in the name of the surviving plaintiff or plaintiffs, against the surviving defendant or defendants; and where either party shall die between verdict and judgment, such death shall not be suggested in abatement, but judgment shall be entered as if both parties were living; and if, on the death of any plaintiff, in actions which survive, before verdict, the heir, legatee or devisee, executor, administrator, or other legal representatives of such deceased party, shall not appear and become a party to such action, on or before the second term of the court next after the death of such party shall have been suggested on the record, such action shall be discontinued, unless good cause be shown to the contrary.

§ 680. When judgment shall have been rendered against two or more persons, and any one or more of them shall die, such judgment shall survive as well against the representatives of the deceased parties as against the survivor, and a *scire facias* may issue against the survivors, jointly with the representatives of the deceased parties, and such judgment may be thereupon revived, and execution issued in like manner.

§ 681. In all suits or actions by husband or wife, touching the separate property of the wife, or where the cause of action survives to the wife, if the husband shall die pending the suit, his death shall be suggested on record, and the suit or action shall proceed to judgment in the name of the wife. In case the wife should die pending the suit, if the cause of action survives to the husband, her death shall be suggested on the record, and the cause shall proceed in the name of the husband; and if the cause of action shall not survive to the husband, but to the representatives of the wife, then, on suggestion of the death of the wife, the suit shall abate as to the husband, and may be revived and prosecuted in the name of the wife. And the like proceedings shall be had in suits against husband and wife, so far as they may be applicable.

§ 682. In like manner, judgments in favor of the husband and wife, may be revived in favor of the survivor, or the representatives of the party to whom the cause of action would survive; and, in case the husband or wife shall die after judgment against them jointly, such judgment shall survive as well against the representatives of the deceased, as against the survivor, and may be revived accordingly.

§ 686. Any Judge of a Court of record, in this State, any Clerk of such Court, or his deputy, any member of the Board of County Supervisors, and any Justice of the Peace, or Master or Commissioner in Chancery, or any Sheriff, is authorized to administer oaths and affirmations, and to take and certify affidavits, whenever the same may be necessary or proper in any proceedings in any Court, or under any laws of this State.

§ 687. In all cases where the oath or affirmation of the party is required, such oath or affirmation may be made by his agent or attorney, and shall be as effectual for all purposes as if made by the party.

§ 303. When any dispute shall arise, respecting the right of a brand or mark, either party may apply to any Justice of the Peace of the county, who shall summon the adverse party to appear before him, on a certain day expressed in the summons, not less than five nor more than ten days from the date thereof; and such Justice shall issue process for witnesses, directed to the Sheriff or any Constable of the county; and such officer, and said witnesses, shall receive the same fees, and be liable to the same penalties, as in other cases before Justices of the Peace; the Justice shall hear the case, and give judgment thereon, which shall be conclusive on the parties; and a transcript thereof, certified by said Justice, shall be sufficient authority for the Clerk to record said brand and mark.

§ 1184. No suit or action shall be brought against any executor or administrator, in such capacity, until after the expiration of six months from the date of the letters testamentary, or of administration.

§ 1783. In addition to the remedies now existing by the common law, by and against married women, the husband and wife may sue jointly, or, if the husband will not join her, she may sue alone for the recovery of any of her property or rights; and she may be sued jointly with her husband, on all contracts or other matters for which her individual property is liable; but if the suit be against husband and wife, no judgment shall be rendered against her, unless the liability of her separate property be first established; and in case of suits against husband and wife, if summons for the husband be returned, "not found," the suit may be prosecuted against the wife alone.

§ 1900. All contracts, judgments, securities, or conveyances whatever, made, given, granted, entered into, or executed, at any time, where the whole or any part of the consideration or foundation of such contract, judgment, security, or conveyance, shall be for money or any other valuable thing whatever, won, laid, or bet at any game or games whatever, or any horse race, cock fight, or any other amusement, sport, or pastime, or on any other wager whatever, or for the reimbursing or repaying any money knowingly lent or advanced for the purpose of such gaming, or to be wagered on any game, play, horse race, cock fight, or on any other sport, amusement, pastime, or wager whatever, shall be utterly void.

§ 1901. Any sale, mortgage, or other transfer or conveyance of any estate or interest, real or personal, to any person, or to another for his use or benefit, or in any manner to satisfy or secure money or other thing won, or any part thereof, or to secure or satisfy any money or other thing lent or advanced on any consideration, foundation or purpose mentioned in the last section, or any part thereof, shall inure to and vest in the wife and children of said mortgagor, seller, vendor, bargainer or lessor, the whole estate, title and interest of such person in the estate or interest, real or personal, so sold, mortgaged, bargained, transferred, or otherwise attempted to be conveyed, as though such person had died intestate.

§ 1902. If any person, by playing at any game whatever, or by betting on the sides or hands of such as do play at any game, or by betting on any horse race, or cock fight, or at any other sport or pastime, or by any wager whatever, shall lose any money, property, or other valuable thing, real or personal, and shall pay or deliver the same, or any part thereof, the person so losing and paying or delivering the same, may, within six months next following, sue for and recover such money, property, or other valuable thing, so lost and paid or delivered, or any part therof, from the person knowingly receiving the same, with costs, before any court having jurisdiction thereof. And in such action, it shall only be necessary to allege that the money or property claimed thereby was so received by the defendant, in violation of the provisions of this chapter, without setting forth the special matter; and the plaintiff may, under such declaration, give in evidence any facts or circumstances tending to prove such violation, and recover the same, or the value thereof.

§ 2254. No court shall permit more than two attorneys to argue on any one side, except in criminal cases, unless good cause be shown therefor.

§ 2255. Any notice required in the progress of any suit or action, in any court of this State, shall be as valid and effectual, when served on the attorney or solicitor of the party in that cause, as if served on the party himself.

SEC. 2. Be it further enacted, That the owner of any dog found killing sheep, shall be held responsible for all losses or damages occasioned by such dog, so killing sheep, to be recovered before any court having competent jurisdiction. [Act ap. Jan. 22, 1875.

SECTION 1. Be it enacted by the Legislature of the State of Mississippi, That hereafter, whenever any suit shall have been commenced in any court of law or equity, in this State, to recover any moneys, public fund, property, or other effects belonging to the State, any county or school fund, by any officer, commissioner or trustee, authorized by law to sue for and recover the same, the said suit shall not abate on account of the death, removal, or resignation of said officer, commissioner or trustee, but the same may be revived, and prosecuted to judgment in the name of the successor of said officer, commissioner or trustee.

SEC. 2. Be it further enacted, That for the purpose of revival under this Act, the suit shall be considered to have been commenced and been pending from the time of filing of the declaration or bill, whether the writ was executed before the vacancy occurred in the office or trust or not.

SEC. 3. Be it further enacted, That the provisions of this Act shall apply to suits now pending, and which have been revived, in the name of the successor of any officer, commissioner or trustee, as well as to suits hereafter to be brought. [Act ap. March 2, 1876.

SEC. 2. Be it further enacted, That in any action founded on any joint and several bond, covenant or other contract, or on any promise, contract, or liability of co-partner, the plaintiff may discontinue his suit, before verdict, against one or more of the defendants, on payment of the costs that have accrued from joining such party or parties, in the suit; that in all such actions the jury may render verdicts against some of the defendants and in favor of others, as the evidence may require; and the Court shall enter the proper judgments and verdicts shall not be reversed or set aside for want of form. New trials shall be granted only as to such defendants as are aggrieved by the verdict; and final judgment shall be entered against the other defendants in pursuance of such verdict. That in all such actions on appeal or writ of error, the Supreme Court may reverse such judgment as to one or more of such defendants and affirm as to others, according to justice and the merits of the case. (Approved ,March 24, 1876.)

Suits Against Estates of Decedents.

SECTION 1. Be it enacted by the Legislature of the State of Mississippi, That in all suits now pending, or that may hereafter be brought against any executor or administrator, in any of the courts of this State, to establish any claim, debt or demand, against the estate of their testator or intestate, or to recover any property belonging thereto, it shall be lawful for any heir of such decedent, or any distributee of such estate, to make him or herself a party defendant to such suit by motion, and shall by leave of the court be admitted to appear and defend such cause, either separately or jointly with the executor or administrator.

SEC. 2. Be it further enacted, If the finding in such suit shall be for the plaintiff, judgment shall be rendered against the executor or administrator alone, to be levied of the goods and chattels, rights and credits of the intestate or intestator, in his hands, to be administered; and if the finding shall be in favor of the party admitted to defend on his separate pleading, judgment shall be in favor of the executor or administrator against the plaintiff.

SEC. 3. Be it further enacted, That estate of such decedent shall not be chargeable with any expense incurred by the party admitted to defend. (Acts 1874, p. 23.)

The Rights of Married Women.

SECTION 1. Be it enacted by the Legislature of the State of Mississippi, That none of the provisions of the Revised Code of 1871, nor of An Act entitled An Act to protect married women in the enjoyment of the fruits of their labor, approved April 18th, 1873, nor of any other statute of this State, shall be so construed as to permit any married woman to contract with her husband so as to establish against him, in any manner whatever, any claim or demand for hire, services or labor performed by such married woman for or on account of her husband, and it shall not be lawful for any married man to contract with his wife, so as to have or maintain against the wife, in any manner whatever, any claim or demand for hire, services or labor performed by such married man for or on account of his wife, and all contracts made between any husband and wife, in violation of this Act, shall be absolutely null and void. (Acts 1876, p. 261.)

Legal Holidays.

SECTION 1. Be it enacted by the Legislature of the State of Mississippi, That the following days, viz: the first day of January, commonly called New Year's Day; the twenty-second day of February, known as Washington's birthday; the fourth day of July, called Independence Day; the twenty-fifth day of December, known as Christmas Day, shall, for all purposes whatsoever, as regards the presenting for payment or acceptance, and of the protesting and giving notice of the dishonor of bills of exchange, bank checks and promissory notes, made after the passage of this Act, be treated and considered as the first day of the week, commonly called Sunday, and as public holidays, and all such bills, checks and notes otherwise presentable for acceptance or payment on the said days, shall be deemed to be presentable for acceptance or payment on the secular or business days next preceding such holidays.

SEC. 2. Be it further enacted, That whenever the first day of January, the twenty-second day of February, the fourth day of July, or the twenty-fifth day of December, shall fall upon Sunday, the Monday next following shall be deemed a public holiday for all or any of the purposes aforesaid; *Provided*, however, that in such case all bills of exchange, checks and promissory notes made after the passage of this Act, which would otherwise be presentable for acceptance or payment on the said Monday, shall be deemed to be presentable for acceptance or payment on the Saturday preceding.

SEC. 3. Be it further enacted, That all Acts or parts of Acts inconsistent with this Act are hereby repealed, but such repeal shall not affect any act done, or proceeding or suit instituted, prior to the passage of this Act. Approved, February 9, 1876.

Jurisdiction of Minors.

SECTION 1. Be it enacted by the Legislature of the State of Mississippi, That parents are entitled to full jurisdiction and control of their male children until twenty-one years of age, if unmarried, and over their female children until eighteen years, if unmarried.

Process and Mode of Service.

§ 1310. All civil process issued by a justice of the peace shall be under his hand and seal, and shall be directed to the officer whose duty it is to execute the same; and every summons shall be issued five days before the return day thereof, unless a shorter day shall be directed by the justice, in pursuance of the preceding section. If such process shall be executed less than five days before the return day, except as aforesaid, such service shall be good to require the appearance of the defendant at the next succeeding the one to which it is returnable.

§ 1311. The sheriff of any county, and his deputies, shall execute any process directed to such sheriff by any justice of the peace; and, in case of emergency, such justice may authorize and depute some reputable person to execute any process, although he be not commissioned as constable; and the sheriff, or the person so deputed, shall be entitled to the same fees as constables for similar services, and be liable to the same penalties.

§ 689. The style of all process issued by the circuit courts of this State, as well as all other courts in the State, shall be, "the State of Mississippi;" and, following this style, shall be the address of the officer who is to execute the same.

§ 691. The date of issuance of process shall be *prima facie* evidence that it issued on that day, but may be disproved, should the matter come in question.

§ 692. If any person shall, for any purpose, ante-date any process he shall forfeit two hundred dollars to the party aggrieved, to be recovered in an action of debt, and he shall, also be liable, in an action on the case, for any damages resulting from such act.

§ 693. The first process in civil suits (except where otherwise expressly provided), shall be a summons, directed to the sheriff, or other proper officer of the county where the suit is pending, commanding him to summons the defendant to appear and answer the action on the return day.

§ 694. The clerk or justice of the peace shall state, in the summons, with brevity, the nature of the action, and upon what it is founded, so as to give the defendant general information as to the nature of the proceeding.

§ 696. In estimating the time within which process has been served, the day it issued, and the day on which it is served, shall not both be counted. One of those days shall be included in the computation, and the other excluded.

§ 697. When any of the defendants reside in a different county from that in which the suit is brought, original process may issue at the same time to each county in which any of the defendants reside ; but the clerk shall indorse on the process to be served in another county, upon what particular defendants it is there to be served, and state, also, on the process thus sent abroad, that it is a duplicate, and that process has been issued to the proper officer of the county where the suit is brought, for the other defendants.

§ 701. Original process from the courts of this state, shall be served upon individuals by the officer to whom the process is directed, in one of the following modes : 1st. Upon the defendant, personally, if to be found in the county, by handing him a true copy of the process. 2d. If the defendant cannot be found in the county, then by leaving a true copy of the process at his usual place of abode, with his wife, or some other person above the age of sixteen years, being one of his family, and willing to receive such copy. 3d. If the defendant cannot himself be found, and if no person of his family, aged sixteen years, can be found at his usual place of abode, who is willing to receive such copy, then by posting such true copy on a door of the defendant's usual place of abode.

§ 702. If the sheriff, or other officer, to whom the original process is addressed, shall execute the same in the mode first stated in the preceding section, his return shall be made substantially as follows : "Executed the within process, this day, upon the defendant, in person, by handing to him a true copy thereof." If the process be executed in the manner secondly above authorized, the return shall be substantially as follows : "Executed this process, this day, by handing to the wife of the defendant (*or, to A. B., a person of his family, of the age of sixteen years, as the case may be*), at his usual place of abode in said county, such person being then and there willing to receive the same, a true copy of this process, said defendant not being found in my county, after diligent search." If the process be executed in the manner thirdly prescribed in the preceding section, the return shall be substantially in the form following : "The within named defendant, A. B., after diligent search, cannot be found in my county, nor could I find, after diligent search, any parson of his family, of the age of sixteen years, at his usual place of abode, who was willing to receive a copy of this process. I therefore executed the same, this day, by posting a true copy thereof on the door of the defendant's usual place of abode, in my county." The returns, however made, shall be dated with the day of service, and signed by the officer serving the process.

§ 703. If the defendant be a corporation, process may be served on the president, or other head of the corporation, upon the cashier, treasurer, or principal clerk, or agent of the corporation, or upon any one of the directors of such corporation. If no such person or persons be found in the county, then it shall be sufficient to post a true copy of the process on the door of the office, or principal place of business of the corporation. In suits against railroad and telegraph companies, brought in any county other than that in which their office or principal place of business may be, the process may be served on any station agent, or sent to any county in which such office or principal place of business may be located, and there served, as herein directed and authorized.

§ 704. If the defendant be an infant, the process shall be served on him personally, and upon his father or mother, or guardian, if he have any in this state.

§ 707. The officer serving process, shall not be permitted to question the truth of his return ; but either of the parties to the action may, in the same action, show the return to be untrue.

§ 708. On motion of either party, and a suggestion that the officer serving process, either by mistake or omission, made a defective return of his proceedings, the return may be amended, but only according to the facts connected with the service.

§ 711. Any process, appearing to be, in other respects, duly served, shall be deemed good, though not directed to any officer.

§ 715. Writs of *scire facias*, for the renewal of judgments, and for reviving suits, may be issued to any county in the State, and shall be executed and returned in the same manner as a summons. If the defendant is a non-resident of the State, or cannot be found to be served with the process, the court or the clerk in vacation, may order publication to be made for one month, in some newspaper, requiring the appearance of the defendant, and, on proof of such publication, may proceed as if the writ of *scire facias* had been returned executed.

§ 718. When the defendant shall not be found, the plaintiff may sue out an *alias* or *pluries* summons, until the defendant shall be served; or he may have a *testatum* writ to another county, where the defendant, after the commencement of suit, shall have gone into another county; or he may have an attachment against the estate of the defendant; and if, upon such attachment, the sheriff shall seize or attach any property of the defendant, the same proceedings shall thereafter be had as if the suit had been originally commenced by attachment.

§ 2937. When process shall be required to be served on notice given any number of days, the day of serving the process, or of giving the notice, shall be excluded, and the day of appearance included, and so in all other cases, when any number of days shall be prescribed, one day shall be excluded, and the other included; when the last day falls on Sunday, it shall be excluded, but in other cases Sunday shall be reckoned in the computation of time.

Service of Process Against Partners.

SECTION 1.   Be it enacted by the Legislature of the State of Mississippi, That in all actions against partners, some of whom are non-residents of the State of Mississippi, or who cannot be served with process, the service of process on such partners as may be found in the State, shall be sufficient notice to maintain the suit against all the partners; *provided*, that any judgment rendered in said suit shall bind the assets of such partnership, and the separate property of such partner or partners as may be actually served with process. (Acts 1876, p. 35.)

TRIAL BY JURY.

§ 724.   All male citizens of the State of Mississippi, and who are also citizens of the United States, between the ages of twenty-one years and sixty years, and who are householders, shall be competent jurors and liable to perform such service in the counties where they reside, but not beyond the limits thereof, except that those persons who have been convicted of any felony shall not be qualified as jurors; but any juror who is over sixty years of age, and who does not plead an exemption, shall be a qualified juror in any case.

§ 1326.   On or before the return day of the process, either party may demand a trial by jury, and thereupon the justice of the peace shall order the proper officer to summon six persons, competent to serve as jurors in the circuit court, to appear immediately, or at such early day as he may appoint, whether at a regular term or not, who shall be sworn to try the case; but each party shall be entitled to challenge peremptorily two of said jurors, and as many more as he can show sufficient cause for. If a sufficient number of jurors shall not appear, by-standers may be summoned until a jury is made up, to consist of six, against whom no sufficient legal objection shall exist. If the jury fail to agree, they may be discharged and another jury summoned as before, and so on until a verdict, and until judgment shall be entered by the justice on the verdict.

§ 1327. Each juror summoned and attending a justice's court, shall be entitled to one dollar per day, to be taxed in the bill of costs, and collected and paid over by the justice to such juror.

§ 1328. If a justice has more jury cases than one on the same day, he shall use the same jury for the trial of each, subject to the right of challenge by either party, and like proceedings in all respects, as in other cases. If more cases than one shall be tried by the same jury, it shall be the duty of the justice to apportion the costs of the jury among the several cases, and tax them in accordance with what he may decide to be a just apportionment.

§ 1329. The justice of the peace shall have power to fine any person summoned as a juror and failing to attend, in any sum not exceeding ten dollars; and if such person, when summoned to appear and show cause why such fine should not be made final, shall not appear and show sufficient cause, execution shall issue for such fine and costs.

§ 1330. Any defendant in a criminal case before a justice of the peace, may, in like manner as in civil cases, demand a jury, and thereupon the justice shall proceed as in other cases where a jury is demanded.

§ 1331. A justice of the peace shall not, on the trial by jury of any case, civil or criminal, express any opinion, or give any instruction or charge to the jury, except that justices may, in such cases, respond to any inquiries by the jurors, or any of them, as to the law of the case.

WITNESSES AND DEPOSITIONS.

§ 1313. The justice of the peace before whom any cause is pending, shall issue all subpœnas for witnesses residing in his county, which either of the parties may require, and such subpœnas shall be returnable on a day certain, giving reasonable time for attendance ; and if any witness, duly summoned, shall fail to appear, in pursuance of the subpœna, he shall forfeit the sum of ten dollars, for the use of the county, for which the justice shall immediately enter judgment *nisi*, which shall be made final, in case such witness, on being duly summoned to appear and show cause, shall fail to appear and show cause for such default, on oath or affirmation, to the satisfaction of said justice ; and the justice may issue attachment for such witness, as a circuit court may do in such cases.

§ 1314. If any witness, in any civil case before a justice of the peace, shall reside without the limits of his county, such justice may issue a commission to some officer of the county where such witness resides, authorized to take depositions in chancery, to take the deposition of such witness, on five day's notice of the time and place of taking the same, to the opposite party ; and such deposition so taken and returned under the hand of the justice taking the same, shall be read in evidence. Depositions of witnesses, in other cases, may be obtained in the same manner, and under the same circumstances, as in other courts of law.

§ 1315. Justices of the peace may examine the parties, or either of them, on oath, when required by the opposite party, and either party shall be admitted to testify in his own behalf. And, on cause shown by either party, such justice shall have power to postpone the trial, from time to time, not longer than three months in all.

§ 756. Parties to the record and persons interested in the result of a suit, or interested in the record as an instrument of evidence, shall not, on that account, be excluded as witnesses in any of the courts of this state.

§ 757. In all civil cases, a plaintiff or defendant, desiring to have the testimony of his adversary, may force him to appear and testify, by process of subpœna or attachment, as in other cases.

§ 758. No person shall testify as a witness to establish his own claim of any amount, for or against the estate of a deceased person, which originated during the lifetime of such deceased person. But such person so interested, shall be permitted to give evidence in support of his demand against the estate of a deceased person which originated after the death of such deceased person, in the course of administering the estate.

§ 759. Husband and wife may be witnesses for each other in all criminal cases, but they shall not be required to testify against each other, as witnesses for the prosecution. Nothing herein contained shall be so construed as to debar full cross-examination by the prosecution, of any husband or wife of an accused party, who may be placed on the stand for the defense.

§ 760. Husband and wife may be introduced by each other as witnesses in all civil cases.

§ 761. The first process to compel the attendance of a witness shall be a subpœna, directed to the sheriff of the county where the witness may reside, mentioning the time and place for the appearance of the witness, the parties to the suit, and the party at whose instance the witness is summoned. The names of all witnesses residing in the same county, shall be inserted in the same subpœna; *Provided*, the number shall not exceed six names in each subpœna.

§ 764. Subpœnas shall be served personally, or if the witness cannot be found, by leaving a copy at his usual place of residence, in the hands of some person over sixteen years of age; and the person so summoned shall appear, and continue to attend, from day to day, and from term to term, until discharged ; and if the suit shall be settled in vacation, notice thereof shall be given to the witnesses; otherwise they shall be entitled to the same compensation for their subsequent attendance, in pursuance of the subpœna, as if the suit had not been settled.

§ 767. Witnesses in criminal cases shall be liable to the same process of subpœna and attachment, and to the like penalties for failure to appear and attend, as in civil cases. The court may cause the witnesses on either side to be bound by recognizance to appear and testify until discharged.

§ 770. Any witness may sue for and recover from the party on whose behalf he was summoned, the amount specified in the certificate of the clerk, before any justice of the peace, or other court having jurisdiction, and the certificate of the clerk shall be good *prima facie* evidence, in such action, of the attendance of such witness, and of the amount of compensation he is entitled to recover.

§ 771. Witnesses in criminal cases shall be allowed the same compensation as in civil cases, but the prosecutor shall not be allowed compensation as a witness, nor shall any person be allowed for his attendance as a witness in more than one criminal case on the same day.

§ 777. If any person summoned as a witness shall refuse to be sworn or affirmed, or to give evidence, he shall be committed to prison by the court, commissioner, referees, or other person authorized to take his testimony, there to remain without bail, until he shall be sworn or affirmed, and give his evidence.

§ 778. Any witness may be examined touching his interest in a cause, or his conviction of any crime, and his answers may be contradicted, and his interest or his conviction of a crime established by other evidence; and no witness shall be excused from answering any question, material and relevant, unless the answer would expose him to a criminal prosecution or penalty, or a forfeiture of his estate; and the court shall decide as to the effect of such evidence, after privately hearing the witness.

§ 779. No conviction for any offense, except perjury or subornation of perjury, shall exclude a witness from testifying in a cause; but if he has been convicted of the offenses herein named, or either of them, he shall not testify, although he may have been pardoned or punished for the same.

§ 781. Any witness summoned to attend court in a civil case, beyond the county of his residence, shall not be bound to attend, unless there be tendered to him, by the officer serving the subpœna, or the party at whose instance he is called, a sum of money sufficient to pay mileage and ferriages and tolls to the court house, and one day's attendance.

§ 788. The depositions of witnesses residing or being temporarily within this state, may be taken in all civil suits in the following cases, and no others, viz: *First :* when the witness shall be about to depart from the state before the cause can be tried. *Second :* when, by reason of extreme age, sickness or other cause, the witness will probably be unable to attend court in person. *Third :* when the claim or the defence shall depend upon the evidence of a single witness, on a point essential to the case. *Fourth :* when the witness shall be a female. *Fifth :* when the witness shall be a judge of any court of record in this state. *Sixth :* when the witness shall be an officer of the state government, or of the government of the United States, and cannot attend court, without neglecting his official duties. *Seventh :* when the witness is a clerk of any court of record, or a sheriff, or justice of the peace, and is required to testify in a county different from that of his residence. *Lastly :* when the witness resides more than sixty miles from the place where the cause is to be tried.

§ 789. Either party may compel the attendance of a female witness to give evidence orally in court, by making and filing an affidavit in the case that he has good cause to believe, and does verily believe, that her presence in court is necessary for the ends of justice. In no other case shall a female be compelled to attend court as a witness in a civil cause.

§ 791. When any party shall desire to take the deposition of any witness absent from or residing out of the state, he shall file interrogatories in the clerk's office, and serve the opposite party or his attorney with a copy thereof, with a notice of the day on which a commission will issue, ten days before issuing the same, in which time the opposite party shall file his cross-interrogatories; and the clerk shall thereupon issue a commission, and shall annex thereto a copy of such interrogatories and cross-interrogatories, and the witness shall be examined by the commissioner thereon.

§ 7. 2. If the opposite party shall not reside in the state, and hath not an agent or attorney at law or in fact within the same, to whom notice of the time and place of taking a deposition within the state can be given, or on whom copies of the interrogatories and notice required for taking a deposition abroad, can be served, it shall be sufficient to file the same with the clerk among the papers in the cause for the time required ; and this provision shall apply to all courts in the state.

§ 793. All commissions to take depositions under this act, may be directed to one or to several commissioners, in the alternative by name, or to any judge of a court of record, justice of the peace, mayor or chief magistrate of a city or town, commissioner appointed by the governor of this state, or other person authorized to administer oaths by the law of the place where the deposition is taken; and the certificate of any such officer shall be *prima facie* evidence of his official character, and of his authority to administer oaths.

§ 794. The witnesses shall be sworn or affirmed by the commissioner to testify the whole truth and nothing but the truth, and the commissioners, or one or more of them, shall carefully and impartially examine the witness, on the interrogatories and cross-interrogatories annexed to the commission; or, if the deposition is taken within the state, upon such interrogatories as may be put verbally or in writing, by the parties, and shall cause the testimony to be fairly written down, by himself or by the witness, or some disinterested person in his presence, and subscribed by the witness; and the testimony, so taken down, with the commission and interrogatories, and every exhibit and voucher relating thereto, and also a certificate by the commissioner of all his proceedings therein, shall be sealed up and directed to the clerk of the court where the action is pending, and transmitted in the most safe and convenient manner, and the clerk shall open the same, and, having indorsed thereon the receipt and opening thereof, shall deposit the same among the papers in the cause. The commissioner shall indorse the style of the case and the word "deposition" on the envelope.

§ 795. The depositions taken, certified and returned, in pursuance of this act, shall be admissible as evidence in the cause ; *Provided,* any of the causes authorizing the taking of depositions under this act shall exist at the time of the trial to prevent the personal attendance of the witness : but the questions and answers thereto shall be liable to all legal objections.

§ 796. Subpœnas for witnesses to appear before any commissioner within this state, to give testimony in any cause pending in a court of this state, shall be issued by the clerk of the court in which the action is pending, or by the commissioner, and shall be executed as in other cases, and returned to such commissioner ; and in case the witness shall fail to appear, the said commissioner shall issue an attachment against him, returnable at such time as the commissioner shall appoint, and the deposition may then be taken without further notice.

§ 797. The commissioner shall have power to continue the taking of depositions from day to day, and may adjourn the taking thereof from time to time, giving notice to the parties, unless they shall be present when such adjournment is made.

§ 798. The sheriff, coroner, and constables of each county, shall serve copies of interrogatories and notices of issuing commissions, and notice of taking depositions, and shall be allowed therefor the same fee as for the service of a summons, to be charged in the bill of costs ; they shall also execute and return all writs of subpœna and attachments; and for any neglect of duty imposed by this article, such officer shall be liable to all the penalties prescribed for neglect of duty in respect to the service of a summons.

§ 799. No exception to any deposition, other than for incompetency or irrelevancy, shall be regarded, unless made in writing and filed one day before the commencement of the trial. The court, on motion of either party, shall determine the exceptions so made and filed, before the commencement of the trial, and if the exceptions are sustained, may, in proper cases, allow time to re-take such depositions.

§ 2252. No attorney or counsellor at law shall be allowed any compensation as a witness in any cause in which he shall be concerned as attorney or counsel.

JUDGMENTS AND ENROLLING.

§ 1318. All judgments rendered by justices of the peace shall operate as a lien upon the property, real and personal, of the defendant or defendants therein, found or situated in the county where rendered, or in any other county where the same may be, which is not exempt by law from execution; *provided,* that an abstract of the judgment shall be filed with the clerk of the circuit court of the county wherein the property is situated, and entered upon the judgment roll, as in other cases of enrolled judgments; said lien to commence from the date of the enrollment and continue until the payment or satisfaction of said judgment, and said judgment may be enrolled as aforesaid, and have the force and effect of a lien, as aforesaid, in all cases where an appeal is taken from said judgment, as well as in other cases; and in the event of a reversal of the judgment of the justice's court, the clerk of the circuit court shall enter a memorandum to this effect, on the judgment roll.

§ 825.   In all civil actions, the party in whose favor judgment shall be given, or in case of non-suit, dismission or discontinuance, the defendant shall be entitled to full costs, except when it may be otherwise directed by law; and the law of costs shall not be interpreted as penal laws.

§ 830.   All judgments and decrees so enrolled shall be a lien upon and bind all the property of the defendant or defendants, within the county where so enrolled, from the rendition thereof, and shall have priority, according to the order of such enrollment, in favor of the judgment creditor, his representatives or assignees, against the judgment debtor or debtors, his, her or their representatives, and purchasers or mortgagees from said judgment debtor or debtors; and no judgment shall be a lien on any property of the defendant or defendants thereto, unless the same shall be enrolled in the manner herein directed. But the priority of lien provided for in this section shall not extend to judgment creditors who fail, refuse or neglect to sue out execution for the satisfaction of his, her or their judgment or judgments, until a junior judgment creditor has, by due diligence, caused his execution to be levied upon the property of the defendant; but in all such cases, the sale by the sheriff or other officer shall vest the title of the defendant or defendants in the purchaser, and the proceeds of such sale shall be applied to the satisfaction of the junior judgment creditor; *provided,* that before said junior creditor shall cause a levy to be made, he shall give notice to older creditors in execution, that unless they proceed in ten days to levy, he will proceed; and in that case, he shall have a preference under his levy.

§ 831.   The purchaser or purchasers of any property sold at execution sale by the sheriff or other officer, shall take the same discharged of all liens of judgment and decrees, whether the same be sold under an execution issued upon the elder or junior judgment or decree.

§ 832.   After the sale of any property by the sheriff or other officer on execution, before the money is paid over by him, he shall examine the "Judgment Roll," to ascertain if there be any elder judgment or judgments, decree or decrees, enrolled against the defendant or defendants in said execution, having a priority of lien; and if there be, he shall apply the proceeds of such sale to such elder judgment or decree, so having priority of lien, and return such application upon the execution on which such sale shall have been made. But should there be any dispute as to which judgment or decree has the priority of lien, then such officer shall make a statement of the fact of such dispute, and return the same, with the execution and the money raised thereon, into the court to which the same is returnable, and the court shall, on motion and examination of the facts, determine to whom the money so raised on execution shall be paid.

§ 833. No judgment or decree rendered in any court of the United States, or of this state, shall be a lien upon or bind any property of the defendants, situate out of the county in which such judgment or decree was rendered, until the plaintiff shall file, in the office of the clerk of the circuit court of the county in which the property may be situated, an abstract of such judgment or decree, certified by the clerk of the court in which the same was rendered, containing the names of all the parties to such judgment or decree. its amount, and the date of the rendition, and the amount appearing to have been paid thereon, if any; and it shall be the duty of the clerk of any circuit court, on receiving such abstract, and on payment of the fees allowed by law for filing, recording and enrolling the same, to file the same and record it in a separate book, plainly indexed, to be kept for that purpose, and to note therein the day on which such abstract was filed for record as aforesaid, and he shall forthwith enroll the same on the "Judment Roll," as in other cases; and such judgment or decree shall from the date of its enrollment as aforesaid, be a lien upon and bind the property of the defendants within the county where it shall be so enrolled.

APPEALS AND CERTIORARI.

§ 1332. Either party may appeal to the circuit court of the county from the judment of any justice of the peace ; *provided,* such appeal be demanded, and bond given, within five days after the rendition of the judgment, and an affidavit filed that such appeal is not made for delay, nor to vex, harass or oppress his adversary, but that justice may be done. The party praying such appeal, shall give bond, with security, to be approved by said justice, payable to the opposite party, in the penalty of two hundred dollars, conditioned for the payment of such judgment as the said circuit court may render against him, and such appeal, when demanded, and bond given, as aforesaid, shall operate as a *supersedeas* of execution on such judgment.

§ 1333. The justice of the peace, from whose decision an appeal shall be prayed, shall, on or before the first day of the next term of the circuit court, to which the same is returnable, transmit to the clerk of such court a certified copy of the record of the proceedings, with all the original process and papers in the case, and the original appeal bond and affidavit given by the appellant, and said clerk shall docket the same, and shall be entitled to the same fees, upon such appeals, as for similar services in suits originating in said court. The justice shall, at all times, be allowed to amend his return according to the facts, and, if the appeal bond shall be defective, the appellant shall be permitted to give a new bond, which shall have the same effect as if given, originally, before the justice, on demand of an appeal.

§ 1334. Appeals to the circuit court shall be tried anew, in a summary way, without pleadings in writing, at the first term, unless cause can be shown for a continuance; *provided*, that, if it shall appear on the trial of such appeal, that suit was brought before a justice of the peace not having jurisdiction thereof, the circuit court shall reverse the judgment of the said justice, if rendered in favor of the plaintiff, and shall dismiss the case at the costs of the plaintiff in the court below. If the defendant be the appellant, and judgment be rendered for the plaintiff in the original suit, ten per cent. damages upon the amount thereof, shall be included in such judgment and costs; and such judgment shall be rendered against the principal and his sureties jointly. If the judgment be for the defendant in the original suit, he shall recover full costs, in like manner; *provided*, that, on such appeals, where the amount in controversy shall exceed twenty dollars, the parties, or either of them, shall be entitled to a trial by jury; and in all such cases, where the amount in controversy exceeds the sum of fifty dollars, either party shall be entitled to an appeal or writ of error, to the supreme court, as in cases originating in the circuit courts.

§ 1336. All cases decided by a justice of the peace may, within six months thereafter, on good cause shown by petition, supported by affidavit, be removed to the circuit court of the county, by a writ of *certiorari*, which shall operate as a *supersedeas*, the party, in all cases, giving bond, with security, as in cases of appeals from justices of the peace ; and in any cause removed by *certiorari* under this act, the court shall be confined to the examination of questions of law, arising or appearing on the face of the record and proceedings. In case of an affirmance of the judgment of the justice, the same judgment shall be given as on appeals. In case of a reversal, the circuit court shall enter up such judgment as the justice ought to have entered, if the same is apparent, or may then proceed to try the cause anew, on its merits.

§ 533. The judges of the circuit courts, in term-time and in vacation, may order the issuance of writs of *habeas corpus*, *mandamus*, *certiorari*, *supersedeas* and attachment, and grant injunctions, *ne exeat*, and all other remedial writs, in all cases where the same may properly be granted, according to right and justice, returnable to any court in this state, whether the suits or proceedings be pending in the district of the judge granting the same, or not. The fiat of such judge shall authorize the issuance of the process or writ, returnable to the proper court.

GARNISHMENT.

§ 1337. When sufficient property cannot be found to satisfy the execution, and the plaintiff shall suggest that any other person is indebted to the defendant, or has effects of such defendant in his hands, the justice shall issue a summons of garnishment against such person, in like manner, and like proceedings shall be had thereon, in all respects, so far as may be applicable, as in cases of garnishment upon judgments rendered in the circuit courts. Such summons may be issued to any county where the party may reside.

§ 874. The clerk of any court of law or equity in this state, on the suggestion of the plaintiff in any judgment or decree therein rendered, that any person is indebted to the defendant therein, or has any effects of such defendant in his hands or possession, and on filing in his office an affidavit of such plaintiff, his agent or attorney, that he does not believe that such defendant has in his possession visible property, upon which a levy can be made, sufficient to satisfy such judgment or decree, shall issue a summons of garnishment, directed to the sheriff or proper officer of the county in which the garnishee may reside, commanding him to summon the said garnishee to appear at the term of the court to which such summons or garnishment may be returnable, to answer on oath, whether he is indebted to the said defendant, and in what sum, and what effects of said defendant he has in his hands or possession, or had at the time of serving such summons, and whether he knows of any other persons indebted to said defendant, or who may have any of the effects of said defendant in their hands or possession; and upon the return of such summons, the like proceedings may be had, as in cases of garnishees in attachment.

§ 875. All property in the hands of such garnishee, belonging to the defendant, at the time of the service of such summons shall be bound by and subject to the lien of the judgment on which such summons shall have been issued, and if the garnishee shall surrender the same to the sheriff or other officer serving such summons, such officer shall receive the same, and make sale thereof, as if levied on by virtue of an execution, and shall return the money arising therefrom, to satisfy the judgment.

EXECUTION AND STAY OF.

§ 1317. No execution shall issue on any judgment of a justice of the peace, until five days after rendering the same, unless the party recovering therein will make oath that he hath reason to believe that he will be in danger of losing his debt or demand by such delay, in which case execution shall issue immediately; but the opposite party shall not be deprived of his right of appeal, within the time prescribed.

Section 1. Be it enacted by the Legislature of the State of Mississippi, That any person, who may hereafter be in possession of personal property of any description, belonging to or claimed by any other person, which property is liable to be levied upon or be seized under any process of *fieri facias renditioni exponas*, attachment, or other process. such person, so in possession as aforesaid, shall point out and deliver such property to any sheriff, constable, coroner, or other officer. who may demand said property, by authority of any legal process in his hands. (Act approved February 19, 1876.)

§ 838. Executions may issue at any time within a year and a day after the rendition of the judgment or decree, or within a year and a day after the expiration of the stay of execution ordered by the court; and in case the issuance of execution has been prevented by injunction or *supersedeas*, then execution may be issued within a year and a day after the dissolution of such injunction, or the discharge or expiration of such *supersedeas*.

§ 842. Land shall not be levied on. if sufficient personal property be found or surrendered by the debtor.

§ 843. When any sheriff or other officer shall serve an execution on horses or other live stock, he shall provide sufficient sustenance for the support of such live stock, until sold or otherwise legally discharged from such execution ; and upon the return of the execution, the court, in cases where the compensation is not fixed by law, shall settle and adjust what such officer shall be allowed for his expenses incurred in supporting such stock ; and such officer shall be allowed to retain the same out of the money arising from the sale of such stock.

§ 844. If any sheriff or officer shall levy, or be about to levy, an execution or attachment on any personal property. and doubt shall arise whether the right to such property is in the defendant or not, such sheriff or officer may demand of the plaintiff a bond, signed by good and responsible persons, payable to such sheriff or officer, in a sufficient penalty, conditioned that the obligors therein will indemnify and save harmless the said sheriff or officer against all damages which he may sustain in consequence of the seizure or sale of the property on which the execution or attachment shall be, or shall have been levied, and, moreover, will pay and satisfy to any person claiming title to said property, all damages which said person may sustain in consequence of such seizure or sale ; and if the plaintiff shall fail to give such bond, the sheriff or officer shall be justifiable in refusing to levy on such property, or, if the levy be made, and such bond be not given, on or before the day of sale, or the return-day of the process, the officer shall be justifiable in releasing the levy, and delivering the property to the party from whose possession it was taken ; *provided*, the plaintiff, or his agent or attorney, had reasonable notice in writing, before the day of sale or return-day of the process, that such bond would be required.

§ 845. If such bond and security be given, it shall be returned with the execution or attachment, and any person claiming the property levied on, may prosecute a suit upon the bond, in the name of the payee, or his representatives, for the use of such claimant, and recover such damages as he may sustain by the seizure or sale of said property, or levy of said process, whether the same shall exceed the penalty of such bond or not ; and such claimant shall,.

after the due execution of such bond, be barred of any action against the sheriff or officer levying such execution, unless the obligors in said bond shall be, or become insolvent, or the bond be otherwise invalid.

§ 851. When the officer shall return on any execution, that no property of the defendant is to be found in his county, and the plaintiff shall suggest, in writing, to the court which rendered the judgment, that the defendant hath property, but hath fraudulently conveyed the same, for the purpose of defrauding his creditors, or to avoid the payment of the execution, a summons shall issue to the person or persons in whose hands such property is supposed to be, or having such fraudulent conveyance ; and, on the return thereof, executed as in other cases, an issue shall be made up and tried by a jury ; and if the jury shall find the conveyance fraudulent, or without valuable consideration, the property thus fraudulently conveyed or made over shall be subject to the plaintiff's execution.

§ 853. If a *distringas* issue in detinue, the court or judge in vacation, on being satisfied that the specific thing cannot be delivered, may order the writ to be superseded, as to the specific thing, and to be executed for the alternative price or value ascertained by the judgment.

§ 855. When a defendant in execution shall own or be entitled to an undivided interest in any property, not exclusively in his own possession, such interest may be levied on, and sold by the sheriff, without taking the property into actual possession, and such sale shall vest in the purchaser all the interest of the defendant in such property.

§ 1343. If the party against whom judgment shall be given, shall, within five days thereafter, procure some responsible person to appear before the justice, and consent to become surety for a stay of execution, the justice shall enter the name of such person on his docket, as surety for a stay of execution on said judgment ; and thereupon, such justice shall grant a stay of execution for thirty days, from the date of such judgment, on all sums not exceeding fifty dollars, and for sixty days, on all sums over fifty dollars; and in case the money be not paid at the expiration of such stay, execution shall issue against the principal and sureties, or either of them, for the principal, interest and costs, on which execution no surety shall be taken.

§ 1344. Any defendant obtaining a stay of execution, shall thereby waive all errors in the judgment, and abandon the right of appeal or *certiorari*.

How Lands Levied on and Sold on Execution from Justice Court.

§ 1319. In all cases in which lands and tenements shall be levied upon by execution or attachment, returnable to a justice's court, it shall be the duty of the officer making the levy, to endorse his return on the writ, by virtue of which the levy is made, at or before the term of the court to which the same is returnable; and it shall be the duty of such justice of the peace, thereupon to make out, and certify to the clerk of the circuit court of the county, a complete transcript of the proceedings had before such justice, together with a copy of the writ of attachment or execution, as the case may be, and the sheriff's return thereon; and said transcript shall be filed, by said justice, in the office of the clerk of the circuit court of the county in which said lands or tenements are situated. It shall be the duty of the clerk of the said circuit court, and he is hereby required, to issue a writ of *venditioni exponas*, directed to the sheriff of his county, who shall advertise and make sale of said lands and tenements, and make return of the said writ, in the same manner as provided by law for the sale of lands and tenements, under and by virtue of a judgment of the circuit court; except that return of said writ, and the proceeds of said sale, shall be made to the justice of the peace by whom judgment was rendered, at or before the term of his court held next succeeding said sale; and it shall be the duty of said justice to tax the fees and commissions due the sheriff and clerk of the circuit court, in all such cases, and when collected, to pay them over to said officer, who shall be entitled to a summary remedy for the same, by motion against said justice, in case of his refusal to pay over said money to the parties entitled thereto, before any other justice of the county, upon giving him ten days' notice of the time and place fixed for the hearing of such motion; and a copy of such notice shall be served on the justice of the peace against whom the motion is made.

CLAIMANT'S ISSUE.

§ 1338. When an execution or attachment, issued by, and returnable before a justice of the peace, shall be levied on property which is claimed by a third person, not a party to the execution or attachment, such claimant shall make oath and give bond, as required where the execution or attachment issues from a circuit court, and the officer shall immediately return the execution or attachment, with the affidavit and bond, to the justice who issued the same; and thereupon the said justice, at the request of either party, shall cause a jury to be summoned and empaneled, as directed by this act, to consist, when sworn, of six persons; and the claim shall thereupon be tried, and like proceedings had, as far as applicable, as directed in cases of claim to property levied on by virtue of an execution or attachment, from a circuit court; *provided*, that where the claimant shall not desire to replevy the property, he shall not be required to give bond, and the property shall remain in the hands of the officer, to abide the result of the trial.

§ 858. When any person, not a party to an execution, shall claim to be the owner of any personal property levied upon by virtue thereof, such person may make oath or affirmation to his right and title to the property so levied on, and may enter into bond, payable to the plaintiff in the execution, with one or more good sureties, in the penalty of double the amount of the fair value of the property so claimed, which value shall be estimated by the officer holding such execution, and shall be endorsed thereon, conditional for the prosecution of said claim, with effect, or, in case he fail therein for the payment to the plaintiff in execution of all such damages as may be awarded against the claimant, in case his claim shall not be sustained, or shall appear to have been made for fraudulent purposes, or for delay, and that he will well and truly deliver the same property to the sheriff or other officer, if the claim thereto should be determined against the claimant; and upon the making of such affidavit and bond, the sheriff or other officer holding the execution, shall receive the same, and shall deliver said property to said claimant, and shall return said affidavit and bond with the execution, and the court shall thereupon direct an issue to be made up between the parties, to try the right of property before a jury, at the same term, unless good cause be shown for a continuance.

§ 859. Further proceedings on such execution shall be stayed, for an amount equal to the value of the property so claimed, as endorsed and returned by the officer, until the final decision of such claim; and on all subsequent executions issued on the same judgment, prior to the final decision of said claim, the clerk shall endorse the amount of said estimated value, for the government of the officer to whom the same may be directed.

§ 860. If, by default of the plaintiff in execution, an issue for the trial of the right of property so levied on and claimed, be not made up at the term to which such execution is returnable, the court shall discharge the claimant from his bond, and the said property shall never thereafter be subject to such an execution; but, if from the default of the claimant, such issue be not made up at the first term of said court, the said court shall cause a jury to be empaneled, at the instance of the plaintiff in the execution, and sworn to execute a writ of inquiry as to the value of the property claimed by said claimant, and also, to inquire whether or not the claim was made for fraudulent purposes, or for purposes of delay.

§ 861. On the trial of an issue made up on a claim of property, the burden of proof shall be on the plaintiff in execution; and such issue shall be tried and governed by the same rules which regulate and govern the trial of an issue in an action of detinue; and either party to such issue shall have all the rights of continuances, new trials or appeals, in the same manner as in any action of detinue; and the final judgment, on any such issue shall have the like effect on the rights of the parties thereto as if the same had been given in an action of detinue; and the jury trying such issue, in case they find in favor of the plaintiff in execution, shall assess the true value of the property so found subject to such execution, and shall also certify whether the claim of the claimant was made for fraudulent purposes, or for purposes of delay; and if the jury shall omit to find such value, a writ of inquiry may be awarded. The valuation of the officer taking the bond of the claimant shall in all cases be *prima facie* evidence of the value of the property; and in case the jury fail to find the value of the property, the plaintiff may, at his election, take judgment for the value assessed by the said officer, without resorting to a writ of inquiry.

§ 862. Whenever a verdict shall be rendered in such case in favor of the plaintiff in execution, either on an issue joined, or an inquiry by default, the court shall pronounce such judgment as would be given in an action of detinue, for the specific property, if to be had, and if not, for its value as assessed by the jury, and costs of suit; and if the jury shall find that such claim was made for fraudulent purposes, or for purposes of delay, the plaintiff shall also recover ten per centum damages, on the assessed value of said property' which judgment shall be rendered jointly against the claimant, or his executors or administrators, and the surety or sureties in his bond given on said claim, or such of said sureties as may be living at the time of said judgment, and execution shall issue thereon accordingly; and the original execution levied on said property shall be credited by the amount of the value of said property, as assessed by the jury, and determined by the judgment of the court thereupon, to bear date of the rendition of such judgment; and if any balance shall then remain unpaid on said original execution, another execution may be issued therefor against the defendant or defendants therein. And in all cases where the value of the property so levied on and claimed, may be assessed at an amount greater than sufficient to satisfy said original execution, the true amount due thereon shall be endorsed by the clerk, on the execution issued against said claimant, and the amount of such original execution, with interest and all costs, shall be received of said claimant, in full satisfaction thereof.

§ 863. Should the plaintiff or claimants, or any one or more of them, die before final judgment on such claims of property, the same may be prosecuted or defended by the executors or administrators of such deceased party, and such executors or administrators, may voluntarily appear and become parties thereto; and in case the executors or administrators of such deceased claimant or claimants shall not voluntarily appear, or shall neglect or refuse to become parties to the said proceedings, after having been duly served with a *scire facias*, five days before the meeting of the court, the court may proceed to render judgment against such executors or administrators of the deceased claimant or claimants, jointly with the other parties, in the same manner, as if such executors or administrators had voluntarily made themselves parties thereto; and in case of the death of a sole plaintiff, or of all the plaintiffs in execution, before final judgment therein, unless the representatives of the proper party or parties, shall appear voluntarily, or on the return of a *scire facias* executed, and become parties to such proceedings, on or before the second term of the court next after the death of such party shall have been suggested on the record, the said claimant shall be released from his bond, and the levy on said property discharged. In case of the death of one or more of the plaintiffs in execution or claimants, after final judgment. the same proceedings shall be had by or against the survivor or survivors, or by *scire facias*, and revival against the representatives of the deceased, as may be had upon other judgments in the circuit court.

§ 864. In case the claimant shall die before judgment, and there shall be no representative of his estate, or such representative shall fail to appear and become a party to such issue, judgment shall be entered against the sureties on his bond, for the property, or the value thereof, as assessed by the sheriff, or to be found by the verdict of a jury empaneled to inquire of the same, at the option of the plaintiff, with interest on such value from the date of the claimant's bond.

§ 865. In case one or more of the sureties on any such claimant's bond shall die before final judgment, and a verdict shall be given in favor of the plaintiff in execution, judgment shall be rendered thereon against the parties living and in court, and the said plaintiff shall have a *scire facias* upon the said verdict, against the executors or administrators of such deceased surety or sureties, to appear and show cause why judgment should not be rendered against them on said verdict; and on return of said *scire facias* executed, unless good cause be shown to the contrary, the court shall give a separate judgment against the representatives of such deceased surety or sureties; and execution may issue thereon.

§ 866. When the sureties on any claimant's bond shall become insufficient or irresponsible, the court, on motion of the plaintiff, may require additional security to be given thereon, or a new bond, and the said additional sureties. or the sureties on such new bond, shall be liable equally, and to the same extent with the original sureties; and if the claimant shall fail to give such additional or new security, judgment shall be given against him, as by default, for not making up the issue, and a writ of inquiry shall be executed.

SALES.

§ 281. Sales by constables shall be held at such convenient times and places as they may appoint, and ten days' notice shall be given thereof, by advertisement, in two or more public places. in the county or neighborhood; and there shall not be more than fifteen days between the levy and the sale of the property levied on. The justice shall make an allowance to the constable, out of the proceeds of the sale, for the keeping of any live stock seized by the constable on execution.

§ 1345. Sales of personal property, under execution from justices of the peace, may be made at any convenient point in the district where it is found. or at the court-house of the county, on ten days' written notice, posted at two or more places in the district best calculated, in the opinion of the officer making the levy. to give public notice, or at the court-house door.

§ 1346. When any property shall be seized under execution, and before a sale, the execution shall expire, or when from any cause property seized shall remain unsold in the hands of an officer, the justice shall issue a *venditioni exponas* for the sale of such property.

§ 846. All sales by any sheriff or other officer, by virtue of any execution or other process, shall be made at the court-house of the county, except when personal property, too cumbersome to be removed, shall be levied on, which may be sold at the place where the same may be found, or at any other convenient place, and also, except where cattle, hogs, sheep, or stock, other than horses and mules, are levied on, the sale of which may be made within the usual hours, on ten days' notice, at the most public place in the neighborhood of the defendant; and such sales may be made on the first Monday of every month, or on the first Monday or Tuesday of each term of the circuit court of the county, and shall not commence sooner than eleven o'clock in the forenoon, nor continue later than four o'clock in the afternoon. Sales of lands shall be advertised in a newspaper published in the county, once in each week, for three successive weeks; and, if there be no such newspaper, or if the publisher thereof shall refuse to publish such advertisement, then such notice shall be given by putting up advertisements, thirty days before the sale, in five public places, one of which shall be at the court-house; and, in case of the sale of any personal property, notice shall be given by putting up advertisements ten days before the day of sale, in five public places in the county, one of which shall be at the court-house door, and the officer shall proceed, at the time and place specified in the notice, to sell, by auction, to the highest bidder, the property levied on, or so much thereof as will satisfy the execution and all costs.

§ 847. Whenever, from a defect of bidders, caused by inclement weather or otherwise, the property shall not be likely to command a reasonable price, the sheriff or officer may adjourn the sale, and re-advertise the same for a subsequent sale day; and whenever the sales advertised for a particular day shall not be completed on that day, the same may be continued from day to day until completed, notice of such continued sale being given to the assembly, at the close of the first day's sale.

ATTACHMENT.

EXTENT OF REMEDY AND GROUND FOR ATTACHMENT.

§ 1419. The remedy, by attachment, shall apply for the enforcement of all liquidated or ascertained debts, of every name and description, whether due by bond, note or open account, or otherwise. It shall extend to all claims for damages, for the breach of any contract, express or implied, and whether written or unwritten, and to all demands or claims founded upon any of the penal laws of this state.

§ 1420. All attachments shall be predicated upon one or more of the following grounds, and no others : 1st, that the defendant is a foreign corporation, or is a non-resident of this state ; or, 2d, that he has removed, or is about to remove himself, or his property, out of this state ; or, 3d, that he so absconds, or conceals himself, that he cannot be served with a summons ; or, 4th, that he has property or rights in action, which he conceals, and unjustly refuses to apply to the payment of his debts ; or, 5th, that he has assigned or disposed of, or is about to assign or dispose of, his property or rights in action, or some part thereof, with intent to defraud his creditors, or give an unfair preference to some of them ; or, 6th, that he hath converted, or is about to convert his property into money, or evidences of debt, with intent to place it beyond the reach of his creditors ; or, 7th, that he fraudulently contracted the debt, or incurred the obligation, for which suit has been or is about to be brought.

THE AFFIDAVIT.

§ 1421. Before any writ of attachment shall issue, the creditor, or his agent or attorney. shall make affidavit, before a judge of the supreme court, a justice of the peace, a clerk of the circuit court, a clerk of the chancery court, or the mayor or chief magistrate of an incorporate city or town, of the amount of his debt or demand, to the best of his knowledge and belief, stating how the same is due, whether by note, open account, or bond, or claimed as damages for breach of contract, or claimed under a penal law of the state.

§ 1422. The affidavit shall contain a statement of the existence of one or more of the seven grounds for attachment set forth in section 1420 of this Act. not stated disjunctively, but conjunctively, except where one of the distinct grounds for attachment contains, within itself, two disjunctive matters.

§ 1423. If the affidavit purport to be made by an agent, or attorney in fact, of the attaching creditor, the statement thereof, in the body of the affidavit, shall be *prima facie* evidence of such character and authority.

§ 1424. The officer taking such affidavit shall carefully preserve the same, and return it to the court having jurisdiction of the case, on or before the return day of the writ of attachment.

THE BOND.

§ 1425. Every officer granting an attachment shall, before he issues the same, take a bond, with good and sufficient security, from the attaching creditor, or his agent or attorney in fact, in double the amount of the principal sum alleged in the affidavit to be due, payable to the defendant in attachment, and his heirs, executors, and administrators, with a condition thereto in the form, or to the effect following :

"The condition of the above obligation is such, that, whereas, the above bound, ..., hath, on the day of the date hereof, prayed an attachment, at the suit of ......, against the estate of the above named ....., for the sum of ......, and and hath obtained the same, returnable to the ..... court, of the ......, of ......, to be held at ....., on the ...... day of ...... next.

"Now, if the said plaintiff, in the said attachment, shall well and truly pay and satisfy to the said defendant, all such damages as he shall sustain, by reason of the wrongful sueing out of the said attachment, and shall also pay all costs which may be awarded against the said plaintiff, in said suit, then the above obligation to be void, otherwise to remain in full force and effect."

§ 1426. If such bond purport to be executed by an agent or attorney in fact of the attaching creditor, a statement thereof, in the bond, shall be *prima facie* evidence that the agent or attorney in fact, had due authority to act.

§ 1427. The attachment bond shall be carefully preserved, by the officer taking the same, and by him returned to the court having jurisdiction of the case, on or before the return day of the writ of attachment, and he shall endorse thereon his approval of the same.

WRIT---HOW ISSUED AND RETURNABLE.

§ 1428. The writ of attachment may be issued by any officer herein authorized to take affidavits for attachments. If issued by a clerk of a court of record, the writ shall be signed by such clerk, with the seal of the court attached. If issued by any other of the officers authorized, it shall be under the hand of such officer, and shall be made returnable to the first day of the next term of the court having jurisdiction of the case.

§ 1429. Attachments shall be in the form, or to the effect following :

"The State of Mississippi :

"To the sheriff, coroner or any constable of .... county, greeting :

"Whereas, A. B. (or C. D., agent and attorney in fact of A. B., as the case may be,) has this day complained by affidavit before me, (describing the character of the officer,) that E. F. is justly indebted to the said A. B. in the sum of .... dollars, or thereabout, due by ..., (describing the nature of the claim,) and oath having been also made before me that (here recite the ground or grounds for attachment contained in the affidavit,) and bond with security having been given to me pursuant to the statute, you are therefore hereby commanded to forthwith attach the estate, real and personal, of the aforesaid E. F., in your county, to the full value of said demand, and the probable cost of this proceeding, and that you safely keep the property so attached or levied upon in your hands, unless replevied according to

law, so as to compel the aforesaid E. F. to appear before the ......
court of said county, to be held at ...., on the .... of ...., 18.., to
answer unto the complaint of the aforesaid A. B., and that you summons the said defendant, if to be found in your county, to be and personally appear at the court aforesaid, on the first day of the term above
named, then and there to answer accordingly.

"Witness (officers issuing the writ) this the .... day of ...., 18..."

§ 1430. If, at the time of issuing the writ of attachment, the attaching creditor shall suggest, that any person is indebted to the debtor,
or has property of his in his hands, or knows of any other person so
indebted, or who has effects or property of the debtor in his hands, the
officer issuing the writ of attachment shall insert therein a command
to the officer, to summon such person to appear on the return day of
the attachment, and answer, in writing, as garnishee of the defendant
in the attachment.

§ 1431. When two or more persons, not residing in this State, are
jointly indebted, the writ of attachment may be issued against such
debtors, or any of them, by their proper names, or by the name of the
partnership, or by whatever other name such debtors may be called, or
known in this State, or against the heirs, executors or administrators
of them, or any or either of them, and may be levied upon the separate
or joint estate, or both, of such debtors, and the lands, tenements,
money, goods, chattels, effects, rights and credits of such debtors, or
or any or either of them, shall be liable to be seized and taken, for the
satisfaction of any debt or demand, for which an attachment will lie
by this chapter.

§ 1432. The officer granting an attachment, may issue duplicate
writs to any other county in which the defendant may have property or
debts due him, which writs shall be returnable to the court to which the
original is returnable, and shall be executed and returned in like manner;
and when the attachment has not been executed, or where no property
has been found, or not sufficient to satisfy the debt, or where the
plaintiff desires to garnishee other persons, the clerk of the court,
to which the same is returnable, may issue *alias* writs, to the same
or other counties, without a renewal of the bond or affidavit.

§ 1433. Affidavits for attachments, and writs of attachment, may
be made and issued on the Sabbath day; and attachments may be
served and executed on that day, if necessary.

MODE OF LEVYING AND SERVING WRIT.

§ 1434. The officer who shall receive such attachment, shall forthwith serve and levy the same, upon the lands and tenements, money,
goods, chattels and debts of the defendants, wherever the same may
be found, or in the hands of any person indebted to, or having effects
of the defendant, and shall summon such person as garnishee, to
appear at the court to which the attachment is returnable, there to
answer on oath what he is indebted, or was indebted to the defend-

ant, at the time of the service of the attachment, or what effects of the defendant he hath in his hands, or had at the time of the service of the attachment, and what effects or debts of the defendant there are in the hands of any other person, to his knowledge or belief; and such officer shall have power to seize the books of account, and other evidences of indebtedness belonging to the defendant, and to summons, as garnishees, all persons appearing thereby to be indebted to the defendant, and to levy on the stock, share or interest which the defendant may have or own in any co-partnership or incorporated company; and all property, debts and choses in action attached, shall be bound by such attachment from the date of the service thereof; if the defendant can be found, the said officer shall also summon him to appear and answer the action.

§ 1435. Every writ of attachment shall be executed in the following manner, that is to say, in case of a levy on real estate, the officer shall go to the house or land of the defendant, or to the person or house of the person in whose possession the same may be, and then and there shall declare that he attaches the same, at the suit of the plaintiff in the said writ named. But in the event the land is wild, uncultivated or unoccupied, a return upon the writ, by the proper officer, that he has attached the land, giving a description thereof by numbers, metes and bounds, or otherwise, shall be a sufficient levy, without going upon the land. In case a levy on the stock, share or interest of the defendant in any co-partnership or incorporated company, the officer shall go to the office or place of business of such partnership or company, and in the presence of such officers, clerks, or agents thereof as may be present, shall make a similar declaration as in the case of real estate. In case of a levy on the rights, credits, and choses in action of the defendant, the officer shall seize and take into possession the books of account and all other evidences of indebtedness, if the same can be had, and shall summon all persons alleged to be indebted to the defendant, or to have effects of said defendant in their hands, to appear and answer as garnishees; and in case of a levy on money, goods or chattels of the defendant, the officer shall take the property into possession, and safely keep the same, to answer and abide the judgment of the court, unless such third person as may have the same in possession, shall enter into bond with security, to be approved by the officer, payable to the plaintiff in attachment, in double the value of the property attached, conditioned to have said property forthcoming to answer and abide the judgment of the court in said suit.

§ 1436. The officer serving an attachment, shall make a full report thereon of all his proceedings, on or before the return day of the writ. He shall deliver to the court or clerk, all bonds which he may have taken, pursuant to the law.

§ 1437. If a writ of attachment, returnable to the circuit court, be served by a constable or coroner, or marshal of a city, or by any other person specially appointed for that purpose, the writ of attachment, with the return thereon, and all property and effects levied on shall forthwith be handed to the sheriff of the proper county, who shall be responsible for the property so seized, unless such sheriff should be a party, in which event, the officer serving the attachment, shall make the return, and likewise retain the property, unless the court or judge, in vacation, shall make some order for the safe keeping and forthcoming thereof.

§ 1438. Any officer to whom a writ of attachment may be delivered, may, either before or after serving the same, demand of the plaintiff, or his agent or attorney, a bond of indemnity, to save him harmless from all claimants of the property seized, or to be seized, under such writ.

HOW PROPERTY MAY BE REPLEVIED.

§ 1439. The defendant, at any time before final judgment, may replevy the personal property seized, and taken into possession by the officer serving the attachment, by giving such officer a bond, with sufficient security, to be approved by him payable to the plaintiff, in double the value of such property, conditioned to have said property forthcoming, to answer and abide the judgment of the court in said suit, or in default thereof, to pay and satisfy the judgment to the extent of the value of said property; and on the execution of such bond, the said officer shall restore to the defendant, the property so replevied, and shall return the bond so taken, with the said writ of attachment, and all his proceedings thereon. Such replevy shall not affect the lien of the attachment. or the proceedings thereon, as to any rights, credits, or choses in action, of the defendant.

§ 1440. If any defendant in attachment shall, at any time before the return thereof, execute and deliver to the officer serving the same, a bond, with two or more sufficient sureties, to be approved by said officer, payable to the plaintiff in attachment, in a penalty double the amount claimed by said plaintiff, conditioned to pay and satisfy any judgment which may be recovered by the plaintiff in said suit, with all costs, the said attachment shall be thereby discharged ; and all the property of every kind levied on, attached, or seized by virtue thereof, shall be released and restored to such defendant. The said bond shall be returned with the attachment ; and in case of any recovery by the plaintiff in said suit, judgment shall be entered up against the defendant and the sureties in the said bond. After the return of said attachment. the bond herein provided for may be given, at any time before final judgment, and may be taken by the sheriff, or officer by whom the attachment was served, in case any of the attached property remains in his hands, or otherwise, by the clerk of the court in which the attachment is pending.

§ 1441. If the plaintiff shall be dissatisfied with the bond or security, given by the garnishee or the defendant, as hereinbefore provided, he may, within* sixty days after the return day of said attachment and bond, by petition to the judge of the court, or to one of the judges of the supreme court, obtain a citation to the sheriff, or other officer taking such bond, to appear before such judge, at such time and place as he may appoint, not less than five days after the service thereof, and show cause, if he can, why the said bond or the security shall not be adjudged insufficient; and such judge shall, then and there, examine said bond, and hear such testimony as either party may offer; and in case such judge shall consider the said bond, or the security, to be insufficient, then such sheriff or other officer shall be subject to the same judgment with the surety in such bond, in the same manner as if he were co-surety thereon.

PROCEEDINGS BY AND AGAINST GARNISHEES.

§ 1442. When any garnishee, duly summoned, shall fail to appear and discover, as by this chapter directed, the court shall enter a judgment against him for the amount of the plaintiff's demand, and all costs, and such judgment shall be final, unless cause be shown to the contrary during the same term, and execution shall issue thereon; *provided*, any such garnishee may answer under oath, to be certified by any person authorized to administer an oath, and forward the answer to the court in which said suit is pending.

§ 1443. Garnishees shall, in all cases, answer within the three first days of the return term, unless the court, for cause shown, shall grant further time ; and if, upon the answer or examination of any garnishee, it shall appear that there is any estate of the defendant's in the hands of any person not summoned, the court shall grant an attachment, to be levied on the property in the hands of such person, who shall appear and answer, and be liable as other garnishees.

§ 1444. If a garnishee admits an indebtedness not then due, execution shall be stayed until its maturity; and if he admits the possession of goods or chattels of the defendant, not seized by the sheriff, such goods or chattels shall be delivered to the sheriff, unless the garnishee shall give bond for the forthcoming thereof, as hereinbefore provided.

§ 1445. When the plaintiff shall allege that the garnishee has not made a full and true discovery of the debt due by him to the defendant, or of the property in his possession belonging to the defendant, he shall, at the term when the answer is filed, unless the court grant further time, controvert the same in writing, specifying in what particulars he believes the answer to be incorrect. The court may direct a jury to be empaneled immediately, unless good cause be shown for a continuance, to inquire what is the true amount due from such garnishee to the defendant, and what goods or chattels are in his possession belonging to the defendant; and the court shall grant judgment upon the verdict of the jury, as if the facts found had been confessed by the garnishee in his answer. If the answer of the garnishee be found true, he shall recover his costs against the plaintiff.

§ 1446. The courts having jurisdiction of an attachment, may summon any garnishee, from one county to another, who shall in all respects be proceeded against in the same manner as garnishees residing within the county where the attachment is returnable. If the garnishee, whose answer is contested, shall not be a resident of the county in which the suit is pending, then, upon an issue being made upon his answer, the venue for the trial of the issue shall be changed, on his application, to the county of his residence. The court in which the issue is tried, shall be authorized to grant new trials and continuances, as in other cases. and the verdict of the jury shall be certified by the clerk, and returned with the issue, to the court in which the suit is pending, and judgment shall be entered thereupon, as if the verdict had there been found.

§ 1447. No final judgment upon a garnishment shall go against a surety or accommodation endorsed, until judgment shall go against the principal, and the preceding endorsers or co sureties, who may be liable to judgment, if they be residents of this State.

§ 1448. If the personal property attached, or any part thereof, shall have been left in the hands of the garnishee, on his giving bond, as hereinbefore prescribed, or shall have been replevied by the defendant, the jury trying the issue between the parties, if they find for the plaintiff, shall assess the value of the property so left in the hands of the garnishee, or replevied by the defendant, as well as the debt or damages due the plaintiff; and if the value of the property shall equal the amount found due the plaintiff, judgment shall be entered against such garnishee and his sureties, or against the defendants and his sureties, on such replevin bond, for the amount of said verdict; and if the value of the property be less than the amount found due the plaintiff, judgment shall be entered against defendant, for the amount of the verdict, and against the sureties in his replevin bond, or against the garnishee and his sureties, for the value of the property so replevied, or left in the hands of such garnishee; and if judgment by default shall be entered, in such case, against the defendant, a writ of inquiry shall be awarded, to assess the value of the property so replevied, or left in the hands of the garnishee; on the execution thereof, judgment shall be entered, as above provided. In all cases provided for in this article, the judgment against the sureties of the defendant, or against the garnishee and his sureties, shall be satisfied and discharged, by the delivery to the sheriff of the county, of the property replevied or left in the hands of the garnishee, within ten day after execution on such judgment shall have come to his hands; and such sheriff shall sell the property so delivered to him, and apply the proceeds to the payment of the execution; and, in all cases, the valuation of the property, by the officer taking such bond, shall be *prima facie* evidence in favor of the plaintiff, of the value of the property.

§ 1449. The defendant, in attachment, may contest the answer of any garnishee, and may allege that the garnishee is indebted to him in a larger sum than he has admitted, or that he holds property of the defendant not admitted by the answer, and shall specify in writing, in what particulars the answer is untrue or defective; and

12

thereupon an issue shall be made up, or the answer and exception shall constitute an issue, to be tried by a jury; but this controversy shall not prevent the plaintiff from taking judgment for the sum admitted by the garnishee, or for the condemnation of the property admitted to be in his hands.

§ 1450. If the issue be found against the garnishee, judgment shall be rendered against him for the amount of money or property in his hands not admitted by him, which judgment shall be in favor of the plaintiff, if necessary to satisfy his judgment or claim against the defendant, or in favor of the defendant, if the judgment of the plaintiff has been satisfied, or for so much thereof as may remain after satisfying said judgment.

§ 1451. When a garnishee, by his answer, or at any time before or after final judgment against him, shall allege that he has been notified that another person claims title to, or an interest in the debt or property which has been admitted by him, or found by a jury to be due, or to be in his possession, and shall, if the question be of a debt due, pay into the court the amount thereof, the court shall suspend all further proceedings, and cause a citation to issue to the person so claiming to appear at the next term of the court, and contest with the plaintiff the right to such money or property ; or, if such claimant be a non-resident, publication shall be made in the same manner as against non-resident defendants in attachment.

§ 1452. If the claimant fail to appear, the court shall adjudge the money or property to the plaintiff. If he appear, he shall propound his claim to the debt or disputed property, in writing, under oath or affirmation, and the plaintiff may take issue thereon, and the same shall be tried and determined as other causes in said court, and the court shall adjudge the money or property to the party that may be found entitled to the same ; and in all such cases the garnishee shall be protected from all further liability to either party, in respect to such debt or property.

§ 1453. If a garnishee in attachment shall pay over or deliver, in pursuance of the judgment or process of the court, any money or property, which has been due, or belonging to the defendant before notice of any sale, assignment or transfer thereof, by the defendant, to any other person, such garnishee shall not thereafter be liable for said debt or property to the vendee or assignee thereof.

§ 1454. The garnishee shall be allowed, by the court, reasonable satisfaction for his attendance, out of the debt or effects in his possession; or against the plaintiff in attachment, in case there be no debt or effects in his possession; *provided*, he shall put in his answer at the return term of the attachment within the time prescribed by law.

ATTACHMENTS FOR DEBTS NOT DUE.

§ 1455. When any creditor, whose debt is not due, shall make affidavit that he has just cause to suspect, and verily believes, that his debtor will remove himself, or his effects, out of the state, before the said debt will become payable, with intent to hinder, delay or defraud his creditors, or that he hath removed, with like intent, leaving property in this state, and shall give bond, as in other cases, he may obtain an attachment in the county where the debtor resides, or last resided, or where his property may be found; which attachment shall be issued, executed and returned, and the like proceedings had thereon, as in other cases of attachment; and if the debtor shall not, on or before the return day thereof, enter into bond to the plaintiff, in double the sum due, with sufficient security, for the payment of said debt, when it shall become payable, and the costs of the attachment, the court, on due proof of the justice thereof, shall grant judgment, as in other cases of attachment; and on giving such bond, the same shall be handed over to the said plaintiff, and the attachment shall thereupon be discharged. When judgment shall be rendered, execution against any garnishee indebted to the defendant shall be stayed, until the claim of the plaintiff, or the garnishee's debt to the defendant, shall become due, and the goods and property attached shall be sold on a credit, until the time when the plaintiff's claim shall be payable. The sheriff, or other officer selling such property, shall take bond from the purchasers, payable to the plaintiff in attachment, for the amount of his debt, interest and costs, which bond shall be returned with the execution, and, if not paid at maturity. shall have the force and effect of a judgment. and execution may issue thereon, as on a judgment of a court of record; and where the property shall sell for more than the debt, interests and costs, the officer shall take a bond for the surplus to the defendant, and deliver the same to him; but no more property shall be sold than is necessary to satisfy the judgment, except where the property cannot be divided; and the officer making the sale shall only be entitled to commissions on the amount of the plaintiff's demand, and the costs and commissions shall be included in the bond or bonds, taken to the plaintiff, who shall be liable therefor to the officers of the court. If the defendant shall have replevied the property, execution against the defendant, and the sureties in the replevin bond, shall be stayed, until the plaintiff's claim becomes due and payable.

CLAIM BY THIRD PARTY.

§ 1456. When property is levied on, under any writ of attachment, and the same is claimed by any third party, as being his property, such third party shall be entitled to all the provisions made by law relative to claimant's issues, in the circuit court. growing out of levies under writs of *fieri facias*. All the proceedings shall conform to the provisions of the statute, relative to claimant's issues, herein referred to.

§ 1457. Such claimant in attachment cases, may have his claim tried without giving bond; but, in that case, the property shall not be replevied. All such issues shall be tried without delay, and the losing party shall pay all costs occasioned by the claim.

ALLEGED GROUND FOR ATTACHMENT CONTESTED.

§ 1458. The ground or grounds, stated in an affidavit for attachment, shall not be considered conclusive on the defendant; but he may, at the first term, proceed to contest the same in the following manner :

§ 1459. At the term to which the attachment is returnable, the defendant may file a plea in abatement of the attachment, traversing the ground or grounds upon which the writ was obtained.

§ 1460. This plea shall be sworn to, and when it is filed, the issue shall be considered as formed, without any response to the plea.

§ 1461. The court shall, at the first term, or as soon thereafter as practicable, and before any trial of the case on its merits, cause a jury to be empaneled, to try such issue, and determine, by their verdict, whether the attachment was wrongfully sued out or not.

§ 1462. On the trial of such issue, both parties may introduce all legal evidence relative to the issue, and the defendant may give evidence as to the damages, if any, which the issuance of such attachment has occasioned him, all damage he has sustained, including lawyer s fees, traveling expenses, hotel bills, loss of trade and special injury to his business ; but the defendant, when he files his plea in abatement, shall give plaintiff written notice of what special damages he will insist upon at the trial.

§ 1463. If such issue be decided for defendant, he shall have judgment in his favor for the damages assessed, and final process shall issue against plaintiff, and the sureties in his attachment bond, and for damages assessed by the jury, and the costs of suit, and the attachment shall be dismissed ; *provided*, that such judgment against the sureties in the attachment bond shall not exceed the penalty thereof.

§ 1464. If the issue be decided for plaintiff, the defendant shall be permitted to plead to the merits, without delaying the cause unreasonably, on such terms as the court may impose.

§ 1465. The plaintiff may dismiss his attachment, but defendant shall have a jury empanneled forthwith, to assess the damage sustained, by reason of suing out the attachment.

SALE OF PERISHABLE PROPERTY.

§ 1466. When goods and chattels are levied upon, under attachment, which are in danger of immediate waste and decay, they shall be sold in the manner following :

§ 1467. The officer levying on such goods, shall immediately summons three male house-holders of the county, and administer to them an oath, to examine such goods, and certify, in writing, whether, in their opinion, the goods are perishable.

§ 1468. If such house-holders certify that the goods are perishable, the officer holding them, shall sell them to the highest bidder, for cash, after a written notice, posted at three public places, in the supervisor's district where the goods were found, for two entire days before the sale ; the proceeds of such sale shall be held by the officer, to abide the result of the suit.

§ 1469. The owner of such goods may replevy the same, as in other cases, at any time before such sale occurs.

ATTACHMENTS BY AND AGAINST NON-RESIDENTS.

§ 1470. Non-resident creditors shall have the full benefit of the attachment laws of this State, for the collection of their claims against all persons residing or being within the State.

§ 1471. Non-resident creditors may also sue out attachments against their debtors residing without the limits of this State, and subject any property, or effects or credits of such non-resident debtors being within the State, to the payment of the demands of such non-residents creditors.

PUBLICATION AND NOTICE.

§ 1472. When a writ of attachment has been levied on the property of defendant, or served on any debtor of defendant as a garnishee, and it shall appear that the defendant has not been found, or that he was attached as a non-resident, it shall be the duty of the plaintiff to file in the court, or with the clerk thereof, an affidavit setting forth that said plaintiff hath been informed and verily believes the fact so to be, that said defendant is not within the State. The affidavit shall also state where said defendant is supposed to be, naming the post office where he receives his letters, if the plaintiff has any knowlege or belief as to that matter; and if plaintiff hath no such information, he shall so state in his affidavit.

§ 1473. When such affidavit is made and filed, it shall be the duty of the court, or the clerk thereof in vacation, forthwith to insert a notice in some newspaper printed and published in the county where the court sits; (if there be one), if not, in some convenient newspaper in another county, stating the pendency of such attachment, at whose suit it is brought, in what court, when returnable, and what sum is claimed; and citing the said defendant to be and appear before such court, and plead to the case; in default of which appearance, judgment by default shall be rendered, and the property sold, and the effects applied to the payment of plaintiff's claim ; *provided*, that in all suits of attachment against non-residents, or absconding debtors, before justices of the peace, advertisement shall be by posting notices in three or more public places, in accordance with this section.

§ 1474. The aforesaid notice shall be published for four consecutive weeks. It shall cite the defendant to appear at the return term of the attachment, if there be time for such appearance after the completion of the publication. If there be not time for such appearance, then the notice shall cite the defendant to appear at the next succeeding term of the court.

§ 1475. If the affidavit, made as herein provided, states the post-office of the defendant, then the clerk of the court or the justice of the peace, as the case may be, shall immediately forward, by mail, postage paid, to the address of such defendant, a copy of the notice inserted in the newspaper ; and the clerk or justice, forwarding such notice, shall make affidavit of the fact, stating the time when, and the place where, such notice was forwarded, and file the same in the papers in the case.

FINAL JUDGMENT AND SALES.

§ 1476. The defendant in attachment, may appear, by himself or attorney, without replevying the property attached, and defend the suit, as in other actions for the recovery of money, at any time before final judgment; but no judgment by default, regularly taken, shall be set aside, except upon cause shown ; and in case the defendant shall have been personally summoned, or shall appear and plead to the action, the judgment therein shall have the same force and effect, against the person and property of the defendant, as in other actions where a summons has been personally served on him: *provided, however*, that such appearance shall not vacate or affect any bond taken under this act, nor discharge any garnishee, nor affect any lien created by the attachment; but the proceedings in respect to any property attached, or any garnishee summoned, shall be the same as if final judgment had been entered by default, without any appearance of the defendant.

§ 1477. If the defendant shall not appear and plead to the action, in pursuance of the notice, the court, on proof of the publication thereof, shall give judgment against him by default, and award a writ of inquiry, if necessary; but on such judgment by default no execution shall issue, except against the property on which the attachment has been served, or against a garnishee who shall have money or property in his hands belonging to the defendant.

§ 1478. All the estate, real and personal, attached, and not replevied as aforesaid, and the stock, share or interest of the defendant, in any copartnership or incorporated company, shall be sold and disposed of towards the satisfaction of the plaintiff's judgment, in the same manner as property taken in execution on a writ of *fieri facias*; and all goods and chattels replevied by the defendant, or found in the hands of any garnishee belonging to such defendant, shall be liable to satisfy such judgment, and shall be delivered to the sheriff, or other officer, and sold in like manner; and judgment shall be entered up, and execution awarded, against every garnishee, for all sums of money due by him to the defendant, or in his custody or possession, for the use of such defendant, or so much thereof as shall be sufficient to satisfy the debt of the plaintiff and all costs.

§ 1479. After judgment obtained by the plaintiff by default, upon any attachments against non-residents, or absent defendants, upon proof of publication only, the plaintiff shall, before any sale be made, or execution issued against any garnishee, enter into bond, with security, to be approved by the court, or the clerk in vacation payable to the defendant, in double the amount of the judgment, conditioned that if the defendant shall, within a year and a day next following, come into court and disprove or avoid the debt recovered by the plaintiff against him, then the plaintiff shall restore to the said defendant the money he may have received towards the satisfaction of his demand, or so much thereof as shall be disproved or avoided; which bond shall be filed with the papers in the cause, and any sale made without such bond being given as aforesaid, shall be utterly void.

§ 1480. In the event that property be in the hands of an officer, levied upon under such judgments as those named in the last precedng section, and if the plaintiff shall fail and refuse, for ten days, to execute the bond named in said section, after due notice, in writing, served by the officer holding such property, then the said officer shall sell said property, according to law, and hold the proceeds for a year and a day, and then pay them to the party entitled to receive the same.

JURISDICTION AS TO ATTACHMENTS.

§ 181. Justices of the peace shall have full cognizance of attachments, in all cases, where the principal of the amount in controversy does not exceed the sum of one hundred and fifty dollars; and a the proceedings in such courts shall, as far as applicable, be conducted conformably to the provisions of this chapter.

§ 182. When a suit shall have been commenced, in any court in this State, the plaintiff may obtain an attachment against the defendants, or any one or more of them, on making affidavit, and givingbond, as required in other cases of attachment, which attachment shall be granted and issued by the same officers, and executed and returned, and the like proceedings shall be had thereon, as in other cases provided for by this chapter; and the affidavit, bond and attachment, when returned, shall be filed with the papers in the original suit, and constitute a part thereof, and the plaintiff may proceed to judgment, and the original suit shall not be delayed thereby.

§ 1483. When it shall appear to the court, on exceptions taken by the defendant, or otherwise, that the sureties on any attachment bond are insufficient, the court shall direct the plaintiff to give a new bond, with good and sufficient security ; and such bond shall be as valid, in all respects, as the original bond; and if the plaintiff shall fail to give a new bond, within the time required by the court, the attachment shall be dismissed ; and in all cases where an attachment bond or affidavit may be defective, in any respect, or may be lost or destroyed, the plaintiff shall be allowed to file a new affidavit and bond, which shall be, in all respects, as valid and binding, as if given at the commencement of the suit.

§ 1484. When an officer shall levy an attachment on live stock of any kind, he shall sell the same, for cash, by giving such notice of the sale as sheriffs are required to give, in making sales of personalty under executions ; but the officer may sell, on any day, after giving the required notice. If the defendant's residence be known, a copy of the notice shall be sent by mail to his post-office. The proceeds of such sale shall be held to abide the final result. Defendant may replevy the property any time before the sale.

§ 1485. Executors and administrators may be garnisheed, for a debt due by their testators or intestate, to the defendant; but no judgment shall be entered, in such case, against an executor or administrator, until the lapse of six months after the grant of his letters.

§ 1486. If the defendant shall die, after the service of the writ of attachment, the action shall not thereby be abated or discontinued, but shall be carried on to judgment, sale, transfer, and final determination, as if the defendant were still alive, and such death had not occured ; and all proceedings and deeds, in such cases are hereby declared to be as valid and effectual in law, as if had and made in the lifetime of such defendant.

§ 1487. Attachments may be executed by any constable, by the sheriff, by the coroner, or by the chief police officer of any incorporated town, or by a person specially appointed for such purpose, and sworn faithfully to perform such duty.

§ 1488. Attachment suits, and all issues growing out of them, shall be tried at the return term, unless good cause be shown for a continuance.

ATTCHMENTS AGAINST SHIPS, ETC.

An Act to provide a remedy by attachment against ships, steamboats and other water-craft.

SECTION. 1. Be it enacted by the Legislature of the State of the Mississippi, That when any person shall have any cause of action other than maritime contract, against the owner, captain, master, supercargo, or other person in charge of any ship, brig, schooner, sloop, steamboat, keel-boat, flat-boat, tug, boat or other water-craft, in any of the navigable waters of this state, or navigating the rivers or seas in or adjacent to this state, for, or on account of any such water-craft, or the business in which said craft may be employed, it shall be lawful to prosecute the same against such water-craft, by the name thereof, or by such description as will enable the officers executing the writ to indentify the same.

Sec. 2. Be it further enacted, That the person having such right of action, his agent or attorney, shall make complaint, on oath, to any judge or justice of the peace, stating the amounts of his demand to the best of his knowlege and belief, and naming or describing the said water-craft therein, and shall give bond, to be approved by said judge or justice, payable to the said water-craft, to the use of such person or persons as may be interested therein, in double the sum for which the complaint shall be made, in such form. and with such condition, as is required in other cases of attachment, and thereupon the said judge or justice shall grant an attachment, directed to the sheriff, or other proper officer, of any county in the state, returnable to the next term of the court, where the suit may be cognizable, and which shall be the leading process in such suit; and such sheriff or other officer shall serve and levy such attachment on said water-craft, wherever the same may be found, or on any personal property belonging to and contained therein, to an amount sufficient to pay said demand and costs.

Sec. 3. Be it further enacted, That all such attachments shall be repleviable at any time before sale of the property, or final judgment in the cause, by the owner, captain, master, supercargo, or other person in charge of the water-craft, against which the same may be issued, on such person giving bond to the sheriff, with sufficient sureties, payable to the plaintiff, in double the amount of the sum sworn to, conditioned that such person will appear at the next term of the court to which the attachment may be returnable, and abide by and perform such judgment or decree as the court may render in the premises, and said bond shall be returned into court, and in case judgment shall be given for the plaintiff, said judgment shall be entered against all the parties bound in said bond, for the amount adjudged in favor of the plaintiff, and all costs, and in the event of the death of any surety on the bond, the court may order a judgment *nisi*, to be entered against the personal representatives of such deceased security.

Sec. 4. Be it further enacted, That the proceedings on such attachments, except as otherwise provided, shall be, in all respects, the same as in case of attachment against absent debtors.

Sec. 5. Be it further enacted, That such attachments may be cognizable before a justice of the peace, for sums within his jurisdiction, and may be proceeded on in the same manner, and with like effect, as hereinbefore provided.

Sec. 6. Be it further enacted, That no such vessel shall be bound in the hands of a *bona fide* purchaser, without notice, for any debts or liabilities contracted or incurred before such sale, unless the action for the same shall be commenced within ninety days after such sale, or if the vessel be absent at sea or elsewhere, then within ninety days after the return of such vessel, if the money be due at the time of such sale; but if the money payable on such debt or liability be not due and payable at the time of such sale, then the action shall be brought within ninety days after the money shall become due and payable, or the return of the vessel as aforesaid.

SEC. 7. Be it further enacted, That the officer serving said attachment, shall summons the owner, captain, or other person having charge of such water-craft, to appear at the return term of said writ and answer accordingly, and such service shall be sufficient to authorize the court trying the same to proceed to final judgment, according to the provisions of this Act. Approved March 4, 1875.

REPLEVIN.

HOW OBTAINED, AND PROCEEDINGS THEREIN.

§ 1528. Whenever any goods and chattels are, or shall be, wrongfully taken or detained, an action of replevin may be maintained by any person having the right of immediate possession, for the recovery thereof, and for the damages sustained by reason of such wrongful taking or detention; *provided,* such action shall be brought within one year next after the plaintiff's right of action has occurred, and not after.

§ 1529. Before any writ of replevin, in such case shall issue, the plaintiff, or his agent or attorney, shall make and file in the office of the clerk of the circuit court, or with a justice of the peace, in cases within the jurisdiction of a justice of the peace, an affidavit, setting forth a description of the property taken or detained, and that the plaintiff is legally entitled to the immediate possession of the same ; that said property was wrongfully taken, or is wrongfully detained, by the defendant, and that the plaintiff's right of action has accrued within one year.

§ 1530. The writ of replevin shall command the sheriff or other lawful officer of the proper county, to take the goods and chattels specified in the affidavit, and to deliver the same to the plaintiff, upon the plaintiff entering into bond to the defendant, with sufficient security, in double the value of the property, to be ascertained by the valuation of the sheriff, or other officer into whose hands the writ may come, conditioned that he will prosecute the writ with effect, and without delay make return of the property to the defendant, if return thereof be adjudged, and pay the defendant such damages as he may sustain by the wrongful suing out of said writ, and also such costs as may be awarded against him, and save harm-

less the sheriff or other officer, as the case may be, for replevying
the said property; unless the defendant shall enter into bond, with
sufficient security in like penalty, payable to the plaintiff, conditioned that the property shall be forthcoming to satisfy the judgment of the court, and to summon the defendant to appear in court
on the return day of the writ, to answer to the action. And upon
the defendant entering into bond as aforesaid, the property shall be
restored to him.

§ 1531. The defendant shall give bond, as above provided,
within two days from the seizure of the property, and failing in that
time, the property shall be delivered to the plaintiff, as above provided; but if the plaintiff, when notified of the failure of the defendant to give bond, shall not himself give the required bond,
within a reasonable time, the property shall remain in the hands of
the sheriff, or other officer, until the trial, subject to the right of
either party, on application to the sheriff or other officer, to
be allowed to give bond and receive the property; and if either
party gives a bond, that shall not affect the suit, but it shall nevertheless proceed.

§ 1532. The declaration may be filed, after the issuance of the
writ; *provided*, it be filed on or before the first day of the return
term, or before any order of *nolle pros.* be taken; and the action
may be tried at the first term of the court. The defendant may
plead that he is not guilty of the premises charged against him, and
this plea shall put in issue, not only the right of the plaintiff to the
possession of the property, but also the wrongful taking and detention thereof. In cases before justices of the peace, the proceedings shall be as in other cases before them.

§ 1533. When the property shall have been permitted to remain
in the possession of the defendant, if the plaintiff recover, the judgment of the court shall be against the defendant and his sureties,
that they restore the property to the plaintiff, or pay him the value
thereof, as assessed by the verdict of a jury, and also for such
damages as shall have been assessed by the jury, for the wrongful
taking or detention; and the valuation of the sheriff, shall in all
cases, under this chapter, be *prima facie* evidence of the value of
the property.

§ 1534. If a plaintiff in replevin, to whom the property has been
delivered, fail to prosecute his suit with effect, the jury shall assess
the value of the property, and the damages sustained by the defendant, and the judgment of the court shall be against the plaintiff and his sureties, that they restore the property to the defendant,
or pay him the value thereof, so assessed, and also the damages so
assessed, for wrongfully suing out the writ. If the plaintiff make
default, or be non-suited, the defendant may have a writ of inquiry,
to assess the value of the property, and the damages sustained by
the wrongful suing out of the writ. And in the event of the death
of any surety upon such bonds, before the termination of the trial,
the court may order judgment *nisi* to be rendered against the personal representatives of such deceased surety, and the party may

have like judgment, upon the finding of the jury, as upon an issue found for him ; and if no bond was given, and the property remains in the hands of the sheriff, or other officer, the value of the property, and the damages sustained, shall be assessed, and judgment shall be for the recovery of the property, and the damages assessed against the party liable, and the sheriff or other officer shall deliver the property to the successful party, and the execution shall issue for damages and costs of suit.

§ 1535. If the party in whose favor the judgment is given be in possession of the property in controversy, he shall retain it, and a writ of *fieri facias* shall issue for the damages and costs of suit ; and if the property be in possession of the losing party, the execution shall command the sheriff to take the property in controversy, if the same may be had, and deliver the same to the successful party, and if not to be had, that he make the value thereof, together with the damages and costs, of the goods and chattels, lands and tenements, of the party and his sureties, against whom the judgment is rendered ; or the successful party may have his *distringas* to compel the delivery of the property, together with a *fieri facias* for the damages and costs.

§ 1536. The bond directed by this chapter to be taken in either case, shall be returned with the writ to the court issuing the same ; and if the sheriff fail to take a proper and sufficient bond, and return the same ; or if the bond taken be adjudged insufficient, and the party giving it shall, if required, fail to perfect the same, the sheriff shall be liable to the party injured, for all damages by him sustained, either by action of debt on his official bond, or by special action on the case : *provided*, the parties shall have the same right of amendment under this chapter as that given by the chapter providing the remedy by attachment.

§ 1537. If either party in such suit, or the sheriff, shall at any time deem any bond taken under this chapter to be insufficient, such party or sheriff, if in vacation, may, upon application to the judge of the court where such writ may be pending, obtain a citation, under the signature of said judge, commanding the obligor in such bond to appear before such judge, at such time and place as the said judge shall therein designate, and if in term time, such party or sheriff may proceed, by motion, against the obligor on such bond, and in either case the judge or court, shall, after hearing the evidence of both parties, determine the sufficiency or insufficiency of such bond ; and if the bond given by the plaintiff shall be adjudged insufficient, he shall give a new and sufficient bond, within the time limited by the court or judge, and in default thereof, the defendant shall be entitled to proceed and enter judgment, as in case the plaintiff should be nonsuited, or otherwise make default ; and if the bond of the defendant shall be adjudged insufficient, and he shall fail to give a sufficient bond, within the time limited by the court or judge, the plaintiff, on giving bond as by this chapter directed, shall be entitled to a judicial writ, commanding the sheriff to take the property in controversy, and deliver the same to the plaintiff ; and thereupon such proceedings shall be had as if the property had been delivered to the plaintiff in the first instance.

FORCIBLE ENTRY AND DETAINER.

IN WHAT CASES A REMEDY.

§ 1582. Any one deprived of the possession of land by force, or intimidation, or fraud, or stratagem, or stealth, and any landlord, vendor, mortgagee, or trustee, or *cestui que trust*, or other person against whom the possession of land is withheld, by his tenant, vendor, mortgagor, or grantor, or other person, after the expiration, of his right by contract, express or implied, to hold possession, and the legal representatives or assigns of him who is so deprived of possession, or from whom possession is so withheld, as against him who so obtained possession, or withholds possession, after the expiration of his right, and all claiming to hold under him, shall, at any time within three years after such deprivation or withholding of possession, be entitled to the summary remedy herein prescribed.

THE COMPLAINT.

§ 1583. The party so turned out of possession, or so held out of possession, may exhibit his complaint before any justice of the peace of the county or corporation within which such lands or tenements may lie, in the following form, or to the following effect, that is to say :

COUNTY, (*or corporation*) of........, to-wit :

A. B., of the said county (*or corporation*) complains that C. D., hath unlawfully turned him out of possession (*or unlawfully withholds from him the possession*) of a certain tenement (*describing it*), containing, by estimation,.... ...acres of land, with the appurtenances, lying and being in the county (*or corporation*) aforesaid, whereof he prays restitution of the possession.

A. B., Plaintiff.

Such complaint shall be verified by the oath or affirmation of the plaintiff, certified at the foot thereof, after the following manner : COUNTY, (*or corporation*) of ....to wit :

This day the above named A. B. made oath (*or affirmed*) before me, a justice of the peace for said county (*or corporation*), that he verily believes the allegations of the above complaint to be correct and true.

Given under my hand this.... ...day of.........

E. FIELD, J. P.

THE WARRANT.

§ 1584. The justice, before whom such complaint shall be made, shall thereupon issue his warrant, to the following effect:

COUNTY (*or corporation*) of........, to wit :

Whereas, A. B. hath made complaint, on oath (*or affirmation*), before me, a justice of the peace for the said county (*or corporation*), that C. D. hath unlawfully turned him out of possession (*or unlawfully, and against his consent, holds him out of possession*) of a certain tenement, and .... of land, with its appurtenances, lying and being in the said county (*or corporation*), and hath prayed restitution of the possession thereof; these are, therefore, in the name of the State of Mississippi, to require you to summon the said C. D. to appear at ...., (*which shall be at the usual place of holding justice's court, in said district*), on the ......day of ......, before the justices of the county (*or corporation*) aforesaid, to answer to the complaint aforesaid, and also require you to give notice of this warrant to two other justices of the peace for the said county (*or corporation*), and to request their attendance at the time and place aforesaid; and have then there this warrant. Witness my hand this......day of
....   E. FIELD, J. P.

§ 1585. The warrant aforesaid shall be directed to the sheriff or coroner, or any constable of the proper county, as the case may require, and shall be made returnable on a day certain, not less than five, nor more then twenty days after its date, and shall be forthwith executed by the proper officer, who shall make due return to the justices, at the time and place therein mentioned, of the manner in which he shall have executed the same.

§ 1586. The said warrant shall be served on the defendant, five days before the return day, either by delivering to him a copy thereof, or if he cannot be found, by delivering a copy thereof to any person of his family, above the age of sixteen years, at his usual place of residence, or if no such person be found, then by setting up a copy in some conspicuous place, on the tenement in the warrant mentioned.

§ 1587. At any time after such warrant shall have been issued, it shall be lawful for the justice issuing the same, upon the application of either party, to issue subpœna for witnesses, requiring them to attend at the court, before the justices, at the time appointed as aforesaid, to give evidence on the trial. Any subpœna so issued, shall be executed in the same manner, and shall have the same force and effect, as a subpœna, issued according to law, in a cause pending in the circuit court.

THE COURT.

§ 1588. It shall be the duty of the justices, notified as aforesaid, and of the justice who shall have issued the warrant, to attend at the place of holding a court, on the day therein specified for the trial of the complaint aforesaid, for which purpose such justices, or any two justices of the county, (*or corporation, as the case may be*), shall constitute a court. Such court shall be considered a court of record; they shall have power to issue all proper process to bring before them witnesses, or other persons whose attendance may be lawfully required by them; and they may adjourn from day to day, and from time to time, until the trial shall be ended. The sheriff or coroner, or constable, as the case may require, shall be attendant upon them, and execute their orders.

THE TRIAL AND FINAL JUDGMENT AND EXECUTION.

§ 1589. When the justices have so met, and formed a court, on the day and at the place aforesaid, if it shall appear to them that the defendant has been duly served with the warrant, they shall proceed, without further pleadings in writing to the trial of the complaint aforesaid.

§ 1590. In any action of unlawful entry, or unlawful detainer, the plaintiff may, on the trial, claim and establish, by evidence, any amount due for arrears of rent, of the tenement of which possession is sought, or reasonable compensation for the use and occupation thereof, during the time the same has been occupied by the defendant, not exceeding the sum of one hundred and fifty dollars; and the said justices shall find, upon the evidence, the said arrears of rent, or reasonable compensation, as aforesaid, and shall cause judgment to be entered up against the defendant in the action, for such arrears of rent, or reasonable compensation, as aforesaid, and award a writ of *fieri facias* thereon.

§ 1591. If the finding be for the plaintiff, the justices shall render judgment in favor of the plaintiff, that he recover possession of the tenement aforesaid, with full costs, and shall award a writ of *habere facias possessionem*, which shall be issued by the justice who commenced the proceedings.

§ 1592. If the finding shall be in favor of the defendant, the justices shall render judgment against the plaintiff, that his complaint be dismissed, and that the defendant recover of him full costs; and the judgment of said justices, rendered as aforesaid, either in favor of the plaintiff or the defendant, shall be executed in the same manner as if it had been the judgment of any other court of record in the state.

§ 1293. If the court shall be composed of but two justices of the peace, and they shall disagree in deciding, the decision of the justice before whom the complaint was made, shall be the judgment of the court.

APPEAL AND PROCEEDINGS.

§ 1594. Either party aggrieved by the judgment of said justices, may, after final judgment, appeal to the circuit court of the county, on the appellant, within five days after the rendition of the judgment, entering into bond and security, in the presence of the justice before whom the complaint was originally made, and approved by said justice, in a penalty of two hundred dollars, payable to the opposite party, conditioned for the payment of the costs before the said justices, and of all costs, that may accrue in the circuit court, in case the appellant fail therein ; but such appeal shall not operate as a *supersedeas ;* and the said justice shall send to the circuit court, all the papers and proceedings, and a transcript of all orders and judgments in said cause, and shall deliver the same to the clerk of the circuit court, to be there docketed for trial; and the said circuit court shall, at the first term, empannel a jury, and hear and determine the said cause anew on its merits, in a summary way, and may award restitution, if necessary.

§ 1595. When the plaintiff shall have claimed and obtained judgment, in any such action, for arrears of rent, or for the use and occupation of the property in controversy, the defendant, before he shall have an appeal, shall give bond in double the amount of such rent or damages, in addition to the penalty required in other cases ; and such bond, besides the condition required in other cases, shall also be conditioned, that the appellant shall pay such sums as may be adjudged against him in the circuit court, for arrears of rent or damages, for the use and occupation of the property in controversy ; and on the trial of the cause in the circuit court, the plaintiff may claim for all arrears of rent due at the time of such trial, or for the use and occupation of the premises up to that time, if the same shall have remained in the possession of the defendant, and the jury shall be charged to inquire and find the same ; and the court shall cause judgment to be entered against the defendant, and his sureties on the appeal bond, for the amount of such verdict, and award a *fieri facias* thereon, with legal interest and all costs ; *provided*, that the judgment against the surety shall not exceed the penalty of the appeal bond.

§ 1596. In all appeals to the circuit court, under this chapter, the said court, on motion of the appellee, may inquire into the sufficiency of the amount of the appeal bond, and of the security thereon, and may require a new bond, or additional security, on pain of dismissal of the appeal.

§ 1597. The clerks of the circuit courts are hereby required to tax in the bill of costs, after final judgment, all the costs that accrued on the trial before the justices, in all cases herein provided for, and include the same in the *fieri facias* by him to be issued for the costs accruing in the same case in said circuit courts.

MISCELLANEOUS PROVISIONS.

§ 1598. No judgment rendered as aforesaid, either for the plaintiff or the defendant, shall bar any action of trespass, or any action of ejectment, or other action between the same parties, respecting the same tenement ; nor shall any verdict, found as aforesaid, be held conclusive of the facts therein found, in any other action between the same parties.

§ 1599. Every justice of the peace, summoned to attend the justice aforesaid, and failing to attend, without sufficient cause therefor, shall be liable to a fine of twenty dollars, to be imposed by the said justice, for the use of said county ; and the said justice shall issue a *scire facias* against such defaulting justice of the peace, returnable to the next term of his court, to show cause why such fine should not be made final; and execution shall issue therefor, if judgment be made final.

§ 1600. The justices holding such court, and the sheriff or other officer attending the same, shall each be entitled to two dollars a day for attending the trial; and all other fees of witnesses and officers, for services rendered in relation to the proceedings and trial aforesaid, shall be the same as the fees for similar services, rendered in a suit at law, respecting the title to land, in the circuit courts, and shall be taxed in the costs.

§ 1601. The justice before whom the complaint is made under this chapter, may, before issuing any process, require the plaintiff to give bond, with security, for the payment of the costs; and in case judgment should go against the plaintiff, judgment shall be entered against him and the sureties on his bond, for the amount of costs.

LIEN OF MECHANICS.

WHEN LIEN ALLOWED.

§ 1603. Every house or other building, bridge, mill, or any addition erected thereto, and any fixed machinery, or gearing, or other fixtures for manufacturing purposes, and every boat or other water-craft, or paling, or other inclosure, hereafter erected or built within this state shall be liable for the payment of any debt contracted and owing for labor performed, or material furnished about the erection and construction or alteration or repairs, and such debts shall be a lien on such building or improvement, and on the land whereon it stands, including the lot or curtilage whereon the same is erected; but such lien shall only take effect as to purchasers and incumbrance in good faith, and for valuable consideration without notice of such lien, from the time of filing the contract, under which such debt was incurred, in the office of the chancery clerk of the county where such land is situated, to be recorded, or of the commencement of a suit in the proper court for the enforcement of such lien.

§ 1604. When any such building or other improvement shall be erected, in whole or in part, by contract, such building or improvement, and the land on which it stands, shall be liable to the contractor alone for work done or materials furnished in pursuance of such contract, and no building or land shall be liable for work done or materials furnished by any person not employed by the owner.

§ 1605. If any such building or improvement be erected by a tenant, or other person not being the owner of the land, then only the building and the estate of the tenant, or other person so erecting such building or improvement, shall be subject to the lien created by this act, unless such building be erected by the written consent of the owner of the land.

§ 1606. When any contractor or master workman shall refuse to pay any person, who may have furnished materials used in the erection of any such building or improvement, or the wages of any journeyman or laborer employed by him therein, such person, or such journey-

13

man or laborer, may give notice, in writing, to the owner of such building or improvement, of the amount due; and thereupon the amount that may be due by such owner, to the contractor or master builder, shall be bound and liable in the hands of such owner, for the payment of the sum so claimed; and if, after such notice, the contractor or master workman shall bring suit against the owner, the latter may pay into court the amount due on such contract; and the person giving such notice shall be summoned to contest the demand of such contractor or master workman; and the court may cause an issue to be made up and tried, and direct payment of the amount claimed by the person giving such notice, out of the money so paid into court; and in case such person giving such notice shall afterwards sue such contractor or master workman, he shall make the owner a party to the suit, and thereupon such owner may pay into court the amount due on such contract, or sufficient to pay the sum claimed, and costs, and the court shall award the same to the person that may be entitled thereto; and in neither of the above cases shall the owner be liable to pay costs; but if the owner, when sued together with such contractor or master workman, shall deny an indebtedness sufficient to satisfy the sum claimed, and all costs, the court, at the instance of the plaintiff, may cause an issue to be made up, to ascertain the true amount of such indebtedness, and shall give judgment, and award costs, according to the justice of the case.

§ 1607. When the contract, by virtue of which any such building or improvement is erected shall be in writing, such contract may be recorded in the office of the clerk of the chancery court of the county in which such building or improvement is situated, and the lien of the contractor shall commence from the time when such contract shall be filed for record.

. § 1608. All carriages, buggies, wagons, plows or any other article constructed or repaired shall be liable for the price of the labor and material employed in constructing or repairing the same; and the mechanic to whom the price of said labor and material may be due, shall have the right to retain possession of such things so constructed or repaired, until the same shall be paid for; and if the same shall not be paid within thirty days, shall commence his suit in any court of competent jurisdiction, and upon proof of the value of the labor and materials employed in such repairs or construction, shall be entitled to judgment against the party for whom such labor or materials were furnished, with costs, as in other cases, and to a special order for the sale of the property upon which the lien exists, for the payment thereof, with costs, and to an execution as in other cases, for the residue of what remains unpaid after sale of the property.

HOW LIEN ENFORCED..

§ 1609. Any person desiring to have the benefit of the lien given by this chapter, shall commence his suit in the circuit court of the county in which the property is situated, within six months next after the time when the money due and claimed by such suit became due and payable, and not after; and such suit shall be commenced by petition, describing with reasonable certainty the property upon which the lien is intended to operate, and setting out the nature of the contract and indebtedness and the amount thereof; and the plaintiff shall file therewith in all cases, except where the whole work or materials, or both were furnished in pursuance of a writen contract for an aggregate price, a bill of particulars, exhibiting the amount and kind of labor performed, and of materials furnished, and the prices at which and times when the same was performed and furnished; and such suit shall be docketed and conducted as other suits in said court.

§ 1610. All persons having an interest in the controversy, and all persons claiming liens on the same property, by virtue of this chapter, shall be made parties to the suit; and should any necessary or proper party be omitted, he may be brought in by amendment, on his own application, or that of any other party interested; and claims of several parties having liens on the same property, may be joined in the same action.

§ 1611. The defendant shall be summoned, as in other actions at law, to appear and defend the action; and in case any necessary party defendant shall be a non-resident of, or absent from the State, or cannot be found, the court may direct publication to be made. in some newspaper published in this state, for the space of one month, requiring such party to appear on a day to be therein named; and in default of such appearance, the same proceedings shall be had, as if such defendant had been duly summoned, and had made default.

§ 1612. The defendant or any of them, may, by answer to said petition, set up any defense they may have against the demands of the plaintiff, and also any counter-claim against the plaintiff, touching the subject matter of the suit; and should any defendant claim to have a lien upon the same property, for any materials furnished, or labor done thereon, he may set the same up by his answer, and the cause shall be deemed at issue, without a replication, and the parties shall be confined, at the trial, to the causes of action and defense set forth in the pleadings.

§ 1613. The court may direct the formation of such issues, to be tried before a jury, as may be necessary for the determination of all matters controverted in the pleadings; and such issues shall be tried by the same rules of evidence and practice, that prevail in other cases at law; and the court may set aside verdicts, and grant new trials, and give judgment, according to the justice of the case.

§ 1614. In case judgment be given for the plaintiff against the builder, it shall, in case he was actually served with process. be entered against him generally, with cost, as in other cases, and with a special order for the sale of the property upon which the lien exists, for the payment thereof, and for an execution. as in other cases, for the residue of what may remain unpaid, after the sale of the property; and when the defendant is brought in by publication only, and has not adpeared in person or by attorney, the judgment shall be entered specially for the debt and costs, to be made of the buildings and lands in the petition described; and in case no general judgment is given against the builder, such proceedings or recovery shall be no bar to any suit for the debt, except for the part thereof actually made under such recovery.

§ 1615. When the judgment shall be against the building and land, or against the building alone, a special writ of execution shall issue, to make the amount recovered, by sale of the property, which shall be described therein; and when both a general and special judgment shall be given, both writs may be issued, either separately or combined in one, or one may be issued after the return of the other for the whole or the residue, as the case may require.

§ 1616. Under such special execution, the sheriff shall advertise, sell and convey said building and lot, or the building alone, in the same manner as in other cases of land levied on for debt; and the deed given by said sheriff, if for the building or improvement alone, shall convey the same to the purchaser, free from any former incumbrance on the land, and shall authorize him to enter and remove the same from the land, with reasonable dispatch; and if such deed shall be for the land also, it shall convey to the purchaser such estate therein as the owner or builder, as the case may be, had at the time when the lien under which the sale is made attached thereon, or at any time afterwards, subject to all prior incumbrances; and moreover, shall convey the building to the purchaser, in the same manner as if the sale was of the building alone.

§ 1617. All lien claims for erecting the same building or improvement, shall be concurrent liens upon the same, and the land whereon the same is erected, and shall be paid in proportion, out of the proceeds thereof, when sold by virtue of this chapter; and in case the sheriff shall have doubts as to the proper application of the money, he may return the same to the court, stating the question, for its determination.

§ 1618. Justices of the peace shall have jurisdiction of cases arising under this chapter, where the amount is within their cognizance, and the proceedings shall be as nearly in accordance with the provisions of this chapter as may be practicable, and the parties shall have the right of appeal, as in other cases.

LANDLORD AND TENANT.

REMEDY FOR RENT BY ATTACHMENT.

§ 1620. If any lessor of lands or tenements, his executor or administrators, agents or attorneys, shall make complaint on oath before any justice of the peace of the county where such lands or tenements are situated, that his tenant, his executor or administrator, is indebted to him for rent due and in arrear on such leased premises, specifying the sum due, and shall give bond and security as required in cases of attachment against absent debtors, such justice shall issue an attachment against the goods and chattels of such tenant, directed to the sheriff or any constable of the county, commanding him to distrain the goods and chattels of such tenant, to an amount sufficient to satisfy the rent so due and in arrear, and all costs.

§ 1621. The officer making a distress, shall give notice thereof, with the cause of such taking, to the tenant or his representatives in person, if to be found, or if not found, by leaving such notice at the dwelling house or other most notorious place on the premises charged with the rent distrained for; and shall forthwith advertise the property distrained for sale, in not less than ten days after such notice, on the premises, or at some convenient public place; and if the tenant or owner of the goods distrained, shall not, before the time appointed for the sale, replevy the same, by giving bond, with security, to be approved by such officer, payable to the plaintiff in such attachment, in double the amount claimed, conditioned for the payment of the rent claimed, with lawful interest for the same, and all costs, at the end of three months after making such distress, the said officer shall sell the goods and chattels so distrained, at public sale, to the highest bidder, for cash, and shall, out of the proceeds of the sale, pay all the costs of the proceedings and shall pay to the plaintiff the amount of his demand, with interest.

§ 1622. When any landlord or lessor, shall have just cause to suspect, and shall verily believe, that his tenant will remove his effects from the leased premises to any other place, within or without the county, before the expiration of his term, or before the rent will fall due, so that no distress for rent can be made, such landlord or lessor, on making oath thereof, and of the amount of rent the tenant is to pay, and at what time the same will fall due, and giving bond, as required in the last preceding section, may, in like manner, obtain an attachment against the goods and chattels of such tenant; and the officer making the distress shall give notice thereof, and advertise the property distrained for sale, in the manner directed in the last preceding section; and if such tenant shall not, before the time appointed for such sale, give bond, with sufficient security, in double the amount of the rent, payable to the plaintiff, conditioned for the payment of the said rent, at the time it shall fall due, with all costs, the goods distrained, or so much thereof as may be necessary, shall be sold by the said officer, at public sale, to the highest bidder, for cash, and out of the proceeds of the sale, he shall pay all the costs, and shall pay to the plaintiff the amount due him for rent, deducting interest for the time until the rent shall become payable.

§ 1623. When any tenant shall have actually removed his effects, from the leased premises, before the rent has become due, so that there be no sufficient property liable to distress, left on the premises, the landlord may, in like manner, obtain an attachment at any time after such removal, or within thirty days after such rent becomes due, and may levy the same on the effects so removed, wherever they may be found, and like proceedings shall be had thereon, as in other cases.

§ 1624. If any tenant shall at any time convey, or carry off from the demised premises, his goods or chattels, leaving the rent, or any part thereof, unpaid, the landlord or lessor may, within thirty days next after such conveying away, or carrying off such goods or chattels, cause the same to be taken and seized, according to the provisions of this article, wherever the same may be found, as a distress for the arrears of such rent, and the same to sell in the same manner, as if they had been distrained in or upon the demised premises; *provided,* that no goods or chattels, so carried off, and sold in good faith, for a a valuable consideration, before such seizure made, shall be afterwards liable to be so taken and seized, for any arrears of rent.

§ 1625. Every replevin bond, taken in pursuance of this chapter, shall mention that the same was entered into for goods or other estate distrained for rent, and restored to the debtor, and shall be forthwith delivered to the lessor for whom distress was made ; and if the money shall not be paid, according to the condition of such bond, any court having jurisdiction of the amount thereof, shall, on motion, award execution against the obligors therein ; said bond being filed in such court, and five days' notice given of such motion.

§ 1626. Any person having rent in arrears, or due upon any lease for life, years or otherwise, ended and determined, or his executors or administrators, may distrain for such arrears, after the termination of the respective leases, in the same manner as if the same had not been determined ; *provided,* that such distress be made within six months after the termination of such lease, and during the continuance of such landlord's title or interest, and during the possession of the tenant from whom such arrears are due.

§ 1627. It shall not be lawful for any person taking any distress to drive or remove the same out of the county where such distress was taken; and if any person shall so remove any goods or chattels distrained as aforesaid, he shall pay to the party aggrieved double the value of the property removed, to be recovered in an action of trespass on the case; and moreover, distresses shall, in all cases, be reasonable and not too great, and any person who shall make an unreasonable distress, under color of this chapter, shall be liable to the action of the party aggrieved for full damages.

§ 1628. Upon any pound breach or rescous, of goods or chattels distrained for rent, the person aggrieved thereby shall, in a special action upon the case, for the wrong thereby sustained, recover treble damages, with costs of suit, against the offenders, or any of them, in any such pound breach or rescous, or against the owner of the goods distrained, in case the same be afterwards found to have come to his use or possession.

TENANT'S REMEDY AGAINST LANDLORD.

§ 1629. In case any distress and sale shall be made, under color of this chapter, for rent pretended to be due and in arrear, where, in truth, no rent is due or in arrear to the party causing such distress to be made, then the owner of the goods and chattels so distrained and sold, his executors or administrators, shall have remedy by action of trespass on the case, against the person in whose name or right such distress was taken, his executors or administrators, and shall recover double the value of the goods and chattels so distrained and sold, together with full costs, or may put the bond of the plaintiff in suit, to recover damages for the wrongful suing out of said attachment, and shall recover therein double the value of the goods and chattels, if the penalty of the bond amount to so much.

§ 1630. The tenant or defendant, his executors or administrators, may replevy the goods and chattels distrained for rent, at any time before sale thereof; but before any writ of replevin shall be granted in such case, he shall enter into bond, to be approved by the clerk granting the same, with one or more sufficient sureties, payable to the party in whose name or right such distress was made, in a penalty of double the amount of rent distrained for, conditioned to perform and satisfy the judgment of the court in such suit, in case he shall be cast therein : and if, upon the trial of such suit, it shall be found that the full amount of rent distrained for was justly due, and the distress lawfully made, the party injured or delayed by suing out said writ, besides a judgment for a return of the goods and chattels replevied, which shall be entered against the party replevying said goods, and the sureties in his replevin bond, shall also have judgment for the amount of the rent in arrear and distrained for, with interest and full costs of suit; and in case the goods replevied shall be restored, the same shall be sold, and if the sale thereof shall not be sufficient to satisfy said judgment, execution shall go against the party replevying, and his sureties, for the residue.

REPLEVIN BY THIRD PERSON.

§ 1631. No goods or chattles found, or being in or upon any demised premises, and not belonging to the tenant, or to some person bound or liable for the rent of said premises, shall be liable to be distrained for the said rent ; but if the tenant, or person liable for said rent, have a limited property or interest in such goods or chattels, the same shall be liable to be distrained and sold for the property or interest such tenant, or other person liable for said rent, may have therein ; and no person claiming title to such property distrained for rent, shall in any manner avail himself of the provisions of this article, unless by a writ of replevin, sued out and levied before the sale of such property under the distress ; such writ of replevin shall issue in favor of such claimant, on his making and filing an affidavit that the goods and chattles distrained are his property, and not the property of the tenant, nor held in trust for the use of the tenant in any manner whatsoever, and that the same, in his opinion, are not liable to such distress, and giving bond and security for double the value of the property attached ; and in case such claimant be cast in the suit, judgment and execution shall be had, as in cases of replevin by the tenant ; and upon such claim being made, the landlord, or person making such distress, may release the property so claimed, and forthwith seize and attach other property of the tenant in lieu thereof.

§ 1632. For the mere speedy determination of all such writs of replevin, every such writ shall be returnable to the next term of the court after the same shall be issued; and the court shall, at the return term, cause an issue to be made up therein, and the same shall be tried at the same term. If the plaintiff in such writ shall make default, or fail to prosecute the same, like judgment shall be entered against him, and the sureties on his bond, as upon an issue found against him, and no new replevin or writ of second deliverance shall be allowed therein.

REMEDY BY ACTION AT LAW TO PERSONS HAVING RENT IN ARREARS.

§ 1633. Any person having rent in arrear or due upon any lease or demise of lands or tenements for life, or lives, for years, at will or otherwise, may bring an action of debt or covenant for such arrears of rent, in case the lease or demise be under seal; or an action of debt or assumpsit in case the lease or demise be by parol or not under seal, against the person who ought to have paid the same, his executors or administrators.

§ 1634. All persons being grantees or assignees of any lands, tenements or hereditaments let to lease, or of the reversion thereof, from any person or persons and the heirs, executors, administrators and assigns of such grantees or assignees shall and may have and enjoy the like advantages against the lessees, their executors, administrators and assigns, by entry for the non-payment of the rent, or for doing of waste or other forfeitures, and also shall, and may have and enjoy all and every such like covenants and agreements contained and expressed in the leases, demises or grants, against all the said lessees, their executors, administrators and assigns, as the said lessors themselves or their heirs ought, should or might have had or enjoyed, at any time or times.

§ 1635. All lessees of lands, tenements and hereditaments, for a term of years, life or lives, their executors, administrators or assigns, shall and may have like action and advantage against all and every person or persons, their heirs and assigns, which have or shall have any gift or grant of the reversion of the said lands, tenements or hereditaments, so letten, or any parcel thereof, for any condition, covenant or agreement contained or expressed in the indentures of their lease or leases, as the same lessees, or any of them, might and should have had against the said lessors, and their heirs, all benefit and advantage of recoveries in value, by reason of any warranty in deed or law, only excepted.

§ 1636. The executors and administrators of any person, unto whom any rent is or shall be due and not paid at the time of his death, shall and may have an action of debt, covenant or assumpsit for all such arrearages, against the tenant or tenants who ought to have paid the said rent, so being behind in the lifetime of their testator intestate, or against the executors or administrators of such tenants; and it shall and may be lawful for every such executor and administrator of any such person to whom such rent is or shall be due, and not paid at the time of his death, to distrain for the arrearages of all such rents on the lands, tenements and hereditaments, which were charged with the payment of such rents, and chargeable to the distress of the said testator or intestate, so long as the same continue in the seizen or possession of said tenant, who ought immediately to have paid the said rent so being behind to the said testator or intestate in his lifetime, or in the seizure or possession of any person or persons claiming the said lands, tenements and hereditaments only by and from the said tenant, by purchase, gift or descent, in like manner and form as their said testator or intestate might or ought to have done in his lifetime; and the said executors and administrators, for the same distress lawfully may make avowry upon the matter aforesaid.

§ 1637. If any man who now hath, or hereafter shall have, in right of his wife, any estate in fee simple, or for term of life of, or in any rents or fee farms, and the said rents or fee farms now are, or hereafter shall be due, behind and unpaid, in said wife's life, then the said husband, after the death of his said wife, his executors and administrators, shall have an action for the said arrearages, against the tenant of the demesne, who ought to have paid the same, his executors or administrators; and also, the said husband, after the death of his said wife, may distrain for the said arrearages, in like manner and form, as he might have done if his said wife had then been living, and may make avowry upon the matter aforesaid.

§ 1638. Any landlord, where the agreement is not by deed, or when there is no contract, may recover a reasonable satisfaction for the lands, tenements or hereditaments, held or occupied by the defendant, in an action on the case upon promises, for the use and occupation of what was so held or enjoyed; and if there shall appear in evidence, on the trial of such action, any parol demise, or agreement, (*not being by deed, whereon a certain rent was reserved*), the plaintiff in such action shall not therefor be non-suited, but may make use thereof, as evidence of the amount of damages to be recovered.

GENERAL PROVISIONS.

§ 1639. When a tenant for life, who shall have demised any lands or tenements, shall die, on or after the day when any rent became due and payable, his executors or administrators may recover from the under tenant, the whole rent due in action of assumpsit, or other proper form of action. If he die before the day when any rent is to become due, they may recover in like manner the proportion of the rent which accrued before the time of his death; and the tenant for the life of another, his executors or administrators, shall have the like remedies, in case of the death of the person by whose life the estate is held, on or before the day when any rent shall become due.

§ 1640. In all cases in which a notice is required to be given by the landlord or tenant, to determine a tenancy, two months' notice in writing shall be given, where the holding is from year to year, and one month's notice shall be given where the holding is by the half year or quarter year; and where the letting is by the month or by the week, one week's notice in writing shall be given.

§ 1641. When any distress shall be made for rent justly due, and any irregularity or unlawful act shall afterwards be done by the party distraining, or his agent, the distress shall not therefore be deemed unlawful, nor the party making it a trespasser from the beginning, but the party aggrieved by such irregularity or unlawful act, may maintain an action of trespass, or on the case, and recover the special damage he may have sustained thereby; *provided*, that such action shall not be sustained, if tender of amends has been made by the party distraining, before suit brought.

§ 1642. When any tenant, being lawfully notified by his landlord, shall fail or refuse to quit the demised premises and deliver up the same as required by said notice, or when any tenant shall give notice of his intention to quit the premises by him holden, at a time specified in such notice, and shall not accordingly deliver up the said premises at the time in said notice contained, then, and in either of such cases, the said tenant shall from thenceforward pay to the landlord double the rent which he should otherwise have paid, to be levied, sued for and recovered at the same times and in the same manner as the single rent or sum, before the giving such notice could be levied, sued for, and recovered, and such double rent shall continue to be paid during all the time such tenant shall continue in possession as aforesaid.

§ 1643. If any tenant of lands or tenements, being in arrear for rent, shall desert the demised premises, and leave the same uncultivated or unoccupied, so as no sufficient distress can be had to satisfy the arrears of rent, any justice of the peace of the county may, at the request of the landlord, and upon due proof, by the affidavit of said landlord, or some other credible person, that the premises have been so deserted, leaving such rent in arrear, and no sufficient distress thereon, go upon and view the said premises, and upon being satisfied, upon such view, that the premises have been so deserted, he shall affix a notice, in writing, upon a conspicuous part of the premises, stating what day he will return to take a second view thereof, not less than five nor more than fifteen days thereafter, and requiring the tenant then to appear and pay the rent due. At the time specified in such notice, the justice shall again view the premises ; and if, upon such second view, the tenant shall not appear and pay the rent due, or there shall not be sufficient distress upon the premises, then such justice may put the landlord into the possession of the said demised premises, and the lease thereof to such tenant, as to any demise therein contained, shall from thenceforth become void. The tenant may appeal to the circuit court from the proceedings of the justice, at any time within thirty days after such possession delivered, by serving notice, in writing, thereof, upon the landlord, and by giving bond, with security, to be approved by such justice, for the payment to the landlord of all costs of such appeal, which may be adjudged against such tenant : and thereupon the justice shall return the proceedings before him to the next term of the circuit court, and said court shall, at the return term, examine the proceedings in a summary way, and may order restitution to be made to such tenant, with costs of appeal, to be paid by the landlord; or in case of affirming such proceedings, shall award costs against the tenant, and the sureties in his bond.

§ 1644. In case either party to any action of replevin shall die, pending the same, the suit shall and may be revived for or against the representatives of the deceased party, in the same manner as other actions at law that survive may be revived.

§ 1645. The officer issuing any attachment for rent shall be entitled to the sum of one dollar and fifty cents for taking the affidavit and bond and issuing the writ, to be paid by the party applying for the same, which shall be collected, together with the rent, and refunded to such party; and the sheriff or other officer serving said attachment shall be entitled to the same fees and commissions as are allowed to sheriffs for serving an attachment against absconding debtors and levying money thereon.

§ 1646. Any tenant or lessee, at will or sufferance, or for part of a year, or for one or more years, of any houses, lands or tenements, and the assigns, under tenants, or legal representatives of such tenant or lessee may be removed from such premises by any justice of the peace of the county, or by the mayor, chief magistrate or justice of the peace of any incorporated city or town, where such premises are situated, in the following cases, to-wit: 1st. Where such person shall hold over and continue in possession of the demised premises, or any part thereof, after the expiration of his term, without the permission of the landlord.

§ 1647. *Second:* where such person shall hold over, without such permission as aforesaid, after any default in the payment of rent, pursuant to the agreement, under which such premises are held, and satisfaction of such rent cannot be obtained by distress of any goods, and a demand for such rent shall have been made, or three days' notice in writing, requiring the payment of such rent, or the possession of the premises, shall have been served by the person entitled to such rent, on the person owing the same, in the manner prescribed by this chapter for the service of the summons.

§ 1648. The landlord or lessor, his legal representatives, agents or assigns, shall make oath or affirmation of the facts, which according to the last two preceding sections, authorize the removal of the tenant, describing therein the premises claimed, and the amount of rent due and when payable, and in the case of a tenancy at will, or at sufferance, that the necessary notice has been given to terminate such tenancy.

§ 1649. On receiving such affidavit, the justice, mayor, or other officer, shall issue a summons, directed to the sheriff, or any constable of the county, or the marshal, police officer, or constable of any incorporated city or town wherein the premises are situated, describing the said premises, and commanding him to require the person in possession of the same, or claiming the possession thereof, forthwith to remove from the same, or to show cause, before such justice or other officer, on a day to be therein named, not less than three nor more than five days from the date of said summons, why possession of the said premises should not be delivered to such applicant.

§ 1650. Such summons shall be served, by delivering a copy to the tenant, and at the same time, showing him the original ; or, if he be absent from his last, or usual place of residence, by leaving a copy at such place, with some person of the age of sixteen years, or if no such person be residing at such place, then by putting up such copy in some conspicuous place on the premises where such tenant last or usually resided ; and the officer serving such summons, shall forthwith make due return thereof to the magistrate who issued the same.

§ 1651. If, at the time appointed, it appear that the said summons has been duly served, and if no sufficient cause be shown to the contrary, the magistrate shall thereupon issue his warrant to the sheriff, or any constable of the county, or to any constable, marshal, or police officer of the city or town where the premises are situated, commanding him to remove all persons from the said premises, and to put the said applicant to said magistrate into the full possession thereof.

§ 1652. The person in possession of such premises, or any person claiming possession thereof, may, at or before the time appointed in such summons for showing cause, file an affidavit with the magistrate who issued the same, denying the facts upon which the said summons was issued, or any such facts, and the matters thus controverted, may be tried by the said magistrate, or, at the request of either party, by a jury.

§ 1653. On the filing of such affidavit by the tenant, and on the request of either party, the magistrate shall issue his precept to the sheriff, or any constable of the county, or any constable, marshal or police officer, of the city or town, commanding him to summons six reputable persons, qualified as jurors in courts of record, to appear before such magistrate, at such time and place as he shall therein appoint, not more than three days from the date thereof, for the purpose of trying the said matters.

§ 1654. The persons so summoned as jurors, if not excepted to, shall be sworn by such magistrate, well and truly to hear, try and determine, the matters in difference between the parties. If, for any cause, a sufficient number of competent jurors shall not be present, the magistrate shall forthwith, without writ, cause others to be summoned. After hearing the allegations and proofs of the parties, the said jury shall be kept together by the officer summoning them, until they agree on their verdict. If such jury cannot agree, the magistrate may discharge them, and issue a new precept, in manner aforesaid, for another jury.

§ 1655. The magistrate may, at the request of either party, adjourn the hearing, from time to time, no one adjournment to exceed ten days, except by consent, and may issue subpœnas and attachments, to compel the attendance of witnesses ; and every person who, being served with such subpœna, shall fail to appear, or, appearing, shall refuse to testify on oath, touching the matters aforesaid, shall be liable to the same proceedings and penalties, provided by law in similar cases ; and the jurors summoned, and failing to attend, without sufficient excuse, shall be liable to the same penalties as in similar cases.

§ 1656. If the verdict of the jury be in favor of the lessor or landlord, or other person claiming the possession of the premises, the magistrate shall issue his warrant to the sheriff, constable, or other officer hereinbefore named, commanding such officer forthwith to put such landlord, lessor, or other person, into the possession of the premises, as hereinbefore directed, and to levy the costs of the proceedings of the goods and chattels, lands and tenements, of the tenant or person in possession of the premises, who shall have controverted the right of said landlord, lessor, or other person ; and whenever a warrant shall be issued, as provided in this chapter, by any magistrate, for the removal of any tenant from any demised premises, the contract or agreement, for the use of the premises, if any such exist, and the relation of landlord and tenant between the parties, shall be deemed to be cancelled and annulled ; *provided*, that nothing in this chapter contained, shall be construed to impair the rights of any landlord or lessor, or of any tenant, in any case not herein provided for.

§ 1657. If the verdict be in favor of the tenant, he shall recover his costs of the applicant, and the magistrate shall issue execution therefor.

§ 1658. In case the proceeding is founded upon the non-payment of rent, under section 1467 of this chapter, the issuance of the warrant for the removal of the tenant shall be stayed, if the person owing said rent shall, before such warrant be actually issued, pay the rent due, and all the costs and charges of the proceedings, or give such security as shall be satisfactory to the said magistrate, to the person entitled to such rent, for the payment thereof, and costs, as aforesaid, in ten days ; and if the said rent and costs shall not be paid accordingly, the warrant shall then issue, as if the proceedings had not been stayed.

§ 1659. The magistrate before whom any proceedings shall be had under this chapter, shall keep a full record of his proceedings, and shall carefully preserve all process and papers in the cause, and the same costs shall be taxed and paid as are allowed for similar service, in cases of forcible or unlawful entry or detainer.

§ 1660. The circuit court of the proper county may award a *certiorari*, for the purpose of examining any adjudication made on any application hereby authorized ; but the proceedings shall not be stayed or suspended, by such writ of *certiorari*, or by any other writ, or order of any court officer ; upon such *certiorori*, the circuit court shall have power to examine into the correctness of all the decisions of the officer before whom the proceedings were had, upon questions of law only ; and also to require the return of such parts of the proceedings, as are material to an examination of such questions upon their merits. Whenever any such proceedings, brought before the circuit court by *certiorari*, shall be reversed or quashed, the court may make restitution to the party injured, with costs, and may make such orders and rules, and issue such process, as may be necessary to carry their judgment into effect; and if the proceedings shall be reversed or quashed, the tenant or lessee may recover against the person making application for such removal, any damages he may have sustained, by reason of such proceedings, with costs, in any action on the case.

BASTARDY.

PROCEEDINGS BEFORE JUSTICE OF THE PEACE.

§ 1802. When any single woman, who shall be delivered of a child, which by law would be deemed and held a bastard, or being pregnant with child, which, if born alive, would be a bastard, shall desire to make complaint against the father of such child, she may make such complaint to any justice of the peace of the county where she may be so delivered ; or in case the child is unborn, then to any justice of the peace where she may reside ; and thereupon such justice shall issue a warrant for the person accused, to be served by the sheriff, or any constable, and shall cause him to be brought before such justice forthwith ; and upon his appearance, the justice shall proceed to question the female, in presence of the party accused, touching the charge against him, which examination shall be taken down in writing ; and if such justice should think the complaint well founded, the said justice shall bind the accused in a bond, with sufficient sureties, in a penalty of not less than five hundred dollars, to be and appear at the next circuit court of the county, to answer the complaint, and in default of such surety may commit the accused.

PROCEEDINGS IN CIRCUIT COURT.

§ 1803. It shall be the duty of the justice to return all the proceedings to the next circuit court; which court, if the woman should desire it, may cause an issue to be made up, whether the reputed father is the real father or not, which issue shall be tried by a jury, as other issues in said court ; and on the trial thereof, both parties shall be competent witnesses.

§ 1807. No proceedings, under this act, shall be instituted after the child is twelve months old.

PRESERVATION OF OYSTERS---THE GAME LAWS.

§ 1889. The boards of supervisors of the respective counties within this state, shall have full power and jurisdiction for the protection and preservation of the oysters growing, or being grown, and of the game running or being produced, in a state or condition of nature, within the territorial limits of each county respectively; and to regulate the times, places and circumstances, under which either may be taken, and by whom and in what quantities, and to what extent made marketable; and with ample power to conserve the same for domestic use, and consumption of the citizens and sojourners of the counties respectively, and also to secure a private right of property, in oysters banked, planted or cultivated in the waters of the county. And to this end, said boards of supervisors may, from time to time, pass all such ordinances, in form of orders or resolutions, as they may respectively deem necessary; and such ordinances shall, from the date of their adoption, or from such prospective date as may be specified, have the same force and effect as if enacted by the legislature of this state, and shall remain in force until repealed by said boards.

§ 1890. The said boards may respectively direct the publication of such ordinances, in such manner as they may judge most expedient; and copies thereof, certified by the clerk of the board, shall at all times be taken as sufficient authentication of said ordinances.

§ 1891. The judicial administration of said ordinances, shall pertain as matters of police, to any justice of the peace in the counties respectively, whether the act complained of transpired in his beat, or elsewhere in said county, or before any magistrate of any city or town, within said county, whether designated as mayor, or by any other title; and the breach of any ordinance prescribed by the board of supervisors, shall be decreed and taken to be a misdemeanor, and a violation of the police order, and subject to forfeiture of the oysters or game taken in violation of such police regulations, and to such fine and imprisonment as may be prescribed by said ordinances, or to one or more of these penalties; and such complaints shall be summarily heard and disposed of, as other matters affecting the public peace and order.

§ 1892. It shall be the duty of all sheriffs, constables, and town and city marshals, within the county, to seize, with or without process, any person or persons, whom they may see and know, or have good reason to believe, to be violating any such police regulations, and to seize all such oysters or game, found in the possession of such person, in violation of said police regulations, together with the boats, casts, or other conveyances or things, in which the oysters or game may be held or contained; and, first securing the same, shall forthwith convey the person or persons from whose custody the game or oysters shall have been taken, before any magistrate or justice of the peace, as aforesaid, to be dealt with according to the rules and regulations prescribed by such boards for such offense.

§ 1893. It shall be competent for the boards of supervisors, in cases of forfeiture of the articles seized, to determine the disposition to be made of them; and if there be any delay given to the party arrested, for the hearing of the case, the magistrate may cause the articles seized, to be disposed of before the hearing, and the proceeds to be held to abide the result.

Section 1. Be it enacted by the Legislature of the State of Mississippi, That it shall be unlawful in any place in this state to catch, kill or injure, or pursue with such intent any wild buck, deer, doe or fawn, between the fifteenth day of May and the fifteenth day of September; and it shall be unlawful to catch, kill or injure, or pursue with such intent, any wild turkey, between the first day of May and the fifteenth day of September; and it shall also be unlawful to catch, kill or injure, or pursue with such intent any quail, sometimes called partridge, between the first day of April and the fifteenth day of September; and it shall be also unlawful to catch, kill or injure, or pursue with such intent, any turtle-dove, sometimes called mourning dove, or any starling, commonly known as field lark, between the first day of April and the fifteenth day of September; and it shall be unlawful at any and all seasons to catch, kill or injure, or pursue with such intent, the mocking bird, cat bird, or thrush.

Sec. 2. Be it further enacted, That no person shall destroy or rob the nests of any wild bird whatever, excepting crows, black birds, blue jays, hawks, owls, and other birds of prey.

Sec. 3. Be it further enacted, That it shall be unlawful for any person to purchase, have in his possession or expose for sale any of the birds or game, mentioned in section one of this act, during the season when the catching, killing or injuring the same is prohibited.

Sec. 4. Be it further enacted, That it shall be unlawful for any railroad company, express company, or other company, steamboat, or carrier, or private individual to have in possession or receive for transportation or carriage, or for any other purpose whatever, any of the birds or game mentioned in section one of this act, during the season when the catching, killing, or injuring the same is hereby prohibited.

Sec. 5. Be it further enacted, That any person or persons violating the provisions of this act, by killing, selling or offering for sale, or having in possession any of the birds, or game mentioned in this act, during the season hereby prohibited, or any fresh venison, during the season mentioned in section one, shall for each of the birds, and each head of game, and each piece of fresh venison so killed, sold, or exposed for sale, or had in possession, on conviction thereof, forfeit and pay a fine of not less than three or more than ten dollars for each bird, and not less than ten, or more than twenty dollars for each buck, deer, doe, or fawn, or piece of fresh venison, and three dollars for each nest of eggs destroyed as aforesaid, together with costs of prosecution.

Sec. 6. Be it further enacted, That any violation of the provisions of this act may be prosecuted before any justice of the peace or any other officer or court having jurisdiction of misdemeanors, and the judgment of such court shall be enforced in like manner, as in other cases of misdemeanor.

Sec. 7. Be it further enacted, That upon collection of any judgment record for any violation of the provisions of this act, one-half of such fine or judgment shall go to the informer and the other half shall go to the common school fund.

Sec. 8. Be it further enacted, That it is hereby made the duty of all sheriffs, constables, market masters, members of boards of supervisors and police officers to arrest all persons violating, or in the act of violating, any\of the provisions of this act, and take them before a justice of the peace or other officer having jurisdiction to hear and try complaints for the violation of the provisions of this act.

Sec. 9. Be it further enacted, That if any person or persons shall take, catch or kill, or attempt to take, catch or kill any of the birds or animals mentioned in this act upon the lands or premises of any owner, who has posted the same, forbidding such trespass, unless he or they shall first have obtained the consent of such owner or owners or other person or persons in charge of such land or premises, shall be deemed guilty of a misdemeanor, and fined not less than ten nor more than fifty dollars, to be recovered in the same manner and appropriated as other fines under this act; *provided*, that this act shall not apply to any one shooting birds on his place to prevent them from depredating upon his vineyard or garden. (Approved, March 31, 1876.)

SUPPLEMENTAL GAME LAW.

Section 1. Be it enacted by the Legislature of the State of Mississippi, That section 1st of an act entitled an act for the preservation of game, animals and birds, in the State of Mississippi, approved March 31st, 1876, be and the same is hereby so amended and supplemented as to substitute the 15th day of March for the 15th day of May and the first day of April, where the same occurs in said section. (Approved, April 14th, 1876.)

Fences, Partition Walls and Trespass by Stock.

WHAT IS A LAWFUL FENCE.

§ 1905. All fences five feet high, substantially and closely built, with plank, pickets, hedges or other good material, and which are strong and close enough to exclude domestic animals of ordinary habits and disposition, shall be taken and considered as lawful fences, as long as they are kept in good repair.

§ 1906. A fence which is constructed by making a strong embankment of earth, two feet and a half high, with sufficient base, and erecting thereon a fence of common rails, planks, pickets or hedges, the same height above the embankment, closely and substantially built, so as to exclude ordinary stock, shall also be taken and considered as a lawful fence, as long as it is kept in good repair.

§ 1907. A fence made of common rails, and built in the form known as a worm fence, and which is six feet high, built of good, sound and heavy rails, well lapped and crooked, shall be considered as a lawful fence, as long as it is kept in repair; *provided*, that such fence be close enough to exclude ordinary domestic animals.

14

§ 1908. Persons owning adjoining land, or lots of land, or being lessees thereof for more than two years, shall be bound to contribute equally to the erection of fences on the line dividing the land or lots, if the land or lots on their respective sites be used by the owner or lessee thereof, for purposes of cultivation, or for horticultural purposes, or for the purposes of depasturing cattle, horses, hogs, or sheep, or if a lot be used as an enclosure for any other purpose; and each party shall be bound to contribute equally towards keeping partition fences in good repair, so long as the land or lot be used as aforesaid; but no owner shall be bound to contribute to the erection of a dividing fence, either now built or to be built, or to the keeping the same in re- repair, who may prefer to erect a fence of his own, and to leave a lane on his own land, between himself and the adjoining owner; but the failure to erect such fence, for the space of sixty days, shall be deemed an abandonment of the intention to do so, and a determination to adopt the fence built; and the party so failing, shall then be bound to pay his proportion of the value of the fence already erected.

§ 1909. In case any owner or lessee of land, shall desire to erect a fence, on a line which divides his land from the land of another person, which is used by that other person for any of the purposes aforesaid, and that other person being requested to do so, will not contribute his proper share of the work, and furnish the requisite materials, suitable for the description of fence necessary to be built, or pay the value of his share, the party desiring to build the fence, may erect or construct the whole of it, of a proper and suitable kind, which shall be a lawful fence, and may thereafter apply, in writing, to any justice of the peace of the county, to appoint proper persons to assess the amount which should be contributed by the other party; and such justice shall, under his hand and seal, appoint three respectable, impartial house-holders of the neighborhood, to view the fence, and determine what amount should be paid to the party who erected the same, by the party who owns the adjoining land, who has failed to contribute to making the · fence. The opposite party shall have five days' notice of the time of the meeting of the house-holders, which notice may be served person- ally, or on an agent, or left at the dwelling of the party, if he be ab- sent, and each party may introduce proof of the value of the fence; and the said house-holders, or a majority of them, may assess the amount to be paid by the one party to the other, and shall give to the party entitled to the compensation, a certificate, under their hands, stating the amount they assess in his favor; and thereupon such party may maintain an action for the amount assessed by the house-holders, or a majority of them, before a justice of the peace, if the amount be within his jurisdiction, or before any court having jurisdiction; and the order of the justice appointing the house-holders, or proof thereof, if it be lost, and the certificate of the house-holders, or proof of notice to the opposite party, of the time of the meeting of the house-holders, shall be sufficient evidence to support the action. The house-holders shall each receive one dollar and fifty cents per day, whilst discharging the duty, to be paid by the party at whose instance they were appointed, who may recover the amount as costs, and the justice shall be entitled to one dollar for issuing the order, to be paid and recovered in like manner.

§ 1910. In case any partition fence has been heretofore built, on a dividing line, and the adjoining land be used by the owner thereof, for any of the purposes aforesaid, the party who built the same, shall, in like manner, be entitled to compensation, to the extent that ought to be contributed by the owner of the adjoining land; and in case of refusal to pay the same, the amount may be assessed, and a recovery had, in the same manner as for erecting a new fence.

§ 1911. Each proprietor of land or lots, separated by a partition fence, on the line, shall be bound to contribute his due proportion of labor and materials, in keeping such fence in good repair, so far as to make it a lawful fence; and on failure to do so, the party who may make the necessary repairs on the same, may, in the manner above described, apply to any justice of the peace, who shall appoint three house-holders to view the repairs, assess the value, and give a certificate thereof; and for the amount assessed, a recovery may be had, as above provided, and the same notice shall be given of the meeting of the house-holders, who shall be entitled to like compensation, and the same fee may be charged by the justice of the peace.

§ 1912. Partition fences erected and paid for, and kept in repair, as provided in the preceding sections, shall be owned jointly by the respective proprietors, either of whom may require the other to contribute to repairing it; but it shall not be taken away, razed, removed, or left down by either party, without the consent of the other; and if either party should violate this provision, he shall be liable to the action of the other party, as a stranger would be; and each party shall be liable to the other for injuries or trespasses committed by his stock, by the breaking of the partition fence; but no party shall be bound to contribute towards keeping a partition fence in repair, after he shall have ceased to use the land which is so divided by it.

§ 1913. When, from natural impediments, it shall be impracticable to erect the entire fence on the line, and it shall become necessary to make some departure on either side, such departure may be made; but the fence shall, notwithstanding, be a partition fence.

§ 1914. In case any joint owner of a partition fence, should desire to have a lane on his own land, between his own and the adjoining land, he shall be at liberty to remove his part of the fence, on giving six months' notice to the other joint owner, but not otherwise; and any proprietor who may remove from his land, and cease to use it for any of the purposes before mentioned, shall thereby abandon his right to the partition fence; but in case of the sale of the premises to another person, the purchaser shall have the same right, and incur the same liabilities, as the original owner, in regard to the partition fences; and a lessee for a longer time than two years, shall stand in the attitude of a purchaser during his term; but if the lease be for two years, or a shorter time, the owner shall still be bound to contribute towards the erection and repair of partition fences, if either the owner or the tenant use the land, as before mentioned, in such cases, the notice served on the tenant, if the owner be absent, shall be sufficient.

§ 1915.   The party who built the partition fence may remove it at pleasure, if the owner of the adjoining land will not pay his proportion thereof; and although the proprietor of any land may desire to retain any fence built by him, on a line which divides his land from that of another person, as a private fence, yet that other person may adopt the same as a partition fence, by paying his proportion of the value thereof; and if the value cannot be agreed upon by the parties, the person desiring to adopt the fence, may apply to a justice of the peace to appoint three house-holders, to assess the proportion that should be paid, in the same manner as provided in section nineteen hundred and nine, article two, of this chapter.

§ 1916.   Any agreement for erecting walls, which parties may make who own adjoining lots, and desire to build partition walls, shall be binding, whether in writing or not; and in case of the failure of either party to comply with his contract, the other may have his appropriate action for damages.

§ 1917.   If the owner of any lot shall build a substantial and durable brick wall, on the line which divides his lot from another, and the owner or lessee of that other, should desire to erect an adjoining building, and connect the same with the building already erected, so as to make the wall of the former building serve as the wall of his own, he may do so, but shall be compelled to pay the owner of the first wall half the value thereof, or half the value of so much of the former wall as he may desire to use as a wall to his own house; but he shall not be at liberty to use the former wall, in any way which may prove dangerous or detrimental to the owner, or which shall interfere with the purposes for which said wall was originally built, except by closing the lights therein, which he may do.

§ 1918.   No person shall be at liberty to join or use such wall, as a partition wall between buildings, without first paying to the owner thereof one-half the value of so much as may be desired to be used; and if the parties cannot agree as to the value, either party may apply to the mayor or chief magistrate of the town, or to any justice of the peace of the town or county, in writing, desiring the appointment of suitable persons to assess the amounts to be paid; and such mayor or justice, shall thereupon appoint three respectable mechanics, skilled in that description of work, to assess the amount which the one shall pay to the other, which shall be equivalent to half the value of so much of the wall as may be desired to be used as a partition wall; and such mechanics, or a majority of them, shall examine the wall, and assess the amount to be paid to the owner thereof, and give a certificate of such examination and assessment, to the party at whose instance they were appointed; but the opposite party shall have five days' notice of the time of the meeting of the appraisers, and their names, which notice may be served personally, or upon an agent, if the party be absent, or it may be left at his dwelling house.   On payment or tender of the amount assessed, the party desiring to use the wall, may proceed to do so, but not otherwise ; and if his work be then interfered with, he may have restraining process by bill in chancery.

§ 1919. If the appraisers appointed should, from any cause, fail to discharge the duty, new appraisers may be appointed ; and if either party should present exceptions to the mayor or justice, to any of the appraisers, and the mayor or justice should be of opinion that the exception is well founded, a new appraiser or appraisers may be appointed, and either party shall be at liberty to introduce proof, before the appraisers, as to the value of the wall.

§ 1920. Any partition wall, which has been so paid for, and is used as such, shall not be removed by either party, without the consent of the other ; nor shall it be so damaged or altered, as to render it less valuable to either ; and if either party should violate this provision, he shall be liable to the other as a trespasser, for all damages that may be sustained.

AS TO TRESPASS BY STOCK.

§ 1921. Every owner of cattle, horses, mules, hogs, sheep, jacks, jennies, or goats, shall be liable for all injuries and trespasses, committed by such animals, by breaking into the enclosure or grounds of another, enclosed by a lawful fence ; and for the first trespass or injury, if the damages do not exceed one hundred and fifty dollars, a recovery may be had before a justice of the peace ; but if the damages exceed one hundred and fifty dollars, suit may be brought in the circuit court ; and for every succeeding offense, after the owner has been notified of the first traspass or injury, double damages shall be recovered, with costs, before a justice of the peace, if the actual damages, when doubled, do not exceed his jurisdiction; but if they do, then before the circuit court ; but in no case shall the damages be assessed at less than two dollars for each horse, mare, mule, ox, bullock or cow, that may break into the enclosure of another. For breaking into a pasture or waste ground, double damages shall not be recoverable, and the damages in such cases may be assessed as low as one dollar for every horse, mare, mule, ox, bullock or cow, that may break into any pasture, or other uncultivated or waste ground.

§ 1922. Any horse, mare, mule, ox, bullock, cow, jack or jenny, habitually addicted to fence breaking, may be taken and confined by any person, into whose enclosure or ground such animal may have broken ; and the owner of such animal, shall pay to the person who has taken up the animal, seventy-five cents per day, whilst it may be so kept, which charge shall be paid before the animal is taken away; *provided*, the owner, if known, be notified of such detention, which, however, shall not affect the right of recovery, unless unreasonable delay has occurred in giving the notice.

§ 1923. The condition of the fence, at the time the trespass complained of was committed, may be shown in mitigation of damages, or to defeat a recovery ; but the party suing shall be notified, at least five days before the trial, that the sufficiency of his fence will be controverted, so that he may come prepared to show its condition, by rebutting testimony.

§ 1924. If any person, whose fence is not a lawful one, shall hurt, wound, lame or kill, by shooting, hunting with dogs, or otherwise, any of the kind of horses, horned cattle, hogs, sheep, goats, jacks, or jennies, that may have broken into his enclosure, he shall pay to the owner thereof, double damages, recoverable before a justice of the peace, if within his jurisdiction, or before the court having jurisdiction; but if the person liable for damages, as aforesaid, will pay to the party injured what shall be deemed reasonable and just, by three respectable neighbors, indifferently chosen, to assess the same, it shall be a bar to such suit; and if the party injured, be thereto requested, will not submit the matter to neighbors, as aforesaid, or will not join in choosing such neighbors, then the party liable to such damages, may choose them; *provided*, the foregoing provisions shall not extend to any joint owner of a partition fence, who has failed to make the proper repairs thereof, as against his co-owner.

§ 1925. If any person shall throw down any gate, bars, fence or fences, enclosing land not his own, without the permission of the owner, or shall in any manner injure or deface any building not his own, he shall pay to the owner twenty dollars for every such offense, to be recovered before a justice of the peace; and shall, moreover, be liable to all damages that may have resulted from such act.

Obstructions to Water-Courses, Mills, Dams, and Duties of Millers.

HOW MILLS AND DAMS MAY BE BUILT.

§ 1927. When any person, owning lands on one side of any water-course, the bed whereof belongs to himself, or owning lands on one side of a water-course, the middle of the bed whereof shall be the dividing line between the lands of himself and another person, and desiring to build a water grist mill, cotton gin, or other machine or engine useful to the public, on such lands, and to erect a dam across the same, for working said mill, cotton gin, or other machine or engine, shall not himself have the fee-simple property in the lands on the opposite side thereof, against which he would abut his dam, he shall make application for a writ of *ad quod damnum*, to the board of supervisors of the county wherein the lands proposed for the abutment are, having given ten days' previous notice to the proprietor thereof, if he be found in the county, and if not, then to his agent therein, if any he have, which court shall thereupon order their clerk to issue such writ, to be directed to the sheriff, commanding him to summon and empanel twelve fit persons, being householders, to meet upon the lands so proposed for the abutment, on a certain day, to be named by the court, and inserted in said writ, of which day notice shall be given by the sheriff to the proprietor, or his agent, as before directed, if neither of them was present in court at the time the order was made.

§ 1928. The jurors taken shall be charged, on oath, by the said sheriff, impartially, and to the best of their skill and judgment, to view the said lands, so proposed for an abutment, and to locate and circumscribe, by certain metes and bounds, one acre thereof, having due regard therein to the interests of both parties, and to appraise the same according to its just value; to examine the lands, above and below, of the property of others, which may be probably overflowed, and say what damage it will be to the several proprietors, and whether the mansion house of any such proprietor, or the offices, curtilage or garden thereunto immediately belonging, or orchards, will be overflowed; to inquire whether, and in what degree, fish of passage and ordinary navigation will be obstructed; whether by any, and by what means, such obstruction may be prevented; and whether, in their opinion, the health of the neighborhood will be damaged by the stagnation of the waters.

§ 1929. The inquest, so made and sealed by said jurors, together with the writ, shall be returned by said sheriff to the succeeding supervisors' court, who shall thereupon order a summons to be issued to the several persons, proprietors or tenants of the lands so located or found liable to damages, if they be found within the county, and if not, then to their agents therein, if any they have, to show cause why the party applying should not have leave to build the said mill, cotton gin, machine or engine, and dam.

§ 1930. If any person, proposing to build such mill, cotton gin, machine or engine, and erect such dam, shall have the fee simple property in the lands on both sides of the stream, or owning the lands on one side of a water-course, shall desire to erect such mill, cotton gin, machine or engine, and to abut his dam on any rock or island in the said water-course, or in any other manner to extend his dam only in part across such water-course, not abutting it on the opposite bank, he shall apply to the board of supervisors of the county wherein the mill house, cotton gin, machine or engine will stand, for a like writ, which writ shall be directed, executed and returned as prescribed in the former case. The owner of such rock or island, or his agent, if to be found, either in the county in which such writ may be applied for, or in the county in which the rock or island may be, shall have like notice of the application for such writ, and of the execution thereof, as is herein provided to be given to the owner of land on the opposite side of the stream, or his agent.

§ 1931. If, on such inquest, or on other evidence, it shall appear to the court that the mansion house of any proprietor, or the offices, curtilage or garden thereto immediately belonging, or orchards, will be overflowed, or the health of the neighbors be annoyed, they shall not give leave to build the said mill, cotton gin, machine or engine, and erect the said dam; but if none of these injuries are likely to ensue, they shall then proceed to consider whether, all circumstances weighed, it be reasonable that such leave should be given, and shall give, or not give it, accordingly; and if given, they shall lay the party applying under such conditions, for preventing the obstruction, if any there be, of fish of passage and ordinary navigation, and for preventing any impediment to the convenient crossing of the water-course on which the dam may be erected, as to them shall seem right.

§ 1932. If the party applying obtain leave to build the said mill, cotton gin, machine or engine, and erect the said dam, he shall, upon paying respectively to the several parties entitled, the value of the acre located, and the damages which the jurors find will be done by overflowing the lands above and below, become seized in fee simple of the said acre of land, and be authorized to proceed to erect such mill, cotton gin, machine or engine, or dam. But if he shall not begin to build the same within one year, and finish it within three years, after such leave of the court obtained, so that it be in good condition for public use; or if such mill, cotton gin, machine or engine be at any time destroyed, or rendered unfit for public use, and the owner or occupier thereof shall not begin to rebuild or repair it within one year, and finish such rebuilding or repair, so that it be in good condition for public use, within three years from the time of such destruction or unfitness for use, the title to any land condemned under this act shall revert to the former owner, his heirs or assigns, and the leave granted by the court to erect any such mill, cotton gin, machine or engine, or dam, shall cease and be void; saving, however, to all persons *non compos mentis*, infants, *femmes covert*, or imprisoned, and to all persons out of the State in the service thereof, or of the United States, three years after their several disabilities are removed, for the purpose of rebuilding or repairing any mill, cotton gin, machine, engine or dam, belonging to them at the time of its destruction, or of its becoming unfit for public use; and saving, also, the right of remainder men and reversioners, in the manner herein provided.

§ 1933. If at any time any tenant, for life or years, of any such mill, cotton gin, machine or engine (except those erected by such tenant himself, after the commencement of his estate), which has been or shall be destroyed, or which has become or shall become unfit for public use, shall have failed to commence or finish the rebuilding or repair thereof, within the time hereinbefore limited, it shall be lawful for the person next entitled in remainder or reversion to such mill, cotton gin, machine or engine, to enter thereupon, and to rebuild or repair the same, and to hold and enjoy it, with its appurtenances, for his own use and benefit; *provided*, that such remainder-man or reversioner, if under none of the legal disabilities herein enumerated at the time when such right shall accrue, shall make such entry, and complete such rebuilding or repair, within three years from the time of the failure of such tenant for life or years, or if *non compos mentis*, an infant, *femme covert*, or imprisoned, or if out of the State, in the service thereof, or of the United States, shall make such entry, and complete such building or repair, within three years after the disability removed.

§ 1934. When any owner of a mill, cotton gin, machine or engine heretofore or hereafter established by law, may think it necessary to raise his dam, the board of supervisors of the county wherein the pond lieth, upon application to them, shall grant a second writ of *ad quod damnum*, to value the additional damage done thereby, under the same rules and regulations as hereinbefore directed.

§ 1935. If any person, not being authorized, as hereinbefore provided, shall make or erect any embankment, levee, dam, or other obstruction, in or over any water course, so as to cause the water to overflow on the land of any other person, to the injury of said land, or of any crop growing or planted thereon, and shall fail to open or remove the same on request, the person thus injured may make complaint, in writing, to any convenient justice of the peace of the county, who shall thereupon issue a summons to the opposite party to appear before him, at a time and place therein to be named, which shall be directed to and executed by the sheriff or any constable of the county, and returned in the same manner as other process issued by a justice of the peace in civil cases; and upon the return of said summons, three householders of the neighborhood shall be chosen, one by the said justice, one by the party complaining, and the third by the defendant, or if he shall fail to choose, then the third shall be chosen by the said justice; and the said householders shall be forthwith summoned to appear before the said justice; and after being sworn, faithfully and impartially to discharge the duties required of them, the said householders shall proceed to examine the obstructions complained of, and they, or a majority of them, shall report, in writing, to the said justice whether, in their opinion, such obstructions injure the land of the party complaining, or do, or may prevent him from planting a crop thereon, or will injure the same when planted; and if they, or a majority of them, report in favor of the party complaining, and the opposite party shall fail immediately to remove such obstruction, the said justice shall issue his precept to the sheriff, or some constable of the county, commanding him forthwith to cause such obstruction to be removed, so as to afford free passage for the water; and it shall be the duty of such officer to employ such force as may be necessary, and to proceed without delay to remove such obstruction, on being indemnified for the expense, by the party complaining, if he shall require it.

§ 1936. Any householder who shall fail to attend, when summoned, without sufficient excuse, or shall fail to discharge the duty herein required, shall be fined, by the said justice, in the sum of twenty dollars; and should any of said householders fail to attend, or serve, or be excused, others may be forthwith summoned to supply their places.

§ 1937. If any person shall, in any manner, stop or cause to be stopped, any embankment, levee or dam, or replace, or cause to be replaced, any obstruction ordered to be opened or removed, in pursuance of the last preceding section, or shall obstruct, impede, or otherwise hinder or interrupt the opening or removing of any embankment, levee, dam or other obstruction, ordered to be opened or removed in pursuance of said article, such person shall be liable to indictment, and, on conviction, may be fined not exceeding five hundred dollars, or imprisoned not exceeding six months, or both, at the discretion of the court.

§ 1938. No inquest taken by virtue of this act, and no opinion or judgment of the court thereupon, shall bar any public prosecution or private action, which could have been had or maintained, if this act had never been made, other than prosecutions and actions for such injuries as were actually foreseen and estimated upon such inquest.

Duties of Millers and Owners of Cotton Gins.

§ 1939. No person shall take any toll, or other compensation, for the grinding of any grain, at any water grist mill hereafter built, unless such mill be established by order of court, pursuant to the provisions of law, except the lands on which such mill is built, and which shall be rendered unfit for cultivation by the dam erected across any water-course, belong, on both sides of such water-course, exclusively to the person or persons erecting such mill and dam; and if any person shall offend herein, he shall forfeit and pay, for every such offense, the sum of five dollars, to be recovered by warrant, before any justice of the peace of the proper county, with costs.

§ 1940. All millers shall well and sufficiently grind the grain brought to their mills, for the usual consumption of the persons bringing the same, and their families, and in due turn as the same shall be brought, and may take for the toll one-eighth part, and no more, of all the grain, of which the remaining part shall be ground into meal, and one-twelfth part, and no more, of all grain of which the remaining part shall be ground into hominy or malt.

§ 1941. Every miller, or occupier of a mill, who shall not well and sufficiently grind, as aforesaid, or not in due turn, as the same shall be brought, or who shall take or exact more toll, shall (whether such mill be established by law or not,) forfeit and pay to the party injured five dollars for each and every offence, recoverable, with costs, before any justice of the peace of the county where such offence shall be committed ; *provided,* that every owner or occupier of a mill shall have a right, at any time, to grind his or her own grain, for the consumption of his or her own family ; *and provided,* that no miller shall be obliged to run more than one pair of stones for the purpose of grinding grain brought to his mill, for the consumption of the persons bringing the same, and their families.

§ 1942. Every owner or occupier of a mill, established or grinding for toll, as aforesaid, shall keep therein sealed measures of half bushel and peck, and toll dish, sealed, and shall measure all grain by strike measure, under penalty of paying five dollars for every such failure, recoverable, with costs, before a justice of the peace of the county where such mill shall be, to the use of the informer.

§ 1943. The owner or occupier of every dam, over which a public road passes, shall constantly keep such dam in repair, at least twelve feet wide at the top, through the whole length thereof, and shall keep and maintain a bridge of the like breadth, with strong rails on each side thereof, over the pier head, flood gates, or any waste-cut through or around the dam, and over any race or canal, leading to or from the mill or pond, over which a public road may pass, under the penalty of two dollars for every twenty-four hours' failure ; but where a mill-dam shall be carried away or destroyed by tempest or accident, the owner or occupier thereof shall not be liable to the said penalties, from thenceforth, until one month after such mill shall have been so repaired as to have ground one bushel of grain.

§ 1944. Nothing in this act contained shall extend to any grist mills propelled by steam, horses, mules or oxen, erected by the owner or proprietor of any plantation, for the use of such owner or proprietor, and which may occasionally be used in grinding for the neighborhood.

§ 1945. Every owner or proprietor of any cotton gin, erected in or within half a mile of any city, town or village, is hereby required to remove or destroy all cotton seed which may fall from such gin, so that the same shall not predjudice the health of the inhabitants of such city, town or village ; and every person, being the owner or proprietor of a cotton gin, situated as aforesaid, who shall neglect or refuse to remove or destroy the cotton seed in and about such gin, having received five days' notice, shall forfeit and pay the sum of twenty dollars for every day he or she shall neglect or refuse to remove or destroy the cotton seed, as aforesaid, to be recovered by warrant, in the name of the state, before any justice of the peace of the proper county, for the use and benefit of the informer.

ARBITRATION AND AWARD.

ARBITRATION OF PENDING SUITS.

§ 1962. In all suits, which may be pending in any of the courts of law or equity, in this state, the parties may, in open court, consent to have all matters in controversy in such suit referred, for decision, to such persons as the parties may have selected as arbitrators.

§ 1963. When the parties have thus appeared in court, and asked for such submission, it shall be the duty of the court to have entered on the minutes a rule for such submission, pursuant to the application of the parties.

§ 1964. When such rule has been entered, further proceedings in court shall be suspended in the cause, until the arbitrators shall have acted, or until the litigating parties shall agree that proceedings may be resumed.

§ 1965. When the award of the arbitrators has been made, according to the submission, and approved by the court, it shall be entered of record, and shall have the force and effect of judgments rendered in the ordinary mode, and may be enforced by the usual final process.

DIFFERENCES BETWEEN MERCHANTS AND OTHERS.

§ 1966. Whenever pecuniary differences, or controversies, arise between merchants, traders or others, and they may desire to terminate the same without litigation, they may proceed as follows :

§ 1967. The parties shall enter into a written agreement, to be signed by each, by which they shall stipulate that the matters in dispute between them (to be distinctly stated in such agreement) shall be submitted to the decision and award of arbitrators, to be named in such agreement, and that such award, when made in writing and signed by the arbitrators, shall be made a rule of some court of competent jurisdiction, to be named in the agreement, and there entered as a rule or judgment of such court, and enforced as other judgments in such court. The agreement shall also contain a clause, binding both parties under such penalty as they may fix and state in the agreement, to abide by and perform the award, when made, pursuant to the terms of submission.

PROCEEDINGS IN COURT.

§ 1968. When either party shall produce, in the designated court, the written agreement made by them, and the written award of the arbitrators, thereto attached, and shall prove to the court the execution of the agreement and written award, the court shall cause the same to be filed by the clerk, and have a judgment, in appropriate form, entered on the minutes, pronouncing judgment, pursuant to the decision or award of the arbitrators, and stating, in such order, that the award shall be final, and that both parties are finally concluded by the same, and the judgment rendered thereon.

§ 1969. On judgments, thus rendered, final process may issue and be enforced, as in ordinary judgments of the court.

§ 1970. Should it be made to appear to the court that the award, made in pursuance of this chapter, was procured by fraud, corruption, or undue means, or that there was partiality and favoritism in the arbitrators, or any of them, the same shall not be confirmed by the court, but rejected. And if such award be confirmed by the court, and it shall be made to appear to the court, at the term next succeeding that at which the award was confirmed, that the same was procured by the means named in this section, it shall be the duty of the court to set the same aside, and vacate the judgment ; and the parties shall occupy the same position toward each other which they did before they submitted their differences to arbitration.

§ 1971. Nothing in this chapter contained shall be so construed as to take away from the chancery courts of this state the powers which they possess over awards, arbitraments, and umpirages, according to the principles of equity jurisprudence.

EXEMPT PROPERTY.

PERSONAL PROPERTY EXEMPT.

§ 2131. The following property shall be exempt from seizure, under execution or attachment, to-wit:

First—The tools of a mechanic, necessary for carrying on his trade.

Second—The agricultural implements of a farmer, necessary for two male laborers.

Third—The implements of a laborer, necessary in his usual employment.

Fourth—The books of a student, required for the completion of his education.

Fifth—The wearing apparel of every person.

Sixth—The libraries of licensed attorneys at law, practicing physicians, and ministers of the gospel, not exceeding two hundred and fifty dollars in value; also, the instruments of surgeons and dentists, used in their professions, not exceeding two hundred and fifty dollars in value.

Seventh—The arms and accoutrements of each person of the enrolled militia of the State; and

Eighth—All globes, books and maps, used by the teachers of schools, academies and colleges. Also, the following property of each head of a family, or housekeeper, to-wit: Two work horses or mules, or one yoke of oxen, two cows and calves, five head of stock hogs, and five sheep, one hundred and fifty bushels of corn, three hundred bundles fodder, ten bushels of wheat or rice, two hundred pounds of pork or bacon, or other meat, one cart or wagon, not to exceed in value one hundred dollars, one sewing machine, and household and kitchen furniture, to be selected by the debtor, not to exceed one hundred dollars in value.

SECTION 1. Be it enacted by the Legislature of the State of Mississippi, That in addition to the property now exempt by law, there shall be one hundred dollars of the wages of all daily, monthly or yearly laborers in this State, exempt to said laborers, and said wages to the amount of one hundred dollars shall not be liable to levy by execution or attachment, and shall not be subject to garnishment in the hands of the employers or in the hands of any other person for said laborer; *provided*, that this act shall not be so construed as to prevent the collection of debts contracted previous to the passage hereof. (Approved March 30, 1872.)

SECTION 1. Be it enacted by the Legislature of the State of Mississippi, That the wages and compensation of married women for services and labor done and performed by them, shall be free from the debts and control of their husbands, and their employees are allowed to pay such wages and compensation directly to such married woman, and payment to them shall be a full discharge and acquittance of the employer. (Approved, April 18, 1873.)

That the following property, and no other, shall be exempt from taxation, to-wit: All cemeteries, used exclusively for burial purposes; property, real and personal, belonging to the United States or to this State, or to any county or incorporate city or town within the same, or to any religious society or incorporated institution for the education of youth, used exclusively for the benefit and support of such society or institution, or held and occupied by the trustees of schools, and school lands of the respective townships, for the use of public schools or property appropriated to, and occupied and used for any court house, jail, house of correction, poor house, hospital or charitable institution, wearing apparel, not including jewelry nor watches, provisions on hand necessary for family consumption, all farming produce raised in this state, in the hands of the producer, all dogs, one gun for private use, all poultry, household furniture, not to exceed in value two hundred and fifty dollars, two cows and calves, ten head of hogs, ten head of sheep or goats, farming utensils used for agricultural purposes, libraries of all persons, pictures and works of art, not kept or offered for sale or merchandise, all property of agricultural and mechanical associations and fairs [so long as the same shall be used for accomplishing the object of such association and fairs, but no longer.—1877], and the tools of any mechanic necessary for carrying on his trade.—Approxed April 15th, 1876.

PROCEEDINGS IN RELATION TO EXEMPTION.

§ 2132. If any sheriff or other officer shall levy, or be about to levy an execution or attachment, on any personal property, and a doubt shall arise as to the liability of said property to be sold, he may demand of the plaintiff a bond, with good sureties, payable to such officer, in a sufficient penalty, conditioned to indemnify and save harmless the said officer, against all damages which he may sustain, in consequence of the seizure or sale of the property on which the execution or attachment shall be, or shall have been levied, and will pay and satisfy to the defendant, all damages which he may sustain in consequence of such seizure or sale; and if such bond be not given, after reasonable notice, in writing, from the officer to the plaintiff, his agent or attorney, that he requires it, the officer may refuse to levy, or, having levied, may dismiss the levy; but if the required bond be given, the officer shall seize and sell, or dispose of the property, according to the command of the process in his hands, and shall return such bond, with the execution or attachment.

§ 2133. The defendant, in execution or attachment, may sue on the bond, in the name of the payee, for his use, and recover double damages, for the loss he has sustained, by the seizure or sale of such property; and after the due execution of such bond, the defendant, in the execution or attachment, shall be barred of any claim against the officer so seizing, or selling such property, unless the obligors in said bond shall be or become insolvent, or the bond otherwise invalid.

§ 2134. If any officer shall seize any personal property, exempt from execution, he shall be liable to an action, at the suit of the owner, for all damages sustained thereby, unless he has taken an indemnifying bond, as hereinbefore provided; and any defendant, whose exempt property is seized, may replevy the same, by giving bond, with sureties, to be approved by the officer seizing it, in double the value of the property, payable to the plaintiff in the execution, and conditioned to have the property forthcoming, to abide the event of an issue, to be made up at the return term of the execution; and in such case, the officer shall deliver the property to such defendant, and shall return the bond with the execution; and at the return term aforesaid, an issue shall be made up, under the direction of the court, and tried, as in case of the trial of the right of property, levied and claimed by a third person; and if found for such defendant, he shall recover costs of the plaintiff; but if found for plaintiff, he shall have judgment against the obligors in said bond, for the value of the property, as assessed by the jury or court, and costs of suit.

HOMESTEAD EXEMPTION.

§ 2135. Every citizen of this state, male or female, being a householder, and having a family, shall be entitled to hold, exempt from seizure or sale, under any execution, attachment, judgment or decree, the land and buildings owned and occupied as a residence by such debtor; *provided*, the quantity of land shall not exceed eighty acres, nor the value thereof, inclusive of improvements, the sum of two thousand dollars.

ALLOTMENT OF HOMESTEAD.

§ 2136. If the land on which such debtor resides shall exceed eighty acres in quantity, or two thousand dollars in value, inclusive of improvements, the officer holding an execution against such debtor, and not finding other property to satisfy the same, shall levy the execution on the whole land, and shall notify the defendant, if to be found in his county, and the plaintiff or his attorney, if in his county, each to select one householder or freeholder, of his county; and each party may select one, and inform the officer of his selection, and the officer shall select a third; or if defendant or plaintiff, or his attorney, be absent from the county, or if he shall not make a selection, as aforesaid, or if the persons selected will not act, the officer shall select the three householders or freeholders, who, on oath, to be administered by such officer, shall set off to such debtor, a portion of said land, embracing the dwelling house and outhouses, and not exceeding eighty acres in quantity, or two thousand dollars in value, which allotment, distinctly indicated by metes and bounds, or other sufficient description, shall be returned with the execution, and the levy of the execution shall be dismissed, as to the part so allotted, and the officer may advertise and sell the remainder of the land.

§ 2137. If the premises shall not be capable of being so divided as to set off to the debtor a part, including the dwelling house, and not exceeding two thousand dollars in value, inclusive of improvements, the said householders or freeholders, shall set off a convenient portion of the land, to include the dwelling house and buildings, and not more land than may be necessary for the convenient use thereof, and they shall appraise the value of the part so set off; and in case the surplus of such valuation, over and above two thousand dollars, shall, within sixty days, be paid by the execution debtor, the part so set off shall not be sold on said execution; but if such surplus shall not be paid, within sixty days after such valuation, the officer may advertise and sell the part so set off: *provided*, the same shall bring a greater sum than two thousand dollars, and out of the proceeds of the sale, he shall pay to the execution debtor the sum of two thousand dollars, which shall be exempt from execution for one year thereafter in order that it may be invested in the purchase of another homestead.

HOW ALLOTMENT CONTESTED.

§ 2138. If, before or after the return of the execution, the plaintiff shall file, in the clerk's office from which the execution issued, or before the justice of the peace who issued it, as the case may be, an affidavit that he verily believes the allotment made to the debtor, by the freeholders or householders, is not correct, and that the land so allotted by them, or some part of it, is liable to sale under his execution, a summons shall be issued by the clerk or justice of the peace, for the defendant, returnable to the next term of his court, requiring him to appear and answer said affidavit; which summons shall be executed as any other summons; on its return, an issue shall be made up under the direction of the court, and tried as in case of the trial of the right of property levied on by execution or attachment, and claimed by a third person; and if the issue be found for plaintiff, a *venditioni exponas* shall be issued for the sale of such of said land as may have been found liable to sale, and the plaintiff shall have judgment for costs; if the issue be found for the defendant, he shall recover cost of the plaintiff.

§ 2139. If a defendant is dissatisfied with such allotment, he may make affidavit before the sale, which affidavit may be made before the officer having the execution, that he verily believes it is not correct, specifying wherein he believes it is not correct; and the officer shall suspend the sale of so much as the said defendant so claims, and return his affidavit, with the execution, to the court to which it is returnable ; and a summons shall issue for plaintiff, or if he is a non-resident of this state, for his attorney of record in said case, if he have one ; and if he be non-resident and have no attorney in this state, publication may be made as in other cases ; and in case of the death of plaintiff, *scire facias* may issue for his representatives, and when proper process shall have been returned, executed, an issue shall be made up, and like proceedings had, as when the plaintiff has filed an affidavit of dissatisfaction; and if the issue, in whole or in part, be found in favor of defendant, judgment shall be entered accordingly, and execution may go according to the judgment.

EXEMPTION IN CITIES, TOWNS AND VILLAGES.

§ 2140. Every person, being a householder, and having a family, residing in any city, town or village, shall be entitled to hold, exempt from seizure or sale, under any execution or attachment, the land and buildings owned and occupied as a residence, by such debtor, not to exceed in value two thousand dollars, and personal property, to be selected by him, not to exceed in value two hundred and fifty dollars.

§ 2141. The foregoing provisions, for allotment and sale, and proceedings of all kinds, in relation to exempt property, real or personal, shall be aplicable to persons and property, in cities, towns and villages.

GENERAL PROVISIONS.

§ 2142. No property shall be exempt from execution, when the purchase money thereof forms, in whole or in part, the debt on which the judgment is founded; nor shall any property be exempt from sale for non-payment of taxes or assessments, or for any labor done thereon, or material furnished therefor. The declaration in the case, the judgment and the execution, shall describe the property for which the purchase money forms, in whole or in part, the debts on which the judgment is founded, and against which the creditor seeks to enforce collection of such claims.

§ 2143. The exempt property, real or personal, may be disposed of, as any other property may be, by the owner, and shall not, by such disposal, become liable to the debts of such owner; and any debtor, leaving this state, may take the personal property he has, which is exempt from execution.

§ 2144. Whenever the debtor shall cease to reside on his homestead, it shall be liable to his debts, unless his removal be temporary, by reason of some casualty or necessity, and with the purpose of speedily re-occupying it, as soon as the cause of his absence can be removed.

15

WIFE JOINS HUSBAND IN SALE OF HOMESTEAD.

SECTION 1. Be it enacted by the Legislature of the State of Mississippi, That it shall not be lawful for a married man to sell or otherwise dispose of his homestead without the consent of his wife, and no deed of conveyance from the husband for the homestead shall be valid unless the wife shall join in such conveyance; her acknowledgment to be taken as in other cases of acknowledgment of deeds by married women. (Approved, April 18, 1873.)

STATUTE OF LIMITATIONS.

PERSONAL ACTIONS.

§ 2151. All actions of debt, assumpsit, or on the case, founded upon promissory note, bill of exchange, contract or liability, not under seal, express or implied, except actions founded upon open accounts, accounts stated, and verbal contracts ; all other actions on the case, except actions for false imprisonment, malicious arrest, or for slanderous words and libels : all actions for waste and trespass upon land ; and all actions of detinue, trover, or action for the recovery of personal property, or damages for taking, converting or injuring the same, shall be commenced within six years next after the cause of such action accrued, and not after. All actions of debt or assumpsit, founded upon any open account, accounts stated, and verbal contracts, shall be commenced within three years next after the cause of such action accrued, and not after.

§ 2152. All actions for assault, battery, maiming, false imprisonment, malicious arrest or menace, and all actions for slanderous words concerning the person or title, and for libels, shall be commenced within one year next after the cause of such action accrued, and not after.

§ 2153. All actions of debt, founded on any judgment or decree, rendered by any court of record in this state, shall be brought within seven years next after the rendition of such judgment or decree, and not after ; and no execution shall issue on any such judgment or decree, after seven years from the date of the issuance of the last preceding execution on such judgment or decree.

§ 2154. All actions of debt, founded on any judgment or decree, rendered by any court of record without the state, shall be brought within seven years after the rendition of such judgment or decree, and not after; *provided*, that if the person against whom such judgment or decree was, or shall be rendered, was or shall be at the time of the institution of the action, a resident of this state, such action, founded on such judgment or decree, shall be commenced within three years next after the rendition thereof, and not after.

§ 2155. No action or *scire facias* shall be brought against any executor or administrator, upon any judgment or other cause of action, against his testator or intestate, but within four years after the qualification of such executor or administrator.

§ 2156. If any person, entitled to bring any of the actions before mentioned, shall, at the time at which the cause of such action accrued, be under any one or more of the following disabilities, that is to say: infancy, coverture, imprisonment, idiocy, lunacy, unsoundness of mind, or absence beyond the limits of the United States, on business of this state or of the United States, such persons may bring the said actions within the times in this chapter respectively limited, after such disability shall be removed.

§ 2157. If, at the time when any cause of action mentioned in this chapter, shall accrue against any person, he shall be out of the state, the action may be commenced within the time herein limited therefor, after such person shall have come into the state; and if, after any cause of action shall have accrued, the person against whom it has accrued shall be absent from, and reside out of the state, the time of his absence shall not be taken as any part of the time limited for the commencement of the action.

§ 2158. If any person, liable to any of the actions mentioned in this article, shall fraudulently conceal the cause of such action from the knowledge of the person entitled thereto, the cause of such action shall be deemed to have first accrued at, and not before, the time at which such fraud shall be, or with reasonable diligence might have been, first known or discovered.

§ 2159. No judgment or decree, rendered in any court held within this state, shall be a lien on the property of the defendant therein, for a longer period than seven years from the rendition thereof; but the time during which the execution of such judgment or decree shall be stayed or enjoined, by *supersedeas*, injunction or other process, shall not be computed as any part of the said period of seven years.

§ 2160. Bills of review in chancery, shall be filed within two years next after the date of the final decree in the cause, and not after; saving to persons under any disability, as hereinbefore mentioned, the like period of two years after the removal of such disability.

§ 2161. Writs of error and appeals shall be sued out or granted, within three years next after the rendition of the judgment or decree complained of, and not after; saving to persons under disability, as aforesaid, the like period after such disability shall have been removed.

§ 2162. If any person, entitled to bring any of the actions hereinbefore mentioned, or liable to any such action, shall die before the expiration of the time herein limited therefor, and if the cause of action does, by law, survive, such action may be commenced by or against the executor or administrator of the deceased person, after the expiration of said time, and within one year after the date of letters testamentary or of administration.

§ 2163. If in any action, duly commenced within the time allowed, the writ shall be abated, or the action otherwise avoided or

defeated, by the death or marriage of any party thereto, or for any
matter of form, or if, after the verdict for the plaintiff, the judgment shall be arrested, or if a judgment for the plaintiff shall be
reversed, on appeal or writ of error, the plaintiff may commence a
new action for the same cause, at any time within one year after
the abatement, or other determination of the original suit, or after
reversal of the judgment therein ; and if the cause of action does,
by law, survive, his executor or administrator may, in case of his
death, commence such new action, within the said one year.

§ 2164.   In all actions of debt or assumpsit, brought to recover
the balance due upon a mutual and open current account, the cause of
action shall be deemed to have accrued at the time of the true date
of the last item proved in such account ; and in all other actions
upon open accounts, the period of limitation shall commence to run
against the several items thereof, from the dates at which the same
respectively became due and payable.

§ 2165.   In actions of debt, assumpsit, or on the case, founded
upon any contract, no acknowledgment or promise shall be evidence
of a new or continuing contract, whereby to take any case out of
the operation of the provisions of this chapter, or to deprive any
party of the benefit thereof, unless such acknowledgment or promise
be made, or contained by or in some writing, signed by the party
chargeable thereby ; and where there shall be two or more joint
contractors, no such joint contractor shall lose the benefit of the
provisions of this chapter, so as to be chargeable, by reason only
of any acknowledgment or promise, made or signed by any other or
others of them ; and in actions against joint contractors, if the
plaintiff is barred as to one or more of the defendants, but is entitled to recover against any other or others of them, by virtue of
a new acknowledgment or promise, or otherwise, judgment shall be
given for the plaintiff, as to any of the defendants against whom
he is entitled to recover, and for the other defendants against the
plaintiff.

§ 2166.   All the provisions of this chapter shall apply to the case
of any debt or demand on contract, alleged by way of set off on the
part of a defendant ; and the time of limitation of such debt or demand, shall be computed in like manner, as if an action had been
commenced therefor, at the time when the plaintiff's action was
commenced.

§ 2167.   All actions and suits for any penalty or forfeiture, on
any penal statute, brought by any person to whom the penalty or
forfeiture is given, in whole or in part, shall be commenced within
one year next after the offence committed, and not afterwards.

§ 2169.   The limitations herein prescribed, for the commencement
of actions, shall apply to the same actions, when brought in the
name of the state, or any county, or in the name of any officer, or
otherwise, for the benefit of the state, or any county, in the same
manner as to actions brought by citizens.

§ 2170.   When any person shall be prohibited by law, or restrained or enjoined by the order, decree or process of any court in

this state, from commencing or prosecuting any action or remedy, the time during which such person shall be so prohibited, enjoined or restrained, shall not be computed as any part of the period of time limited by this chapter for the commencement of such action.

§ 2171. None of the provisions of this chapter shall apply to suits brought to enforce payment of notes, bills, or evidences of debt, issued by any bank or moneyed corporation.

SECTION 1. Be it enacted by the Legislature of the State of Mississippi, That all actions of debt or covenant, founded upon any bond, obligation, or contract under seal or upon the award of arbitrators, shall be commenced within seven years next after the cause of such action accrued, and not after. (Approved, April 19, 1873.)

PROMISSORY NOTES, ENDORSEES AND PROTEST.

PROMISSORY NOTES AND OTHER PROMISES TO PAY, AND HOW ASSIGNED.

§ 2227. Every promise in writing, not under seal, whereby any person or persons, or body politic or corporate, promises or agrees to pay a sum of money, or acknowledges the same to be due, shall be deemed and treated as a promissory note, and the sum of money therein mentioned shall be deemed to be due to the payee and his assigns, and any instrument, to which the person making the same shall attach or affix a scroll, or any printed impression intended as a seal, shall be held and deemed a sealed instrument.

§ 2228. All promissory notes, and all other writings for the payment of money, or for the payment of any other thing, may be assigned by endorsement, whether the same be payable to order or assigns, or not, and the assignee, or endorsee, may maintain such action thereon, in his own name, as the assignor or endorser could have maintained; and in all actions, on any such assigned promissory note, bill of exchange, or other writing for the payment of money or other thing, the defendant shall be allowed the benefit of all want of lawful consideration, failure of consideration, payments, discounts and sets-off, made, had or possessed against the same, previous to notice of assignment, in the same manner as though the suit had been brought by the obligee or payee; and the assignee or endorsee of any such instrument, may maintain an action against the person or persons who may have endorsed the same, as in case of inland bills of exchange; *provided,* that when any debt shall be lost, by the negligence or default of any assignee or endorsee, the assignor shall not be liable on such assignment or endorsement.

§ 2229. When any person is bound in any bond, bill single, obligation, promissory note, or other writing, for money or other thing, or endorses any bill of exchange that shall be protested, and the amount of money or other thing due thereon shall be tendered or paid by the surety or endorser, the holder thereof shall be obliged to transfer such instrument to the person who paid or tendered the amount due ; and such assignee shall have a right of action thereon, in his own name, against the principal debtor.

BILLS OF EXCHANGE AND CHECKS.

§ 2230. When any person or persons, or body politic or corporate, shall, by order in writing, signed by such person, or by a proper agent, direct the payment of any sum of money, in the hands of any other person, the sum therein specified shall be due, by virtue thereof, to the person in whose favor the order is drawn, and may be put in suit against the drawer thereof, or against the drawee, if accepted, and the amount recovered, with interest and cost.

§ 2231. All bills of exchange, drawn upon any person, or body politic or corporate, resident within the United States, and out of this state, and protested for non-acceptance, shall draw damages at five per centum on the sum drawn for, and interest on the principal ; and the damages on bills drawn by any person, or body politic or corporate, payable, out of the United States, which shall be protested for non-acceptance, or non-payment, shall be ten per centum on the amount drawn for, the principal to draw interest also ; and in all cases the holder shall be entitled to all costs and charges.

§ 2232. Domestic bills of exchange, drawn on, and payable in this state, for the sum of twenty dollars or upwards, shall be protested for non-acceptance, or if accepted, for non-payment, in like manner as foreign bills ; but no damages shall accrue, and in every other respect they shall be subject to, and governed by the same customs and usages which govern foreign bills of exchange.

§ 2233. Bills of exchange may be protested by any justice of the peace, in this state, or by the mayor or chief magistrate of any incorporated town ; and the protest may be in the following form, or to the following effect, to-wit:

FORM OF PROTEST.

" Be it known that I, A. B., a justice of the peace of the county of ......, state of Mississippi, on the ..... day of ...., at the usual place of abode of C. D., presented to him the bill, of which the annexed is a copy, for acceptance, [*or payment, if for payment,*] which he did not accept [*or pay,*] wherefore I do protest the said bill. Dated at ......, this .... day of ...."

A copy of this bill shall be attached to the protest, and the drawer, such protest, or notice thereof, in writing, being sent to him, or left at his usual place of residence, within a reasonable time, shall be bound to pay the money mentioned in such bill, to the person entitled to it, with interest and damages.

§ 2234. In case of the loss of any bill of exchange, before it is payable, the drawer shall be obliged to give another bill, of the same tenor with that first given, the person demanding the same, giving sufficient security to the drawer, to indemnify him against the payment of such first bill.

§ 2235. If any person shall take an inland bill of exchange, for any previous debt, the same shall be accounted a complete payment, if the person accepting the same does not take proper and due course to obtain payment of the drawer, by endeavoring to get the same accepted and paid, or protested.

Remedies on Bonds, Notes, and Bills of Exchange.

§ 2236. In any action, founded on any joint, or joint and several bond, covenant, bill, promissory note, or other contract, or on any promise, contract, or liability of copartners, it shall be lawful to sue any one or more of the parties liable on such bond, covenant, bill, note, contract, promise, or liability.

§ 2237. In all actions, founded on bills of exchange, or promissory notes, the maker or makers, acceptor or acceptors, drawer or drawers, and endorser or endorsers, living and resident within this state, shall be sued in a joint action; and such suit shall be brought in the county where the party to said suit, who is first liable on said note or bill, shall reside.

§ 2238. Separate suits may be brought against the representatives of such of the parties to said bills and notes, as have died, or joint suits may be brought against the representatives of such deceased party, with those who are alive, and bound thereon.

§ 2239. The clerk shall issue duplicate writs to the several counties where the various defendants may reside; and he shall endorse on all executions issued in such suits, the names of the makers, drawers, acceptors and endorsers, so as to designate the order in which they are liable.

§ 2240. The plaintiff may discontinue his suit, before verdict, against any of the endorsers, or parties secondarily liable, on payment of the costs that have accrued from joining such party in the suit.

§ 2241. The jury may render verdicts against some of the defendants, and in favor of others, as the evidence may require; and the court shall enter the proper judgments upon such verdicts, and said verdicts and judgments shall not be reversed or set aside for want of form. New trials shall be granted only as to such defendants as are aggrieved by the verdict; and final judgment shall be entered against the other defendants, in pursuance of the verdict.

§ 2242. The sheriff shall make the money, on executions issued upon judgments hereafter rendered, in pursuance of this chapter, out of the property of the maker or makers, acceptor or acceptors; and it shall not be lawful to levy on the property of the endorsers or sureties, unless sufficient property of the principal or principals cannot be found by the sheriff, out of which the plaintiff's money and costs can be made; and, in that case, the sheriff may proceed with the execution against the defendant not liable, and so on, until the execution be satisfied; and if any sheriff shall levy such execution on the property of the endorser or surety, when the principal has sufficient property in his county to satisfy such execution, the party so offending shall be deemed a trespasser, and shall be liable to an action, by the party aggrieved, and exemplary damages shall, in such cases, be given by the jury.

SURETIES AND JOINT DEBTORS.

HOW SURETIES MAY BE RELIEVED.

§ 2257. Any person who is, or shall be bound as surety or accommodation endorser for another, may, at any time after the debt has become due, or liability been incurred, give notice, in writing, to the creditor to commence and prosecute legal proceedings against the principal debtor, if living and resident within this state, for the recovery of said debt; and if such creditor shall fail to commence such legal proceedings, by the next term of the proper court, in which suit can be brought, so be held after the expiration of thirty days after the giving of such notice, and to prosecute the same to effect, the surety, who shall have given such notice, shall be discharged from liability, and the creditor shall be barred of all recovery against him.

§ 2258. When any judgment or decree shall be rendered, or shall have been rendered, against a principal debtor and his sureties, or against the sureties only, and any one or more of such sureties shall pay off and satisfy the same, such judgment shall, by operation of this act, be transferred and assigned to the surety, or sureties, so paying off and satisfying the same, who shall have all the liens and equities which the judgment creditor may have had, by virtue of such judgment, or of the debt or claim on which it is founded ; and such surety, on making affidavit of his suretyship, and of the payment of said judgment, and filing the same, together with evidence of such payment, with the clerk of the court in which the judgment was rendered, shall be entitled to have execution issued on such judgment, in the name of the plaintiff, against the defendants on the record, in the same manner as if the judgment had not been satisfied, and the clerk shall endorse thereon that the same is issued for the use of the surety so having paid such judgment, and the sheriff shall proceed to collect the money from the principal debtor therein, for the use of such surety, if the principal debtor be a party to such judgment ; and if the principal debtor be not a party to the judgment, then he shall collect a ratable proportion of the money from each of the co-securities, for the use aforesaid.

§ 2259. When any person, who is or shall be bound as surety or endorser for another, in any writing, for the payment of money or other thing, which shall remain unpaid, in whole or in part, by the principal debtor, after the maturity thereof, shall pay or tender to the creditor or holder of such writing the amount due thereon, such creditor or holder shall assign such writing to the surety or endorser paying or tendering the money or other thing due as aforesaid; and such assignee shall and may have an action at law, in his own name, against the principal debtor upon the said writing, to recover the amount so paid in satisfaction thereof.

§ 2260. No surety or endorser shall suffer judgment to be entered against him by confession or default, without the consent of the principal debtor; and any surety or endorser, who shall be sued alone, shall give notice thereof to the principal debtor, if resident in this state, and set up such defense to the action as the principal debtor might set up, in case he has knowledge or notice of the existence of such defenses; and if such surety or endorser, sued alone, shall fail to give such notice, in case the principal debtor be a resident of the state, or to set up such defenses, of which he has notice, he shall be barred of all recovery against the principal debtor; *provided*, such principal debtor has a good defense against the action of the creditor.

§ 2261. When execution shall issue on any judgment, rendered against a principal or surety, or sureties, the sheriff, or other officer, shall make the money, or as much thereof as possible, out of the property of the principal debtor, if he have any property in the county to which the execution is issued; *provided*, the surety shall make oath that he is only surety on the instrument upon which the judgment is founded, and file the same with the sheriff, who shall return such affidavit with the execution.

§ 2262. The provisions of this article shall apply to proceedings before justices of the peace, and such justices shall perform the duties required to be performed by the clerks of the circuit court.

How One of Several Joint Debtors May be Relieved.

§ 2263. In all cases of joint, or joint and several indebtedness, the creditor may settle or compromise with, and release any one or more of such debtors; and such settlement or release shall not affect the right or remedy of the creditor against the other debtors, for the amount remaining due and unpaid, and shall not operate to release any of the others of the said debtors; and all mortgages or securities, for the said indebtedness, shall remain in full force against such debtors, not so released, in favor of the creditor, and also in favor of such of the said debtors as may be entitled to contribution, payment, or reimbursement from others of said debtors, and the right of payment, contribution or reimbursement, as among themselves, shall not be affected by this act; and if any such debtor, so released, shall have paid more than his ratable share of the whole debt, the whole amount paid by him shall be credited, and if less than his ratable share, then the full amount of his ratable share shall be credited, and the other debtors shall be liable for the residue.

§ 2279. The legal rate of interest on all bonds, notes, accounts, judgments and contracts, shall be six per cent. per annum; but contracts may be made, in writing, for the payment of a rate of interest as great as ten per cent. per annum. And if a greater rate of interest than ten per cent. shall be stipulated for, in any case, such excess shall be forfeited, on the plea of the party to be charged therewith; and all judgments and decrees, founded on any contract, shall bear interest after the rate of the debt on which such judgment or decree was rendered.

§ 2280. The issues, bills, notes, bonds, or certificates of deposit, of any bank, corporation, or association of persons, formed for banking purposes, or possessing banking privileges, situated without the limits of this state, shall not be loaned in this state, by any agent, officer, or person employed by, or having any interest in, or connection with any such bank, corporation, or association of persons, at a greater rate of discount or interest than such bank, corporation, or association of persons formed for banking purposes, or possessing banking privileges, is allowed to take or receive on the loan of money, under or by virtue of the charter of such bank, corporation or association, or by the laws of the state where the same may be situated, or by the laws of this state; and all contracts and agreements, made in violation of the provisions of this section, shall, as to the whole of the discount or interest allowed or paid, or agreed to be allowed or paid, be utterly void, and of no effect, and such discount or interest may be recovered back, by the person suffering such discount, or paying such interest.

§ 2281. All judgments not specified in this chapter shall bear interest at the rate of six per cent. per annum.

§ 2282. When partial payments are made on bonds, contracts, or assurances that bear interest, the interest that has accrued up to the time of such payment, shall be first credited, and the residue of such partial payment shall be placed to the payment of the principal; and the same rule shall apply to all debts due by the judgment, sentence or decree of any court.

Public Roads, Bridges and Fences---Penalties.

§ 2354. Every overseer may appoint, in writing, one male person, liable to work on the road, to notify the hands, whose labor may be required for the time being, who shall be furnished with a list of the persons to be summoned; and it shall be the duty of the person so appointed, to summon the hands named in such list, in the same manner that overseers are required to do, and to return said list to the overseers, upon oath, designating the hands warned, and the date thereof; and such return shall be *prima facie* evidence of the facts therein contained, in all prosecutions for penalties for not appearing and working, in pursuance of such notice. The person so appointed shall be exempt from working the road, at that time; and for any failure to give the notice, in pursuance of such appointment, he shall be liable to a penalty of ten dollars.

§ 2355. When teams, plows or scrapers are required in working the roads, the overseer may notify any person in his district, having them, to furnish the same, who shall be entitled to a credit as follows, that is to say : for each two-horse plow and team, with gears, and a hand to manage the same, three days' labor; for each ox-plow and team of three yoke of oxen, and two hands to manage the same, five days' labor ; for a good iron or steel-shod scraper and two horses, with a hand to manage the same, four day's labor ; and for every wagon, with a team of four horses, mules or oxen, and a hand to manage the same, four day's labor. And if any person shall fail to furnish the same, when required, he shall forfeit, for each day's failure, two dollars, for as many day's labor as he would have been entitled to credit for, in case the same had been furnished. Each overseer shall make a list of the names of all persons who have been summoned to work on the roads, and have failed to appear and perform the service required, or to furnish a proper substitute, or to pay the commutation money, and stating the number of days of such failure, and which of said persons were required to furnish plows, scrapers or teams, and shall report the same to some convenient justice of the peace, under oath, in which oath he shall state that the list contains the names of all delinquents ; and such return shall be *prima facie* evidence against such persons, of their having been duly summoned, and having failed to appear, as required by this chapter, and of the number of days of such failure, in any proceedings to recover any penalties imposed by this chapter.

§ 2356. Any person summoned to work on the road, and failing to attend and perform the services required, or to bring with him such tools, implements or teams, as he may have been required to bring, shall be guilty of a misdemeanor ; and the justice of the peace, on receipt of the report of the overseer, shall issue his warrant for the arrest of the delinquent reported by the overseer, and proceed as in other criminal cases, and, on conviction of delinquency, each person shall be fined two dollars a day, for each day's failure; and if the amount of such fine and costs of such case shall not be immediately paid, the justice of the peace, before whom the trial is had, shall sentence such person to imprisonment in the county jail, for one month, or until the payment of such fine and costs, and jail fees. But if such person will enter into bond or recognizance, in the sum of one hundred dollars, with sufficient sureties to be approved by the justice of the peace, payable to the overseer of the road and his successors, conditioned that such delinquent road hand shall immediately report himself to the overseer of the road, and perform, under his direction, labor on said road, for the period for which he is delinquent, at such time as the overseer may appoint, and pay the costs of the proceedings against him, he shall be discharged from custody, and the justice shall preserve such bond or recognizance; and if any of the obligors or recognizors shall, within thirty days after giving said bond or recognizance, produce to such justice satisfactory evidence of the required work having been faithfully performed, for the requisite period, under the direction of the overseer, the justice shall mark such bond or recognizance "cancelled," and deliver it to the obligor or recognizor applying for it; but if the bond or recognizance shall not be thus cancelled within thirty days, the justice of the peace shall issue a notice to the obligors or recognizors, to appear before him, on a day to be named, not less than five days from the service of such notice, and on the day named shall, unless sufficient cause be shown, render final judgment against said obligors or recognizors, and issue execution thereon, and when the money is collected, pay it over to the overseer of the road, to be expended on his road.

§ 2357. It shall be the duty of overseers of roads, to receive all moneys paid by road hands, at the rate of one dollar and fifty cents per day, in lieu of the work of one hand, at any time before his report to a justice of the peace, of the delinquency of hands, and with such commutation money, and with the money collected by justices of the peace, from delinquents, or from any other source, to employ labor on his road district, to the best advantage; and it shall be the duty of overseers to direct the labor of delinquent hands, who may be sentenced by a justice, and may report to them for service.

§ 2358. Any overseer, failing or refusing to apply all money received by him as herein provided, shall, on conviction thereof, be imprisoned, not exceeding six months, in the county jail, and be fined equal to double the amount by him received, and not applied.

§ 2359. Every overseer, if required by a majority of the workmen on the road assigned him, shall lay off such road into equal divisions, for the ease and convenience of the laborers, and assign the same or agree with the laborers for keeping said divisions in repair; and if any person, to whom any such division shall be assigned, shall fail to keep the same in good repair, he shall be liable to all the penalties imposed upon overseers, for failing to keep the road in repair; and moreover, the overseer shall order out the hands on said division, and cause the same to be put and kept in repair.

§ 2360. If any road, bridge, or causeway, be, at any time, so damaged by high water, or otherwise, as to render the same dangerous or unfit for travelers, the overseer for the district may order out the working hands assigned to said road, to repair the same, though they may have already worked ten days on said road; and if any overseer shall fail to do so, after notice, any member of the board of supervisors may employ sufficient hands to repair such road, bridge, or causeway, the expense to be paid out of the county treasury; and in addition to the other penalties, for not keeping the road in repair, the overseer shall be liable to refund to the county, the money so expended, to be recovered by action, in the name of the board of supervisors.

§ 2361. If any person shall fell any bush or tree, into any public highway, or obstruct the same in any manner whatever, and not re-move the same, within twenty-four hours, the overseer of the road of the district, shall remove the same; and the person so felling such tree or bush, or otherwise obstructing said road, shall forfeit and pay all expenses of removing the same, to be recovered before any justice of the peace of the county, in the name of the board of supervisors, and it is hereby made the duty of said overseer to cause suit to be commenced therefor.

§ 2362. When hedges are planted along any public road, the owner of the land shall trim said hedges on the side next to the road, and keep them trimmed. so that travelers will not be incon-venienced thereby, and if said hedges intrude upon the road, the overseer of the district shall give written notice to the owner, over-seer, or occupant of the land, to have said hedges trimmed, so as not to obstruct the road, or interfere with travelers, within ten days after such notice. otherwise such owner, overseer, or occupant, shall forfeit two dollars per day, for every day's failure to comply with such notice, to be recovered as is provided in the last preceding section.

§ 2363. Every overseer, within six months after his appointment, shall cause the road of which he has superintendence, leading to the court house, or principal town in the county, to be measured, if not already measured ; and shall erect, if not already erected, a post, of durable material, at the termination of each mile, marking thereon, in large Roman characters or figures, the number of miles from said court house, or principal town ; and every overseer failing herein, shall forfeit the sum of twenty-five dollars, one-half to the use of the county, and the other half to the use of the person who will sue for the same.

§ 2364. Every overseer of the road, who shall neglect to replace such posts as shall become destroyed or displaced, within the time aforesaid, shall forfeit the sum of five dollars for each post, to be recovered in the manner provided in section two thousand three hundred and sixty-one, article four, of this chapter.

§ 2365. Every overseer shall, within the time aforesaid. cause posts to be erected, when trees are not convenient, at the intersec-tion or forks of all public roads in his district, with guide-boards and index hands, pointing in the direction of said roads, on which shall be inscribed, in legible characters, the name of the town or place to which they severally lead, and the computed distance thereto, in miles; and any overseer, who shall neglect to put up and keep in repair, such posts and guide-boards, shall forfeit the sum of five dollars, to be recovered as provided in section two thousand three hundred and sixty-one, article four, of this chapter.

§ 2366. The overseers of roads shall be authorized to employ a suitable person to prepare and paint the mile-posts and guide-posts and boards; and all expenditures required by this section and sec-tion two thousand three hundred and sixty-three, article four, of this chapter, shall be reported, by the overseer, to the board of su-pervisors, who shall order the same to be paid out of the county treasury; *provided*, the same is reasonable and just.

TRAVELING ON PUBLIC ROADS.

§ 2370. All drivers of carriages, or other vehicles, whether of burden or pleasure, using any public road in the state, when met by another carriage or vehicle, shall keep on the right hand, and when overtaken by another carriage or vehicle, shall also keep to the right hand, so as, in both cases, to permit the carriage or vehicle, so meeting or overtaking, to pass free and uninterrupted; and any person willfully offending against this provision, shall forfeit and pay the sum of five dollars for each offense, and such offenses are hereby made cognizable before any justice of the peace of the county, and the person so offending shall be subject to an action for damages, at the suit of the party injured.

§ 2378. It shall not be lawful for any person to drive any wagon, carriage, or other vehicle of any description, or to ride, leap, or drive any horse, mule, or any description of cattle, over or upon any bridge, erected in any county, by authority of the legislature, or the board of supervisors of said county, at a faster gait than a walk; and every person, so offending, shall forfeit, for every offense, the sum of five dollars, to be recovered before any justice of the peace, in the name of the board of supervisors, for the use of the county; and it is hereby made the duty of every overseer of the road, and member of the board of supervisors, to institute prosecutions for all offenses under this article; but this article shall not extend to any physician, or to any person going for a physician, or returning therefrom, or riding express, by order of any public officer of the United States or of this State, or pursuing a fugitive from justice; *provided*, the board of supervisors shall cause to be fixed up, and kept, at each end of such bridge, in some conspicuous place, a board, on which shall be painted, in large letters, " five dollars fine for traveling over this bridge at a faster gait than a walk;" and on neglect of such notice, no such fine shall be incurred.

§ 2380. The board of supervisors shall, at all times, have full authority to fix and establish the rates of toll to be charged on all public ferries, bridges, and causeways, established, or hereafter to be established, and to alter the same, from time to time, at pleasure; and if any owner or keeper of any ferry, bridge, or causeway, shall charge or demand a greater sum for ferriage or toll, than the rate fixed by the said board, he shall forfeit and pay, for every such offense, the sum of ten dollars, to be recovered before any justice of the peace of the county, by any person of whom such charge or demand may be made.

§ 2382. The owner or keeper of every ferry, toll bridge or causeway, shall put up, in a convenient place, so as to be open and visible to travelers, a copy of the table of rates of toll and ferriage, established by the board of supervisors, printed, written or painted in legible characters; and for every failure to put up and maintain such table of rates, such owner or keeper shall forfeit and pay the sum of ten dollars, to be recovered before any justice of the peace of the county, by any person who will sue for the same.

§ 2383. The owner or keeper of every ferry shall at all times be provided with good and tight boats, flats or other vessels, suited to such ferry, sufficient in size, strength, steadiness and accommodation, for the safe and speedy transportation of passengers, carriages, horses, cattle and goods, well furnished with all necessary machinery, oars, poles and other implements, and men, prudent, skilful and competent to such business and service; and the banks and landing places shall be kept in good order, so as to be safe and easy for travelers; and if any such owner or keeper of a ferry shall convey or attempt to carry any person over any ferry in a boat, flat or other vessel, not good and sufficient, and furnished and manned, according to this section, or without having such banks and landing places in good order, he shall be liable to a penalty of ten dollars for each offense, to be recovered before any justice of the peace of the county, by any person who will sue for the same, besides being liable to the parties injured, for any damages sustained.

§ 2384. Every ferryman shall give constant and diligent attendance at his ferry, and shall not deny or unreasonably delay carrying over any passenger, horses, cattle, carriages or goods, and all persons shall be received into the ferry-boat, and carried over the ferry in the order of their arrival, or first coming to the ferry; and any ferryman offending against this provision shall forfeit the sum of ten dollars for every offense, to be recovered before any justice of the peace of the county, by any person who will sue for the same, and shall moreover be liable to an action for damages, at the suit of the party aggrieved; *provided*, that no ferryman shall be obliged to pass said ferry, when it manifestly appears to be dangerous to do so, on account of any storm or freshet; *and provided, also*, that all public officers, and such as go on public and urgent occasions, as posts, expresses, physicians and the like, shall be carried over first, or with the first.

§ 2385. Every ferryman shall have authority to keep out, or put out, of his ferry-boat or other vessel, any person who shall attempt or press to enter, or who shall enter or stay in his said boat or vessel contrary to his orders; and any person so doing, contrary to order, shall forfeit the sum of ten dollars for each offense, to be recovered before any justice of the peace, by any person who will sue for the same, besides being liable to any other civil or criminal prosecution.

§ 2386. The owner or keeper of any ferry, established according to law, on any stream of water, being the dividing line between two counties, shall have the right of landing on the opposite side of such stream in the other county, and to unload any passengers, wagons, carriages and their loading, and stock of all kinds, without any hindrance or molestation; and any person hindering or molesting such landing or unloading, shall forfeit and pay to the owner or keeper of such ferry the sum of ten dollars for every offense, recoverable before any justice of the peace.

RAILROADS.

§ 2421. Any railroad company, having the right of way, may run locomotives and cars, by steam, through towns, cities and villages, at the rate of six miles an hour, and no more; and if, in passing through any town, city or village, any locomotive or car should be run at a greater rate of speed, the company shall pay one hundred dollars, to be recovered by suit, in the name of such town, city or village, and for its use; and the company shall, moreover, be liable for any damages or injury which may be sustained by any one, from such locomotive or cars, whilst they are running at a greater speed than six miles an hour, through any town, city or village.

§ 2422. Every railroad company shall cause each locomotive engine, run by it, to be provided with a bell, of at least thirty pounds weight, or a steam whistle, which can be heard distinctly at a distance of three hundred yards, and shall cause the bell to be rung, or the whistle to be blown, at the distance of at least three hundred yards from the place where the railroad crosses over any highway; and the bell shall be kept ringing, or the whistle shall be kept blowing, until the engine has crossed the highway, or has stopped.

§ 2423. Every railroad company, upon stopping a train at any place where such railroad shall cross a highway, shall so uncouple their cars as not to obstruct travel upon such highway for a longer period than five minutes.

§ 2424. Every such company shall cause a board to be erected, and keep up, upon a post or frame sufficiently high, at every place where the railroad may cross a highway, with this inscription: "Look out for the locomotive." And on failure to observe the three last foregoing provisions, such company shall be liable to a fine of fifty dollars for each failure, for the use of the county where the offense is committed, and such offense shall be cognizable before any justice of the peace of the county. A failure to erect the board, as directed, shall be deemed to have occurred once every day the company may continue so to fail or neglect to have the same set up; and, moreover, such company shall be liable to any party injured by such failure or neglect, for all damages that such party may have sustained thereby.

§ 2425. If any person shall willfully obliterate, injure or destroy, any board put up as above required, he shall forfeit, for every such offence, the sum of fifty dollars, to be recovered by the company, in an action of debt, before a justice of the peace of the county where the offence was committed.

§ 2426. Any such company may erect any enclosure around any depot, where the public safety requires it, to prevent persons, other than travelers, from coming near the locomotives and cars, and may exclude from within such enclosures all persons, except travelers.

§ 2427. When the consignee, or owner of any goods or articles, transported on any railroad, and which remain in the possession of the company, can not be found, or refuses to receive the same, or pay the charges, or neglects to do so, for an unreasonable time, application may be made by the company, or its agent, to any justice of the peace, or to the mayor, or chief magistrate of any incorporated town, for an order of sale ; and if it shall be made to appear, to such justice or mayor, that the goods have been transported by the company, and that the consignee or owner cannot be found, or refuses or neglects to pay the costs and charges of transportation, or to receive the goods, such justice or mayor shall isssue an order under his hand, directed to the sheriff, or any constable or marshal of a town, directing the sale of the goods, at public vendue, at such time as the justice or mayor may direct ; and out of the proceeds of sale, to pay the charges on such goods, and all costs which have accrued, in procuring the order and making the sale ; and should there be a balance left, it shall be paid into the county treasury, and the owner of such goods may receive the same out of the treasury, on the order of the board of supervisors, if applied for in one year, but not afterwards.

§ 2428. Where a railroad has been, or shall hereafter be constructed, so as to cross any highway, and it shall be necessary to raise or lower the highway, it shall be the duty of the company to make proper and easy grades in such highway, so that the railroad may be conveniently crossed, and to keep such crossing in good order; and in like manner, it shall be the duty of such company to erect, and keep in order, all bridges on any highway, at such points as bridges may be necessary to cross such railroad; and any company which may fail to comply with these provisions, shall forfeit the sum of one hundred dollars, to be recovered by action, which action may be brought by any person authorized, or employed by the president of the board of supervisors of the county in which the failure occurred, in the name and for the use of said county.

§ 2429. Every railroad company shall be liable for all damages which may be sustained by any person in consequence of the neglect or mismanagement of any of their agents, engineers or clerks, or for the mismanagement of the engines.

HANDLING BAGGAGE ON RAILROADS.

§ 2910. That it shall be the duty of every railroad company chartered by this state, to instruct all its station agents and baggage masters, whose services are rendered in this state, to receive any trunk or baggage which the regulations of such company allow to be transported, with every passenger, from any person, immediately upon the exhibition by such person of a ticket over the road of such company; and immediately upon receiving such trunk or baggage, to issue to the owner thereof, or his agent, a check for the same, bearing upon it the number or name of the station, marked as the destination of such person, upon said ticket; *provided* the same be within the limits of this state, and that said baggage masters, upon the arrival of the train of which they have charge, at any regular station in this state, shall put off any trunk or baggage, which may be checked to such station, upon the platform thereof ; and it

16

is hereby made the further duty of such railroad company, to safely keep such trunk or baggage at such station, until the owner thereof, or his agent, shall demand the same ; and said company shall instruct their station agents accordingly.

§ 2911.   That any such railroad company, whose agents or employees shall carelessly or willfully injure, or allow to be in injured, or lost, any trunk or baggage, bearing a check as provided in section two thousand nine hundred and ten, of this article, either by improper handling or otherwise, shall be liable for damages, in a sum not less than double the amount of the actual damage.

§ 2912.   That for any violation of any of the provisions of this act, by any railroad company, or its agents, in this state, such company may be proceeded against, in the proper court of the county where such offence is committed, by service of process upon any agent of said company, in said county ; and the agent or employee of any such company, who shall willfully violate any of the provisions of this act whether he has received proper instructions from the company or not, shall also be liable to prosecution in such court, for a misdemeanor, and fined not less than twenty-five dollars, nor more than one hundred dollars.

AS TO THE RUNNING OF TRAINS : ACCIDENTS, ETC.

Section 1. Be it enacted by the Legislature of the State of Mississippi, That if any engineer of any locomotive running upon any railroad track, upon and over which passengers or freight are or may be transported, shall run his locomotive across or upon the track of any other railroad, upon and over which passengers or freight are or may be transported, without first coming to a full stop before crossing such other track, or if he shall run or permit his locomotive to cross such track, without first coming to a full stop, he shall, on conviction, be fined in any sum not less than one hundred dollars, and not more than one thousand dollars, or be imprisoned in the county jail for any period not less than three months, nor more than one year, or both, at the discretion of the court, and if any person shall be injured or killed by reason of such crossing, he shall be imprisoned in the state prison, for a period not less than two years, nor more than fifteen years.

Sec. 2. Be it further enacted, That if any conductor of any train shall order and direct the engineer to violate the provisions of the first section of this act, or, if by reason of the gross carelessness or willful neglect of duty of the brakeman of any train of cars, such train or locomotive shall run across or upon such crossing, or if the brakeman or other person in charge of any switch, shall carelessly or willfully leave the same open, and through such carelessness or willful neglect of duty, any person shall be injured or killed, such conductor, brakeman, or other person so offending, shall suffer the penalties prescribed for the engineer for like offense, in the first section of this act.

Sec. 3. Be it further enacted, That if any such engineer shall permit his locomotive to run upon or cross such other track, until the locomotive or train upon the other track has passed over such crossing, if the signal man from the locomotive or train on the other track shall arrive at the crossing first, he shall suffer the same penalty prescribed in the first section of this act.

Sec. 4. Be it further enacted, That it shall not be lawful for any locomotive or train to be stopped or remain stationary on any railroad crossing, unless the same is done by the united agreement, and under specific regulations adopted by the directors of such crossing railroads, and if the provisions of this section shall be violated, the person or persons so offending, shall suffer the same punishment prescribed in the first section of this act.

Sec. 5. Be it further enacted, That if any person shall, while in charge of a locomotive engine running upon railroad, in this state (or while acting as the conductor of a car or train on any such railroad), be intoxicated, he shall, on conviction, be punished in the manner prescribed in the first section of this act. [Approved, April 6, 1874.]

JUMPING UPON OR CLINGING TO ENGINES OR CARS.

Section 1. Be it enacted by the Legislature of the State of Mississippi, That no person or minor shall climb, jump, step, stand upon, cling to, or in any way attach himself to any locomotive engine or car, either stationary or in motion, upon any part of the track of any railroad, unless in so doing he shall be acting in compliance with law, or by permission, under the lawful rules and regulations of the corporation then owning or managing such railroads.

Sec. 2. Be it further enacted, That whenever any officer, agent, or employee of any railroad corporation shall have any information that any person or minor has violated any of the provisions of the first section of this act, and has thereby endangered himself, or caused reasonable alarm to others, said officer, agent, or employee, shall, without unnecessary delay, make complaint of such offense against such persons or minor, before some justice of the peace.

Sec. 3. Be it further enacted, That any person or minor who shall violate any of the provisions of section one of this act, shall be punished by a fine, not exceeding twenty-five dollars, to be recovered in an action of debt, in the name of the people of the state of Mississippi, before any justice of the peace, or, upon conviction, by imprisonment in the county jail, or other place of confinement, for a period not exceeding ten days.

LIABILITY FOR DAMAGE TO PERSONS OR STOCK.

Section 1. Be it enacted by the Legislature of the State of Mississippi, That a railroad company shall be liable for any damage to persons, stock, or other property, by the running of the locomotives or cars, or other machinery of such company, or for damage done by any person in the employment and service of such company, unless the company shall make it appear that their agents have exercised all ordinary and reasonable care and diligence, the presumption, in all cases, being against the company. [By limitation, March 21, 1876.]

SUITS AGAINST RAILROADS, EXPRESS, AND TELEGRAPH COMPANIES.

SECTION 1. Be it enacted by the Legislature of the State of Mississippi, That the venue of actions and suits against railroad companies in this State, shall be in any county in which any part of the road-bed of the company which may be sued, lies; and the venue of suits and actions against any express company doing business in this state, shall be in any county in which any part of the line on which it does business, may run; and the venue of actions and suits against telegraph companies, whose lines run through any part of this state, shall be in any county through which any part of the line of any such company, which may be sued, shall run; and if the President or other principal officers of said corporation, cannot be found in the county in which suit is brought, it shall be the duty of the sheriff or other officer having process to execute against said corporation, to deliver a true copy of said process to any operator, clerk, or agent of any telegraph or express company, in said county; and said service shall be as good and as effectual as if served on the president or other principal officer of such corporation. [Approved, March 4, 1873.]

CUTTING TIMBER, AND OTHER TRESPASSES.

§ 2473. If any person shall cut down, deaden, or take away, if already cut or fallen, or destroy, any cypress, white oak, black oak, or other oak, pine, poplar, black walnut, cherry, or pecan tree, on land not his own, without the consent of the owner of the land, he shall pay to the owner of such tree or trees, fifteen dollars for every such tree so cut down, taken away, or destroyed; and for every other tree, not herein described, so cut down, carried away, or destroyed, the sum of five dollars shall be paid; and the party injured may recover, for such trespass, before a justice of the peace, if the amount claimed be within his jurisditiion, if not, then before the circuit court; but any party injured, may elect to charge less, for any tree cut, carried away, or destroyed, than the amount herein fixed, and may recover accordingly, before any court having jurisdiction of the amount claimed.

§ 2474. If any person shall cut down, girdle, destroy, or carry away, if already cut down, any live oak tree, or any main limb thereof, on land not his own, without the consent of the owner, he shall pay to the owner fifty dollars for every such tree or limb so cut down, girdled, destroyed, or carried away, which may be recovered before any court having jurisdiction.

§ 2475. If any person shall cut down, girdle, or destroy, by any means whatever, any ornamental tree of any kind, of the dimensions of four inches or more in diameter, which is enclosed in any pleasure ground, yard, or garden, without the consent of the owner, the person so offending, shall pay the owner of such tree forty dollars for every tree so cut, girdled, or destroyed ; for any ornamental tree of less dimensions, which may be cut, girdled, or destroyed, being enclosed as aforesaid, the person offending shall pay twenty-five dollars ; and the party injured may sue for and recover the penalties hereby given, before any court of competent jurisdiction.

§ 2476. If any person shall cut down, dig up, or destroy any ornamental shrub, bush or plant, which is enclosed in any pleasure ground, flower garden, or yard, without the consent of the owner, the person so offending shall pay to the owner thereof the sum of twenty dollars, for every shrub, bush or plant, so cut or destroyed, to be recovered before a justice of the peace, if the amount be within his jurisdiction ; if not, then before the circuit court.

§ 2477. If any person shall cut down, dig up, girdle or destroy, any fruit tree, enclosed in an orchard, yard or garden, without the consent of the owner, the person so offending shall pay to the owner of such tree, the sum of fifty dollars, for each tree so cut down, dug up, girdled or destroyed, which may be recovered before a justice of the peace, if the amount claimed be within his jurisdiction ; if not, then before the circuit court ; but any party so injured may elect to charge less for each fruit tree, so cut down, dug up, girdled or destroyed, and shall recover accordingly, before any court having jurisdiction of the amount claimed.

§ 2478. Every person who, without leave of the owner, or person in charge, shall lose or take away any boat or water craft, shall pay the owner thereof twenty dollars, over and above the expenses for bringing back such boat or water craft, which may be recovered before a justice of the peace, if the amount be within his jurisdiction, but if not, then before the circuit court ; and the party so offending shall, moreover, be liable to the party aggrieved, for further damages, to be recovered by the proper action ; and when several persons are concerned, in the act of losing or taking away any boat or water craft, each person shall be liable for the whole penalty ; *provided*, that the penalty in this article shall be fifty dollars, as to water craft on the Mississippi river.

§ 2479. Every action, for any specific penalty, given by this act, shall be prosecuted, within twelve calendar months, from the time the injury was committed, and not after ; and nothing herein contained, nor the recovery of any penalty hereby given, shall be a bar to any action for further damages. or to any criminal prosecution, for any such offence, as herein enumerated.

§ 2480. Any person who shall cut, or raft any cypress, or ash timber, for sale or transportation, upon lands belonging to the State of Mississippi, or held by said state, in trust, for purposes of internal improvement, levees or schools, or upon the land of any other person or corporation, without permission in writing, from the owner or other person, authorized to grant the same, shall be liable for double damages, to be recovered by action, in the name of the state, or other party aggrieved.

JUSTICE AS CORONER.

§ 245. Every coroner shall, upon view of the body, take inquests of deaths in prison, and of all violent, sudden, or casual deaths within his county, and the manner of such deaths; and as soon as he shall have notice, or be certified of any death, as aforesaid, he shall make out a precept, directed to the sheriff or any constable of the county, where the dead body is found or lying, requiring him to summon six good and lawful men of the same county to appear before him, at the time and place in such precept mentioned; but if a person is killed in the presence of witnesses, or come to his death by a known accident, it shall not be necessary to have an inquest, which precept shall be in the form or to the effect following, to-wit:

THE STATE OF MISSISSIPPI, ⎫
.... COUNTY.   ⎬ ss.
                           ⎭

To the sheriff, or any constable of said county:

You are required, immediately upon sight hereof, to summon six good and lawful men of the said county of ...., to appear before me, A. B., coroner of said county, at ......, in said county, on the ..... day of ......, at the hour of ......, in the ...... noon of said day, then and there to inquire of, do, and execute all such things as, on behalf of the state, shall be lawfully given them in charge, touching the death of C D, (or a person unknown, as the case may be;) and be you then and there, to certify what you shall have done in the premises, and further to do and execute what, in behalf of the state, may then and there be enjoined on you.

Given under my hand, at ...., in the said county, the ...... day of ...., A. D. ....

§ 246. The sheriff or constable, to whom such precept shall be delivered, shall forthwith execute the same, and shall repair to the place, at the time mentioned therein, and make return of the said precept, with his proceedings thereon, to the coroner who issued it.

§ 247. The coroner shall also issue process for witnesses to come before him to be examined, and to declare their knowledge concerning the matter in question; and the coroner shall administer to each witness an oath or affirmation in the form, or to the effect following:

"You do solemnly swear (or affirm) that the evidence you shall give to this inquest, on behalf of the state, touching the death of C D, (or person unknown,) shall be the truth, the whole truth, and nothing but the truth."

§ 248. The coroner shall swear or affirm the jurors, upon view of the body, "diligently to inquire, and true presentment make, on behalf of the State of Mississippi, how or in what manner C D (or a person unknown, as the case may be,) here lying dead, came to his death, and of such other matters relating to the same, as shall be lawfully required of you, according to evidence; so help you God."

§ 249. If any sheriff or constable shall neglect or refuse to execute the services and duties, or any of them, by this article prescribed, or if any person summoned as a juror or witness, shall fail to appear, the coroner shall certify and return the facts to the next circuit court held in and for the county; which court, unless a reasonable excuse be offered, shall set such fine upon the sheriff, constable, juror or witness so offending, as shall be fit and reasonable, not exceeding one hundred dollars, to be paid into the county treasury; and the coroner shall have power to issue an attachment to compel the attendance of defaulting witnesses.

§ 250. When the jurors are sworn or affirmed, as aforesaid, the coroner shall give them a charge, upon their oaths or affirmations, to declare of the death of the person, whether he or she died by murder, manslaughter, misadventure, misfortune, accident or otherwise, and when and where, and by what means, and in what manner; and, if by murder, who were principals, and who were accessories, and, if by manslaughter, who were the perpetrators, and with what instrument the stroke or wound was, in either case, given, and so of all prevailing circumstances which may come by presumption; and if by misadventure, misfortune, accident or otherwise, whether by the act of God or man, and whether by hurt, fall, stroke or drowning, or in any other way; to inquire what persons were present at the death, from whence the deceased came, and who he or she was, and his or her parents, relatives or neighbors; who were the finders of the body, whether killed in the same place where he or she was found, or, if elsewhere, by whom, and how he or she was brought from thence, and of all the circumstances relating to the said death; and if he or she died in prison, whether by hard usage there or not; and if so, how and by whom; and if he or she put an end to his or her own life, then to inquire of the manner, means or instrument, and of all the circumstances concerning it.

§ 251. If any person be found guilty, by inquisition taken in the manner directed by this article, and be not in custody, the coroner shall forthwith issue his warrant to apprehend the person so found guilty, and the accessories, if any; and the person accused, if apprehended, shall forthwith be taken before some justice of the peace of the county where the offense was committed, to be dealt with according to law.

§ 252. Every coroner, upon an inquisition before him found, whereby any person or persons shall be charged on account of murder or manslaughter, or as accessory or accessories to the said crime of murder or manslaughter, either before or after the commission thereof, shall put in writing so much of the evidence given to the jury before him, as shall be material; and every such coroner is hereby authorized and required to bind all such, by bond or recognizance, as do declare anything material to prove the said murder or manslaughter, or to prove any person or persons to be accessory or accessories as aforesaid, to the said murder, to appear at the next circuit court, to be holden within the county, where the trial thereof shall be, then and there to give evidence against such offender or offenders, at the time of his, her or their trial; and shall certify, as well, the same evidence, as such bonds and recognizances, in writing, as he shall take, together with the inquisition before him taken and found, to the said circuit court, at or before the time of trial of the party so charged or accused.

§ 253. Whenever it may be necessary, in order to ascertain the cause of the death, the coroner, at the written request of a majority of the jurors, may cause some surgeon or physician to appear as a witness upon the taking of such inquest; and the fee of said surgeon or physician shall, in no case exceed ten dollars; *provided*, that if the examination of said surgeon or physician be made by dissection or chemical analysis, before the body has been interred, he shall be allowed the sum of fifty dollars; but if made after the body has been interred, the sum of one hundred dollars shall be paid, as the coroner's fees are paid by law; and it shall be the duty of the coroner to deliver to said surgeon or physician the said written request of the jurors, and a copy of the verdict, both certified by him, and the fee shall be paid on the presentation thereof.

§ 254. In all cases, the finding of the jury, together with the precept and all the proceedings before the coroner, shall be returned by him to the clerk of the circuit court, to be carefully preserved in his office.

§ 255. If, upon a murder, or other untimely or accidental death, there be no coroner in the county where such case shall happen, or if, from any cause, the coroner cannot be had, in due time, to hold an inquest, it shall be lawful for any justice of the peace in such county, to do and perform all the duties appertaining to the office of coroner in such case, and to receive the same fees; and the inquest, so taken and returned, shall be as effectual in law, as if taken and returned by the coroner.

§ 256. When an inquest shall be held upon the body of any person who has died by the violence of another, the cost of such inquest shall be paid from the treasury of the state; and in case of an inquest on the body of a person who has died by casualty, or suicide, such cost shall be paid from the county treasury; and in either case, a copy of the verdict of the jury, certified by the clerk of the circuit court, shall be a sufficient voucher to the auditor, or treasurer, to authorize such payment.

JUSTICE AS NOTARY PUBLIC.

SECTION 1. Be it enacted by the Legislature of the State of Mississippi, That all justices of the peace in this state, mayors of any incorporated town or city, and the clerks of the circuit and chancery courts of this State, shall be notaries public by virtue of their office, and shall possess all the powers, and discharge all the duties belonging to the office of notary public, and may authenticate all their acts, instruments and attestations, by their seal of office; and and all acts done by them of a notarial character, shall receive the same credit and legal effect as are attached to the acts of notaries public within the United States.

§ 2. Be it further enacted, That there may be appointed by the Governor, one notary public for each incorporated city or town in the state having a population of three thousand inhabitants, from among the qualified electors of said city or town, who shall hold his office for the term of four years, and until his successor is qualified: *provided*, that the term of office of the notaries first appointed under this act shall commence on the first day of January, 1872.

§ 3. Be it further enacted, That every notary public appointed under this act, shall, before he enters upon the duties of his office, take the oath of office, and enter into bond in the same manner as county officers, in the penalty of two thousand dollars, conditioned that he will well and truly perform all the duties of his office. Any party interested may proceed on such bond, in the manner provided for summary proceedings on bonds of justices of the peace.

§ 4. Be it further enacted, that every notary public shall have the power of administering oaths and affirmations in all matters incident to their notarial office; and any person who shall be convicted of having knowingly and wilfully made, or taken, a false oath or affirmation before any notary public, in any matter within his official duty, shall suffer the penalty of perjury.

§ 5. Be it further enacted, That every notary public shall have power to receive the proof or acknowledgment of all instruments of writing relating to commerce or navigation, letters of attorney, and such other writings as are commonly proved or acknowledged before notaries within the United States; and, also, to make declarations, and testify the truth thereof, under his seal of office, concerning all matters by him done in virtue of his office.

§ 6. Be it further enacted, That notaries public, appointed under this act, may also receive the proof or acknowledgment of deeds, conveyances, or other contracts or agreements necessary to be recorded in this state.

§ 7. Be it further enacted, That every notary public shall keep a fair register of all his official acts, and shall give a certified copy of any record in his office to any person applying for the same, such person paying the legal fees therefor.

§ 8. Be it further enacted, That in case of the death, resignation, disqualification, or expiration of office of any notary, his registers and other public papers shall be lodged, within thirty days, in the office of the clerk of the circuit court of the county where he resided; and said clerk may bring and maintain an action of detinue for the same; and any person detaining the same contrary to this act shall forfeit the sum of one thousand dollars, to be recovered by action in any court of competent jurisdiction, in the name and for the use of the county; which action shall be brought by the district attorney, when required to do so by the board of supervisors of the county in which the delinquency occurs.

§ 9. Be it further enacted, That when any notary public shall protest any bill of exchange, promissory note, or other instrument, he shall make a full and true record, in his register, or book kept for the purpose, of all his proceedings in relation thereto, and shall note thereon whether demand was made, of whom, when and where, whether he presented such bill or note, whether notices were given, to whom and in what manner, where the same were mailed, and when and to whom, and where directed, and every other fact touching the same.

§ 10. Be it further enacted, That the board of supervisors of the several counties shall provide a notarial seal for each notary within their county; the seals for the notaries appointed under this act shall have the inscription : '' Notary Public of ———'' (naming the town or city) around the margin, and an eagle in the center ; the seals for all other notaries shall have the inscription: '' Notary Public of —— county,'' around the margin, and an eagle in the center ; which seals shall be delivered by said notaries to their successors in office.

§ 11. Be it further enacted that a notary protesting a bill or note, shall not be compelled to go out of his county to give evidence in relation thereto, but either party may obtain from the clerk of the court where the action is depending, a commission to take the deposition of such notary, on giving the same notice as required in other cases.

§ 12. Be it further enacted, That the record of the notary protesting any bill or note, or other instrument, or a copy thereof, verified by the affidavit of such notary, taken before a justice of the peace, shall be conclusive evidence of the fact of the protest, and *prima facie* evidence of all other facts touching the dishonor of said bill or note ; such copy shall be competent evidence in all the courts of this state, including the courts in the county in which the notary protesting the bill or note resides.

§ 13. Be it further enacted, That it shall be lawful for notaries public to demand, receive and take the fees hereinafter mentioned, for any business done by them, that is to say :

For protesting bill or note for non-acceptance or non-payment, and giving one notice.................................$	2 00
Each additional notice......................................	25
Registering such protest and making record,.................	1 00
Attesting letters of attorney and seal	50
Notarial affidavit to an account or other writing, and seal.....	50
Each oath or affirmation, and seal.........	50
Notarial procuration and seal..............................	1 00
Taking proof of debts to be sent abroad....................	50
Taking protest in insurance cases, and seal.................	1 00
Copy of record and affidavit..............................	1 00
Taking acknowledgment to deed or other writing, and seal....	25

§ 14. Be it further enacted, That all laws now in force in reference to officers undertaking or exercising the duties of their office, before taking the oath of office, and giving the bond required by law, shall apply to the notaries appointed under this act.

§ 15. Be it further enacted, That when any notary appointed under this act shall remove out of the town for which he was appointed, all his powers as such shall cease, and his office become vacant, and if such notary public fails to qualify as herein provided, within thirty days after his appointment, then the appointment shall be void. In all cases where the office of a notary appointed under this act shall become vacant, by reason of the death, removal or resignation of such notary, then the Governor shall appoint a person to fill the office.

§ 16. Be it further enacted, That if any notary public shall swear falsely in regard to the facts stated in his notarial record, or a copy thereof, he shall be guilty of perjury, and on conviction, shall be punished as in other cases of perjury.

Approved April 5, 1872.

AGRICULTURAL LIEN LAWS.

(ACT OF 1876.)

SECTION 1. Be it enacted by the Legislature of the State of Mississippi, That there shall be a lien in favor of all landlords, on all the agricultural products raised on the land of such landlord, for the rent agreed to be paid by the tenant, and also a lien upon such products for all necessary family and farming supplies and farming implements, and stock furnished or advanced to such tenant, during the year that such products are raised ; *provided,* such lien for supplies, stock, and implements, shall not operate as against other persons to whom such tenant shall have given a deed of trust or mortgage for supplies, for said year, and of which said landlord had notice [the word "notice" shall be construed to mean actual, not merely constructive notice—Acts 1877, page 83], before such advancing by such landlord ; and *provided, further,* that such lien for rent shall exist only on the products raised during the year for which such rent is claimed.

SEC. 2. Be it further enacted, That there shall be a lien in favor of all employers of laborers upon the wages to be paid such laborers, and upon all the shares or interest of such employees, while so employed, for the indebtedness for all necessary and farming supplies, working stock, and implements furnished or advanced to such employees, by such employers, during the time of such employment.

SEC. 3. Be it further enacted, That there shall be a lien in favor of the laborers or employees, upon all agricultural products raised by such laborers or employees for their share or interest in such crops, and a lien for their wages upon all crops raised by them, or with their assistance, and for the hauling or handling of any such crops or products.

SEC. 4. Be it further enacted, That the liens provided for in the foregoing sections of this act, shall be prior to all other liens, claims, or incumbrances, and shall exist without recording, and whether the contract be in writing or not, and shall be concurrent, except that the lien for rent shall be prior to all others.

SEC. 5. Be it further enacted, That the enforcement of the liens provided for in the foregoing sections of this act, may be had in the courts of law in this state, and in the following manner : When the amount of indebtedness or value of the share or portion of the crops claimed, is not more than one hundred and fifty dollars, exclusive of interest, the plaintiff, his agent, or attorney, may make and file with any justice of the peace having jurisdiction of the case, an affidavit, setting forth a statement of the claim, the amount claimed, and the names of all persons known or supposed to have any interest in the property sought to be subjected to the enforcement of such lien, and also describing the property upon which such lien is claimed to exist. Upon the filing of which affidavit, such justice of the peace shall issue a writ, directed to some officer authorized by law to execute such writ, commanding such officer to seize the property described, or a sufficiency thereof to cover the amount claimed, and costs of suit, and to summon the persons named in such affidavit, to appear, as in other suits, to answer the claim of the plaintiff, and such officer shall execute such writ in pursuance of its terms, and shall hold such property so seized, subject to the result of the suit.

SEC. 6. Be it further enacted, That on the return day of such writ, the defendant or defendants, who shall make defense or set up any claim in or to such property, or any part of it, shall file a succint statement, in writing, of his or their claim, or defense, and such cause shall then be considered at issue, and shall be tried, as other causes, in justices' courts, and the judgment of such court may be for a part, or the whole, of plaintiff's demand, or for the defendant or defendants, or such of them as shall be entitled to judgment, or for both plaintiffs and defendants, in accordance with the finding of the court or jury. Such judgment may be for a part of the specific property, or for a specified sum of money, as the finding in the case may warrant, and the costs shall be taxed and collected by an equitable apportionment by the court.

SEC. 7. Be it further enacted, That after judgment rendered in such suits, the court or justice shall issue a special execution, not sooner than three days after such judgment is rendered, commanding the proper officer to execute such judgment in accordance with the terms of such judgment, which terms shall be stated in such special execution, and such officer shall execute the execution, by division of the property in question, and distribution to the different parties having an interest in it, or by sale, as in other cases of sales of personal property under execution, or by division in part, and sale in part, as the execution may direct.

SEC. 8. Be it further enacted, That when the amount claimed by plaintiff, exclusive of interest, exceed one hundred and fifty dollars, proceedings shall be instituted in the manner hereinbefore provided, except that the justice issuing such writ of seizure, shall make the same returnable to the next term of the circuit court in the county where such property claimed to be subject to the lien, is situated, and the affidavit shall be sent up to the circuit court, as in cases of attachment, and the officers executing such writ of seizure, shall return the same to the circuit court, as in cases of attachment, together with his return, showing his proceedings under such writ; and shall safely keep and hold the property seized by virtue of such writ, subject to the result of the suit in the circuit court, unless the defendant or defendants against whom the indebtedness is charged, or the defendant or defendants in possession of the property, when the same was seized, or the plaintiff, defendant having the first right, as in replevin, shall enter into bond, in double the value of the property, with two or more good sureties, to be approved by the officer executing the writ, who shall make affidavit that they are worth the amount of such bond, in property liable to execution, over and above their legal exemptions, payable to the other parties to the suit, conditioned to have such property forthcoming, to abide the result of such suit, and in default thereof to pay and satisfy such judgment as shall be rendered in such cause, to the extent of the value of such property and costs of such suit, in which event the property shall be delivered to such defendant or defendants, or plaintiff, so entering into such bond. This provision for bond shall extend to suits heretofore instituted.

Sec. 9. Be it further enacted, That on or before the return day of such writ in the circuit court, the plaintiff shall file with the papers in such cause, a statement, setting forth in full, his claim, and the defendant or defendants, making any defense or claim, shall, in like manner, file a statement of his or their defense or claim, when such suit shall be considered at issue, and shall be tried as other suits in the circuit court, at the first term, unless good cause for continuance be shown, and the proceedings shall be the same as hereinbefore provided to be had in justices' courts, except that judgment may be rendered in the cause, upon the bond, in case one be given, instead of against the property; and full powers are hereby invested in the circuit court to render judgment in accordance with the finding of the court or jury.

Sec. 10. Be it further enacted, That in all suits instituted under and by virtue of this act, the court, in which such suit shall be pending, shall allow all amendments of the proceedings necessary to a full development and settlement of the rights of the different parties to such proceedings, and all persons, not parties to such suit, claiming any interest in the property involved in such litigation, if they shall have actual notice of such suit, shall become parties in the same, upon petition by them, and an order of the court, to that effect, and in default thereof, shall have no other right of action as to the property in which the plaintiff or plaintiffs, or defendant or defendants, shall have acquired rights by virtue of, and under the judgment in such cause.

Sec. 11. Be it further enacted, That it shall be lawful for persons to make and execute mortgages or deeds of trust upon growing crops, or upon crops to be grown within fifteen months from the making of such mortgage or deed of trust, which incumbrance shall be valid and binding upon the interest of such mortgagor or grantor, in such crop, but shall not be, in any case, prior to the liens hereinbefore provided for in this act.

SEC. 12. Be it further enacted, That there shall be no property exempt from execution, where the claim sued for is for labor performed ; *provided*, the fact that such claim is for labor performed, shall appear in the judgment on the same, and shall also appear in the execution issued on such judgment.

SEC. 13. Be it further enacted, That appeals from judgments rendered in suits instituted under this act, in justices' courts, shall be in the same manner as in other cases in such courts ; *provided*, the same be taken in three days from the rendition of such judgment.

SEC. 14. Be it further enacted, That an act entitled an act to secure the payment of wages for labor and liabilities for supplies, approved April 5, 1872, and an act entitled an act to amend an act entitled an act to secure the payment of wages for labor and liabilities for supplies, approved April 5, 1872, approved April 17, 1873, be and the same are hereby repealed, but this act is not intended to affect civil or criminal proceedings instituted, or contracts entered into under said acts, before the passage of this act.

SEC. 15. Be it further enacted, That no judgment shall constitute a lien upon growing crops, nor shall any execution be levied on any such growing crops; *provided*, that this section shall not affect judgments and executions rendered and issued for the enforcement of liens provided for in this act.

SEC. 16. Be it further enacted, That if any person shall sell, remove, or dispose of any crop, or part thereof, upon which any other person shall have a claim, by virtue of the provisions of this act, such person so selling, removing, or disposing of such crop, or part thereof, if without the consent of the person so interested, shall be deemed and held to be guilty of a misdemeanor, and upon conviction, shall be fined not less than ten dollars, nor more than five hundred dollars, or by imprisonment in the county jail, not more than six months, or by both such fine and imprisonment. [Approved, April 14, 1876.]

LIEN ON WATER CRAFT.

SECTION 1. Be it enacted by the Legislature of the State of Mississippi, That there shall be a lien in law, in favor of every merchant, coal merchant, supply man, material man, or repairer upon any domestic vessel, steamboat, or other water craft, owned by citizens of this state, or plying between any ports or landing in this state, or exclusively upon any of the navigable waters of this state, and upon all the furniture, tackle, apparel and equipments of the same to secure the price or value of any merchandise, fuel, material or supplies furnished to such domestic vessel, steamboat or other water craft, or the price or value of any repairs which may be made upon the same ; and such lien shall be upon the vessel, steamboat, or other water craft itself, and upon all the furniture, tackle, apparel and equipments of the same, without reference to the ownership thereof, and shall be superior to any mortgage on the same, created by the owners thereof, and shall be enforceable against such vessel, steamboat, or other water craft, and the furniture, tackle, apparel, and equipments of the same, in the hands of any subsequent purchaser, whether *bona fide* or otherwise; *provided,* that proceedings to enforce such lien shall be commenced within ninety days after the purchaser shall have purchased the same. [Approved, April 5, 1876.]

CONSTABLES.

DUTIES OF CONSTABLES.

§ 278. Constables shall take the oath of office prescribed by the constitution, and enter into bond in like manner as other county officers are required to do, conditioned according to law, which bond shall be in the penalty of one thousand dollars, or such other sum as the board of supervisors of the county may, at any time, require.

§ 279. Vacancies happening in the office of constable, shall be filled by election for the unexpired term, in the manner provided for filling vacancies in the office of justice of the peace; the person elected to fill any such vacancy, giving bond, and taking the oath of office as required in the last preceding section of this article.

§ 280. It shall be the duty of every constable to keep and preserve the peace within his county; to prevent all intoxication, or sale, barter or use of intoxicating liquors on election days, and prevent all disturbances; preserve peace and good order at the polls and places of voting, and faithfully to aid and assist in executing the criminal laws of this State; to give information, without delay, to some justice of the peace, or other proper officer, of all riots, routs, and unlawful assemblies, and of every violation of the penal laws, which may come to his knowledge in any manner whatsoever; and also to execute and return all process, civil and criminal, lawfully directed to him according to the commands thereof, and to pay over all moneys, when collected by him, to the justice of the peace, or to the person lawfully authorized to receive the same.

§ 281. Sales by constables shall be held at such convenient times and places as they may appoint, and ten days' notice shall be given thereof, by advertisement, in two or more public places, in the county or neighborhood; and there shall not be more than fifteen days between the levy and the sale of the property levied on. The justice shall make an allowance to the constable, out of the proceeds of the sale, for the keeping of any live stock seized by the constable on execution.

§ 282. If any constable, or other officer, shall fail to execute and return, according to law, any execution to him directed by any justice of the peace, on or before the return day thereof, the plaintiff, in such execution may recover the amount thereof, with interest and costs, and five per cent. damages thereon, by motion before the justice to whom said execution was returnable, against said officer and his sureties, on giving five days notice of such motion. And when any constable, or

other officer, or his sureties, shall have paid the amount of money
and damages recovered as aforesaid, the original judgment and execution shall be vested in the person so paying, for his benefit; and further, the said justice, on like motion and notice, may fine the said officer
not exceeding fifty dollars, for failing to return such execution.

§ 283. If any constable or other officer, shall collect or receive any
money, by virtue of an execution issued by a justice of the peace. and
shall not pay the same over, on demand, to the plaintiff, in execution,
or other person authorized to receive the same, the said plaintiff, or
other person authorized to receive the same, may recover the amount
thereof, with interest and costs, and twenty-five per cent. damages, by
suit or motion, before any justice of the peace, or other court having
cognizance, against such officer and his sureties, on giving two day's
notice.

§ 284. If any constable, or other officer. shall make a false return
on any execution, or other process issued by a justice of the peace,
such officer shall forfeit and pay the sum of fifty dollars, to be recovered against such officer, and his sureties, by suit or motion, before the
justice by whom such process was issued, or any other justice of the
peace having jurisdiction, on two days notice, in case of a motion, for
the use of the party injured by said false return, and such justice or
justices shall have full power to try and determine such suit or motion.

§ 285. In all suits or motions against constables or other officers,
under this article, either party may appeal to the circuit court as in
other cases.

§ 286. Any constable who shall fail to discharge any of the duties
required of him by this article, when no other penalty is provided for
such failure, shall be liable to be fined not exceeding ten dollars, by
the justice of the peace before whom the proceeding may be pending,
to be collected by such justice, and paid into the county treasury, and
he shall be liable on his bond to the action of the party injured for all
damages.

AS A CRIMINAL COURT.

JURISDICTION.

§ 1304. Justices of the peace shall have jurisdiction concurrent
with the circuit court of the county, of all cases of offenses against the
laws of this state, occurring in their several counties, where the punishment prescribed does not extend beyond a fine and imprisonment in
the county jail; and they shall be conservators of the peace for the
whole county.

§ 2750. The several courts of justice. organized under the constitution and laws of this state, shall possess the sole and exclusive jurisdic-

tion of trying and punishing all persons, in the manner prescribed by law, for crimes and offenses committed in this state, except such as are exclusively cognizable by the courts deriving their jurisdiction from the constitution and laws of the United States.

§ 2751. The local jurisdiction of all offenses, unless otherwise provided by law, shall be in the county where the offense was committed.

§ 2752. Where an offense is commenced out of this state, and consummated in it, or where an offense is consummated in this state, by any means or agency, proceeding from a person out of this state, the person so commencing such offense, or putting in operation such means or agency, although out of the state at the time such offense was actually consummated, shall be liable to indictment and punishment therefor, in the county where the offense was consummated.

§ 2753. Where an offense is commenced in this state, and consummated out of it, either directly by the accused, or by any means or agency procured by, or proceeding from him, he shall be tried in the county where such offense was commenced, or from which such means or agency proceeded.

§ 2754. When an offense is committed, partly in one county and partly in another, or where the acts, effects, means or agency occur, in whole or in part, in different counties of this state, the jurisdiction shall be in either county in which said offense was commenced, prosecuted or consummated, where indictment shall be first found.

§ 2755. Where property is stolen in another state or country, and brought into this state, or is stolen in one county in this state, and is carried into another, the jurisdiction shall be in any county into, or through which the property may have passed, or where the same may be found.

§ 2756. Where the mortal stroke, or other cause of death, occurs or is given or administered in one county, and the death occurs in another county, the offender may be tried in either county; and so, also, if the mortal stroke or cause of death occurs, or is given or administered, in another state or country, and the death happens in this state, the offender shall be tried in the county where the death happened.

PRACTICE.

§ 1322. On affidavit of the commission, within his district, of any criminal offense of which he has jurisdiction, lodged with any justice of the peace, he shall issue a warrant for the arrest of the offender, returnable forthwith, or on a certain day to be named, and shall issue subpœnas for witnesses, as in civil cases, and shall proceed to try and dispose of said case, according to law; and on conviction, shall order such punishment to be inflicted as the law provides.

§ 1323. It shall be lawful for a justice of the peace to order any one found guilty by him, who shall not immediately pay any fine imposed on him, and all costs, to stand committed to the county jail, until payment of such fine and costs.

§ 1324. The keeper of the jail of any county shall receive and

17

keep any prisoner committed by a justice of the peace, according to the order of commitment.

§ 2821. The justices of the peace of the several counties of this state shall be conservators of the peace within their respective counties, and shall have power to take all manner of bonds or recognizances, with or without security, for good behavior, to keep the peace, or for appearance at the circuit court, as the case may require, to answer any charge against the obligor or cognizor, or any offense committed in the view of such justices, or any of them, and whereof they have not jurisdiction to hear and determine; and in case any person shall refuse to enter into bond and recognizance as aforesaid, and to find security, when so required, it shall be lawful for said justices, or any of them, to commit the person so refusing to jail, there to remain until he shall comply with the order of such justices. And all bonds and recognizances so taken, shall be returned by the justices taking the same, to the next circuit court; and if any person shall forfeit his bond or recognizance, the same shall be so adjudged, and proceeded with, as is provided in this code.

§ 2822. Any justice of the peace may, by warrant under his hand, cause any person charged on oath with having committed, or being suspected of any offense against the laws of this state, to be apprehended and brought before him, or some other justice of the peace of his county, and on examination, any justice may commit such offender to jail, when the offense is not bailable, or where the offender is unable or unwilling to give bail, in bailable cases.

§ 2823. Any justice of the peace, or other committing officer or court, may require any prosecutor or witness, appearing before him, to enter into bond or recognizance, in such sum as he may think fit, with or without security, for his appearance to prosecute, or give evidence in any cause or matter, and in default of such prosecutor or witness, may commit him to jail, until he shall give such bond or recognizance, or until he shall be discharged by due course of law.

§ 2824. Any justice of the peace, on the affidavit of any credible person, may issue warrants to search for stolen goods, particularly describing the goods, and the place to be searched. If other persons claim any property thus seized, not over the value of one hundred and fifty dollars, the justice shall try the claim in his own court. If the value thereof be over that sum, then he shall send the claim to the circuit court of the proper county for trial, taking bond according to the statute relating to claimant's issues.

§ 2825. In all criminal cases, brought before any justice of the peace, he shall take the voluntary confession of the accused, and the substance of the material testimony of all the witnesses examined before him, in writing, and shall inform the accused of his right to interrogate such witnesses, which questions, and the answers thereto, he shall also reduce to writing; and the said proceedings and testimony, so taken and had, the said justice shall certify and send up, together with the bonds or recognizance of the accused, and the prosecutor and witnesses, to the next term of the circuit court of the proper county, on or before the first day of the term. And any justice failing so to do, shall be fined by such circuit court, on motion of the district attorney, on reasonable notice thereof, not more than fifty dollars.

§ 2826. When any person, accused of any offence, removes or escapes to another county, any justice of the peace of any county, where the accused may be supposed to have removed or escaped, shall, on application, endorse any warrant purporting to have been issued by any justice in another county, which shall authorize the arrest of any such offender in the county of such endorsement, and his removal to the county where the offence was committed, or is triable.

§ 2827. Any justice of the peace, in criminal cases or inquiries before him, may issue subpœnas to any county in the state, returnable immediately, and shall have power to enforce obedience thereto, as in other cases.

§ 2828. Any justice of the peace, of any county in this state, into which any offender may have removed himself, or escaped, on the oath of some credible person, may issue his warrant for the arrest of such offender, returnable before any justice of the peace of the county where the offence is properly cognizable, which shall authorize such arrest, and the removal of such offender to the proper county, for examination.

§ 2829. All offences, cognizable before a justice of the peace, shall be prosecuted by warrant, under the hand of such justice, returnable on a day, and at a place therein specified ; the person accused shall have the benefit of counsel in his defense, and the privilege of cross-examining the witnesses against him, as in other cases.

§ 2830. If any person shall pull down any advertisement, authorized by law, he shall, on conviction thereof, before any justice of the peace, be fined by such justice, not more than fifty dollars, to be paid into the county treasury.

§ 2831. Persons who have no visible means of support, but who, for the most part support themselves by gaming, shall be deemed, held and taken, as vagrants, and dealt with as such.

§ 2836. The following persons shall be deemed adjudged and punished as vagrants, to-wit : All able bodied persons, who live without employment or labor, and have no visible means of support or maintenance ; any person who shall abandon his wife or family, without just cause, leaving them without support, and in danger of becoming a public charge ; keepers of houses of public gaming, or houses of prostitution, and all common prostitutes, who have no other employment for their support or maintenance ; any able-bodied person, who shall be found begging for a livelihood, and common gamblers, or persons, who for the most part, maintain themselves by gaming.

§ 2837. It shall be the duty of any justice of the peace, upon his own knowledge, or on oath or information of any credible person, to issue his warrant to the sheriff or constable of any county, for the arrest of any vagrant, or person suspected or believed to be such vagrant, and to examine him in relation thereto ; and on satisfactory evidence of his being a vagrant, such justice shall commit him to the common jail of the county, for ten days, unless he shall give bond or recognizance, with good security, in the sum of two hundred dollars, for his good behavior for twelve months; which bond or recognizance, such justice shall return to the next term of the circuit court, and the same shall have like effect, and be subject to like proceedings, as bonds or recognizances in criminal cases. And if such vagrant shall so continue, after the execution of such bond or recognizance, or shall, at any time within the said twelve months, act as a vagrant, or otherwise violate the law, the said bond or recognizance shall become forfeited.

§ 2838. It shall be the duty of any justice of the peace, upon his own knowledge or information, of any subsequent violation of the provisions of this code, in relation to vagrants, to commit such vagrant to jail, for twenty days ; and no bond or recognizance shall be allowed on such second or other offence.

§ 2839. In all commitments for vagrancy, the justice shall order the offender to be confined for the time specified, and until he shall pay the costs of such imprisonment, and all proceedings relative thereto, or until discharged by due course of law, after ten days' notice to such justice, of his intended application for such discharge.

§ 2840. All the fines collected by such justice, or other officer, shall be paid into the state treasury, to the credit of the school fund.

§ 2854. Every court, before whom any person shall be convicted of an offence, less than felony, may, in addition to the penalty prescribed by law, require such convict to enter into recognizance, in a reasonable sum, with or without security, to keep the peace, and to be of good behavior, for any time not longer than two years, and may order such person to stand committed, until such recognizance be executed.

§ 2863. Offenses, for which no penalty is provided in this code, or indictable, as at common law, shall be punished by fine, in any sum not more than five hundred dollars, and imprisonment in the county jail, for a term not more than six months.

§ 2867. In all petty misdemeanors, except those committed by or on any officer or minister of justice, if the party complaining, or injured, shall appear before the court where the same shall be pending, and acknowledge to have received satisfaction therefor, the court, in its discretion, may discharge the defendant, and dismiss the proceedings, upon payment of all costs.

§ 2873. All bonds and recognizances taken in criminal cases, whether they shall describe the offense actually committed or not, shall have the effect to hold the party bound thereby, to answer to such offense as he may have actually committed, and shall be valid for that purpose, until he be discharged by the court.

§ 2877. When a prisoner shall be brought before any conservator of the peace, charged with the commission of an indictable offense, and when, in the course of the investigation, it shall appear to such conservator, that the prisoner was insane, when the offense was committed, and still is insane, he shall not be discharged ; but such conservator of the peace shall remand the prisoner to custody, and forthwith report the case to the chancellor of the proper county, whose duty it shall be to proceed with the case, according to the directions contained in the chapter and article of the chancery court law relating to persons *non compos mentis.*

§ 2880. Wherever, in the criminal laws of this state, the male gender is named, it shall include the feminine, and *vice versa*, when applicable. The singular shall include the plural, in all applicable cases.

§ 2881. Every person charged with any offense, committed in another state, territory, or country, may plead a former conviction or acquittal, for the same offense, in such other state, territory, or country; and if such plea be established, it shall be a bar to any further proceedings for the same offense here.

§ 2882. Where a defendant is acquitted of a criminal charge, upon trial, on the ground of a variance between the indictment and proof, or upon an exception to the form or substance of the indictment or record, he may be tried and convicted, upon a subsequent indictment, for the offense actually committed, notwithstanding such acquittal; and it shall be the duty of the court to order the accused into the custody of the proper officer.

§ 2887. Every person who shall design and endeavor to commit any offense, and shall do any overt act toward the commission thereof, but shall fail therein, or shall be prevented from committing the same, on conviction thereof, shall, in case where no provision is made by law, for the punishment of such offense, be punished as follows: If the offense attempted to be committed is capital, such offense shall be punished by imprisonment in the penitentiary, not exceeding ten years; if the offense attempted, be punishable by imprisonment in the penitentiary, or by fine and imprisonment in the county jail, then the attempt to commit such offense shall be punished for a period, or for an amount not greater than is prescribed for the actual commission of the offense so attempted, in the discretion of the court.

§ 2888. It shall be the duty of all grand jurors, justices of the peace, constables, coroners, members of the board of county supervisors, sheriffs, and all other civil or peace officers of the county, without delay, to give information against, and prosecute every person who shall be guilty of a violation of any of the penal laws of this state, and all necessary costs and expenses incurred therein, shall be paid, on due proof thereof, out of the state treasury, if the defendant is acquitted, or unable to pay the same.

§ 2504. It shall be sufficient, in an indictment under this article, to charge that the defendant did pass, or issue, or circulate, as money, or as a substitute for money, a note, bill, certificate, or other evidence of debt whatever, not being United States currency, or national bank notes, under the value of five dollars, in violation of the provisions of this article, without further describing said evidence of debt or liability than by its usual name. And proof that such defendant did pass, issue, or circulate as money, or as a substitute for money, any note, bill, certificate, or other evidence of debt or liability whatever, of the character or denomination prohibited by this article, shall be *prima facie* evidence of the truth of such charge.

§ 2510. When the right of property, in any unmarked animal, shall be in doubt, any person *bona fide* claiming the title to the same, may call in two or more of the neighbors nearest to, and adjoining the range where such animal usually runs, and in their presence, and with their approbation, may mark or brand such animal.

§ 2519. Upon the trial of any indictment, for any offense specified in sections two thousand five hundred and eighteen and two thousand five hundred and nineteen, of this article, it shall not be necessary to prove the conviction of any offender, for the offense in relation to which any agreement or understanding, therein prohibited, shall have been made.

§ 2532. If any person shall give or accept such challenge, or knowingly carry or deliver such challenge, or the acceptance thereof, or be second of either party to any duel, such person shall, on conviction, be incapable of holding or being elected to any post of vonor, profit, or emolument, civil or military, under the constitution and laws of this state ; and the appointment of any such person to office, as also all votes given to any such person, are hereby declared illegal, and none of the votes given to such person, for any office, shall be taken or counted.

§ 2535. If any person shall offend against any of the provisions of this article, such person shall be a competent witness against any other person offending in the same transaction, and may be compelled to appear and give evidence, in the same manner as other witnesses ; but the testimony so given shall be statutory pardon for any offense against the provisions of this article, and shall not be used in any prosecution or proceeding, civil or criminal, against the person so testifying, and may be plead as a defense in any prosecution against him, made under this article, for that offense.

§ 2558. If any prisoner, confined in a county jail, or in the penitentiary, for a criminal offense, shall escape therefrom, he may be pursued, retaken, and imprisoned again, notwithstanding the term for which he was sentenced to be imprisoned, may have expired at the time he shall be retaken, and shall remain so imprisoned until tried for such escape, or until discharged, on a failure to prosecute therefor.

§ 2650. Every offense prohibited in section 2649, may be tried, either in the county where the same may have been committed, or in any county into, or through which, any person so kidnapped or confined, shall have been taken, while under such confinement.

§ 2651. Upon the trial of any such offense, the consent of the person so kidnapped or confined, shall not be a defense, unless it appear satisfactorily to the jury, that such consent was not extorted by threats or duress.

§ 2571. Every person who shall be convicted of having forged, counterfeited, or falsely altered any will of real or personal property, or any deed or other instrument, being or purporting to be the act of another, by which any right or interest in real or personal property shall be, or purport to be, transferred, conveyed, or in any way changed or affected, or any certificate or endorsement of the acknowledgment of any person, of any deed or other instrument, which, by law, may be recorded, made, or purporting to have been made, by any officer duly authorized to make such certificate or endorsement, or any certificate of the proof of any deed or other instrument, which, by law, may be recorded, made, or purporting to have been made, by any officer duly authorized to make such certificate, with intent to defraud, shall be adjudged guilty of forgery.

§ 2572. Every person who shall be convicted of having forged, counterfeited, or falsely altered, any certificate or other public security, issued, or purporting to have been issued, under the authority of this state, by virtue of any law thereof, by which certificate or other public security, the payment of any money, absolutely or upon contingency, shall be promised, or the receipt of any money, goods. or valuable thing, shall be acknowledged, or any certificate of any share, right or interest, in any public stock, created by virtue of any law of this state, issued, or purporting to have been issued, by any public officer, or any other evidence of any debt or liability of this state, either absolute or contingent, issued, or purporting to have been issued, by any public officer, or any endorsement or other instrument, transferring, or purporting to transfer, the right or interest of any holder of any such certificate, public security, certificate of stock, evidence of debt or liability, or of any person entitled to such right or interest, with intent to defraud this state, or any public officer thereof, or any other person, shall be adjudged guilty of forgery.

§ 2573. Every person who shall forge or counterfeit the great seal of this state, the seal of any public office, authorized by law, the seal of any court of record, including the seal of the court of chancery, and the seal of the board of county supervisors, or the seal of any body corporate, duly incorporated by or under the laws of this state, or who shall falsely forge or counterfeit any impression, purporting to be the impression of any such seal, with intent to defraud, shall, upon conviction, be adjudged guilty of forgery.

§ 2574. Every person who, with intent to defraud, shall falsely alter, destroy, corrupt or falsify any record of any will, conveyance, or other instrument, the record of which shall, by law, be evidence, or any record of any judgment or decree of a court of record, or the enrollment of any such judgment or decree, or the return of any officer, court or tribunal, to any process of any court, or who shall falsely make, forge or alter, any entry in any book of records, or any instrument purporting to be any such record or return, with intent to defraud, shall, upon conviction, be adjudged guilty of forgery.

§ 2575. If any officer, authorized to take the proof or acknowledgment of any conveyance of real or personal estate, or of any other instrument which, by law, may be recorded, shall wilfully and falsely certify that any such conveyance or instrument was acknowledged by any party thereto, when in truth no such acknowledgment was made, or that any such conveyance or instrument was proved, when in truth no such proof was made, he shall, upon conviction, be adjudged guilty of forgery.

§ 2576. Every person who shall be convicted of having counterfeited any of the gold or silver coins which shall be at the time current, by custom or usage, within this state, shall be adjudged guilty of forgery.

§ 2577. Every person who shall be convicted of having counterfeited any gold or silver coin, of any foreign government or country, with the intent of exporting the same, to injure or defraud any foreign government, or the subjects thereof, shall be deemed guilty of forgery.

§ 2578. Every person who shall be convicted of having made or engraved, or having caused or procured to be made or engraved, any plate in the form or similitude of any promissory note, bill of exchange, draft, check, certificate of deposit, or other evidence of debt, issued by any incorporated bank in this state, or by any bank incorporated under the laws of the United States, or of any state or territory, or under the laws of any foreign country or government, without the authority of such bank, or of having or keeping in his custody or possession, any such plate, without the authority of such bank, with the intent of using or having the same used, for the purpose of taking therefrom any impression, to be passed, sold or altered, or of having made, or caused to be made, or having in his custody or possession, any plate upon which shall be engraved any figures or words, which may be used for the purpose of falsely altering any evidence of debt, issued by any such incorporated bank, with the intent of having the same used for such purpose, or of having or keeping in his custody or possession, without the authority of such bank, any impression taken from any such plate, with intent to have the same filled up and completed, for the purpose of being passed, sold or uttered, shall be adjudged guilty of forgery.

§ 2579. Every plate specified in the last section shall be deemed to be in the form and similitude of the genuine instrument imitated, in either of the following cases: when the engraving on such plate resembles, and is intended to conform to such parts of the genuine instrument as are engraved; or when such plate shall be partly finished, and the part so finished resembles, and is intended to conform to similar parts of the genuine instrument.

§ 2580. Every person who shall be convicted of having sold, exchanged or delivered, for any consideration, any forged or counterfeited promissory note, check, bill, draft, or other evidence of debt, or engagement for the payment of money, absolutely, or upon contingency, knowing the same to be forged or countefeited, with the intent to have the same uttered or passed, or of having offered any such notes or other instruments for sale, exchange or delivery, for any consideration, with the like knowledge and like intention, or of having received any such note or other instrument, upon a sale, exchange or delivery, for any consideration, with the like knowledge, and with the like intention, shall be adjudged guilty of forgery.

§ 2581. Every person who, with the intent to injure or defraud, shall falsely make, alter, forge or counterfeit any instrument or writing, being or purporting to be, any process issued by any competent court, magistrate or officer, or being or purporting to be, any pleading or proceeding, filed or entered in any court of law or equity, or being, or purporting to be, any certificate, order or allowance, by any competent court or officer, or being, or purporting to be, any license or authority, authorized by any statute, or any instrument or writing, being, or purporting to be, the act of another, by which any pecuniary demand or obligation shall be, or shall purport to be, created, increased, discharged or diminished, or by which any right or property whatever, shall be, or purport to be, transferred, conveyed, discharged, diminished, or in any manner affected, by which false making, forging, altering or counterfeiting, any person may be affected, bound, or in any way injured in his person or property, shall be adjudged guilty of forgery.

§ 2582. Every person who, with intent to defraud, shall make any false entry, or shall falsely alter any entry made in any book of accounts, kept in the office of the auditor of public accounts of this state, or in the office of the treasurer of this state, or in the office of any county treasurer, or in any other public office, by which any demand, or obligation, claim, right or interest, either against or in favor of this state, or any county or town, or any individual, shall be, or purport to be discharged, diminished, increased, created, or in any manner affected, shall, upon conviction thereof, be adjudged guilty of forgery.

§ 2583. Every person who, with intent to defraud, shall make any false entry, or shall falsely alter any entry made, in any book of accounts kept by any moneyed corporation within this state, or in any book of accounts kept by any corporation or its officers, and to be delivered, or intended to be delivered, to any person dealing with such corporation, by which any pecuniary obligation, claim or credit, shall be, or shall purport to be, discharged, diminished, increased, created, or in any manner affected, shall be adjudged guilty of forgery.

§ 2584. Every person who shall have in his possession any forged, altered or counterfeited negotiable note, bill, draft, or other evidence of debt, issued, or purporting to have been issued, by any corporation or company, duly authorized for that purpose, by the laws of the United States, or of this state, or of any other state, government or country, or any other forged, altered or counterfeit instrument, the forgery of which is hereinbefore declared to be punishable, knowing the same to be forged, altered or counterfeited, with intention to utter the same as true, or as false, or to cause the same to be so uttered, with intent to injure or defraud, shall also be adjudged guilty of forgery.

§ 2585. Every person who shall have in his possession any counterfeit of any gold or silver coin, which shall be at the time current in this state, knowing the same to be counterfeited, with intention to defraud or injure by uttering the same, as true or false, or by causing the same to be so uttered, shall be adjudged guilty of forgery.

§ 2586. Every person who shall be convicted of having uttered or published as true, and with intent to defraud, any forged, altered or counterfeit instrument, or any counterfeit gold or silver coin, the forgery, altering or counterfeiting of which is hereinbefore declared to be an offense, knowing such instrument or coin to be forged, altered, or counterfeited, shall suffer the punishment herein provided for forgery.

§ 2587. If any person shall, with intent to injure or defraud, make any instrument in his own name, intended to create, increase, discharge, defeat or diminish, any pecuniary obligation, right or interest, or to transfer or affect any property whatever, and shall utter and pass it, under the pretense that it is the act of another who bears the same name, he shall, upon conviction, be adjudged guilty of forgery, in the same degree as if he had forged the instrument of a person bearing a different name from his own.

§ 2589. The total erasure, obliteration, or destruction of any instrument or writing, with the intent to defraud, by which any pecuniary obligation, or any right, interest, or claim to property, shall be, or shall be intended to be, created, increased, discharged, diminished, or in any manner affected, shall be deemed forgery, in the same manner, and in the same degree, as the false alteration of any part of such instrument or writing.

§ 2590. When different parts of several genuine instruments shall be so placed or connected together, as to produce one instrument, with intent to defraud, the same shall be deemed forgery, in the same manner as if the parts, so put together, were falsely made or forged.

§ 2591. Every instrument, partly written and partly printed, or wholly printed, with a written signature thereto, and every signature of an individual, firm, or corporate body, or of any officer of such body, and every writing purporting to be such signatures, shall be deemed a writing, and a written instrument, within the meaning of the provisions of this chapter.

§ 2592. Whenever, by any of the foregoing provisions, an intent to defraud is required to constitute forgery, it shall be sufficient if such intent appear, to defraud the United States, any state or territory, any body corporate, city, town or village, or any public officer in his official capacity, any copartnership, or any one of such partners, or any real person whatever.

§ 2593. The false making, forging or counterfeiting, of any evidence of debt, issued, or purporting to have been issued, by any corporation having authority for that purpose, to which shall be affixed the pretended signature of any person, as an agent or officer of such corporation, shall be deemed forgery, in the same manner as if such person was, at the time, an officer or agent of such corporation, notwithstanding there never was any such person in existence.

§ 2594. If any person shall falsely or fraudulently make, forge or alter any writing, being, or pretending to be, an auditor's warrant on the state treasury, or any order or warrant on the treasury of this state, or the treasury of the United States, or any county, or any incorporated city or town, with intent to defraud the state, or any county, incorporated city or town, or any person, he shall be deemed guilty of forgery.

§ 2608. In all indictments, under the provisions of this article, it shall be sufficient to charge the general name or description of the game at which the defendant may have played, without setting forth or describing, with or against whom he may have bet or played; and no exception shall be sustained to any such indictment, for any defect or want of form, but the court shall proceed to give judgment, according to the very right of the case. And in addition to the penalties hereinbefore provided, it shall be the duty of the jury to find, in their verdict, the amount won, and it shall be the duty of the court to enter up judgment against the winning party, for the amount so won, to be collected as other fines, and to be appropriated for the use of common schools.

§ 2609. Betting upon any horse race, or shooting match, shall not be indictable.

§ 2603. All moneys exhibited for the purpose of betting, or alluring persons to bet at any game, and all moneys staked or betted, shall be liable to seizure, by any justice of the peace of the county in which such offence shall be committed, or by any other person, under a warrant from such justice or other peace officer; and all such moneys, so seized, shall be accounted for by the person making the seizure, to the justice of the peace, or other officer issuing such warrant, and be paid by him into the treasury of the county, deducting thereout fifty per centum upon all moneys so seized, to the person making the said seizure.

§ 2610. All laws made, or to be made, for the suppression of gaming, are hereby declared to be remedial, and not penal statutes, and shall be so construed by the courts.

§ 2611. On the trial of all indictments, under the provisions of this article, the district attorney shall not be confined, in the proof, to a single violation, but under the indictment charging a single offence, may give in evidence any one or more offences, of the same character, committed anterior to the day laid in the indictment, and not barred by the statute of limitations; *provided,* that in such case, after conviction or acquittal on the merits, the accused shall not be again liable to prosecution for any offence of the same character, committed anterior to the day laid in such indictment.

§ 2612. It shall be the duty of the sheriffs, coroners, justices, constables, and all other civil officers of the county, when they know, or have reason to suspect, any person to be guilty of a violation of the provisions of this article, to apprehend, or cause to be seized, such person, with or without warrant, and to bring him before some officer having jurisdiction thereof, and to appear and prosecute such offender at the next term of the circuit court.

§ 2663. Whenever it shall appear to any court of record, that any witness or party, who has been legally sworn or examined in any case, matter or proceeding, pending before the court, has testified in such manner as to induce a reasonable presumption that he has willfully and corruptly testified falsely, to some material point or matter, such court may immediately commit such party or witness, by an order or process for that purpose, to prison, or take recognizance, with sureties, for his appearing and answering to an indictment for perjury.

§ 2664. Such court shall thereupon bind over the witnesses to establish such perjury, to appear at the proper court, to testify before the grand jury, and on the trial, in case an indictment be found for such perjury.

§ 2667. In all prosecutions against any person, for willful and corrupt perjury, it shall be sufficient to set forth the substance of the offence charged upon the defendant, and before what court, or before whom the oath or affirmation was taken ; averring such court, or person, to have competent authority to administer the same, together with proper averments to falsify the matter wherein the perjury is assigned, without setting forth the bill, answer, information, indictment, declaration, or any part of any record, or proceeding, either in law or equity, other than as aforesaid, and without setting forth the commission or authority of the court, or the commission or authority of the person before whom the perjury was committed.

§ 2668. In all prosecutions for subornation of perjury, or for corrupt bargaining, or contracting with others to commit willful and corrupt perjury, it shall be sufficient to set forth the substance of the offence charged upon the defendant, without setting forth the bill, answer, information, indictment, or declaration, or any part of the record or proceeding, either in law or equity, and without setting forth the commission or authority of the court or person before whom the perjury was committed, or was agreed, or promised to be committed.

§ 2674. Every person who shall be convicted of feloniously taking the personal property of another in his presence, or from his person, and against his will, by violence to his person, or by putting such person in fear of some immediate injury to his person, shall be adjudged guilty of robbery.

§ 2675. Every person, who shall be convicted of feloniously taking the personal property of another, in his presence, or from his person, which shall have been delivered or suffered to be taken, through fear of some injury, threatened to be inflicted at some different time, to his person or property, or to the person of any relative or member of his family, which fear shall have been produced by the threats of the person so receiving or taking such property, shall be adjudged guilty of robbery.

§ 2655. If any person shall sever from the soil of another, any produce growing thereon, or shall sever from any building, gate, fence, railing or other improvement or enclosure, any part thereof, and shall take and convert the same to his own use, with intent to steal the same, he shall be deemed guilty of larceny, in the same manner, and of the same degree, as if the article so taken had been severed at some previous and different time.

§ 2628. The killing of a human being, without the authority of law, by any means, or in any manner, shall be murder in the following cases : when done with a deliberate design to effect the death of the person killed, or of any human being ; when done in the commission of an act eminently dangerous to others, and evincing a depraved heart, regardless of human life, although without any premeditated design to effect the death of any particular individual; when done, without any design to effect death, by any person engaged in the commission of the crime of rape, burglary, arson, or robbery, or in any attempt to commit such felonies.

§ 2629. Every person who shall, by previous appointment, agreement, or understanding, fight a duel, without the jurisdiction of this state, and in so doing shall inflict a wound upon his antagonist, or any other person, whereof the person thus injured shall die within this state, and every second engaged in such duel, shall be deemed guilty of murder in this state, and may be indicted, tried and convicted, in the county where such death shall happen.

§ 2631. The killing of a human being, by the act, procurement or omission of another, shall be justifiable in the following cases: when committed by public officers or those acting by their command, in their aid and assistance, in obedience to any judgment of a competent court; or when necessarily committed in overcoming actual resistance to the execution of some legal process, or to the discharge of any other legal duty; or when necessarily committed in re-taking any felon who has been rescued, or has escaped; or when necessarily committed in arresting any felon fleeing from justice; such homicide shall also be justifiable when committed by any person, in resisting any attempt unlawfully to kill such person, or to commit any felony upon him, or upon, or in any dwelling house in which said person shall be; or when committed in the lawful defence of such person, or any other human being, where there shall be reasonable ground to apprehend a design to commit a felony, or to do some great personal injury, and there shall be imminent danger of such design, been accomplished; or when necessarily committed in attempting, by lawful ways and means, to apprehend any person for any felony committed; or in lawfully suppressing any riot, or in lawfully keeping and preserving the peace.

§ 2632. The killing of a human being, by the act, procurement, or omission of another, shall be excusable, when committed by accident and misfortune, in lawfully correcting a child or apprentice, or in doing any other lawful act, by lawful means, with usual and ordinary caution, and without any unlawful intent; or by accident or misfortune, in the heat of passion, upon any sudden and sufficient provocation; or upon any sudden combat, without any undue advantage being taken, and without any dangerous weapon being used, and not done in a cruel or unusual manner.

§ 2633. The killing of a human being without malice, by the act, procurement or culpable negligence of another, while such other is engaged in the perpetration of any felony, except rape, burglary, arson or robbery, or while such other is attempting to commit any felony besides such as are above enumerated and excepted, shall be deemed manslaughter; or the killing of a human being, without malice, by the act, procurement, or culpable negligence of another, while such other is engaged in the perpetration of any crime or misdemeanor, not amounting to felony; or in the attempt to perpetrate any crime or misdemeanor, in case such killing would be murder at common law, shall be deemed manslaughter.

§ 2634. Every person deliberately assisting another in the commission of self-murder, shall be deemed guilty of manslaughter.

§ 2635. The willful killing of an unborn quick child, by an injury to the mother of such child, which would be murder, if it resulted in the death of the mother, shall be deemed manslaughter.

§ 2636. Every person who shall administer to any woman pregnant with a quick child, any medicine, drug, or substance whatever, or shall use or employ any instrument or other means, with intent thereby to destroy such child, unless the same shall have been necessary, to preserve the life of such mother, or shall have been advised by a physician, to be necessary for such purpose, shall be deemed guilty of manslaughter.

§ 2637. The killing of a human being without malice, in the heat of passion, but in a cruel or unusual manner, without authority of law, and not in necessary self-defense, shall be deemed manslaughter.

§ 2638. Every person who shall unnecessarily kill another, either while resisting an attempt by such other person to commit any felony or to do any other unlawful act, or after such attempt shall have failed, shall be deemed guilty of manslaughter.

§ 2639. The killing of another, in the heat of passion, without malice, by the use of a dangerous weapon, without authority of law, and not in necessary self-defense, shall be deemed manslaughter.

§ 2640. The involuntary killing of a human being by the act, procurement or culpable negligence of another, while such other person is engaged in the commission of a trespass or other injury to private rights or property, or engaged in an attempt to commit such injury shall be deemed manslaughter.

2641. If the owner of a mischievous animal, knowing its propensity, willfully suffer it to go at large, or shall keep it without ordinary care, and such animal, while so at large, or not confined, kill any human being, who shall have taken all the precaution which the circumstances may permit, to avoid such animal, such owner shall be deemed guilty of manslaughter.

§ 2642. Any person navigating any boat or vessel for gain, who shall willfully or negligently receive so many passengers, or such quantity of other lading, that by means thereof such boat or vessel shall sink or overset, and thereby any human being shall be drowned, or otherwise killed, shall be deemed guilty of manslaughter.

§ 2643. If any captain, engineer, or any other person having charge of any steamboat, or railroad engine, connected with any car or cars, used for the conveyance of passengers, or if the engineer or other person having charge of the boiler of such boat or engine, or of any other apparatus for the generation of steam, shall, from ignorance or gross neglect, or for the purpose of excelling any other boat in speed, or for the purpose of unusual speed, create, or allow to be created, such an undue quantity of steam as to burst or break the boiler, or other apparatus in which it shall be generated, or any apparatus or machinery connected therewith, or shall thereby cause the said engine or cars to run off said railroad track, or from any other ignorant or gross neglect, shall permit or cause said cars or engine to be thus thrown, by which bursting, breaking, or running off the track, as aforesaid, any person shall be killed, every such captain, engineer, or other person, shall be deemed guilty of manslaughter.

§ 2644. If any physician, or other person, while in a state of intoxication, shall, without a design to effect death, administer, or cause to be administered, any poison, drug, or other medicine, or shall perform any surgical operation on another, which shall cause the death of such other person, he shall be deemed guilty of manslaughter.

§ 2645. Every other killing of a human being, by the act, procurement, or culpable negligence of another, and without authority of law, not provided for in this chapter, shall be deemed manslaughter.

§ 2682. Offenses against the provisions of this article—(Sabbath—violation of—chapter 58, article 29)—shall be cognizable before any justice of the peace of the county where they may occur, or by indictment in the circuit court; and the said offenders, in lieu of such fine, may, at the discretion of the court, be imprisoned in the common jail, not longer than one week.

§ 2686. Every person engaged, or who shall be about to engage in cutting or rafting cypress, pine, or ash timber, for sale or transportation, shall file, in the chancery clerk's office of the county where he shall engage in such business, an affidavit of such intention, and a particular description of the tract of land from which he designs cutting such timber, and the authority by which he so intends to cut such timber, as well as the name of the person from whom he derives such authority; which affidavit, said clerk shall record in a book, to be called the "rafting record;" and such clerk, for such service, shall be entitled to receive fifty cents; and the failure to file such affidavit, by any person cutting such timber, shall be deemed and taken as *prima facie* evidence of the guilt of such person, on any trial or indictment which may be had or found against him, for a violation of this article, and shall subject him, even if he shall prove his innocence of such cutting, without permission, to the payment of the costs of such prosecution, and he may, in the discretion of the court, be ordered to stand committed, until such costs shall be paid.

§ 2687. It shall be the duty of any justice of the peace, in this state, on information, on oath, that any person is engaged in the violation of this article (§§ 2684 and 2685), to issue his warrant, directed to the sheriff or any constable of the county, commanding him to arrest all persons found illegally cutting or rafting such timber, and to bring such person, so offending, whether named in such warrant or not, before some justice of the peace of the county, to be dealt with according to law; and if such person shall have cut any timber, or made any raft, contrary to the provisions of this article, it shall be the duty of such officer, serving such warrant, to take possession of such timber, and hold the same subject to the order of such justice. And should the said justice, on examination, be satisfied that such timber was illegally cut, such justice shall order the said officer to sell such timber or raft, and to pay over the proceeds thereof to the county treasurer ; and if the accused shall be convicted, on indictment for such offense, then, after deducting the costs, one-half of the proceeds of the sale of such timber as may have been cut from state land, shall be paid to the informer, and the other half into the state treasury ; and in case of lands belonging to any individual or corporation, the proceeds of sales shall be paid to the owner of such land.

§ 2707. In every criminal prosecution for libel or actionable words, it shall be lawful for the defendant, upon the trial, to give in evidence in his defense, the truth of the matter, written, spoken, or published.

§ 2698. No indictment under this article (chapter 58, article 32), shall be quashed or abated for want of form ; nor shall it be necessary to aver in any indictment the name or description of the kind of vinous or spirituous liquors charged to have been sold, nor the name of the person to whom it was sold.

§ 2721. It shall be unlawful for any person or persons to be, or appear, in any mask or disguise, in the country or towns, or in any public place in this state, or to prowl or travel in such mask or disguise ; *provided*, this section shall not be so construed as to apply to innocent amusements.

§ 241. When any person accused of treason, felony, or other crime or misdemeanor, shall be committed to the jail of any county, and the sheriff shall have cause to suspect that such person or persons will attempt to escape, such sheriff shall apply to any justice of the peace for the same county, who, upon satisfactory proof of danger of the escape of such prisoner, shall issue his warrant to the said sheriff for a sufficient guard for securing such prisoner, so long as the necessity therefor shall continue, and said guard shall be entitled to two dollars and fifty cents per day, to be paid by the county treasurer, on the certificate of said sheriff.

§ 2500. All notes and other securities, for the payment of money or other things, made or given to any such association, institution, or company, that may be formed, for any of the purposes expressed in the first section of this article (article 7, chapter 58), or made or given to secure the payment of any money loaned or discounted by any incorporated company, or its officers, contrary to the provisions of this article, shall be void.

ARRESTS.

§ 2773. Arrests for crimes and offenses may be made by any officer acting as sheriff, or his deputy. or any constable, marshal, or policeman, of any city or town within their county, or by private persons.

§ 2774. Every person, when commanded by an officer, seeking to arrest an offender, must obey such command.

§ 2775. Arrests for criminal offenses may be made at any time or place, and so, also, to prevent a breach of the peace, or the commission of a crime.

§ 2776. An officer or private person may arrest any person, without warrant, for an indictable offense committed, or a breach of the peace threatened, or attempted, in his presence ; or when such person has committed a felony, though not in his presence : or when a felony has been committed, and he has reasonable ground to suspect and believe the person proposed to be arrested, to have committed it, or on a charge made upon reasonable cause, of the commission of a felony by the party proposed to be arrested. And in all cases of arrests without warrant, the person making such arrest, must inform the accused of the object and cause of such arrest, except when he is in the actual commission of the offense, or is arrested on pursuit.

§ 2777. To make an arrest, as provided for in this article. any officer or private person, after notice of his office and object, if admittance is refused, may break open a window or outer or inner door of any dwelling or other house, in which he has reason to believe the offender may be found.

§ 2778. If any offender escape, or be rescued, the person from whose possession or custody he escaped or was rescued, may immediately pursue and retake him, at any time, and in any county in this state, without warrant.

§ 2779. Every person making an arrest, shall take the offender before some magistrate, or other convenient law officer, without unnecessary delay, for examination of his case.

§ 2780. Officers and others, who, in the discharge of their duty, shall make arrests, as authorized or required by the provisions of this article, shall not be liable, on account thereof, civilly or criminally, notwithstanding it may turn out that the party arrested was innocent of any offense.

§ 2782. Justices of the peace, officers and others, engaged or assisting in the arrest of offenders, shall be entitled to the same fees as are usual, or allowed by law to officers for similar services, in civil cases. to be allowed by the court, on due proof of the services, in the circuit court, and taxed, collected and paid, as other costs in criminal cases.

§ 2783. If any person be dangerously wounded, the party accused shall be committed to prison, until it be perfectly known whether the person so wounded shall recover or not, unless it shall appear to the court of inquiry that the case, in any event, would not amount to murder ; in which case, or in the event that the person wounded shall recover, the offender shall be recognized to appear, at the next term of the circuit court, to answer said offence.

§ 2786. Any person, who shall arrest any one who has killed another, and is fleeing, or attempting to flee, before arrest, and shall deliver him up for trial, shall be entitled to the sum of two hundred dollars, out of the state treasury, upon the production of a certificate of the allowance of said claim, by the circuit court of the proper county.

WITNESSES AND EVIDENCE.

§ 771. Witnesses in criminal cases shall be allowed the same

18

compensation as in civil cases, but the prosecutor shall not be allowed compensation as a witness, nor shall any person be allowed for his attendance as a witness in more than one criminal case on the same day.

§ 2613. Every witness, when summoned, shall appear and give evidence of all offences against the provisions of this article, of which he shall have any knowledge ; and such witness, so summoned and giving evidence, without procurement or contrivance on his part, shall be thereafter exempt from criminal prosecution, for any offence against the provisions of this article, in relation to which he shall have so testified, *bona fide*.

§ 2654. If any person shall steal any bond, covenant, note, bankbill, bill of exchange, draft, order, receipt or other evidence of debt, or chose in action, or any public security issued by the United States, or any state, or any instrument whereby any demand, right or obligation, shall be created, increased, released, extinguished or diminished, the money due thereon, or secured thereby, and remaining unsatisfied, or which, in any event, might be collected thereon, or the value of the property transferred or affected thereby, as the case may be, shall be deemed the value of the article stolen, without further proof thereof.

§ 2665. If, on hearing of such cause, matter or proceeding, in which such perjury shall be suspected to have been committed, any papers or documents produced by either party, shall be deemed necessary to be used in the prosecution for such perjury, such court may, by order, detain such papers or documents from the party producing them, and direct them to be delivered to the district attorney.

§ 2848. Any person, desiring to prosecute another, for a violation of the criminal laws of the state, may apply to the clerk of the proper court, in vacation, for writs of subpœna, for any witnesses to attend before the grand jury at the next term. It shall be the duty of the clerk to issue all subpœnas thus applied for, and it shall be the duty of all witnesses, thus summoned, to attend, in obedience to the command of such subpœna; and if they fail to appear, the foreman of the grand jury may apply for and obtain an attachment, as in other cases of defaulting witnesses.

§ 2849. Every witness summoned on a criminal prosecution, inquiry or plea of the state, shall attend, from day to day, and from term to term, without further notice, until discharged by the court, or by the party summoning him, or in default thereof, he shall be fined by the court, not more than five hundred dollars, for the use of the school fund, unless on the return of a *scire facias*, as provided in this chapter, in relation to bonds and recognizances, and before final judgment thereon, he shall show good cause for such default ; and such witness shall be further liable to attachment, as in civil cases.

§ 2871. In all trials of indictments for assault and battery, or for an assault, the defendant may give in evidence, in excuse or extenuation, any insulting words used by the person, on whom such assault or assault and battery was committed, at the time of the commission thereof, towards the defendant, and the jury may consider and determine whether such insult was or was not a sufficient excuse or justification of the offense committed.

APPEALS.

§ 1335. Any one convicted of a criminal offense, by the judgment of a justice of the peace, shall have the right of appeal to the next term of the circuit court of his county, upon his entering into bond or recognizance, in a sum, to be prescribed by the justice, not less than fifty, nor more than five hundred dollars, with good and approved security, conditioned for the payment of all costs, and for the appearance of the defendant, at the next term of said circuit court ; and on his appearance in said court, such case shall be tried anew, on its merits, and disposed of, as other cases pending in said court ; and on default of such defendant, a forfeiture shall be entered against him and his sureties.

BAIL.

§ 1325. It shall be lawful for any officer, having any person in custody, by virtue of the warrant of a justice of the peace, in the cases hereinbefore provided for, to take bond or recognizance, with good and sufficient sureties, in a sum not less than fifty, nor more than five hundred dollars, conditioned for the appearance of such person, at the day named in the warrant, before the justice of the peace before whom it is returnable, and to fix the amount of the bond or recognizance, which bond or recognizance, shall be returned to such justice, and proceeded on, in case of forfeiture, as in like cases in the circuit court, as far as may be, with the difference in the constitution of the courts ; and so, any justice of the peace, before whom a prisoner is brought, on adjourning from day to day, or to a subsequent day, for the hearing of such case, may take bond or recognizance, in such sum as he may prescribe, not less than fifty, nor more than five hundred dollars, with sufficient sureties, properly conditioned for the appearance of such prisoner ; which bond shall be filed by the justice, and may be proceeded on by him, as in like cases in circuit courts. But when the bond or recognizance, taken as above, by the justice, or any officer, shall exceed in its penalty one hundred and fifty dollars, it shall be returned to, and filed in the clerk's office of the circuit court of the county, by the justice of the peace, with his certificate of the breach that occurred, in the non-appearance of the prisoner before him ; and judgment *nisi* shall be entered by the circuit court, on such bond or recognizance and certificate ; and thereupon, such other proceedings shall be had, as in case of a bond or recognizance, conditioned for the appearance of a party in the circuit court.

§ 2787. When a defendant charged with a criminal offence, shall be committed to jail by any court, judge, justice, or other officer, for default in not giving bail, it shall be the duty of such court or officer, to state in the *mittimus*, the nature of the offence, the county where committed, the amount of bail required, and the number of sureties ; and to direct the sheriff of the county where such party is ordered to be confined, to release him, on his entering into recognizance, as required by the order of the court, or committing officer.

§ 2788. It shall be the duty of the sheriff having custody of any defendant as aforesaid, upon his compliance with the order of said committing court or officer, to release him from custody. Said sheriff shall approve the sureties on the recognizance, and for that purpose shall examine them on oath, or take their affidavit in writing, and may administer such oath.

§ 2789. It shall be the duty of any sheriff taking recognizance as aforesaid, to return the same to the clerk of the circuit court of the county where the offence is alleged to have been committed, on or before the first day of the next term thereof ; and if any sheriff shall neglect to take recognizance as aforesaid, or if the same, from any cause, be insufficient at the time he took and approved the same, on exceptions taken and filed before the close of the next term, after the same should have been returned, and upon reasonable notice thereof to said sheriff, he shall be deemed and stand as special bail, and judgment shall be rendered against him as such.

§ 2790. When the defendant is not entitled to bail, or where he neglects or refuses to give bail, as required by law, and the jail of the county in which the offence was committed, or where the case stands for trial, is, in the opinion of the court or committing officer, insufficient for the safe keeping of criminals, it shall be the duty of the court or officer, to make an order for the removal of the accused to the nearest or most convenient and safe jail, of some convenient county, there to be kept, until the court shall sit for the trial of the offender ; and it shall be the duty of the jailor of such county to safely keep him, according to the order of the court or officer having jurisdiction thereof ; and it shall further be the duty of said sheriff or jailor, to have the body of the defendant, without further order, before the circuit court of the proper county, at its next term thereafter, on the first day of the term, unless he shall have been discharged by due course of law.

§ 2791. All bonds and recognizances taken for the appearance of any party, either as defendant, prosecutor or witness, in any state case or other criminal proceeding or matter, shall be made payable to the state of Mississippi, and shall have the effect to bind the accused, and his sureties on said bond or recognizance, until the principal shall be discharged by due course of law, and shall stand in full force, from term to term, without renewal.

§ 2792. If any defendant, prosecutor, or witness in any criminal case, proceeding or matter, shall fail to comply with the terms of his bond or recognizance, the court may, at any time after such default made, enter judgment *nisi* against the obligor and his sureties in such bond or recognizance, and thereupon a *scire facias* may issue as against bail, returnable to the next term of such court, as in other cases. And upon the return of service of such *scire facias*, or two writs of *scire facias* to the proper officer of the county where such bond was entered into " not found," such return shall be equivalent to personal service, and judgment may be made absolute thereon, unless a sufficient showing to the contrary be made to the court, at the time such case is called in its order on the docket.

§ 2873. All bonds and recognizances taken in criminal cases, whether they shall describe the offense actually committed or not, shall have the effect to hold the party bound thereby, to answer to such offense as he may have actually committed, and shall be valid for that purpose, until he be discharged by the court.

§ 2874. All justices of the peace, and all other conservators of the peace are authorized, whenever a person is brought before them, charged with any offense less than murder, arson or treason, for which bail is now allowed by law, to take the recognizance or bond of such person, with good and sufficient security, in such penalty as such justice or conservator of the peace may require, for his appearance before such justice or conservator for an examination of his case, at some future day, not more than five days from the time of taking such recognizance or bond. And if the person thus recognized, or thus giving bond, shall fail to appear at the appointed time, it shall be the duty of such justice or conservator to return the recognizance or bond, with his certificate of the default, to the court having final jurisdiction of the case, that a recovery may be had therein, by *scire facias*, as in other cases of forfeiture. The justice, or other conservator, shall also issue an *alias* warrant for all such defaulters.

PROCESS AGAINST CORPORATIONS.

§ 2769. When an indictment shall be found against any corporation, a summons shall be issued against it by its corporate name, to appear and answer such indictment, which summons may be executed in the same manner as a summons against a corporation in a civil suit; and upon such summons being returned executed, the corporation shall be considered in court, and appearing to the said indictment, and the court shall cause an appearance and a plea of not guilty to be entered; and such proceedings may then be had thereon, in the same manner as if the corporation had appeared and pleaded " not guilty" thereto; and if the said corporation shall be convicted on the said indictment, the court may pass judgment thereon, and cause process of execution to be issued against the goods and chattels, lands and tenements of the said corporation, for the amount of the fine and costs, which may be awarded against it, in the same manner as on a judgment in a civil suit; and the sheriff shall proceed to sell the goods and chattels, or lands and tenements of such corporation, on the said execution, in the same manner as on an execution issuing against a corporation in a civil suit.

§ 2770. If such summons shall be returned not executed, and the sheriff or other officer shall make affidavit that he hath made diligent inquiry, and cannot ascertain any place of business of said corporation in his county, or the name of any officer of said corporation, resident in the county in which such indictment shall have been found, upon whom such summons could be executed, then the court shall make an order, directing said corporation to cause their appearance to be entered, and to plead to said indictment, on or before the first day of the next term of the court; a copy of which order shall, within thirty days, be inserted in one of the public newspapers printed in this state, as the court may direct, and continued therein for at least four weeks; and if the said corporation shall not appear within the time limited by such order, or within such further time as the court shall appoint, then, on due proof of such publication, the said court shall order the clerk to enter an appearance and plea of not guilty for said corporation; and thereupon, further proceedings may be had on such indictment, in the same manner as if the said corporation had appeared and pleaded thereto; and in case of conviction, execution may be issued, and proceedings had thereon, as in the preceding section mentioned.

§ 2771. Like process and proceedings may be had before justices of the peace, in any prosecution or proceeding against a corporation, for any offense made cognizable before a justice of the peace; and in case publication shall be necessary, the day of appearance may be fixed for such time as will allow the order to be published for the required period.

§ 2772. When any corporation shall be convicted, on indictment for a nuisance, for not repairing, or keeping in repair, any road, causeway, bridge or ferry, and shall neglect to pay the fine and costs awarded against them therefor, for the space of three months after an execution shall have been issued against them for the same, then it shall not be lawful for any such corporation, their officers, agents, or any other person, to demand or take any toll upon any part of their road, or any causeway, bridge or ferry, not kept in repair, until the said fine and costs shall be paid; and if any person shall demand, or take, any toll, upon any part of the road, causeway, bridge or ferry, of any corporation so indicted and convicted, after such neglect to pay, as aforesaid, and notice in writing thereof to such person, and until said fines and costs are paid, such person shall be liable to indictment, and, on conviction, may be fined, not exceeding one hundred dollars.

ACTIONS AGAINST JUSTICES, CONSTABLES AND OTHER OFFICERS.

§ 326. Every justice of the peace, or other officer, to whom the statute laws, or other books, have been or may be furnished by the state, shall carefully preserve the same, and at the expiration of his term, shall deliver the same to his successor, and take his receipt therefor, and file the same in the office of the clerk of the circuit court of the county where such offices are exercised; and in default thereof, the said court, on motion of the clerk, or of the successor in office (whose duty it shall be to make such motion), shall enter judgment in favor of the state, against such justice, or officer, so in default, for the sum of ten dollars for each volume missing, and not satisfactorily accounted for, five days' notice being given of such motion.

REMEDIES FOR MONEY COLLECTED.

§ 1339. When any justice of the peace shall fail to pay over to the person authorized to receive the same, any money collected by him in his official capacity, or shall fail to account for and pay into the state or county treasury, as the case may be, according to law, all fines and penalties which may be assessed by and paid to him, or which shall come into his hands, by any other means whatsoever, on complaint of any such failure, to any other justice of the peace, of the county, such justice shall issue his summons, commanding the justice so failing to appear before him; and if it appear that such justice of the peace has failed to pay over the money collected by him, as aforesaid, the justice trying the same shall enter judgment against such delinquent, for the money so detained, with costs and ten per cent. damages, and no stay of execution shall be given on such judgment, and in addition thereto, such defaulting justice of the peace shall be liable to indictment, and to fine in double the sum collected by him and not accounted for, and imprisonment not more than six months, and such justice shall be removed from office.

§ 1341. In case any justice of the peace shall resign, or remove from the district, or otherwise go out of office, he shall, within ten days thereafter, deliver his docket, with all process and papers relating to his said office, to the clerk of the circuit court of the county, to be by him kept as public records, and who shall be authorized to certify copies thereof; and if any such justice of the peace shall die, it shall be the duty of his executors or administrators to deliver his docket and papers to the clerk of said circuit court; and if any justice of the peace, vacating his office as aforesaid, or the executors or administrators of any such justice who shall die, shall neglect or refuse to deliver said docket and papers to the clerk of the circuit court of the proper county, on demand made, he or they shall forfeit and pay the sum of one hundred dollars; and on such failure, an action for the recovery of such forfeiture shall be brought by the district attorney, in the name and for the use of the county in which such failure occurs, on complaint, verified by affidavit, of any person aggrieved; and such ex-justice of the peace shall, in addition thereto, be liable, on conviction, to imprisonment not exceeding six months, in the county jail. If there shall remain on said docket any suits undetermined, or any judgments unexecuted, any justice of the peace of the same county, at the request of the plaintiff therein, may have access to said docket and papers, and may hear and determine such suits, or issue execution on such judgments, in the same manner as business originally commenced by him; and when a successor to the justice who may have resigned, removed, or died, shall be elected and qualified, the clerk shall deliver the docket so deposited with him to such successor, and the justice so receiving the docket may proceed to conclude all business pending thereon, as if the proceedings had been originally instituted before him, and he shall preserve the docket and records delivered to him, as in other cases, and deliver them to his successor.

§ 1342. It shall be the duty of every justice of the peace in this state, on the first Monday of January, in each year, to make a return to the auditor of public accounts, of all fines and penalties, which he shall have assessed during the twelve months preceding such return, and to pay as much thereof as he shall have received, where the same is directed by law to be paid; and any justice of the peace who shall fail to make such return, or to pay the money by him received, as aforesaid, in addition to the remedy prescribed in section number 1339, article twelve, shall be deemed guilty of a misdemeanor in office, and, on conviction thereof, shall be removed from office, and may be fined not more than five hundred dollars, and imprisoned in the county jail not more than six months.

§ 1759. If any minister, judge, or justice, shall join any persons together as husband and wife, without lawful license, as by this chapter required, or shall go out of the state and marry persons belonging to the state, without such license, such minister, judge, or justice, shall, in either case, be liable to indictment, and on conviction, to imprisonment in the county jail, not less than one month, nor more than six months.

§ 1761. A certificate of marriage, signed by the minister, judge, or justice celebrating the same, or in case of Quakers, Menonists, or other societies that solemnize their marriages by consent of parties taken in open congregation, by the clerk of the society, shall be transmitted, by such minister, judge, justice, or clerk, within six months thereafter, to the clerk of the circuit court of the county wherein the marriage is solemnized, to be recorded, and exemplification of which shall be evidence of such marriage; and every minister, judge, justice, or clerk of a religious society, failing to transmit such certificate to the clerk, within the time above prescribed, shall forfeit and pay to the person suing for the same, the sum of fifty dollars, to be recovered before any court having cognizance thereof.

§ 2599. If any judge of any court, or any justice of the peace, or attorney-general, or district attorney, or any constable, sheriff, or coroner, or any person, charged by law with the custody of public money, shall violate the provisions of the foregoing section (2591), such person so offending, on conviction thereof, shall be fined in the sum of five hundred dollars, and be imprisoned for the space of twenty days, or less, at the discretion of the court; and in case any public officer shall, in any manner, use or loan public money, in his hands by virtue of his office, in any game, wager, or bet, on conviction thereof, his commission shall thereby be deemed vacated, and the vacancy supplied, as in case of death, resignation, or removal from office.

§ 2712. If any judge, justice, sheriff, coroner, constable, assessor, collector, clerk, or any other officer, shall knowingly demand, take, or collect, under color of his office, any money, fee. or reward whatever, not authorized by the laws of this state, or shall demand and receive, knowingly, any fees for service not actually performed, such officer, so offending, shall be deemed guilty of extortion, and on conviction thereof, shall be punished by fine not exceeding five hundred dollars, or imprisoned not more than three months, or both, in the discretion of the court, and shall be removed from office.

§ 2889. If any grand juror, justice of the peace, constable, member of the board of county supervisors, sheriff, coroner, or other civil or peace officer, shall willfully neglect or refuse to return any person committing an offense against the laws of this state, committed in his view or knowledge, or of which he has any notice, or shall willfully absent himself, when such offense is being, or about to be committed, for the purpose of avoiding a knowledge of the same, he shall, on conviction, be fined not less than one hundred dollars, nor more than five hundred dollars, and may, in the discretion of the court, be removed from office.

TO SECURE PROMPT PAYMENT OF FINES COLLECTED BY JUSTICES OF THE PEACE.

SECTION 1. Be it enacted by the Legislature of the State of Mississippi, That it shall hereafter be the duty of each judge of the circuit court, in this state, at each regular term of his court, in each county, to require every justice of the peace and *ex-officio* justice of the peace in the county in which such term of court is being held, to appear on the first or second day of such term of court, with a transcript of his docket, and submit the same for examination and inspection by the grand jury, which transcript shall contain a full and complete report of all fines imposed, and the amount of the same, collected by such justice of the peace, and what disposition has been made of the same, which shall be certified and sworn to by such justice or *ex-officio* justice of the peace, before the circuit clerk of such county; and any justice or *ex-officio* justice of the peace, willfully making a false entry upon such transcript, shall be guilty of perjury, and, on conviction thereof, shall be subject to all the pains and penalties prescribed by law.

SEC. 2. Be it further enacted, That it shall be the duty of the grand jury to carefully examine the transcript of each justice's docket, in the presence of the district attorney, and make a report of their action thereupon, to the judge of the court, in open court; and if, upon such examination, it shall appear that any justice or *ex-officio* justice of the peace has failed to pay over or account for any money or moneys, in the manner and time required by law, it shall be the duty of said grand jury to present a bill of indictment against such defaulting justice or *ex-officio* justice of the peace, as now provided by law; and when such indictment shall have been prosecuted, it shall be the duty of the court to proceed to the trial of said case, instanter, unless good cause can be shown for a continuance.

SEC. 3. Be it further enacted, That if any justice or *ex-officio* justice of the peace, shall neglect or refuse to appear with a transcript of his docket and report, at the time provided in the first section of this act, it shall be the duty of the judge of the court, on the application of the district attorney, to issue such summary process as is now provided by law in the cases of defaulting jurors or witnesses; and it shall be the duty of the sheriff of the county to serve the same promptly, for which he shall be entitled to receive and collect the same fees as provided by law in similar process; and the clerk of the circuit court shall, likewise, receive the same fees as in like cases; *provided*, that the district attorney shall have authority to compel any justice or *ex-officio* justice of the peace to present his docket, for the inspection of the grand jury, whenever, in his judgment, it may be necessary.

SEC. 4. Be it further enacted, That it shall be the duty of the foreman of each grand jury to deposit the transcript of the docket of each justice or *ex-officio* justice of the peace, so furnished him, in the office of the clerk of the circuit court, at the end of the court term, which shall be carefully filed and preserved by such clerk, and subject, at all times, to the inspection of any person desiring to do so. It shall be the duty of the judges of the several circuit courts in this state, to give this act in charge to the grand jury, at each regular term of his court. (Approved, March 31, 1876.)

RETAILING LIQUORS, LICENSES, PENALTIES.

MODE OF OBTAINING LICENSE.

§ 2456. It shall not be lawful for any person, except druggists and physicians, (under the restrictions hereinafter named,) to sell any vinous or spirituous liquors, in a less quantity than one gallon, without first having obtained a license therefor.

§ 2457. The corporate authorities of every incorporated city or town, shall have power to grant to any person, resident in such city or town, license to sell by retail, in any quantity, vinous and spirituous liquors, within the same, for the period of twelve months; and to assess and collect such tax therefor, as they may see proper, not exceeding one thousand dollars, nor less than two hundred dollars, having reference to the situation of the place, as affording more or less profit to the applicant; the sum received for such licenses, to be for the use of the common school fund, and paid into the county treasury for that purpose.

§ 2458. The boards of supervisors shall have power to grant license to any person resident within their respective counties, and not within an incorporated city or town, to sell, by retail, vinous and spirituous liquors, in any quantity, within such county, and to assess and collect such tax thereon as such board may see proper, having reference to the situation of the place, as affording more or less profit to the applicant, and not exceeding one thousand dollars, nor less than two hundred dollars, for a period of twelve months; and all sums, received for such licenses, shall be paid into the state treasury, and placed to the credit of the common school fund; but no city, town or county, shall have power to levy an additional tax or per centage, on the license tax herein provided for, for city, county or town purposes.

§ 2459. No license shall be granted to any person to retail vinous or spirituous liquors, in less quantities than one gallon, unless the applicant shall first produce a petition for the issuance of such license, recommending the said applicant to be of good reputation, and a sober and suitable person to receive such license, which petition shall be signed by a majority of the legal voters, resident in the supervisor's district, where the liquors are intended to be sold; and if such liquors are intended to be sold within the limits of any incorporated city or town, then, by a majority of the legal voters therein; and all such petitions, after being presented and filed, shall lay over one month, for consideration and the reception of counter petitions, before being acted upon; and any name found on both petitions, shall be counted against the granting of the license; and if any supervisor's district or incorporated town shall, by a majority of legal voters therein, petition the board of supervisors against the granting of license to retail spirituous liquors, such license shall not be granted to any applicant, within the bounds of such district or incorporated town, for twelve months after said petition is so presented.

§ 2460. Before any license shall be issued, the applicant shall pay, to the treasurer of the county or corporation, the tax assessed thereon, and all other charges, and shall give bond, with two or more good and sufficient sureties, to be approved by the board of supervisors or corporate authorities of the city or town, as the case may be, payable to the state, in the penalty of one thousand dollars, conditioned that the person, to whom such license shall be granted, shall, during the continuance of his license, keep a quiet, peaceable and orderly house, for retailing vinous and spirituous liquors, in said district, town or city, and will not suffer or permit any riotous or disorderly conduct, or any drunkenness, or any unlawful gaming, in or about the same, or on the premises thereunto belonging, and will, in all things, faithfully observe and keep all the provisions of this chapter; and all such bonds shall be filed and carefully preserved in the office of the clerk of the chancery court of the county.

§ 2461. No license shall be granted for a longer or shorter period than one year; and such license shall be a personal privilege, and not transferable to another. The particular place and house in which the liquors are to be sold, shall be designated in the license, and no license shall authorize any person to sell vinous or spirituous liquors at any other place or house than that specified in such license; *provided*, that the boards of supervisors, or the corporate authorities of any incorporated town or city, may, in their discretion, and for sufficient cause, allow a change in the place or house in which liquors may be sold, under the provisions of this chapter;

but, in no case, shall this license admit of liquors being sold at more than one place, at the same time, within the district in which license is granted.

MISCELLANEOUS PROVISIONS.

§ 2462. The board of supervisors of each county of the state, or the corporate authorities of any city or town, as the case may be, shall have power, and it is hereby made their duty to revoke any retail license, which may be granted under this chapter, whenever it shall be made to appear that the person holding such license has become unfit to sell under such license, or has in any way violated the provisions thereof ; but before such revocation is made, the person proceeded against shall have ten days' notice of the intention to revoke his license, with a brief statement of the ground upon which the revocation is sought to be made.

§ 2463. Before any druggist or physician shall sell any vinous or spirituous liquor, in less quantity than one gallon, he shall make, in writing, and file in the office of the chancery clerk of the county where he does business, an affidavit that he will only sell vinous or spirituous liquors, for medicinal, culinary or sacramental purposes, and not for such purposes, unless the applicant satisfies him, by evidence produced, that such are *bona fide*, the purposes for which the purchase is made ; and that he will not sell such liquors, in any case, where he has cause to doubt that they are absolutely required for such purposes.

§ 2464. Debts created for liquors at any establishment where liquors are retailed, shall not be recoverable at law, and all notes or securities given for such debts shall be absolutely null and void.

§ 2465. No license shall be granted, under the provisions of this chapter, to retail liquors, at any place where a special or local act of the legislature provides that no liquors shall be retailed.

§ 2466. The clerk of the board of supervisors of each county, and the clerk or mayor of any incorporated town or city, on the first day of every term of the circuit court, shall furnish the grand jury or district attorney with a list of all persons who have obtained licenses to retail vinous and spirituous liquors within the county, within one year next preceding such court, with the date of each license; and for failing to furnish such list, the clerk or mayor shall be fined fifty dollars, on motion of the district attorney, whose duty it shall be to make such motion; and the said list shall be good *prima facie* evidence on the trial of any indictment under this chapter, of the granting of any license, and the date thereof, and also that no person not named in said list has obtained such license.

§ 2467. Every justice of the peace, sheriff, constable and other county officer, is hereby required and enjoined to cause this chapter to be strictly enforced within their respective counties, and to give information of all violations thereof, and to cause all offenders to be arrested and bound over to answer for the same.

§ 2468. It shall be the duty of the district attorneys of this state to bring suit upon any and all bonds, take under this chapter, which may be violated, and conduct the suits to judgment, and collect the proceeds, and pay them over, according to law.

§ 2469. All county treasurers, and the officers of incorporated cities and towns, who may receive money for license to retail liquor in less quantities than one gallon, shall pay the same into the state treasury, within thirty days from the time of receiving the same; and if they should fail to do so, shall be liable, on indictment and conviction, to a fine, not exceeding the amount of money so received, and not paid over, or to imprisonment in the county jail, not more than six months, or by both such fine and imprisonment.

§ 2470. Merchants and others, carrying on any business or trade, who may sell or give away liquors at their places of business, either vinous or spirituous, in less quantities than one gallon, for any purpose whatever, shall be subject to pay the regular retail tax, fixed by the county, or corporate authorities of the place where such business is conducted; and it shall be the duty of the sheriff to assess and collect such tax, whenever he is informed that such sales or gifts have been made; and such persons, on conviction, shall be fined in a sum not exceeding one hundred dollars.

§ 2471. It shall not be lawful for any person, having license to retail vinous and spirituous liquors, to keep open the bar, or place where such liquors are sold, or to sell any such liquors, on the first day of the week, commonly called Sunday; and any person so offending, shall be liable to a fine of not less than fifty, nor more than one hundred dollars, for each offense.

RETAILING LIQUORS—PENALTY FOR.

§ 2690. If any person shall sell any vinous or spirituous liquor, in any quantity less than one gallon, without having a license therefor, in pursuance of the laws of this state; or if any person having such license, shall sell any such liquor in a quantity less than one gallon, at any other place or house than that specified in such license; or if any druggist, apothecary, or physician, shall sell any vinous or spirituous liquor in a quantity less than one gallon, except in good faith for medicinal, sacramental or culinary purposes, or shall permit the drinking of said liquors in his store, or upon his premises; or if any person, having such license, shall fail to keep a quiet, peaceable and orderly house, or shall suffer or permit any riotous or disorderly conduct, or any drunkenness, or any unlawful gaming, in or about the house or place where such liquors are kept, or on the premises thereunto belonging, or shall sell any vinous or spirituous liquor to any person then being intoxicated; or if any person shall directly, or by any evasion or subterfuge, violate any provision of this act, then the person so offending (and also any person who may own or have any interest in any vinous or spirituous liquor sold contrary to this act) shall be liable to indictment, and on conviction, shall be fined not less than twenty-five dollars, nor more than five hundred dollars, or be imprisoned not less than one week, nor more than three months, or both, at the discretion of the court.

§ 2691. It shall not be lawful for any person having license to retail vinous or spirituous liquors, to keep open the bar or place where such liquors are sold, or to sell any such liquors, on the first day of the week, commonly called Sunday; and any person so offending, shall be liable to be punished as is prescribed in the last preceding section.

§ 2692. If any person, whether having a license to retail liquor or not, shall knowingly sell any vinous or spirituous liquor, in any quantity, to any minor, he shall, on conviction, be fined in a sum not less than one hundred dollars, nor more than one thousand dollars.

§ 2693. If any candidate, for any public station, shall treat or bestow any vinous or spirituous liquor upon any voter, with intent to influence his vote, he shall be liable to indictment, and, on conviction, shall be fined twenty-five dollars.

§ 2694. If any owner, lessee or occupant of any house, outhouse, or other building or tenement, shall knowingly permit or suffer any person to retail vinous or spirituous liquor, contrary to law, in such house, outhouse, building or tenement, without giving immediate information thereof, and prosecuting the offender, according to law, such owner, lessee or occupant shall be liable to indictment, and on conviction, may be fined not more than five hundred dollars, or imprisoned not more than one month, or by both such fine and imprisonment.

§ 2695. No spirituous or fermented liquors shall, on any pretense whatsoever, be sold within any county prison, or the penitentiary, nor shall any kind of spirituous or fermented liquors be brought into any county prison, for the use of any convict confined therein, without a written permit, signed by the physician to such prison, specifying the quantity and the quality of the liquor which may be furnished to any prisoner, the name of the prisoner for whom, and the time when the same may be furnished, and that the same is necessary as a medicine, which permit shall be delivered to and kept by the keeper of the prison.

§ 2696. Any person who shall sell in, or bring to any of the said prisons, any spirituous or fermented liquors, contrary to the foregoing provisions, and every keeper or other officer employed in or about any such prison, or penitentiary, who shall suffer any spirituous, or other liquor, to be sold and used therein, contrary to the foregoing provisions, shall be deemed guilty of a misdemeanor, and, upon conviction thereof, shall be subject to imprisonment, not exceeding one year, in a county jail, or to a fine not exceeding three hundred dollars, or both, at the discretion of the court; and every sheriff, or other officer, so convicted, shall forfeit his office.

§ 2697. Any person who shall sell any vinous or spirituous liquors, prepared by them or their agents, or knowing it to be prepared, according to any certificate or formula for adulteration, or shall adulterate the same, such person shall be subject to indictment therefor, and, upon conviction, shall be imprisoned in the penitentiary not less than one year, nor more than five years.

§ 2834. No person shall sell, or offer for sale, any liquor, vinous or spirituous, or other intoxicating drink, or any merchandise or provisions, at or within two miles of any meeting house, or other place of public worship, during the time appointed for the continuance of such worship ; and any such offender, on conviction thereof, before any justice of the peace of the county, shall be fined thirty dollars for each offense, and stand committed until such fine and costs are paid ; *provided*, that this section shall not extend to any incorporated town, or persons residing permanently within the limits prescribed, and complying with the requisitions of the law, in other respects.

§ 2835. If any sheriff or constable of the county, where such offense may occur, shall refuse or neglect to carry into effect the provisions of the lest preceding section, he shall, on conviction thereof, before any justice of the peace, be fined ten dollars.

PROVIDING AGAINST EVIL RESULTS FROM THE SALE OF INTOXICATING LIQUORS IN THE STATE.

SECTION 1. Be it enacted by the Legislature of the State of Mississippi, That it shall be unlawful for any person or persons, by agent, or otherwise, without first having obtained a license to keep a grocery to sell, in any quantity, intoxicating liquors, to be drank in, upon or about the building or premises where sold, or to sell such intoxicating liquors to be drank in any adjoining room, building or premises, or other place of public resort connected with said building ; *provided*, that no person shall be granted a license to sell or give away intoxicating liquors, without first giving bond to the municipality or authority authorized by law to grant license, which bond shall run in the name of the people of the state of Mississippi, and be in the penal sum of two thousand dollars, with at least two good and sufficient sureties, who shall be freeholders, conditioned that they will pay all damages to any person or persons, which may be inflicted upon them, either in person or property, or means of support, by reason of the person so obtaining a license, selling or giving away intoxicating liquors ; and such bond may be sued and recovered upon, for the use of any person or persons, or their legal representatives, who may be injured by reason of the selling of intoxicating liquors, by the person, or his agent, so obtaining the license.

SEC. 2. Be it further enacted, That it shall be unlawful for any person or persons, by agent, or otherwise, to sell intoxicating liquors to minors, unless upon the written order of their parents, guardians, or family physician, or to persons who are intoxicated, or who are in the habit of getting intoxicated.

SEC. 3. Be it further enacted, That all places where intoxicating liquors are sold or given away, in violation of this act, shall be taken, held, and declared to be common nuisances ; and all rooms, taverns, hotels, eating-houses, bazaars, restaurants, drug stores, groceries, coffee-houses, cellars, or other places of public resort, where intoxicating liquors are sold, in violation of this act, shall be shut up and abated as public nuisances, upon conviction of the keeper thereof, who shall be punished as hereinafter provided.

SEC. 4. Be it further enacted, That every person who shall, by the sale of intoxicating liquors, with or without license, cause the intoxication of any other person, shall be liable for and compelled to pay a reasonable compensation to any person who may take charge of and provide for such intoxicated person, and two dollars per day in addition thereto, for every day such intoxicated person shall be kept, in consequence of such intoxication, which sums may be recovered in an action of debt, before any court having competent jurisdiction.

SEC. 5. Be it further enacted, That every husband, wife, child, parent, guardian, employer, or other person, who shall be injured in person or property, or means of support, by any intoxicated person, or in consequence of the intoxication, habitual or otherwise, of any person, shall have a right of action, in his or her own name, severally or jointly, against any person or persons who shall, by selling or giving away intoxicating liquors, have caused the intoxication, in whole or in part, of such person or persons; and any person or persons owning, renting, leasing, or permitting the occupation of any building or premises, and having knowledge that intoxicating liquors are to be sold therein, or who, having leased the same for other purposes, shall knowingly permit, therein, the sale of any intoxicating liquors (that have caused, in whole or in part, the intoxication of any person or persons, selling or giving away intoxicating liquors), aforesaid, for all damages sustained, and for exemplary damages ; and a married woman shall have the right to bring suits, and to control the same, and the amount recovered as a *femme sole*; and all damages recovered by minors, under this act, shall be paid, either to such minor, or to his or her parent, guardian, or next friend, as the court shall direct, and the unlawful sale or giving away of intoxicating liquors, shall work a forfeiture of all rights of the lessee or tenant, under any lease or contract of rent upon the premises, where such unlawful sale or giving away shall take place; and all suits for damages, under this act, may be by any appropriate action in any of the courts of this state having competent jurisdiction.

SEC. 6. Be it further enacted, That for violation of the provisions of the first and second sections of this act, every person so offending shall forfeit and pay a fine of not less than twenty, nor more than one hundred dollars, and be imprisoned in the jail of the county not less than ten nor more than thirty days, and pay the costs of prosecution ; and for every violation of the provisions of the third section of this act, every person convicted as the keeper of any of the places therein described to be nuisances, shall forfeit and pay a fine of not less than fifty, nor more than one hundred dollars, and be imprisoned in the jail of the county for not less than twenty, nor more than fifty days, and pay the costs of prosecution; and such place or places, so kept by such person or persons so convicted, shall be shut up and abated, upon the order of the court before whom such conviction may be had, until such a time as such person or persons keeping such places, shall give bond and security, to be approved by said court, in the penal sum of one thousand dollars, payable to the state of Mississippi, conditioned that he, she, or they will not sell intoxicating liquors contrary to the laws of this state, and will pay all fines, costs, and damages assessed against such keeper or keepers for any violation thereof; and in case of forfeiture of such bond, suit may be brought thereon, for the use of any person interested, or for the use of the common school fund of the county, in case of a fine or costs due such county ; *provided*, that the penalties in the nature of fines mentioned in this section, may be enforced separately from the imprisonment, before any justice of the peace having jurisdiction.

Sec. 7. Be it further enacted, That the giving away of intoxicating liquors, or other shift or device to evade the provisions of this act, shall be deemed and held to be an unlawful selling, within the provisions of this act.

Sec. 8. Be it further enacted, That for the payment of all fines, costs, and damages assessed against any person or persons, in consequence of the sale of intoxicating liquors, as provided in section five of this act, the real estate and personal property of such person or persons of every kind, except such as may be exempt under the homestead laws of this state, or such as may be exempt from levy and sale upon judgment and execution, shall be liable : and such fines, costs, and damages shall be a lien upon such real estate, until paid : and in case any person or persons shall rent or lease to another or others, any building or premises, to be used or occupied, in whole or in part, for the sale of intoxicating liquors, or shall permit the same to be so used or occupied, such building or premises so used or occupied, shall be held liable for, and may be sold to pay all fines, costs, and damages assessed against any person or persons occupying such building or premises ; proceedings may be had to subject the same to the payment of any such fine and costs assessed, or judgment recovered, which remain unpaid, or any part thereof, either before or after execution shall issue against the property of the person or persons against whom such fine and costs or judgment shall have been adjudged or assessed ; and when execution shall issue against the property so leased or rented, the officer shall proceed to satisfy said execution out of the building or premises so leased or occupied as aforesaid, and in case such building or premises belong to a minor, insane person, or idiot, the guardian of such minor, insane person, or idiot, and his or her real and personal property shall be held liable instead of such minor, insane person, or idiot, and his or her property shall be subject to all the provisions of this section, relating to the collection of fines, costs, and damages.

Sec. 9. Be it further enacted, That the penalty and imprisonment mentioned in the sixth section of this act, may be enforced by indictment, in any court of record having criminal jurisdiction, and

19

all pecuniary fines or penalties provided for in any of the sections of this act (except the fourth and fifth), may be enforced and prosecuted for before any justice of the peace of the proper county, in an action of debt, in the name of the people of the state of Mississippi, as plaintiff; and in case of conviction, the offender shall stand committed to the common jail until the judgment and costs are fully paid, and the magistrate or court in which conviction is had, shall issue a writ of *capias ad satisfaciendum* therefor; and justices of the peace shall also have jurisdiction of all actions arising under the fourth and fifth sections of this act, where the amount in controversy does not exceed one hundred and fifty dollars, such actions to be prosecuted in the name of the party injured or entitled to the debt or damages provided for in said fourth and fifth sections.

SEC. 10. Be it further enacted, That in all prosecutions under this act, by indictment or otherwise, it shall not be necessary to state the kind of liquor sold, or to describe the place where sold, and for any violation of the third section of this act, it shall not be necessary to state the name of the person to whom sold, and in all cases, the person or persons to whom intoxicating liquors shall be sold, in violation of this act, shall be competent witnesses to prove such fact, or any other, tending thereto.

SEC. 11. Be it further enacted, That the provisions of this act shall take effect and be in force from and after the first day of July, A. D. 1873, so far as it affects licenses already granted, but as to those hereafter granted, it shall be in force from and after its passage. (Approved, March 17, 1873.)

IN RELATION TO LICENSES AND THE SALE OF LIQUOR.

SECTION 1. Be it enacted by the Legislature of the State of Mississippi, That it shall be unlawful for any druggist or druggists, to sell or give away any spirituous liquors, except on the prescription or certificate of a physician; and any druggist or druggists who shall violate the provisions of this section, shall be deemed and held guilty of a misdemeanor, and on conviction thereof, before any court having competent jurisdiction, he or they shall be fined in a sum of not less than ten dollars, nor more than fifty dollars, for each offense.

SEC. 2. Be it further enacted, That if any physician, or pretended physician, shall give a prescription or certificate to any person or persons, for spirituous liquors, to be used otherwise than as medicine, he shall be deemed and held guilty of a misdemeanor, and on conviction thereof, before any court having competent jurisdiction, he shall be fined in a sum of not less than ten dollars, nor more than fifty dollars, for each offense.

SEC. 3. Be it further enacted, That if any person or persons shall forge or counterfeit a prescription or certificate, in the name of any physician, he or they shall be deemed and held guilty of a misdemeanor, and on conviction thereof, before any court having competent jurisdiction, he or they shall be fined in a sum of not less than fifty dollars, nor more than one hundred and fifty dollars, or by imprisonment in the county jail, for a term of not less than ten days, nor more than thirty days, or by both such fine and imprisonment, at the discretion of the court. (Approved, April 17, 1873.)

TAX FOR RETAILING LIQUORS.

SECTION 1. Be it enacted by the Legislature of the State of Mississippi, That from and after the passage of this Act, no license shall be granted for a longer period after its date than twelve months, nor for a less sum than two hundred dollars, nor more than one thousand dollars, and said amounts shall be regulated by the boards of supervisors, and authorities of incorporated cities and towns, with reference to the advantages of situations, and classified as follows, to wit : Two hundred dollars, four hundred dollars, seven hundred dollars, one thousand dollars ; and shall be paid into the state treasury to the credit of the common school fund ; *provided*, that any incorporated city or town, of one thousand inhabitants or over, the minimum shall be three hundred dollars.

SEC. 2. Be it further enacted, That after any license is granted as now provided by law, the person or persons obtaining the same, shall furnish the collector of the county with a certified copy of the order granting such license and fixing the amount to be paid, and a certificate from the chancery clerk, or clerk of the incorporated city or town, that the bond has been filed as required by law, and the collector shall issue the license upon the blank furnished by the auditor, to such person or persons, for twelve months from the date of the granting of the same, and the collector shall be allowed, as full compensation for the collection of money under this act, to charge the parties taking out a license two per cent. in currency on the amount collected, in addition to the amount of license, and the full amount paid for such license shall be paid into the treasury. (Approved, February 12, 1875.)

PETITION AGAINST GRANTING LICENSE.

SECTION 1. Be it enacted by the Legislature of the State of Mississippi, That said section two thousand four hundred and fifty-nine of said code, be and the same is hereby amended in the final clause thereof, so that said clause shall read as follows, to-wit : If a majority of the legal voters of any supervisor's district, or of an incorporated city or town, shall petition the board of supervisors, or the board of mayor and aldermen, or other municipal board of any city or town, as the case may be, against the granting of any license to retail vinous or spirituous liquors therein, then it shall be unlawful to grant any such license ; and no such license shall be granted to any applicant, to retail such liquors within such district, city or town, for three months from and after the presentation of such petition. (Approved March 26, 1874.)

PAYMENT OF LICENSES TO COUNTY TREASURERS.

Section 1. Be it enacted by the Legislature of the State of Mississippi, That sections 2457 and 2459 of the revised code of 1871, be so amended as to require the tax assessed and collected arising from license to retail vinous and spirituous liquors under the general laws of this state, within incorporated towns and cities in this state, shall be paid to the county treasurer in the manner hereinafter provided, and be by him paid into the state treasury as is now required by law, for account of fines collected by justices of the peace.

Sec. 2. Be it further enacted, That section 2409 be so amended as to require the treasurer of any incorporated town or city, who may receive money for license to retail liquor in accordance with the foregoing section, to pay the same into the county treasury within ten days after collecting the same, and it shall be his further duty on or before the first Monday of July annually to make a report to the board of supervisors, showing the amount of such collections and of whom collected since the date of the last report as herein required; *provided*, that the first report under the provisions of this act shall show all collections made since the first day of January, 1872.

Sec. 3. Be it further enacted, That when any money is paid to the county treasurer as aforesaid, or for account of fines collected by justices of the peace, he shall give to the person paying the same duplicate receipts therefor, one of which such person shall forthwith transmit to the auditor of public accounts, in order that the county treasurer may be charged with the amount thereof. (Approved, April 11, 1873.)

CIVIL RIGHTS BILL.

Section 1. Be it enacted by the Legislature of the State of Mississippi, That section two thousand seven hundred and thirty-one, (2731,) and section two thousand seven hundred and thirty-two, (2732,) of the revised code, approved May 13, A. D. 1871, be and they are hereby amended to read as follows, to-wit : That all citizens of this state, without distinction of race, color or previous condition of servitude, are entitled to the equal and impartial enjoyment of any accommodation, advantage, facility or privilege furnished by common carriers running in or through, or plying within this state, whether upon land or upon waters, by any keeper, owners or lessee of any hotel, inn or restaurant, by any owner, managers or lessees of any theater or other place of public amusement, or of public entertainment or accommodation, and the equal and impartial enjoyment of any such accommodation, facility, privilege or advantage is hereby declared to have always been, is now, and shall forever remain a right inherent in every citizen or person, and which right shall not be denied, abridged or infringed on account of any distinction of race, color or previous condition of servitude ; and any person who shall violate any of the foregoing provisions, or who shall deny to, or withhold from any person the enjoyment of any of the foregoing accommodations, facilities, privileges or advantages, equally and impartially on any such account, or for any such reason, or who shall abridge or infringe the same, or who shall incite thereto, shall be deemed guilty of a misdemeanor, and shall, on conviction before any justice of the peace or any court having jurisdiction thereof, for each and every such offense, forfeit and pay to the person aggrieved thereby a sum of money which, in any case shall not be less than three hundred (300) dollars, to be recovered in any action on the case, with full costs and such allowance for counsel's fees as the court shall deem just ; and shall be fined not less than one hundred (100) dollars, or be imprisoned not less than thirty (30) days, nor more than one (1) year, or both, in the discretion of the court. And any corporation, association or individual violating the aforesaid provisions, or any of them, or denying, withholding, abridging or infringing, in any manner, any of the aforesaid rights, privileges, accommodations, facilities or advantages of any citizen or person, shall, upon conviction thereof, forfeit their, his or her charter or license, or other authority or power, under or by virtue of which they, he or she are, or may be, by the laws of this state, permitted or authorized to conduct, manage, or run any business or employment, and any person or association of persons assuming or continuing to use or act under or by virtue of any such charter, license or authority, so forfeited or aiding in the same, or inciting thereto, shall be deemed guilty of a misdemeanor, and on conviction thereof, shall be fined for each and every offense not less than one thousand (1000,) nor more than five thousand (5000) dollars, and shall be imprisoned not less than three (3) years, nor more than seven (7) years, and the corporate and joint property of such corporation or association, or individual, shall be held liable for the forfeitures, fines and penalties incurred by any violation of this act.

SEC. 2. Be it further enacted, That the circuit courts of this state shall have appellate jurisdiction in all causes arising under or by virtue of this act, and it shall only be necessary for the plaintiff or plaintiffs in any action under or by virtue of this act, in any court to show that he, or she, or they, as the case may be, were refused, denied or withheld equal and impartial accommodation, facility, privilege or advantage furnished by any public carriers, by any innkeeper, owner, manager or lessee of any theater, or other place of public amusement, or of entertainment or accommodation, or that theirs, his or her right or rights as declared by this act were abridged or infringed, and no sufficient cause was assigned, given or made known to the plaintiff, then and there, at the time of such refusal, denial, or withholding, or abridging, or infringing of such accommodation, facility, privilege or advantage applied for ; and the burden of proof shall be upon the defendant to show that such refusal, denial or withholding of such accommodation, facility, privilege or advantage, or abridging or infringing of the same was not on account of race, color or previous condition of servitude.

Sec. 3. Be it further enacted, That the judges of the several circuit courts of this state shall specially give this act in charge to the grand jury of their respective courts at the commencement of each term thereof, and district attorneys of the several districts of this state shall institute and prosecute in their several districts proceedings for any violation of this act ; and any district attorney who shall fail, neglect, or refuse compliance herewith, shall be deemed guilty of misdemeanor in office, and on conviction thereof shall be fined not less than five hundred (500) dollars, nor more than one thousand (1000) dollars, and shall be dismissed from office.

Sec. 4. Be it further enacted, That every law, statute, ordinance, regulation or custom, inconsistent with this act, or the act to which this is amendatory, is hereby repealed and annulled, and that this act take effect and be in force on and after thirty days from the date of its passage. (Approved, February 7, 1873.)

LIMITATION OF PROSECUTIONS.

§ 2766. No person shall be prosecuted for any offence, (murder, manslaughter, arson, forgery, counterfeiting, robbery, larceny, rape and embezzlement, and obtaining money or property under false pretenses, excepted,) unless the prosecution for such offense, shall be commenced within two years next after the commission thereof ; *provided,* that nothing herein contained shall be so construed as to bar any prosecution against any person who shall abscond or flee from justice, in this state, or shall absent himself from this State, or out of the jurisdiction of the court, or so conduct himself, that he cannot be found by the officers of the law, or that process cannot be served upon him.

§ 2767. A prosecution may be commenced, within the meaning of this code, by the issuance of a warrant, or by binding over or recognizing the offender, to compel his appearance, to answer the offense as well as by indictment or presentment

§ 2768. When an indictment shall be lost or destroyed, or quashed or abated, or the judgment thereon arrested or reversed, for any defect herein, or in the record, or for any matter of form, or other cause, not being an acquittal on the merits, the further time of six months, from the time when such indictment shall be lost, destroyed, quashed or abated, or judgment thereon arrested or reversed, as aforesaid, shall be allowed for the finding of a new indictment.

CERTAIN PENAL SUITS—TRIABLE BEFORE JUSTICE.

§ 227. If any sheriff, coroner, or other officer, shall fail to return any execution to him directed, on the return day thereof, the plaintiff in such execution shall be entitled to recover judgment against such sheriff, coroner, or other officer, and their respective sureties, for the amount of such execution, and all costs, with lawful interest thereon, until the same shall be paid, with five per cent. on the full amount of such judgment for his damages, to be recovered by motion, before the court to which such execution is returnable, on five days' notice first given thereof; *provided*, that after the sheriff, coroner, or other officer, or his or their sureties, shall have paid the amount of money and damages recovered as aforesaid, then the original judgment and execution shall be vested in the sheriff, coroner or other officer, or his or their sureties paying the said recovery and damages for his or their benefit, and executions may issue on said original judgment, in the name of the plaintiff, for the use and benefit, and at the cost and charges of the officer, or his sureties, in whom the said judgment may be vested as aforesaid; but nothing herein contained shall affect any other remedy against officers for failing to return excutions, and the remedy given by this section shall apply in favor of county treasurers, clerks, and other officers and witnesses, for the recovery of all jury taxes, fees and costs, with interest and damages thereon, in the same manner as to plaintiffs in executions. In any proceeding against a sheriff, or other officer, for failing to return any process, proof, that said process was put in the post-office, duly addressed to him, and that the postage was paid thereon, shall be sufficient *prima facie* evidence of the receipt thereof by such officer, unless he will make oath that he did not receive it himself, and that he verily believes it was not received by any of his deputies.

§ 229. If any sheriff, deputy sheriff, coroner, or other officer shall collect, by virtue of any execution or attachment, the whole, or a part of the money which, by such writ, he is required to levy, and shall not immediately pay the same to the party entitled thereto, or his attorney, on demand made, or shall return, upon any writ, of *capias ad satisfaciendum*, or attachment, for not performing a decree for the payment of money, that he hath taken the body or bodies of defendant or defendants, and hath the same ready to satisfy the money in such writ mentioned, and shall have actually received such money from the defendant or defendants, or hath voluntarily suffered him or them to escape, and shall not immediately pay such money to the party to whom the same is payable, or his attorney, or shall make any other such return upon any such execution or attachment, as will show that such sheriff, deputy sheriff, coroner, or other officer, hath voluntarily and without authority omitted to execute the same, or to levy the money therein mentioned, or as would entitle the plaintiff to recover from said sheriff or other officer, by any action, the debt, damages or costs in said execution mentioned, then or in either of said cases, the said sheriff, or other officer, and his sureties, shall be liable to pay to the plaintiff in said execution or attachment, or to any person entitled to said money, or any part thereof, the full amount of the money due upon the said execution or attachment, with twenty-five per cent. damages, and lawful interest until paid, to be recovered with cost, by motion before the court to which such execution is returnable, on five days' notice of such motion to said sheriff, or other officer, and his sureties; *provided*, that in case the said sheriff, or other officer, shall have received only a part of the money due by said execution or attachment, and shall not be otherwise liable to a judgment for the whole amount thereof, the recovery shall be limited to the amount received by him, with damages and interest as aforesaid ; but the court, at the request of either party, in case any matters of fact shall be in issue between them, shall immediately cause a jury to be empaneled to try the same, and if the verdict shall be against the said sheriff, or other officer, judgment shall be entered up with damages and costs, as above directed.

§ 230. When the amount of the sale of property under execution or attachment shall exceed the debt, damages, interest and costs, for which the execution issued, the sheriff or other officer, shall pay such surplus or excess to the debtor, or such other person as may be entitled to receive the same ; and if any sheriff, or other officer, shall fail or refuse to pay such surplus or excess when required, to the person entitled thereto, such sheriff, or officer, and his sureties, and his or their representatives, shall be liable to the like penalty and judgment in favor of the person entitled to said surplus or excess, as is authorized and directed by law, in favor of the plaintiff, against the sheriff and his sureties, for not paying money levied on an execution to them.

§ 232. Every sheriff, who shall have levied any writ of execution, or other process on goods and chattels, which shall remain in his hands and possession unsold, at the expiration of his term of office, shall deliver over such goods and chattels remaining unsold, to his successor in office, taking his receipt for the same ; and the sheriff, to whom such goods and chattels are delivered as aforesaid, shall proceed to sell the same, in like manner as his predecessor ought to have done, had he remained in office, and shall account for and pay the proceeds of such sale to the parties entitled thereto by law. And if any sheriff shall fail to deliver over to his successor in office any goods and chattels so levied on, and remaining in his hands as aforesaid, on demand thereof made, it shall be lawful for the plaintiff in such execution, or other process, upon five days's notice thereof, to move the court from which the same issued, against the sheriff so failing, and his sureties, and their heirs, executors and administrators, upon which motion judgment shall be entered for the amount of the execution or other process which came to the hands of such defaulting sheriff, with interest, and five per cent. damages and costs.

§ 296. If any person shall take up any horse, mare, mule, jack, cattle, sheep or hog, as an estray, contrary to the provisions of this article; or if any person, having taken up such animal, shall fail to send, or notify the owner, if known, or to give information, as required by section two hundred and eighty-nine of this article; or shall fail to perform any duty required of him by this article, or shall abuse such animal, or shall use the same in an unreasonable or improper manner, so that damage shall be done to the owner, or the value of the animal impaired; or if any person shall take or send away any estray out of this state, or shall trade, sell or barter the same, or if any taker up shall fail to deliver said estray to the ranger, at the court house, on the day of the sale of said estray, such person shall for every such offense, forfeit an amount of money equal to the appraised value of the estray, one-half to the use of the county where the offense shall have been committed, and the-other half to any person who shall sue for the same; and in addition thereto, shall be liable to the owner for the value of such animals, of which the appraisement, made in pursuance of this article, shall, in favor of such owner, be admissible as evidence; and such taker up shall forfeit all compensation for taking up and keeping such estray.

§ 300. It shall not be lawful for any drover, or other person, to drive any horses, mules, cattle, hogs or sheep, of another, from the range to which the same may belong; but it shall be his duty, if any other such stock shall join his, immediately to halt at the nearest pen, or some other convenient place, and separate such stock as does not properly belong to him, or to the person for whom he may be employed to collect or drive stock; and if any person shall violate the provisions of this section, he shall forfeit twenty dollars for every offense, with costs, recoverable before a justice of the peace, by and for the use of any person who will sue for the same, and shall also be liable in damages to the party injured; and when any person employed in driving stock shall violate the provisions of this section, he and his employer shall be liable to the like penalties.

§ 282. If any constable, or other officer, shall fail to execute and return, according to law, any execution to him directed by any justice of the peace, on or before the return day thereof, the plaintiff in such execution may recover the amount thereof, with interest and costs, and five per cent. damages thereon, by motion before the justice to whom said execution was returnable, against said officer and his sureties, on giving five days' notice of such motion. And when any constable, or other officer, or his sureties, shall have paid the amount of money and damages recovered, as aforesaid, the original judgment and execution shall be vested in the person so paying, for his benefit; and further, the said justice, on like motion and notice, may fine the said officer, not exceeding fifty dollars, for failing to return such execution.

SUITS BY AND AGAINST THE BOARD OF SUPERVISORS.

§ 1384. Any person having a just claim against any county in this state, which the board of supervisors may refuse to allow, may bring suit against such board in any court having jurisdiction, and in case such party should recover, the board shall allow the same, and a warrant shall issue, as in other cases; but either party shall have the right of appeal, or writ of error, in such cases, and should the board still refuse to issue a warrant to satisfy such judgment, the property of the county shall be liable for the satisfaction of the same, as in other cases; and the board of supervisors are authorized to sue, and may be sued, in the name of the board of supervisors of the county of ...., in all matters in which the county may be interested. Process in suits against the board may be served on the president, or by filing a copy with the clerk, or leaving the same at his office.

§ 1739. If any person shall be found hawking, peddling or trav-cling from house to house, or place to place, to vend any goods, wares or merchandise, without having first obtained a license as aforesaid, he shall, for every such offense, forfeit the sum of one hundred dollars for the use of the county, to be recovered by action in the name of the president of the board of supervisors, to be recovered by attachment as in case of absconding debtors, or otherwise; and if any person, having obtained such license, shall lend, hire or transfer the same to another, for the purpose of using the same, the person lending, hiring or transferring such license, and the person using the same under color thereof, shall each be liable to a like penalty as for hawking without a license, to be recovered in the same manner, and such license shall thereby become void.

§ 1740. Any person found hawking or peddling as aforesaid, who shall, on demand being made by any person of the age of twenty-one years, in the county, fail or refuse to produce and show such license as aforesaid, shall forfeit the sum of ten dollars for every offense, to be recovered before any justice of the peace, for the use of the county.

§ 1744. If any transient auctioneer, vender or trader, after demand made as aforesaid, for such bond or deposit, shall sell any of such merchandise or chattels, without first having given such bond or made such deposit, he shall, for every offense, forfeit and pay the sum of one hundred dollars, to be recovered by action, commenced by attachment or otherwise, for the use of the county.

§ 1942. Every owner or occupier of a mill, established or grinding for toll, as aforesaid, shall keep therein sealed measures of half bushel and peck, and a toll dish, sealed, and shall measure all grain by strike measure, under penalty of paying five dollars for every such failure, recoverable, with costs, before a justice of the peace of the county where such mill shall be, to the use of the informer.

§ 1943. The owner or occupier of every dam, over which a public road passes, shall constantly keep such dam in repair, at least twelve feet wide at the top, through the whole length thereof, and shall keep and maintain a bridge of the like breadth, with strong rails on each side thereof, over the pier-head, flood-gates, or any waste-cut through or around the dam, and over any race or canal, leading to or from the mill or pond, over which a public road may pass, under the penalty of two dollars for every twenty-four hours' failure; but where a mill dam shall be carried away or destroyed by tempest or accident, the owner or occupier thereof shall not be liable to the said penalties, from thenceforth, until one month after such mill shall have been so repaired as to have ground one bushel of grain.

§ 1945. Every owner or proprietor of any cotton gin, erected in or within half a mile of any city, town or village, is hereby required to remove or destroy all cotton seed which may fall from such gin, so that the same shall not prejudice the health of the inhabitants of such city, town or village; and every person, being the owner or proprietor of a cotton gin, situated as aforesaid, who shall neglect or refuse to remove or destroy the cotton seed in and about such gin, having received five days' notice, shall forfeit and pay the sum of twenty dollars for every day he or she shall neglect or refuse to remove or destroy the cotton seed, as aforesaid, to be recovered by warrant, in the name of the state, before any justice of the peace of the proper county, for the use and benefit of the informer.

§ 1986. The father and grandfather, the mother and grandmother, and the descendants of any poor person not able to work, shall, at their own charge, relieve and maintain any poor person, as the board of supervisors shall direct; and in case of refusal, shall forfeit and pay to the county the sum of eight dollars per month, for each month they may so refuse, to be recovered in the name of the county, before any justice, or other court having jurisdiction.

§ 2253. Every attorney or counselor at law, receiving money for his client, and failing or refusing to pay the same, when demanded, may be proceeded against in a summary way, by motion before the circuit court of the county where such attorney or counsellor usually resides, or where he may be found, or before the court in which the money was collected, in the same manner that sheriffs are liable to be proceeded against for money collected on execution, ten days' notice of such motion being given; and in addition to the principal and legal interest, damages at ten per centum on the amount thereof shall be awarded; and in case the failure to pay over said money shall appear to have been willful, and without any reasonable excuse, the court shall fine and imprison such attorney or counsellor, as for a contempt, and strike his name from the roll, and revoke his license.

§ 2271. Any person, or persons who shall, knowingly and willfully sell, hold, or offer for sale, within this state, any tainted, putrid, unsound, unwholesome, or unmerchantable flour, having the ends, sides, or other parts of any barrel or barrels, containing the same, marked with words or letters, expressing or meaning sound, good flour, or who shall practice any fraud or deception to put off or sell any damaged, unsound, or unmerchantable provisions, shall forfeit the whole of such flour or other provisions, to the use of the poor of the county where the same may have been sold, held, or offered for sale ; *provided*, that nothing herein contained shall be construed to affect any flour or other provisions wrecked descending or ascending any navigable waters, connected with the commerce of this state.

§ 2273. Any person, or persons, who shall sell, hold, or offer for sale, within this state, any barrel or barrels of flour that shall weigh or contain less than one hundred and ninety-six pounds of net flour, shall for every such offense, forfeit and pay, at the rate of twenty cents per pound, for any less quantity than ten pounds that each and every barrel, so sold, held, or offered for sale, may be deficient, with costs ; and if any barrel of flour sold, held, or offered for sale, shall weigh or contain ten or more pounds less than one hundred and ninety-six pounds of net flour, the whole of such barrel or barrels, so found deficient, shall be forfeited to the use of the school fund. And if any vinous or spirituous liquors, upon such inspection, shall be found to have been adulterated, they shall be condemned ; the said inspector shall seize the same and destroy them, and the owner shall pay the expenses of inspection.

§ 2274. Thirty days after the publication required by the provisions of article two, of this chapter (chapter 50), if any person. or persons, shall sell any article of provisions, or other article or commodity whatever, within any county or corporation where such standard of weights and measures have been obtained, agreeable to the provisions of this act, not correspondent to such county or corporation standard, or shall keep any weights and measures, or other implements for weighing and measuring, for the purpose of buying or selling thereby, not correspondent with the county or corpora tion standard aforesaid, such person shall, for every such offense, forfeit and pay twenty dollars, to the use of the school fund.

§ 2276. If any inspector of flour and other provisions, appointed within this state, shall, directly or indirectly, demand and receive any other or greater fee, perquisite, reward, or other compensation whatever, for any service or duty he shall perform as inspector. than what shall be allowed him by law, the regulation and order of the court of his county, or the ordinance of his corporation (as the case may be), for the first offense he shall forfeit and pay twenty dollars, the said forfeiture for the use of the school fund ; and for the second offense. he shall forfeit his commission as inspector, and be liable to a fine of forty dollars.

DUTIES OF OVERSEERS OF ROADS.

§ 2351. Every overseer, immediately after his appointment, shall demand of every person within his district, a list of all the hands he may have, liable to work on the road, which demand shall be made personally. or in writing, left at the usual place of abode of the person applied to ; and, if any person shall refuse or neglect, for the space of ten days, to deliver to the overseer the list so required, such person shall forfeit and pay the sum of six dollars for each hand liable to work, so neglected or refused to be given in, as aforesaid, to be recovered by an action, in the name of the board of supervisors of the county, for the use of the county ; and it is hereby made the duty of the overseer to cause such action to be instituted.

FERRIES.

§ 2385. Every ferryman shall have authority to keep out, or put out, of his ferry-boat, or other vessel. any person who shall attempt or press to enter, or who shall enter or stay in his said boat or vessel, contrary to his orders ; and any person so doing, contrary to order. shall forfeit the sum of ten dollars for each offense, to be recovered before any justice of the peace, by any person who will sue for the same, besides being liable to any other civil or criminal prosecution.

§ 2386. The owner or keeper of any ferry, established according to law. on any stream of water, being the dividing line between two counties, shall have the right of landing on the opposite side of such stream, in the other county, and to unload any passengers, wagons, carriages, and their loading, and stock of all kinds, without any hindrance or molestation : and any person hindering or molesting such landing or unloading, shall forfeit and pay to the owner or keeper of such ferry, the sum of ten dollars, for every offense, recoverable before any justice of the peace.

CRIMES AND OFFENCES PUNISHABLE BY FINES ALONE.

§ 223. When any deputy sheriff hath served any writ, execution, attachment, or other process whatever, he shall endorse thereon the date of the service thereof, and the proper return of his proceedings, and subscribe his own name, as well as that of his principal, thereto; and any deputy sheriff failing herein, shall be fined by the court, not exceeding one hundred dollars, for the use of the county, on motion, and reasonable notice to said deputy.

§ 225. Every sheriff, by himself or his deputy, shall, from time to time, execute all writs and other process to him legally issued and directed within his county, and shall make due return thereof to the proper court, on the day to which the same is returnable ; and, if any sheriff shall fail herein, he shall, for every such offense, be fined by the court to which such writ or process is returnable, in any sum not exceeding one hundred dollars, on motion, five days' previous notice thereof being first given to said sheriff; one moiety of said fine to the party aggrieved, and the other moiety to the use of the county in which said fine is imposed : and such sheriff and his sureties shall likewise be liable to the action of the party aggrieved by such default, for all damages sustained thereby, and also to all other penalties provided by law for such offenses.

§ 226. If any sheriff, or his deputy, coroner, or other officer, shall make a false return on any process whatever, to him directed, such sheriff, deputy, coroner, or other officer shall, for every such offense, be liable to pay the sum of five hundred dollars, one-half to the plaintiff in such process, and the other half to the use of the county in which such fine is imposed, recoverable against such officer and his sureties, or such officer alone, by motion before the court to which such process is returnable, after five days' notice of such motion, to such sheriff, deputy, coroner, or other officer, and their respective sureties. If the return alleged to be false, does not appear on the face of the record to be so, the court before which such motion is made, shall, at the request of either party, immediately proceed to empannel a jury, to ascertain whether such return be false, or not, on an issue joined under the direction of the court ; and if such jury shall find that the said return is false, judgment shall be entered for the sum aforesaid, against such sheriff, deputy, coroner, or other officer, and their respective sureties, with double costs.

§ 243. If any person, by any means whatever, shall willfully, mischievously, injure or destroy any of the work, materials or furniture of said court-house or jail, or deface any of the walls or other parts thereof, or shall write any obscene words, or shall make any drawing or character, or do any other act, either on said building or the walls thereof, in violation of decency or propriety, or shall deface or injure the trees, fences, pavement, or soil, on the grounds belonging thereto, such person, for every such offense, shall forfeit and pay a sum not less than twenty dollars, nor more than fifty dollars ; and such offense is made cognizable before a justice of the peace of the county or town where committed.

§ 320. If any person, elected to any county office, shall undertake to execute the same, or discharge the duties thereof, before he shall have taken the oath of office, and given bond, as required by law, he shall be liable to indictment, and on conviction, may be fined not exceeding five hundred dollars, to the use of the common school.

§ 1729. Any tax collector, who shall willfully fail or refuse, within ten days after the time appointed by law, for any monthly payment or final settlement, to make the same, or willfully fail or refuse to discharge any other duty required of him by this chapter, shall be deemed guilty of a misdemeanor, and on indictment and conviction thereof, he shall be removed from office, and fined not exceeding one thousand dollars, by any any court of competent jurisdiction.

§ 1733. It shall not be lawful for any person, not appointed and qualified as an auctioneer, to expose to sale at auction, by public outcry, any goods, wares, merchandise or stock, under the penalty of five hundred dollars for each offense ; *provided*, that this section shall not apply to sales of the property of deceased persons, or to any sale required by law, or made under the judgment, decree, order or process of any court, or under any deed of trust, or mortgage with a power of sale, or to sales made by any one of his own property.

DUTY OF MASTERS OF VESSELS IN REGARD TO CERTAIN POOR.

§ 1989. If any person commanding a ship, vessel, steamboat or other water craft, shall import into this state, or bring to the shores thereof, any infant, lunatic, maimed, aged or infirm person, or vagrant, who is likely to become chargeable on the county or town in which said person may be landed, on the requisition of any supervisor of the district, or the chief magistrate of any town in which such person may be landed, the captain, master, or commander of such ship, vessel, steamboat or other water craft, shall enter into bond, with sufficient sureties, payable to the county or town, conditioned to indemnify such county or town, against all charges that may be incurred in the support and care of such person ; and any captain, master or commander, who shall fail or refuse to give the bond required by this section, shall forfeit and pay to the county or town, the sum of two hundred dollars for each infant, lunatic, maimed, aged or infirm person, or vagrant, so brought into the state, to be recovered by action, before any court having jurisdiction; and may also be indicted before any court having cognizance thereof, and fined in the sum of one hundred dollars, for every person so unlawfully landed, or brought into the state.

§ 1990. When any ship, vessel or steamboat, shall arrive at any port or harbor within this state, with alien passengers on board, who are to be landed or left in this state, and who may become a charge as paupers, the master or commanding officer of such vessel, shall, before the said passengers, or any of them, leave such ship, vessel or steamboat, deposit with the supervisor of the district where such passengers are to be landed or left, a complete list of their names, and shall forthwith enter into bond, with sufficient sureties, payable to the county or to the town, in a sum sufficient to indemnify the county or town, with condition to indemnify and save harmless the said county or town, from all expenses which may arise from supporting or maintaining such alien passengers; and in default of such bond, such captain, master or commander, may be committed, by any justice of the peace, or mayor of any town, until the bond be executed; and, moreover, such captain, master or commander, shall be liable to be indicted for a violation of this section, on conviction before a court having jurisdiction, shall be fined in a sum of one hundred dollars, for each passenger landed in violation of this section; and any justice of the peace, or mayor or chief magistrate of any town, shall have power to issue a warrant for the immediate apprehension of any person who may violate the provisions of this section, and take proper recognizance from the offending party, for his appearance before the proper court, to answer the charge against him; *provided*, that the supervisor of the district, or the mayor or chief magistrate of any town, may dispense with such bond, if it shall be deemed unnecessary; *and provided, also*, that such bond may be dispensed with, if the master or commander will pay to the supervisor of the district, or to the mayor of any town, the sum of ten dollars for each passenger landed; and in either case, the supervisor, or the mayor or chief magistrate of the town, shall give to such captain, master or commander, a written permit to land such passengers as may be designated therein.

§ 2431. The board of supervisors of any county, or the corporate authorities of any town or city, through which any telegraph line may run, shall have full power and authority to regulate, within their respective limits, the manner in which the same shall be constructed and maintained, with a view to the safe and convenient use of the public highways, by persons traveling thereon; and if the proprietors of any telegraph line shall refuse or omit to comply with such regulations, they shall be liable to indictment, and, on conviction, may be fined, not exceeding one hundred dollars for each offense; and, moreover, the said board of supervisors, or corporate authorities of such town or city, may cause such line to be abated, within their respective jurisdictions, as a nuisance.

BANKING AND BANK NOTES.

§ 2498. No person, who is not authorized by law, shall subscribe to, or become a member of, or be in any way interested in any association, institution or company formed, or to be formed, in this state, for the purpose of issuing notes or other evidences of debt, to be loaned, or put in circulation, as money ; nor shall any person, unauthorized by law, subscribe to, or become in any way interested, in any bank or fund created for the like purpose; and any person who shall subscribe to, or become a member of any such company, or interested in any such bank, shall forfeit and pay the sum of one thousand dollars, on conviction before any court of competent jurisdiction.

§ 2499.　No incorporated company, without being authorized by law, shall employ any part of its money or effects, or be in any way interested in any fund employed for receiving deposits, making discounts, or issuing notes or other evidences of debt, to be loaned or put in circulation ; and any director, agent or officer of any incorporated company, who shall violate the provisions of this section, may be indicted therefor, and on conviction, shall pay a fine of one thousand dollars.

§ 2501.　No person, without express authority by law to do so, shall keep any office for issuing any notes, bills, certificates of deposits, or evidences of debt, to be loaned or put in circulation as money ; and every person offending against the provisions of this section shall be liable to indictment, and on conviction, shall be fined in a sum not exceeding one thousand dollars.

§ 2502.　No person, without express authority by law, shall issue any note, bill, certificate of deposit, or other securities, payable to order or bearer, with intent to put the same in circulation as money, or as a substitute for money ; and no person shall pass, or offer to pass or circulate, any such note, bill, certificate of deposit, or other security, so issued without authority of law; and any person offending against the provisions of this section shall be liable to indictment, and on conviction, may be fined not exceeding two hundred dollars.

§ 2503.　It shall not be lawful for any person to circulate or pass, or offer to pass, any bank note, or certificate of deposit, given or made by this or any other state, or any bill or other issue made for circulation by any such corporation or bank, in or out of the state, of a less denomination than five dollars; and should any person offend against the provisions of this section, such person shall be liable to indictment, and on conviction, shall be fined not less than twenty-five dollars; *provided*, that this prohibition shall not extend to the fractional currency of the United States, or national bank notes.

§ 2601.　If any guest or other person shall play at any game, bank or table, contrary to law, in a tavern, or any outhouse, or under any booth, arbor or other place upon the premises in possession of any tavern keeper, and the said tavern keeper shall not forthwith give information of the offense, together with the names of the offenders, to some justice of the peace of his county, and prosecute the same, the tavern keeper so in possession of said premises shall, upon conviction thereof, be fined not less than twenty dollars, nor more than one hundred dollars ; and, moreover, his license shall be revoked, either before or after conviction, by the court granting the same, whenever, after being duly summoned to show cause to the contrary, he shall fail to appear before the court and satisfy such court that he did not know of, and had no reason to suspect, such playing, gaming or betting.

§ 2602. Any owner, lessee or occupant of any house, outhouse, or other building, who shall knowingly permit or suffer any of the before-mentioned tables, banks or games, or any other game prohibited by law, to be carried on or exhibited, in his said house, outhouse or other building, or on his lot or premises, being thereof convicted, shall pay a fine of not less than one hundred dollars, nor more than two thousand dollars.

§ 2605. If any person, in order to raise money for himself or another, shall publicly or privately put up a lottery to be drawn or adventured for, or any prize or thing to be raffled or played for, or if any person shall sell, or expose for sale, any lottery ticket, or any prize or prize boxes, such person shall be adjudged guilty of gaming, and on conviction thereof, shall be fined not less than twenty, nor more than two thousand dollars.

§ 2614. Every owner, lessee or occupant of any house or other building, who shall suffer or permit any unlicensed billiard table to be carried on or exhibited for public play in his house, outhouse or other building, being convicted thereof, shall pay a fine of not less than one hundred dollars, nor more than one thousand dollars.

§ 2620. If any person shall willfully obstruct, break, injure or destroy any bridge, causeway or ferry, or any appurtenances thereof which shall have been established for the convenience of the public by the proper authority, he shall, on conviction thereof, be fined not more than one hundred dollars for each violation of this section, to be paid into the state treasury, and shall be liable, further, for all damage occasioned by such wrongful act.

§ 2621. All overseers of roads who shall refuse or neglect to do their duty in any respect, as required by law, after notice of their appointment as such, shall, on conviction, for each neglect, be fined not more than fifty dollars, in addition to the penalties recoverable by law before a justice of the peace.

§ 2622. Any person who shall willfully destroy, deface or pull down any mile-post, sign-board, or index board, shall, on conviction thereof, be fined not more than one hundred dollars, and imprisoned not more than one week.

§ 2623. If any person shall fell any bush or tree into any public highway, or obstruct the same in any manner whatever, and shall not remove the same immediately, it shall be deemed a nuisance, and on conviction thereof, the offender, in addition to the penalty now recoverable by law, shall be fined not more than fifty dollars, and be imprisoned not more than one week.

§ 2624. If any captain or master of a vessel, or any other person, shall obstruct, or cause to be obstructed, any of the navigable

20

bays, rivers, creeks, or other navigable channels or passes thereof, in any manner whatever, on conviction thereof, the offender shall be fined not more than one thousand dollars, or imprisoned not longer than six months, or by both such fine and imprisonment.

§ 2625. If any overseer of any road shall suffer any public road in his district to remain out of repair for more than ten days at any one time, unless hindered by extreme bad weather, or other unavoidable cause, on conviction thereof shall be fined not more than fifty dollars; *provided*, that the indictment shall be found in six months after the expiration of his term of office.

SABBATH—VIOLATION OF.

§ 2679. If any person, on a sabbath day, commonly called Sunday, shall himself be found laboring at his own, or any other trade, calling or business, or shall employ his apprentices, or servant, or servants belonging to any other person, in labor, or other business, except it be in the ordinary household offices of daily necessity or other work of necessity or charity, he shall, on conviction be fined not more than twenty dollars for every offense, deeming every apprentice or servant so employed, as constituting a distinct offense ; *provided*, that nothing in this section shall apply to railroads, or steamboat navigation in this state.

§ 2680. No merchant, shopkeeper, or other person, except apothecaries and druggists, shall keep open store, or dispose of any wares or merchandise, goods or chattels, on Sunday, or sell or barter the same ; and every person so offending, shall, on conviction, be fined not more than twenty dollars for every such offense.

§ 2681. If any person shall show forth, exhibit, act, represent, or perform, or cause to be shown forth, acted, represented or performed, any interludes, farces, or plays of any kind, or any games, tricks, juggling, slight of hand, or feats of dexterity, agility of body, or any bear baiting, or any bull baiting, horse racing, or cock fighting, or any such like show or exhibition, whatsoever, on Sunday, every person, so offending, shall be fined not more than fifty dollars.

§ 2683. If any person shall be found hunting with a gun, or with dogs, on the Sabbath, or fishing in any way, he shall, on conviction thereof be fined not less than five, nor more than twenty dollars.

§ 2711. If any person shall knowingly cut, fell, alter, remove or destroy, or shall cause to be cut, felled, altered, removed or destroyed, any boundary tree, or other allowed boundary land-mark, to the wrong of his neighbor, or any other person, he shall, on conviction, be fined not more than two hundred dollars, nor less than fifty dollars.

§ 2740. It shall not be lawful for any person to hunt deer, or other game or animals, in the night time, with fire, except within his own enclosure; and any person violating this law, shall, on indictment and conviction, be liable to a fine, not exceeding one hundred dollars, for each offense, and shall, moreover, be liable in a civil action, to the owner of any horse, neat cattle, hog, sheep or other domestic animal, which may be killed or wounded in such unlawful hunting, in double the amount of the injury sustained.

§ 2747. If any person or persons, shall hereafter willfully disturb, molest, or interrupt any literary society, or school or society formed for the intellectual improvement of its members, or any other school or society, organized, under any law of this state, or any school, society or meeting, formed or convened for the improvement in music, letters, or for social amusement, such person or persons, so offending, shall be deemed guilty of a misdemeanor, and on conviction thereof, shall be fined in any sum not less than ten dollars, nor more than fifty dollars with cost of prosecution, and shall stand committed until such fine and all costs are paid.

§ 2832. If any person shall assault, beat, challenge to fight, or provoke to fight any person, on account of betting or gaming, or winning or losing money at any game, or any other thing, of value, the person so assaulting, beating, challenging to fight, or provoking to fight, being thereof convicted, before any justice of the peace, in addition to the penalties provided in this code, in the circuit court, shall forfeit and pay fifty dollars, to be collected by execution, and paid into the state treasury, for school purposes.

§ 2833. If any person shall profanely swear or curse, or shall be drunk in any public place, in the presence of two or more persons, he shall, on conviction thereof, before any justice of the peace of the county, where the same may happen, be fined, not more than ten dollars for each offense, and shall stand committed to jail, until such fine and costs are paid ; such fine and costs to be for the use of public schools.

Sec. 13. Be it further enacted, That all persons collecting dues to the State are hereby prohibited from exchanging any coin or currency received by them for such dues to the state, for certificates of indebtedness, and all officers, or other persons, shall, upon payment into the state treasury of any such certificates collected by them, take and subscribe to the following oath, which shall be required by the state treasurer, and which he or his deputy, or any other officer, authorized to administer, viz: I ———— of ———— Mississippi, do solemnly swear that each and all of the certificates of indebtedness herewith presented to the treasurer, in settlement for dues to the State collected by me, were received by me for taxes (or dues to the State), and that I have not exchanged with any person or persons, any coin, or United States currency received by me in the collection of taxes, or other dues to the State, for certificates of indebtedness or Auditor's warrants issued subsequent to the first of April, 1874; so help me God.

Sec. 14. Be it further enacted, That any tax collector, or other officer, violating the provisions of section 13 of this act, shall be deemed guilty of a misdemeanor, and, on conviction, shall be fined not less than five hundred dollars for each violation, and such conviction shall work a forfeiture of his office and render him forever thereafter ineligible to any office of profit or trust in this state.

Crimes and Offenses Punishable by Fines or Imprisonment, or Both,

§ 1750. Any person who shall exercise, in this state, any of the privileges above enumerated (Art. 19, Chap. 22) without first paying the price, and procuring the certificate of the chancery clerk, as required shall be deemed guilty of a misdemeanor, and on conviction before a justice, or other court of competent jurisdiction, shall be fined not less than double the tax imposed by said section, or shall be imprisoned in the county jail, not exceeding six months, or be punished by both fine and imprisonment, at the discretion of the court.

§ 2436. If any superintendent, operator, or person connected, in any capacity whatever, with any line of telegraph, in this state, shall use, or cause to be used, or make known, or cause to be made known, the contents of any dispatch, which may be sent or received over such telegraph line, without the consent or direction of the party sending or receiving the same, or shall fail to transmit all dispatches filed at the office of which he is the superintendent or operator, for transmission to any other point, without divulging or making public the contents or purport thereof, without like consent, as aforesaid, such person, on conviction thereof, shall be liable to be fined not exceeding five hundred dollars, or imprisonment not exceeding six months, or both, at the discretion of the court ; but this article shall not apply to any dispatch of a public nature, sent with a view to general publicity.

§ 2486. If any man and woman shall live together, in unlawful cohabitation, whether the same shall be in adultery or fornication, upon conviction thereof, they shall be fined in any sum, not less than one hundred dollars, nor more than five hundred dollars each, and imprisoned, not more than six months, or by such fine or imprisonment alone, at the discretion of the court.

ELECTIONS—BRIBERY, THREATS, ETC.

§ 2515. If any person shall offer or give a reward to another, for the purpose of inducing him to persuade, or by any other means, not amounting to bribery, to procure any person to vote at any election, for or against any person, the person so giving or offering such reward, shall, upon conviction thereof, be imprisoned in the county jail, for not more than one year, or fined not more than five hundred dollars, or both, at the discretion of the court.

§ 2516. Whoever shall procure, or endeavor to procure, the vote of any elector, or the influence of any person, over other electors, at any election, for himself or any candidate, by means of violence, threats of violence, or threats of withdrawing custom, or dealing in business or trade, or of enforcing the payment of a debt, or of bringing a suit or criminal prosecution, or by any other threat or injury to be inflicted by him, or by his means, shall, upon conviction, be punished by imprisonment in a county jail, not more than one year, or by fine, not exceeding one thousand dollars, or by both such fine and imprisonment.

§ 2536. If any person shall unlawfully disturb any election for any public office, in this state, such person shall be liable to indictment, and on conviction, may be fined not exceeding five hundred dollars, and imprisoned, not exceeding six months, or both ; and if the returning officer shall willfully fail to report to the district attorney any offender against the provisions of this section, he shall be liable to indictment, and on conviction, may be fined not exceeding five hundred dollars.

§ 2537. Any person who shall vote at any election, not being legally qualified, or who shall vote in more than one county, or at more than one place in any county, or in any city or town, entitled to separate representation, or who shall vote for members of the board of supervisors, justice of the peace, or constable, out of the district in which he resides, shall be liable to indictment, and on conviction, shall be fined not exceeding two hundred dollars, or be imprisoned in the county jail, not more than six months, or by both such fine and imprisonment.

§ 2539. Any such inspector, or other officer, who shall proceed to any election, without having the ballot-box locked and secured, in the manner directed by law, or who shall open and read, or consent to any other person opening and reading any ballot given to him to be deposited in the box, at such election, before it is put into the box, without the consent of the voter giving the same, shall, upon conviction, be punished by imprisonment in a county jail, not exceeding six months, or by fine, not exceeding three hundred dollars, or by both such fine and imprisonment.

§ 2540. Any inspector or returning officer, of a general or special election, who, before the votes are counted, shall dispose of, or deposit the ballot box, in a manner not authorized by law, or shall, at any time after the election has begun, and before the ballots are counted, give the key of the ballot-box, with which he is entrusted, to any other, shall, upon conviction, be punished by imprisonment in a county jail, not exceeding three months, or by fine not exceeding three hundred dollars, or by both such fine and imprisonment.

§ 2541. When any one who offers to vote at an election, shall be objected to by any challenger, as a person unqualified to vote, if any inspector of such election shall permit him to vote, without producing proof of such qualification, in the manner directed by law, or if any such inspector shall refuse the vote of any person who shall comply with the requisites prescribed by law, to prove his qualifications, knowing him to be entitled to vote, or if any inspector shall, knowingly permit an unqualified person to vote, he shall, upon conviction, be punished by imprisonment in a county jail, not exceeding three months, or by fine not exceeding two hundred dollars, or by both such fine and imprisonment.

§ 2543. It shall not be lawful for any military officer, or other persons, to order, bring, or keep any troops of armed men at any place within a mile of the place where any general or special election is held, unless it be for the purpose of quelling a riot or insurrection, in the manner provided by law, or for the purpose of defense, in time of war; and whoever shall violate the provisions of this section, shall, on conviction, be punished by imprisonment in the county jail, not exceeding one year, or by fine, not less than five hundred dollars, or by both such fine and imprisonment; and if the offense shall be committed with intent to influence such election, the person convicted thereof, shall forever be disqualified to hold any office or place of trust, honor, or profit under the laws or constitution of this state, and shall be punished by imprisonment in the penitentiary, for a term not exceeding two years, and be forever excluded from the right of suffrage.

§ 2545. If any person, elected to any office in this state, shall undertake to exercise the same, or discharge the duties thereof, without first having taken the oath of office, and given bond, as required by law, he shall be adjudged guilty of a misdemeanor, and on conviction thereof, shall be fined not more than five hundred dollars, or imprisoned not longer than one year, at the discretion of the court, or by both such fine and imprisonment.

DUELING.

§ 2531. Every person who shall challenge another to fight a duel, or who shall send, deliver, or cause to be delivered, any written or verbal message, purporting or intended to be such challenge, or who shall accept any such challenge or message, or who shall, knowingly carry, or deliver any such message or challenge, or who shall be present at the time of fighting any duel with deadly weapons, either as second, aid, or surgeon, or who shall advise or give assistance to such duel, shall, on conviction thereof, be fined in a sum not less than three hundred dollars, nor exceeding one thousand dollars, or be imprisoned, not less than six months, in the county jail, or by both such fine and imprisonment.

§ 2534. If any person shall be guilty of fighting, and shall, in such fight, use any rifle, shot-gun, sword, sword-cane, pistol, dirk, bowie-knife, dirk-knife, or any other deadly weapon, or if any person shall be second or aid in any such fight, the person so offending shall be fined not less than three hundred dollars, or shall be imprisoned, not less than three months, or punished by both such fine and imprisonment ; and if any person shall be killed in such fight, the person so killing the other, may be prosecuted and convicted, as in other cases of murder.

ESCAPE OF PRISONERS.

§ 2553. Every person who, by any means whatever, shall aid or assist any prisoner, lawfully committed to any jail or place of confinement, in execution of any conviction for any criminal offence, other than felony, whether such escape be effected or not, or who shall convey into such jail or place of confinement, any disguise, instrument, arms, or other things, proper or useful to facilitate the escape of any prisoner so committed, whether such escape be effected or attempted, or not, shall be punished by imprisonment in a county jail, not exceeding one year, or by fine, not exceeding five hundred dollars, or by both such fine and imprisonment.

§ 2555. Every person who shall aid or assist any prisoner in escaping, or attempting to escape, from the custody of any sheriff, coroner, marshal, constable, or other officer or person, who shall have the lawful charge of such prisoner, upon any criminal charge, shall, upon conviction, be punished by imprisonment in a county jail, not exceeding one year, or by fine, not exceeding five hundred dollars, or by both such fine and imprisonment.

§ 2556. If any private person have any prisoner in his keeping, arrested on suspicion of felony, treason, murder, or other offense, and the person who is so arrested escape, by his willful act or negligence, then the person from whom such prisoner so escaped, shall, upon conviction, be fined in a sum not more than one thousand dollars, and imprisoned in a county jail, not longer than one year, or by both such fine and imprisonment.

§ 2557. If any sheriff, jailor, coroner, marshal, constable, or other officer, shall willfully and corruptly refuse to execute any lawful process, directed to him or any of them, requiring the apprehension or confinement of any person, charged with a criminal offense, or shall corruptly and willfully omit to execute such process, by which such person shall escape, or shall willfully refuse to receive, in any jail under his charge, any offender lawfully committed to such jail, and ordered to be confined therein, on any criminal charge or conviction, or any lawful process whatever, or shall suffer any person, lawfully committed to his custody, to escape and go at large, either willfully or negligently, or shall receive any gratuity or reward, or any security or engagement for the same, to procure, assist or connive at, or permit any prisoner in his custody, on any criminal charge or conviction, to escape, whether such escape be attempted or effected, or not, he shall, upon conviction, be punished, by imprisonment in the county jail, not exceeding one year, or by fine, not exceeding one thousand dollars, or by both such fine and imprisonment.

§ 2562. Every person lawfully imprisoned in a county jail, who shall escape therefrom, or who shall attempt, by force or violence, to escape therefrom, shall, upon conviction, be imprisoned in the county jail, not more than one year.

COUNTERFEITING MERCANTILE LABELS, ETC.

§ 2595. Every person, who shall knowingly and willfully forge or counterfeit, or cause or procure to be forged or counterfeited, any representation, likeness, similitude, copy or imitation, of the private stamps, wrappers or labels, usually affixed by any mechanic or manufacturer to, and used by such mechanic or manufacturer on, in or about the sale of any goods, wares or merchandise, with intent to deceive or defraud the purchaser or manufacturer of any goods, wares or merchandise whatsoever, upon conviction thereof, shall be deemed guilty of a misdemeanor, and shall be punished by imprisonment in the county jail, for a term not less than three months, nor more than two years.

§ 2596. Every person who shall have in his possession any die, plate, engraving, or printed label, stamp or wrapper, or any representation, likeness, similitude, copy or imitation of the private stamp, wrapper or label usually fixed by any mechanic or manufacturer to, and used by such mechanic or manufacturer, on, in or about the sale of any goods, wares or merchandise, with intent to use or sell the said die, plate or engraving, or printed stamp, label or wrapper, for the purpose of aiding or assisting, in any way whatever, in vending any goods, wares or merchandise, in imitation of, or intended to resemble and be sold for the goods, wares or merchandise of such mechanic or manufacturer, shall, upon conviction thereof, be deemed guilty of a misdemeanor, and shall be punished by imprisonment in the county jail, for a term not less than three months, nor more than one year.

§ 2597. Every person who shall vend any goods, wares or merchandise, having thereon any forged or counterfeit stamp or label, imitating, resembling or purporting to be the stamp or label of any mechanic or manufacturer, knowing the same to be forged or counterfeited, and resembling and purporting to be imitations of the stamps or labels of such mechanic or manufacturer, without disclosing the fact to the purchaser thereof, shall, upon conviction, be deemed guilty of a misdemeanor, and shall be punished by imprisonment in the county jail, for a term not exceeding one year, and by a fine, not less than fifty, nor more than five hundred dollars, or by both such fine and imprisonment.

GAMING.

§ 2598. If any person shall encourage, promote or play at any game, play or amusement, for money or other valuable thing, or shall wager or bet, promote or encourage the wagering or betting, any money or other valuable thing upon any game, play, amusement, cock fight or duel, or upon the result of any election whatever, upon conviction thereof, shall be fined in a sum, not less than twenty dollars, nor more than five hundred dollars ; and unless such fine and costs be immediately paid, shall be imprisoned for any period, not more than twenty days, nor less than five days, at the discretion of the court.

§ 2599. If any judge of any court, or any justice of the peace, or attorney-general or district attorney, or any constable, sheriff, or coroner, or any person charged by law with the custody of public money, shall violate the provisions of the foregoing section, such person so offending, on conviction thereof, shall be fined in the sum of five hundred dollars, and be imprisoned for the space of twenty days, or less, at the discretion of the court : and in case any public officer shall, in any manner, use or loan public money in his hands by virtue of his office, in any game, wager, or bet, on conviction thereof, his commission shall thereby be deemed vacated, and the vacancy supplied, as in case of death, resignation or removal from office.

§ 2600. If any person shall be guilty of keeping or exhibiting any game, or gaming table, commonly called A B C or E O, roulette, or rowley-powley, or *rouge-et noir*, rondo, pool, keno, monte, or any faro bank, or other game, gaming table, or bank of the same or like kind, or any other kind or description, under any other name whatever, or shall be in any manner, either directly or indirectly, interested or concerned in any of the aforesaid gaming tables, bank or games, either by furnishing money or articles for the purpose of carrying on the same, being interested in the loss or gain of said table, bank or games, or employed in any manner in conducting, carrying on, or exhibiting said gaming tables, games or banks, every person so offending, and being thereof convicted, shall pay a fine, at the discretion of the court, not exceeding two thousand dollars, or imprisoned, not longer than six months in the county jail, or by both such fine and imprisonment.

§ 2603. All moneys exhibited for the purpose of betting, or alluring persons to bet at any game, and all moneys staked or betted, shall be liable to seizure, by any justice of the peace of the county in which such offense shall be committed, or by any other person, under a warrant from such justice or other peace officer; and all such moneys, so seized, shall be accounted for by the person making the seizure, to the justice of the peace, or other officer issuing such warrant, and be paid by him into the treasury of the county, deducting thereout fifty per centum upon all moneys so seized, to the person making the said seizure.

§ 2604. Any person or persons, who shall oppose the seizure of any such money as above described, by any person so authorized to make it, shall be liable to a penalty of fifteen hundred dollars, on conviction thereof; and any person who shall take and carry away any part of said money, after the said seizure shall be declared, shall be guilty of a misdemeanor, and on conviction thereof, shall be fined and imprisoned, at the discretion of the court.

§ 2606. Any person of full age, who shall bet any money, or thing of any value, with a minor, or allow a minor to bet at any game or gaming table exhibited by him, or in which he is interested or in any manner concerned, on conviction thereof, shall be fined not less than three hundred dollars, and imprisoned not less than three months.

§ 2616. If any person shall keep or exhibit any billiard table, for public play, or shall, in any way, be concerned or interested in such billiard table, without having a license therefor, he shall pay a fine of not less than five hundred dollars, or be imprisoned not less than six months, or by both such fine and imprisonment.

OBSTRUCTING ROADS.

§ 2626. If any person shall wantonly or negligently obstruct or injure any railroad, or plank road, in this state, or any covered road, on conviction thereof, he shall be fined not more than two thousand dollars, or imprisonment not longer than twelve months in the county jail, or by both such fine and imprisonment.

STEALING OR REMOVING PERSONAL PROPERTY.

§ 2653. If any person, who shall feloniously take, steal, and carry away, any personal property of another, under the value of ten dollars, he shall be deemed guilty of petit larceny, and shall be punished by imprisonment in a county jail, for a term not exceeding three months, or by fine, in any sum not exceeding one hundred dollars, or by both such fine and imprisonment, at the discretion of the court.

§ 2658. If any person shall move, or cause to be removed, to any place beyond the jurisdiction of this state, any personal property, which shall, at the time of such removal, be under written pledge, or mortgage, or deed of trust, and liens by judgment, in this state, with intent to defraud the pledgee, mortgagee, trustee, or *cestui que trust* of said property, said person shall be deemed guilty of a misdemeanor, and upon conviction thereof, before any court of competent jurisdiction, shall be fined not less than one thousand dollars, or imprisoned in the county jail, not less than three, nor more than twelve months, or by both such fine and imprisonment, at the discretion of the court.

§ 2659. If any person shall remove, or cause to be removed, or shall aid or assist in removing, to any place beyond the jurisdiction of this state, any personal property, upon which there shall, at the time of such removal, be any judgment or execution lien, within this state, with intent to deprive the person entitled to the benefit of such lien, shall be deemed guilty of a misdemeanor, and upon conviction thereof, shall be fined in any sum not more than five hundred dollars, or be imprisoned in the county jail, not less than one, nor more than six months, or by both such fine and imprisonment, at the discretion of the court.

IMPROPER USE OF DANGEROUS WEAPONS.

§ 2699. If any person, having, or carrying any dirk, dirk-knife, sword, sword-cane, gun, pistol, or other fire-arms, or other deadly weapon, shall, in the presence of three or more persons, exhibit the same, in a rude, angry, or threatening manner, not in necessary self-defense, or shall, in any manner, unlawfully use the same, in any fight or quarrel, the person so offending, upon conviction thereof, shall be fined in a sum not exceeding five hundred dollars, or be imprisoned in the common jail, not exceeding three months, or by both such fine and imprisonment. [And such gun, pistol, or other fire-arms, when exhibited in a rude, angry, or threatening manner, shall be held and deemed *prima facie*, a deadly weapon, without any proof that the same was loaded with powder, shot, or ball.]

CONCEALING OR DESTROYING WILLS.

§ 2700. If any person shall willfully alter or destroy any will or codicil, without the consent of the party making the same, or shall willfully secrete the same for six months after the death of the testator shall be known to him, the person so offending, on conviction thereof, shall be fined or imprisoned in the common jail, or both, at the discretion of the court.

DAMAGE TO TELEGRAPH LINES.

§ 2702. Any person who shall intentionally or negligently, in anywise obstruct, injure, break, or destroy, or in any manner interrupt any telegraph line, in this state, or communication thereon, between any two points, by or through which the said line may pass, shall, on conviction thereof, be fined, at the discretion of the court, not more than one thousand dollars, or imprisonment not longer than twelve months, or by both such fine and imprisonment.

§ 2435. If any person shall willfully injure, or in any manner obstruct, or interrupt, the working of any telegraph line in this state, or shall willfully destroy, cut down, or injure any post, or other support of the wires, insulators, or other fixtures necessary to the working of said telegraph lines, or shall cut, break or destroy the wires, or shall place any wires, or other substance whatever, in contact with, or touching the wires or other fixtures of said telegraph line, so as to impede, or in anywise interfere with the operations thereof, or shall take, carry away, injure or destroy, any of the posts, wires, insulators, or other fixtures or things belonging to such telegraph lines, during any temporary suspension of the operations thereof, from accidental causes, such person shall be liable to indictment, and on conviction, may be fined not exceeding five hundred dollars, or imprisoned not exceeding six months, or both, at the discretion of the court; and shall, moreover be liable to all damages suffered by reason thereof.

DAMAGED PROVISIONS.

§ 2704. Any person who shall knowingly and willfully sell, or hold, or offer for sale, any tainted, putrid, unsound, unwholesome, or unmerchantable flour, or other provisions, as sound and good, or shall practice any fraud or deception, to put off and sell any damaged, unsound, or unmerchantable provisions, shall, upon conviction thereof, be punished by fine not exceeding five hundred dollars, or imprisoned in the common jail, not more than thirty days, or by both such fine and imprisonment.

LIBEL.

§ 2706. Any person who shall be convicted of writing or publishing any libel, or speaking words made actionable by law, shall be fined in such sum, or imprisoned for such term, as the court, in its discretion, may adjudge, having regard to the nature and enormity of the offense, or by both such fine and imprisonment.

MALICIOUS INJURY TO PROPERTY.

§ 2708. Any person who shall maliciously, either out of a spirit of revenge, or wanton cruelty, or who shall mischievously kill, maim or wound, or injure any horse, mare, gelding, mule, sheep, cattle, hog, dog, poultry, or other live stock, or cause any person to do the same, shall be fined, in any sum not less than fifty, nor more than three hundred dollars, or be imprisoned, for any term not exceeding six months, or by both such fine and imprisonment; but the penalty in this section mentioned, shall not apply to any person who may injure animals found in the act of trespassing within his enclosure, and who has paid or tendered to the owner of the animal, full compensation for the injury inflicted.

§ 2709. Every person who shall maliciously or mischievously destroy, disfigure or injure, or cause to be destroyed or injured, any property of another, either real or personal, shall be deemed guilty of malicious mischief, and, upon conviction thereof, shall be fined in a sum two-fold the value of the property destroyed, or of the damage done, and be imprisoned, for any time, not exceeding twelve months.

ACTING AS BROKER WITHOUT LICENSE.

§ 2718. If any person shall buy, sell, barter or exchange, any gold, silver or bank notes, or any drafts, or bills for the payment of money, as a broker or factor, without a license first had, on conviction thereof, he shall be fined not more than five hundred dollars, and imprisoned in the common jail, not longer than six months.

IMPORTING CONTAGIOUS DISEASES.

§ 2719. If any person shall wilfully and knowingly import or bring into this state, or into any county thereof, from another county, the small-pox, or any other contagious or infectious disease or matter thereof, with the design to spread the same by inoculation or otherwise, or shall inoculate, or procure inoculation, for said diseases, or any or either of them, after such disease may have been introduced, except as provided by law, the person so offending shall, on conviction, be fined not more than two thousand dollars, and be imprisoned not more than one year, for each offense so committed, or by both such fine and imprisonment.

FRAUDULENT PACKING OF COTTON.

§ 2720. If any person shall fraudulently pack or bale cotton, he shall, on conviction thereof, be fined not more than five hundred dollars, and imprisoned not more than six months, at the discretion of the court.

BUYING STOLEN COTTON, CORN, ETC.

SECTION 1. Be it enacted by the Legislature of the State of Mississippi, That hereafter, it shall be a misdemeanor, under the laws of this state, for any person or persons, to buy or sell, either by paying or receiving money thereof, or by exchange or barter of property of any description thereof, or deliver or receive under contract of sale of purchase, any cotton in the seed, or ginned but not baled, between the hours of sunset on any day and sunrise on the day next succeeding.

SEC. 2. Be it further enacted, That it shall also be a misdemeanor for any person, not regularly engaged as principal, or clerk, in the mercantile, warehouse, grocery, livery or feed stable business, paying a privilege tax under the laws of the state, to sell, or exchange, or barter any indian corn, or wheat, between the hours of sunset on any day, and sunrise on the day next succeeding, saving and excepting that green corn for table use may be bought and sold by any person between daybreak and sunset of any day.

SEC. 3. Be it further enacted, That it shall also be a misdemeanor for any principal, clerk, or employee, engaged in the mercantile, warehouse, grocery, livery or feed stable business, or any other person, not being at the time a wayfaring man or traveler who buys corn to feed immediately to his beast, to buy or exchange, trade or barter for any Indian corn or wheat, between the hours of sunset on any day, and sunrise on the day next succeeding. (Approved, March 15, 1876.)

FRAUDULENT WEIGHING OF COTTON.

SECTION 1. Be it enacted by the Legislature of the State of Mississippi, That it shall not be lawful for any person or persons who are employed by any merchant, warehouseman or other person, as weighers of cotton or other article of produce, to give a certificate for a less amount than the actual weight of the same, deductions for mud and water only excepted.

SEC. 2. That any receipt, memorandum or other instrument of writing, by which it is made to appear that the producer receives credit for a less amount than the actual weight of the article or articles weighed, shall be deemed and held to be a fraudulent certificate under the provisions of this act.

SEC. 3. Be it further enacted, That any person or persons who shall be found guilty of a violation of this act, by any court of competent jurisdiction, shall, upon conviction, be fined not less than five nor more than one hundred dollars, or shall be imprisoned not exceeding six months, or both fine and imprisonment, at the discretion of the court. (Approved, March 6, 1872.)

MASKS AND DISGUISES.

§ 2722. If any person or persons, masked or in disguise, shall prowl or travel, or ride or walk, or be in the country or towns, or in any public place, in this state, to the disturbance of the peace, or the terror or the alarming of the citizens of any portion of this state, on conviction thereof, he or they shall be fined, not less than one hundred, nor more than five hundred dollars, and imprisoned in the jail of the county wherein convicted, at the discretion of the court before which the conviction is had.

§ 2725. Any person or persons, not masked or disguised, who shall be found to be voluntarily associating and keeping company with any person or persons, found prowling or traveling, masked or disguised, in the country, or in any town, or in any public place in this state, shall be deemed guilty of a violation of this article, and upon conviction, shall be punished in the same manner, and to the same extent, as he or they might have been, had they been found prowling or traveling, masked or disguised, as hereinbefore provided.

§ 2726. Whenever any person or persons shall be found prowling or traveling, masked or in disguise, in the country, towns, or in any public place in this state, it shall be the duty of every peace officer, and other person or persons, to demand of such offender or offenders, that he or they immediately unmask, or take off his or their disguise, as the case may be ; and upon the neglect or refusal of such person or persons, so masked or disguised, to immediately comply with such demand, it shall be the duty of said peace officer, or other person or persons, to arrest the offender or offenders, either with or without process, and take him or them before the nearest magistrate, having jurisdiction thereof, which he or they can find, to be dealt with according to law ; and to this end, such peace officer, or other person or persons, so authorized to make such arrest, may call to his or their aid, any and all by-standers necessary to make such arrests; and it shall be the duty of such magistrate to take cognizance of such cases, and proceed therein, at the earliest time practicable ; which proceedings shall be the same as though said offender or offenders, had been brought before said magistrate, upon process issued by him.

§ 2727. Whenever said peace officer, or other person or persons, shall call to his or their aid, to make such arrest, any person or persons, as provided in the next preceeding section, it shall be the duty of such person or persons, so called, to proceed at once to assist in making such arrest, and take such offender or offenders before said magistrate; and every person who shall wilfully neglect or refuse to assist, shall be deemed guilty of a misdemeanor, and upon conviction, shall be punished by fine or imprisonment, or both, at the discretion of the court before which such conviction shall be had, said fine not to exceed five hundred dollars, and said imprisonment not to exceed six months.

§ 2728. If any peace officer, whose duty it is to make such arrest, or to take such offender or offenders before said magistrate as hereinbefore provided, shall willfully neglect or refuse to perform such duty, he shall be deemed guilty of a misdemeanor, and upon conviction, shall be punished by fine or imprisonment, or both, at the discretion of the court before which such conviction is had; said fine not to exceed one thousand dollars, and said imprisonment not to exceed one year.

APPROVAL OF BONDS.

SEC. 4. Be it further enacted, That the official bond of all the officers named in the second section of this Act (Chap. V, Acts 1876) shall be approved by the chancery clerk, (or if there be no chancery clerk, then by the clerk of the circuit court,) and by the president of the board of supervisors of the county; and if any chancery or circuit clerk, or president of any board of supervisors shall approve any official bond, knowing or having good reason to believe that said bond is not good and sufficient for the amount thereof, such chancery clerk, circuit clerk, or president of the board of supervisors, shall be deemed guilty of a misdemeanor, and shall be punished accordingly.

PROTECTION OF STOCK RAISERS.

SECTION 1. Be it enacted by the Legislature of the State of Mississippi, That it shall not be lawful for any person to pen or confine any milch cow, calf or yearling, not his own, with the intent, or for the purpose of procuring milk, without the consent of the owner of such cow, calf or yearling.

SEC. 2. Be it further enacted, That on proof that any person shall have penned or confined any cow, calf or yearling, not his own, it shall be deemed and held *prima facie* evidence of an intent to violate the provisions of the first section of this act.

SEC. 3. Be it further enacted, That any person violating the provisions of this act, shall be deemed guilty of a misdemeanor, and, on conviction thereof, shall be fined not less than five dollars for each offense, or imprisonment in the county jail not more than twenty days, or both such fine and imprisonment, at the discretion of the court. (Approved, April 14, 1876.)

DECOYING MINORS.

SEC. 2. Be it further enacted, That any person enticing, decoying away, or employing any minor, male or female child, knowing that said minor has a parent, and without the consent of said parent or parents, shall be liable for a misdemeanor, and shall be punished by fine not exceeding twenty dollars, or imprisonment not exceeding twenty days, or both, and shall be liable to pay the further sum of one dollar per day, to the parent for each day said minor is kept, to be recovered in any court having jurisdiction. (Approved, March 29, 1876.)

SALE OF IMPURE CANDIES.

SECTION 1. Be it enacted by the Legislature of the State of Mississippi, That it shall not be lawful for any person to manufacture, sell or keep, offer or exhibit for sale, in this state, any candy in which terra alba, or any other preparation of lime, or other deleterious or injurious earth, drug or mineral, shall be mixed or used in the manufacture or preparation thereof; and any person violating the provisions of this act, shall, on conviction thereof, be fined any sum not exceeding five hundred dollars, or imprisoned in the county jail not exceeding sixty days, or both, such fine and imprisonment, at the discretion of the court. (Approved, April 5, 1876.)

HOLDING STOLEN PROPERTY.

SEC. 2. Be it further enacted, That any person in possession of personal property, belonging to or claimed by another who shall willfully omit, or refuse to deliver such property, or to point out the same to any officer demanding the same, in the mode and manner named in section number one of this act, shall be deemed guilty of a misdemeanor, and, on conviction thereof, in any court of competent jurisdiction, shall be punished by fine, not less than the full value of such property, and not exceeding double the value thereof, or by imprisonment in the county jail for a period not less than twenty days, and not exceeding six months, or both such fine and imprisonment at the discretion of the court. (Approved, February 19, 1876.)

STEALING TIMBER.

§ 2733. If any person shall cut down, deaden or destroy, or take away, if already cut down or fallen, any cypress, white oak, black oak, or other oak, pine, poplar, walnut, cherry or pecan tree, on land not his own, and without the consent of the owner, he shall be guilty of a misdemeanor, and, if found guilty, shall be imprisoned in the county jail, not more than three months, or fined not less than five dollars nor more than three hundred dollars, or by both such fine and imprisonment; but if the party injured, elects to proceed in a civil action for damages, no prosecution, under this section, shall be had. it being the intent hereof, that there shall be both a prosecution and civil action action maintained for the same offense.

LOTTERIES.

§ 2734. To carry into force and give effect to section fifteen, of article twelve, of the constitution of the state of Mississippi, it is provided, that every lottery and gift enterprise, of whatever name or description, regardless of the authority of law heretofore creating the same, be and the same are hereby prohibited, and declared a nuisance and misdemeanor, against the public policy of the state; and whoever is concerned therein, directly or indirectly, making, drawing, setting up, purchasing, or controlling any lottery or gift enterprise, within this state, in any way or manner whatsoever, or in any manner aids therein, or is connected therewith, shall, upon conviction, before a court of competent jurisdiction, be punished by a fine, not less than than five hundred dollars, nor more than five thousand dollars, and by imprisonment, not less than six months, nor more than five years, at the discretion of the court having jurisdiction thereof; *provided*, that the fine imposed by the court, shall be awarded, one-half to the informers, and the other half to the use of the public school fund of this state.

§ 2735. If any person or persons, hereafter shall sell, or expose, or keep for sale, any lottery ticket, to be drawn in any lottery or gift enterprise, of any kind, within this state, or any device, in the nature of a lottery ticket, or any lottery policies, or any paper with letters or figures that evidence the same, or in any way represents the drawing of any such lottery or gift enterprise whatever, or act as agent or broker in effecting the sale of the same, on conviction thereof, before any court of competent jurisdiction in this state, shall for each offense, be sentenced to pay a fine not exceeding five hundred dollars, and imprisoned, not exceeding one year, at the discretion of the court; and the purchaser of any such lottery ticket, or device in the nature of a lottery and gift enterprise, ticket or policy, or paper, as above mentioned, shall not be held liable to punishment by this or any other law of this state, but shall be a competent witness in the cause; and any indictment shall be held good, which charges the crime in the language of the law, without setting forth therein the number or date of the ticket, or the device, or anything in the nature thereof, or policy, or that which represents the same, of the name of the lottery or gift enterprise, or where the same is located; *provided*, that the proviso to section two thousand seven hundred and thirty-four, of this article, and relating to the distribution of fines by the court thereof, be and the same is extended, and made part of this section.

SETTING WOODS ON FIRE.

§ 2741. It shall not be lawful for any person willfully to set on fire any woods, marshes, or prairies, within any of the counties of this state at any time between the first day of May, and the first day of February; and any person so offending, shall be liable to indictment, and on conviction, shall be fined, not less than twenty, nor more than one hundred dollars, or imprisoned, not less than one month, nor more than three months, or both; and if such offense be commited, so as to occasion any loss, damage or injury, to any other person, then the fine shall not be less than fifty, nor more than five hundred dollars; and such person shall, moreover, be liable to an action at the suit of the party aggrieved, for all loss, damage or injury sustained thereby, but any person may at at all times, set fire to his own marshes, prairies, or woods, at any season of the year, being responsible in a civil action, for any damages thereby occasioned to another person.

DEFACING CHURCHES OR SCHOOL BUILDINGS.

§ 2746. If any person shall wilfully injure any church edifice, school house, or other building used for school purposes, or in any way disfigure the same, by painting, writing or printing thereon any obscene words, figures or devices, or by pasting thereon any paper or other material, bearing such words, figures, cuts or devices, he shall be punished by fine, not exceeding one hundred dollars, or by imprisonment in a county jail, not exceeding ninety days, or both of said punishments, in the discretion of the court,

RACING OR SHOOTING IN PUBLIC HIGHWAY.

§ 2870. If any person shall be found guilty of racing or shooting in any street or public highway, he shall, on conviction thereof in the circuit court, be fined, not more than five hundred dollars.

DOG STEALING.

§ 2875. Every person who shall feloniously steal, take and carry away, any dog, the property of another, shall be guilty of petit larceny, and on being indicted and found guilty, shall be punished as in other cases of petit larceny.

POISONING FISH.

§ 2876. Every person, who shall poison any fish in any of the navigable streams of this state, or in any other other stream or lake, without the consent of the owner of the soil, by mingling in the water any substance calculated and intended to stupify or destroy fish, shall be guilty of a misdemeanor, and on conviction thereof, in the circuit court of the proper county, shall be fined in a sum not less than five dollars, and imprisoned in the county jail for a period not less than ten days, or by both such fine and imprisonment.

REPORTS BY COUNTY TREASURER.

§ 1377. The county treasurer shall, at each regular meeting of the board of supervisors of the county, and at such other times as the said board may require, make a report of the state of the treasury, exhibiting the receipts and disbursements, and the balance for or against the county, and shall exhibit the money to be counted by said board ; and in case any treasurer shall willfully fail to make such report, he shall be deemed guilty of a misdemeanor, and on conviction shall be punished by fine of not more than one hundred dollars, or imprisonment not longer than one month in the county jail. A book shall be kept in the office by the clerk, to be styled "The Treasurer's Docket," in which all such reports shall be recorded, after being carefully examined and compared with vouchers, and approved by the board ; and a copy thereof shall, within five days after the same is recorded, be posted up at the court-house door. And it shall be the duty of the chancery clerk to post such copy, and on failure to do so, said clerk shall be deemed guilty of a misdemeanor, and on conviction, shall be punished by fine of not more than one hundred dollars, or by imprisonment in the county jail not longer than one month.

21

COLLECTING UNAUTHORIZED FEES.

§ 1379. If any sheriff, clerk, assessor, or other person, shall claim and receive from the board of supervisors of any county, any fee or compensation, not authorized by law, or if any member of such board shall knowingly vote for the payment of any such unauthorized claim, or any appropriation not authorized by law, he shall be subject to indictment, and on conviction, fined not exceeding double the amount of such unlawful charge, or may be imprisoned in the county jail, not more than three months, or by both such fine and imprisonment.

SUPERVISORS NOT TO BE INTERESTED IN CONTRACTS.

§ 1389. No board of supervisors shall empower or authorize any one or more members of said board, or other person, to let or make contracts for the building or erection of public works of any description in vacation, or during the recess of such board; but all such contracts shall be made and approved by the board in open session.

§ 1390. It shall be unlawful for any member of any board of supervisors in this state to have or own any interest or share, either directly or indirectly, in any contract made or let by any board of supervisors, for the construction of court houses, jails, bridges, or other public buildings or works, or for any member of such board to receive any portion or share, either directly or indirectly, of the money or other things paid for the construction of such buildings, bridges or other public works.

§ 1391. A violation of any of the provisions of the preceding sections of this article shall be deemed a misdemeanor, and punishable, on conviction, by fine of not less than one hundred dollars, nor more than five hundred dollars, and by imprisonment in the county jail, not less than one, nor more than six months, and by dismissal from office.

SALES BY AUCTIONEERS.

§ 1734. The assessor, or in case of his failure to do so, the collector of each county, shall every year demand of each auctioner, in his county, a statement, on oath, of the aggregate amount of all sales at auction made by him since the last assessment, and shall assess the taxes thereon to such auctioneer, at the rate of one-half of one per cent. on such amount, and collect them, as in other cases; and if any auctioneer shall omit or refuse to furnish such statement, on oath, to be administered by the assessor, or collector, when required, or to pay the taxes thereon, he shall be liable to a fine of five hundred dollars, and six months' imprisonment in the county jail, or either, on conviction; and the board of supervisors shall cause his bond to be put in suit, and the whole penalty shall be recovered, in case of a failure to give such statement, for the amount of taxes, with thirty per cent. per annum damages thereon, in case of failure to pay over taxes assessed. The board of supervisors may relieve from the penalty, in case such auctioneer shall come forward and furnish the proper statement, and pay over the taxes due, with damages as aforesaid, and all costs.

ROAD OVERSEERS.

§ 2353. Overseers shall keep advised of the condition of their road districts, and shall, from time to time, as occasion may require, call out such limited number of hands as may be necessary, to stop washes, fill up mud-holes, causeways, bogs, marshes, or swampy places, or repair any damages occasioned by rains, cuts, or otherwise, without waiting for the regular road working; any such labor shall be justly apportioned, if practicable; and any overseer failing in this, shall be liable to indictment, fine and imprisonment, or either.

DUTY OF TELEGRAPH COMPANIES.

§ 2434. Such companies or associations shall be bound, on application of any officer of this state, or of the United States, in case of any war, insurrection, riot, or other civil commotion, or resistance of public authority, or for the prevention and punishment of crime, or for the arrest of persons suspected or charged therewith, to give to the communications of such officers, immediate dispatch, at the price of ordinary communications of the same length; and if any officer, agent, operator or employee, of any such company or association, shall refuse or willfully omit to transmit such communication, as aforesaid, or shall designedly alter or falsify the same, for any purpose whatever, the person, so offending, shall be liable to indictment, and on conviction, may be fined and imprisoned, at the discretion of the court.

INSURANCE WITHOUT LICENSE.

§ 2453. Any person violating the provisions of this article, (Article 8, chapter 55,) shall, upon conviction thereof, in any court of competent jurisdiction, be fined in any sum not exceeding one thousand dollars, or imprisoned in the county jail, not more than thirty days, or by both such fine and imprisonment.

WILLFUL NEGLECT OF DUTY.

§ 2890. If any person, being sheriff, clerk of any court, coroner, constable, assessor, or collector of taxes, or holding any county office whatever, shall willfully neglect or refuse to perform any of the duties required of him by law, or shall violate his duty in any respect, he shall, on conviction thereof, be fined not exceeding one thousand dollars, or be imprisoned in the county jail, not exceeding six months, or both; and in case such officer shall have given bond for the faithful performance of his duties, the president of the board of county supervisors shall cause suit to be brought thereon, for the recovery of such damages as the state or any county may have sustained thereby.

SECURITY FOR COSTS.

§ 572. When any suit shall be commenced in any court of law or equity, in this state, the plaintiff or complainant may be required, on motion of the clerk, or any party interested, to give security for all costs accrued or to accrue in such suit, within sixty days after an order of court, made for that purpose; *provided*, the party making such motion, shall make and file an affidavit that such plaintiff or complainant is a non-resident of the state, and has not sufficient property in this state, out of which the costs can be made, if adjudged against him; or if the plaintiff or complainant be a resident of the state, that he has good reason to believe, and does believe, that such plaintiff or complainant will not be able to pay the costs of such suit, in case the same shall be adjudged against him ; and if the security be not given, the suit shall be dismissed, and execution issued, for the costs that have accrued, or the court may, on cause shown, extend the time for giving such security.

§ 573. Security for costs may be given by recognizance entered into in open court, or by a written undertaking endorsed on, or filed with the papers in the cause ; and if the costs shall not be paid when due, judgment shall be rendered by the court against said security, as well as against the plaintiff or complainant, and execution issue as in other cases.

§ 2851. All the property of any convict shall be liable, first, in preference to all other demands, except jointure and dower, to the discharge of costs and expenses incurred by the state, or any county, in such prosecution or conviction.

Preservation of Fish in Pearl River.

Sec. 1. Be it enacted, That it shall not be lawful for any person to place or maintain in said Pearl river at any point fish traps of any description, nor to erect or maintain dams of any description across said river at any point; and it shall hereafter be lawful for any person or persons, when they may do so without a breach of the peace, and shall be the duty of all peace officers of the state to destroy any and all fish traps and dams in said river which may be within their jurisdiction.

Sec. 2. That any person who shall hereafter construct or maintain or be instrumental or interested in constructing or maintaining any fish trap or dam in or across said river at any point, shall be deemed guilty of a misdemeanor, and upon conviction thereof shall be fined in a sum not less than ten dollars, or be imprisoned not less than ten days, or both, at the discretion of the court, for each and every day that such trap or dam shall have been maintained in said river, and the court shall order its officers to forthwith destroy such fish trap or dam, for which he shall receive the sum of five dollars, to be taxed in the costs of the case. [Acts 1877, p. 92.]

To Encourage the Breeding of Good Stock.

Sec. 1. That in order to encourage the propagation of good stock in this state, there shall hereafter be a lien in favor of the owner of all stallions, jacks and bulls, upon the colts and calves sired by such stallions, jacks and bulls, for and to the extent of the value of the price agreed on for the services of said animals between the owners of the colts and calves so sired.

SEC. That such lien shall be enforced by suit before any magistrate having jurisdiction of the debt; the writ, judgment and execution shall describe the colt or calf on which the lien is claimed under the provisions of the first section of this act, and when the judgment is rendered, such colt or calf shall be declared liable to be sold to pay the debt and costs in such suit, and when so declared, shall be levied on and sold as property is usually levied on and sold under execution at law. [Acts 1877, p. 93.]

Fences.---Malicious Injury to Stock.

Sec. 1907, Revised Code 1871 (see page 209 of this volume), is amended by act approved February 1st, 1877, so that a fence made of common rails, and built in the form known as a worm fence, and which is *six* instead of five feet high, is a lawful fence.

Sec. 2708, Revised Code, 1871 (see page 315 of this volume), is amended by act approved Feb. 1st, 1877, so as to make the fine not less than five, nor more than three hundred dollars, instead of not less than fifty, etc.

APPENDIX.

COMPILED BY THE PUBLISHERS.

TAXATION.

Sec. 5, act approved Feb. 1st., 1877 (Acts 1877, p. 21), fixes the State tax for general purposes at three mills for the year 1877; and boards of supervisors are prohibited from levying taxes which, with the entire State taxes, will exceed $15 00 on the thousand dollars in valuation, except taxes to pay interest on county bonds ; provided, that in Warren and Monroe counties, supervisors may levy a tax which, added to the State tax, will not exceed twenty-five mills ; in Oktibbeha, ten mills additional to State tax can be levied for general purposes, and such special taxes as may be necessary to pay interest and principal on account of branch railroad from Artesia to Starkville.

Sec. 6 of said act provides for a special tax of two mills on all taxable property, for 1877 and subsequent years, for the payment of the principal and interest on bonds issued in funding the floating debt of the State, under act approved March 28th, 1874.

Sec. 2, Revenue Act 1876, levies a poll tax on each and every male inhabitant of the State over twenty-one and under fifty years of age, to be paid by collectors directly into county treasuries, in aid of common school fund.

Taxable property, other than real estate, consists of: cattle (over two cows and calves), horses, mules, sheep (over ten head), swine (over ten head), carriages and other wheeled vehicles, pianos, melodeons, organs, watches, jewelry, gold and silver plate, guns (over one), pistols, bowie knives, dirks and sword canes—the value of each to be sworn to; amount of money employed in merchandise or manufacturing; amount of money, solvent credits, notes, accounts; amount of household furniture, over $250 00 in value ; value of State bonds, warrants or certificates ; value of county or city bonds; value of cotton, not in hands of producer; and all other personal property not here enumerated, to be valued and reported.

TAX ON PRIVILEGES.

An act approved March 1st, 1875, and amendatory acts 1876, impose the following tax upon privileges:

On each express company...	$2,000 00
On each telegraph company operating three hundred miles or more of wire.	2,000 00
On each telegraph company operating over one hundred dred, and less than three hundred miles of wire.	1,000 00
On each company operating over twenty-five, and less than one hundred miles of wire.	500 00
On each company operating less than twenty-five miles of wire, for each mile.	1 00
On each foreign insurance company.	1,000 00
On each home insurance company, with principal office and assets within the State of Mississippi.	1,000 00

Or such home companies may pay, in lieu of such sum, an amount equal to two (2) per cent. of capital paid in, which shall be in full of all State and county taxes: *provided*, that all mutual companies having less than $10,000 paid capital upon which to pay taxes, shall pay fifty (50) cents upon each policy issued or in force, or pay the privilege tax of $1,000 00, as they may elect.

On each sleeping-car company.	1,000 00
On each distillery of grain.	200 00
On each insurance agent.	10 00
On each billiard or Jenny Lind table, nine or ten-pin alley, or similar contrivance, kept for public use.	20 00
On each trading boat, with produce, provisions, and provender, exclusively.	25 00
On each wharf-boat.	100 00
On all other trading boats.	200 00
On each tavern or hotel, in city or town of five thousand inhabitants, or over, with capacity for thirty or more guests.	100 00
Same, with capacity for less than thirty guests.	50 00
On each tavern or hotel, in city or town of two thousand, and not over five thousand inhabitants, with capacity for twenty-five or more guests.	50 00
Same, with capacity for less than twenty-five guests.	25 00
On each tavern or hotel, in city or town of less than two thousand inhabitants.	15 00
On each private boarding-house, not boarding students exclusively.	10 00
On each railroad eating-house, where two or more trains stop for meals daily.	125 00
On each railroad eating-house, where not more than one passenger train stops for meals.	50 00

Provided, That no hotel or eating-house shall be required to pay more than once under the foregoing provisions; but when subject to the conditions of more than one provision, the highest shall be paid.

Each restaurant, in city or town of over two thousand inhabitants... 50 00
Same, in city or town under two thousand inhabitants... 25 00
On each circus or menagerie, or both combined, for each day's performance.. 50 00
On each side-show, per day.... .... 10 00
On each show, exhibition, concert, or other performance, where a fee is charged for admission, and not devoted exclusively to religious, benevolent, or educational purposes, per day... .... 5 00
On each room or hall used as theater or opera-house, for public exhibition, in city or town under five thousand inhabitants, per year........ .... 100 00
On such room or hall, in city of over five thousand inhabitants, per year.......................... .... 200 00
On each store, stock under $1,000..................... 5 00
On each store, stock of $1,000 to $2,000.............. 10 00
On each store, stock of $2,000 to $3,000............. 15 00
On each store, stock of $3,000 to $5,000.. .... 20 00
On each store, stock of $5,000 to $8,000.............. 30 00
On each store, stock of $8,000 to $12,000.............. 50 00
On each store, stock of $12,000 to $15,000........ 60 00
On each store, stock of $15,000 to $20,000.............. 85 00
On each store, stock of $20,000 to $25,000.............. 100 00
On each store, stock of $25,000 to $35,000.............. 150 00
On each store, stock over $35,000................... 200 00
Each auctioneer in towns of one thousand inhabitants, or less.... .... 10 00
Same, in town or city of one thousand to three thousand inhabitants........ .... 25 00
Same, in city of over three thousand and under five thousand inhabitants............................... 30 00
Same, in city or town of over five thousand inhabitants.. 40 00
Each peddler, on foot.............................. 10 00
Each peddler, with one horse, or mule, or other animal.. 20 00
Each peddler, with one horse or mule, or other animal, with wagon or other vehicle 30 00
Provided, Persons peddling exclusively, goods, wares, or merchandize manufactured in the State, shall be exempt.
On each peddler, with two horses or mules, or other animals, with wagon, or other vehicle................. 40 00
On each cotton broker, or factor, engaged in buying or selling cotton, and not licensed as a merchant 20 00
Each public cotton-weigher, where less than two thousand bales are weighed............................. 5 00
Over two thousand, and less than three thousand five hundred, and less than five thousand bales.......... 10 00
Over three thousand five hundred, and less than five thousand bales...................................... . 15 00

Over five thousand, and less than eight thousand bales..	20	00
Over eight thousand, and less than ten thousand bales...	25	00
Over ten thousand bales............................	40	00
Each coal-yard, except where charcoal alone is sold.....	25	00
Each brewery, or establishment for the manufacture or bottling of ale, beer, soda, or mineral water..........	40	00
Each drug store, where vinous and spirituous liquors are sold in less quantities than one gallon	100	00
Each store or establishment selling vinous or spirituous liquors, by gallon, or more............	50	00
Each pawnbroker or firm......................	100	00
Each established broker, keeping an office.............	200	00
Each street broker................................	25	00
Each practicing lawyer...	10	00
Each and every person receiving or forwarding goods, wares, or merchandize, for profit, and not paying $20 privilege tax as a merchant, nor keeping a licensed wharf-boat........................	20	00
Each commission merchant..........................	50	00
Each dentist.....................................	5	00
Each civil engineer or architect.....................	10	00
Each gas company, in city or town of less than four thousand inhabitants................................	50	00
Same, in city or town of over four thousand inhabitants.	100	00
On each toll-bridge................................	25	00
Each steam ferry on the Mississippi river, whose point of landing or departure is from a town or city of five thousand or more inhabitans........................	150	00
On same, from city or town of less than five thousand inhabitants.....	75	00
On all other ferries where the receipts exceed five hundred dollars per annum..............................	25	00
On each dealer in ale, beer, or other malt liquors, in city or town of five thousand inhabitants, or more, and not licensed as a retail liquor dealer.....................	100	00
On same, in towns of over two thousand, and under five thousand inhabitants..........................	60	00
On all other such dealers.........................	30	00
On each soda fountain............................	5	00
Each cotton compress company.....................	100	00
Each agency established for sewing machines..........	40	00
Each sewing machine agent, except one for each established agency.....	5	00
Each photograph gallery..........................	10	00
Each livery, feed, or sale stable, in town of over one thousand, and less than two thousand inhabitants.........	10	00
On same, in city or town of over two thousand, and under three thousand inhabitants....	20	00
On same, in city or town of over three thousand, and under five thousand inhabitants........................	40	00

On same, in city or town of over five thousand, and less
than ten thousand inhabitants.... ....   50 00

On each such stable, in city or town of over ten thousand
inhabitants........ ....   100 00

On each transient vendor of horses or mules.... ..   30 00

Each real estate agent............... ....   10 00

Each bank of discount or deposit, in city or town of less
than two thousand inhabitants.....................   200 00

Which shall be in lieu of all taxes on ten thousand dollars
of the capital of such bank.

Each bank of discount or deposit, in city or town of over
two thousand, and less than four thousand inhabitants.   300 00

Which shall be in lieu on all taxes or fifteen thousand dollars of capital.

Each bank of discount or deposit, in city or town of over
four thousand inhabitants........................   1,000 00

Which shall be in lieu of all taxes on fifty thousand
dollars of capital of such bank : *Provided,* That any person or persons doing a banking business in city or town
of over four (4) thousand inhabitants. whose business is
based on a capital of less than twenty thousand dollars,
including all stocks, bonds, credits of every description,
whether deposited in or out of the State, and will furnish
to the Auditor of Public Accounts, under oath, a statement showing such fact, shall not be required to pay a
privilege tax of over $500, which shall be in full for all
taxes on twenty thousand dollars of capital.

On each and every person selling prize or gift packages,
or any goods not exposed or exhibited on the cars passing through this State........ ....   25 00

On each transient vendor of jewelry, whether the same is
offered for sale in the store of a resident dealer or not.   25 00

[On each transient vendor or peddler of clocks, or pumps, or
stoves, or pinchbeck jewelry, and on all transient vendors, whatever, not provided for in an Act relating to privileges, approved
March 1, 1875, the sum of $1,000. And on all trappers, from other
States, of beaver, or other animals captured for their fur, $100. All
counties, towns, and cities, shall be authorized to levy an additional
tax on the above privilege, not to exceed fifty per centum on the
above sums. Act approved February 1, 1877.]

And the license herein provided, shall be a personal privilege tax,
and not transferable; and a license shall not be construed to exempt
from taxation the property used in the license business, except as
specially provided in this Act. The tax on privileges imposed by
this section, shall not be liable to taxation by any incorporated city
or town, to an amount exceeding fifty per centum of the State tax
herein provided, nor by any county, in any amount whatever: *Provided,* That no additional tax shall be collected by county, city, or
town, on any insurance, telegraph, express, or sleeping car companies. All licenses upon telegraph companies, express companies,

insurance, and sleeping-car companies, and also upon banking companies, in the cities of Jackson and Vicksburg, shall be paid by them into the State Treasury; and no person or persons shall be allowed to collect or receive commissions for the same. And in case of the failure of any such person or corporations to pay the same, the Auditor is hereby required to place the same in the hands of any sheriff or district attorney, who shall collect the same, with the fifty per cent. damages, and who shall be entitled to the usual fees, out of such damages.

* * * * * * * * * * *

SEC. 5. That any person desiring to enjoy any of the privileges enumerated in the first section of this Act, shall first pay the price above fixed, to the collector, and obtain his license, or that of the Auditor, for such privilege; and the person receiving such license, shall post or put up the same in his office or place of business, in some conspicuous place; and any person or persons, or corporation, who shall exercise, in this State, any of the privileges enumerated in this Act, without first paying the price, and procuring the license, as required, shall be guilty of a misdemeanor, and, on conviction before any justice of the peace, or other court of competent jurisdiction, shall be fined not less than double the tax imposed by this Act, or shall be imprisoned in the county jail not exceeding one month, or be punished by both, at the discretion of the court, as now provided by section 1750 of the Code of 1871; and any debts or claims that may accrue to any person on account of the business herein taxed, who shall fail or neglect, within thirty days after such license is due, to pay the same, shall be null and void, and no suit shall be maintained in any court of law or equity, in this State, to enforce the payment of such claims, or a compliance with contracts in favor of any person or persons failing to pay the privilege tax required by this Act; and the collector shall have the power to distrain and sell any property liable for the tax imposed upon privileges, as he now has for the collection of the State taxes.

SALARIES AND FEES OF PUBLIC OFFICERS.

Governor, per annum.. $4,000 00
Lieutenant-Governor, allowed per diem when Senate is in
   session, same as is allowed to Speaker of House.
Private Secretary Executive Department................... 1,000 00
Clerk to Governor, during session of Legislature, per day   5 00
Secretary of State.. 2,500 00
One clerk to Secretary of State.......................... 1,000 00
Auditor of Public Accounts............................... 2,500 00
One Deputy Auditor....................................... 1,250 00
Four clerks, Auditor's office, each...................... 1,000 00

State Treasurer	2,500 00
One clerk, State Treasurer's office	1,250 00
One clerk, as treasurer of educational and charitable institutions	1,000 00
Attorney General	2,000 00
Judges of Supreme Court	3,500 00

(Those in office March 21st, 1876, not being affected by this rate of compensation.)

Judges of Circuit Court	2,500 00
Chancellors	2,500 00

(See special Act for Warren county, Acts 1876, p. 237.)

District Attorneys, the perquisites allowed by law, and..	1,200 00
State Superintendent of Public Education	2,000 00
Librarian and Keeper of the Capitol	800 00
Superintendent of the Penitentiary	1,600 00
Superintendent Lunatic Asylum	2,000 00
Superintendent Blind Asylum	1,000 00
Superintendent Deaf and Dumb Asylum	1,000 00
Adjutant General	500 00
Commissioner of Swamp Lands	500 00
Commissioner of Immigration and Agriculture.	100 00
Secretary of State Board Registration	150 00

Registrars—the three for each county not to receive exceeding $600 00 in the aggregate, or $3 00 per day, payable by county.

County Superintendent of Education—20 per cent., or one-fifth of the salaries fixed by Acts in relation to public education, approved April 11th, 1873, March 19th, 1874, except that in Sumner and Sharkey, the salary is $100 00, and in Leake, $75 00.

MEMBERS AND OFFICERS OF LEGISLATURE.

An act approved March 28, 1874, provides that members of the Legislature shall receive a salary, each, of the sum of five hundred dollars; Speaker of the House, eight hundred dollars per annum; mileage, twenty cents per mile. An act approved January 11, 1877, (Acts 1877, p. 84,) provides that whenever the office of Lieutenant Governor shall be vacant, the President *pro tem.*, of the Senate, shall receive the same pay as the Speaker of the House. One-third of the salary, and all of the mileage, is payable at the beginning of the regular session; one-third of salary thirty days thereafter, and remainder at the end of session.

At the special session of December, 1874, an act was passed to "explain and amend" the act of March 28, 1874, by making it take effect January 1, 1875, allowing mileage at special sessions convened by the Governor; and for the special session of December, 1874, per diem for three days was allowed.

The rate of compensation fixed by the Legislature for its members, officers and employees, is subject to approval of Governor.

and is not subject to alteration during the same session, and is to continue until a subsequent session. The allowance may, in like manner, be changed to take effect thereafter. (Revised Code, 1871, § 333.)

Acts of February 2d, and March 24th, 1876, fixed the compensation of officers and employees as follows :

Secretary of the Senate, per diem...................... $20 00
Clerk of the House, per diem........................... 25 00
Reading Clerk of House, per diem...................... 7 00
Sergeant-at-Arms, of Senate, per diem.................. 16 50
Sergeant-at-Arms, of House, per diem................... 6 00
Assistant Sergeant-at-Arms, of House, per diem........ 5 00
Doorkeeper, Senate and House, each.................... 4 00
Two Messengers, for House, each....................... 1 00
Three Porters, for House, each......................... 2 50
Six Pages, for House, each............................. 1 00

The compensation of Secretary of Senate and Clerk of House is in full for all clerical help employed by them.

Fees of Clerks, Sheriffs, Justices, Etc.

(Act of March 6, 1875, including Amendments of 1876, 1877.)

SECTION 1. Be it enacted by the Legislature of the State of Mississippi, That it shall be lawful for the clerks of the supreme court, clerks of the circuit court, clerks of the chancery court, commissioners in chancery, clerks of the boards of supervisors, sheriffs, coroners, constables, justices of the peace, notaries public, and other persons hereinafter named, in this state, to demand, receive and take the several fees hereinafter mentioned and allowed, for any business by them respectively done by virtue of their several offices, or otherwise, and no more; that is to say:

TO THE CLERKS OF THE SUPREME COURT.

For filing records on writ of error or appeal, or any other
  paper required by law to be filed...................... $ 25
Entering appearance of each party. 25
Every order of court.................................. 25
Filing and entering each rule or motion 50
Docketing and indexing each case on general docket... 50
Docketing the same on district docket, each term....... 25
Every writ issued by order of court, or on application of
  party according to law............................... 1 25
Each continuance...................................... 25
Final judgment, or decree of general affirmation or refusal 1 00

Same against principal and sureties on bond 1 50
Each special decree in chancery....................... 2 00
Copy of judgment or decree, every hundred words ..   20
Taxing cost and copy thereof, to be charged but once....   50
Issuing execution.............. ....   1 25
Entering issuance and return thereof on docket, each...   25
Administering oath or affirmation, when required by law.   25
Qualifying and entering attorney on roll.........   50
For recording the opinions of said court, furnishing
    transcript of record, or copies of papers on file, of which
    any person is entitled to demand and receive copies,
    per hundred words.....   15
Recording process and return thereon, in each cause..... 1 00

For other services not herein provided for, the same compensation given for like services to clerks of the circuit courts, and
on the return of *nulla bona* on any execution for costs issued
against a defendant in error, or appellee adjudged to pay the same,
the clerk of the supreme court shall be entitled to issue execution
against the party who brought the cause into said court, for such
services as shall have been performed therein at his instance, and
the clerk of the supreme court is hereby allowed, annually, the sum
of fifty dollars for each supreme court district, payable out of the
state treasury, by order of said court, as compensation for cases
adjudged against the state, in all cases brought to and determined
by the supreme court.

TO THE CLERKS OF CHANCERY COURTS.

For filing and marking each bill, answer or other paper   5
Copies thereof, for every hundred words...............   10
Entering each dismission or discontinuance...........   25
Setting down cause for hearing....   10
Enrolling or recording each decree, for every hundred
    words   15
Each injunction or other bond.......................   50
Administering each oath and certifying the same.........   25
Entering sheriff's return, on every writ   10
For registering the probate of any will or testament, and
    for letters testamentary thereon 1 00
Recording a will, testament, or codicil, for every hundred
    words   10
Administering oath to executors, administrators, collec-
    tors or guardians, and taking bond and recording the
    same........................... .... 1 25
Letters of administration, collections, or guardianship,
    and order granting the same........ .... 1 00
Order appointing appraisers and copy.   50
Issuing warrant of appraisement.....................   50
Registering claims against decedent   15
Recording an inventory, appraisement, or account of ex-

ecutors, administrators, collectors or guardians, for every hundred words...................................... 10

Filing and recording the bond of a county officer, to be paid by the officer...................................... 1 50

Issuing tavern license and taking bond 1 50

Copy of tavern rates and certificates................ 50

Issuing license to retail spirituous liquors............. 1 00

Taking bond thereon................................. 1 50

Issuing license under the privilege tax ....,...... 50

Certifying the official act of a justice of the peace, or other certificate, with seal......................... 50

For each day attending the supervisor's court........... 3 00

Copying personal assessment rolls, not less than twenty, nor more than fifty dollars, payable out of the county treasury..................................... 50 00

Copying land assessment rolls, not less than twenty, nor more than one hundred dollars, payable out of the county treasury....................................... 100 00

TO CLERKS OF CIRCUIT COURTS, IN CIVIL CASES.

For each writ, other than those hereinafter mentioned... 75

Docketing each case, to be charged but once......... ... 15

Filing and marking all the papers in each cause......... 25

Entering each appearance of a defendant, to be charged but once.. 10

Entering each motion or rule on the docket, and order thereon..................................... 15

TO THE CLERKS OF THE SUPREME COURT, CHANCERY AND CIRCUIT COURTS.

Taking bond.... 50

Entering non-suit, discontinuance, or *nolle pros*........ 25

Order and copy of rule of reference................... 50

Swearing each witness............................. 5

Entering each continuance........................... 15

Scire facias, except against jurors when excused....... 1 00

Swearing and impaneling every jury.................. 10

Receiving and entering every verdict................. 10

Recording each judgment in court, except of non-suit, discontinuance or *nolle pros*........................ 25

Each subpœna for one witness....................... 25

Each additional name inserted....................... 10

Each commission to take depositions.................. 50

Copies of interrogatories, for every hundred words...... 15

Taking a recognizance.............................. 50

Recording return on execution....................... 25

Administering oath and certifying the same 25

Each certificate to witness........................... 15

Each separate certificate, except to jurors, required to be
under seal.. 25
Enrolling judgment, for first defendant 1 00
Each additional defendant........... 25
Filing and recording abstract of judgment or decree, and
indexing the same.... .... 1 00
Taxing cost, to be charged but once 25
Each marriage license...... .. .. 2 00
Bond for same....⨳.................................. 1 00
For each day attending the circuit court, to be paid out
of the county treasury............................ 2 00

No clerk shall charge a fee for affixing the seal of his office, but
the same shall be a part of his official signature.

IN CRIMINAL CASES.

For entering filing of indictment, or filing information... 25
Each writ, other than subpœnas.... 50
Arraigning prisoner and entering plea................... 75
Taking recognizance................................. 50
Entering surrender of principal by bail............... 25
Swearing and impaneling every jury.................. 25
Entering verdict or judgment, each.................. 25
Swearing every witness............................. 5
Each subpœna, with one witness..................... 25
Each additional name inserted 5
Each motion and order thereon..................... 15
Special *venire* in capital cases....................... 50
All copies, for every hundred words.................. 10

For all public services not herein particularly provided for, the
clerk shall, at each term, exhibit a detailed fee bill, to be examined
by the attorney general, or district attorney previous to the allowance by the court, and the court is hereby authorized to allow the
same, not exceeding fifty dollars for any one year, to be paid out of
the county treasury; *Provided,* No part of such bill shall be for
fees which may accrue on prosecutions in which the State may fail,
and the cost be not taxed on the prosecution.

TO THE CLERKS OF THE SUPREME COURT, CHANCERY, AND CIRCUIT COURTS:

For making final records, furnishing transcripts of records, or
copies of papers on file, recording deeds, and all other writings and
instruments required by law to be recorded and copied, or which
any person is entitled to demand and receive copies, ten cents for
every hundred words, and the same fees shall be allowed to all officers in the state for making and certifying copies of records, or
papers which they are authorized to copy and certify; but no fees
shall be allowed the clerk of the supreme court for making final
records, or to the clerks of the chancery or circuit courts, for making

final record in any case, unless they are required to make a final record by the judgment or decree of the court rendering the same.

SEC. 2. *Be it further enacted,* That the county surveyors be allowed the following fees, and no more :

TO COUNTY SURVEYORS :

For each day's service, in making survey..........	5 00
For each single plat, with certificate of survey, with calculations of contents.....................	2 50
With each adjoining plat, with note of reference........	50
For every additional copy of plat, with certificate of survey, notes of reference, where there are not more than three plats contained in one, in said copy............	1 50
For every additional plat in said copy..................	50
For surveying town lots, not exceeding for each day.....	5 00
Each chain carrier, for each day.....	1 50

SEC. 3. *Be it further enacted,* That the fees, chargeable as aforesaid, shall be paid by the parties desiring the services to be performed, and when the services are rendered in obedience to an order of court, in a suit therein pending, the surveyor shall state an amount of the fees for such services, written on the back of one of the plats by him returned to the court, and the same shall be allowed in the bill of costs, and taxed against the losing party, as other costs, unless such party shall already have paid the same.

TO SHERIFFS :

For executing the process, judgments, and decrees of the circuit courts, and for similar services in other courts, levying an attachment on an absent, absconding, or other debtor.......	2 00
Summoning each garnishee.........................	50
Serving summons or other *mesne* process, for each defendant	1 50
Levying an execution.............................	1 50
Entering each writ in his office......................	25
Returning the same...............................	25
Each bail bond and recognizance....................	50
Summoning each witness...:	50
Executing a writ of possession and return............	3 00
Making deed to purchasers of real estate..............	2 00
Serving *scire facias* on each defendant, except defaulting jurors when excused......	50
Taking bond of every kind	50
Impaneling each jury sworn.........................	20
Summoning a special jury...........................	2 00
Serving any person with a summons or citation not herein provided for.........................	50
Serving *ca. sa.* on each defendant and commitment......	1 50
Serving attachment for contempt and return............	1 50

Serving interrogatories and notice, or notice alone......	1 50
Summoning jury on any inquisition in the county, attending the same, and taking inquest, per day............	3 00
Removing a prisoner on *habeas corpus*, each day in vacation....	3 00
Removing a prisoner on *habeas corpus*, change of venue, or otherwise, for every mile going or returning.......	10
Each commitment or release......................	1 00
Victualing prisoners, each day	40

[And no allowances for feeding prisoners shall be made made until after the board of supervisors shall have examined the authority by which each prisoner was confined, and the discharge, if the prisoner or prisoners be discharged, and shall be satisfied, by a computation based thereon, that the account is correct. Acts 1876, p. 220.]

Advertising any sale, besides printer's charge......... .	1 00
Executing death warrant, to be paid out of the county treasury...........	12 00

On all money made by virtue of any decree, execution, attachment or other process, the following commissions, to-wit :

On the first one hundred dollars, three per cent.
On the second one hundred dollars, two per cent.
On all sums over two hundred dollars, one per cent.

For attending in person, or by deputy, upon the terms of the supreme court, chancery courts, circuit courts and supervisors' courts, for himself and each deputy, (not exceeding two persons in all, except by special order of the court,) each day, to be paid out of the county treasury on the allowance of the court.................. 2 00

For attending elections, either himself or deputy, two dollars for each day. to be paid out of the county treasury.. 2 00

For impaneling grand juries, serving all public orders of court in his county, and for all other public services not otherwise provided for, a sum not exceeding fifty dollars for each year, to be allowed by the circuit court, after examination by the district attorney, and paid out of the county treasury.

For executing all judgments, decrees, orders, or process of the supreme court, chancery courts, and supervisors' courts, the same fees as are allowed for similar services in the circuit courts.

The sheriff's fees, in state cases, when the state fails in the prosecution, to an amount not exceeding fifty dollars in any one year, shall be paid out of the county treasury, on the certificate of the clerk, of the failure of the prosecution, and that the account of said sheriff, for his fees, has been allowed by the court, and entered on the minutes. The sheriff shall, also, be allowed the reasonable expenses of keeping any live stock, and, also, all reasonable expenses of keeping and preserving any personal property levied on by virtue of any execution, attachment, or other process, and such expenses shall be allowed by the court to which the process is returnable, and taxed in the cost of suit.

TO TAX COLLECTORS :

The compensation of sheriff's, when acting as tax collectors, shall be five per centum on the first ten thousand dollars of taxes collected for the state, in any one year, and five per centum of the first ten thousand dollars of taxes collected for the county, in any one year, including county, school, bond, and privilege taxes, and on all other sums so collected, three per centum : and that upon all taxes collected by them, after the same shall become delinquent, they shall be allowed a compensation up to March 1st, ensuing, of ten (10) per cent., after which date, the sum of five (5) per cent. shall only be allowed, which said additional compensation shall be collected out of the delinquent tax payer, and never out of the state or county treasuries. [Acts 1877, p. 13.]

TO MEMBERS OF THE BOARDS OF SUPERVISORS.

The compensation of members of the boards of supervisors shall be four dollars per day.

TO CORONERS :

For taking inquisition on a dead body................. $10 00
And if a justice of the peace perform said duty, he shall receive the same fees as provided for the coroner.
For all services performed by them, the same fees as are allowed sheriffs for similar services.

TO JUSTICES OF THE PEACE:

For celebrating a marriage, and certificate thereof....... $1 00
Each warrant in criminal case......................... 40
Witness or recognizance.............................. 40
Mittimus or recognizance............................. 40
Warrant, summons, or *scire facias*, in civil cases........ 50
Proceedings thereon, to judgment..................... 25
Each subpœna containing one name.................... 25
Each additional name................................. 5
Entering each suit.................................... 10
Entering each judgment............................... 20
Swearing each witness................................ 5
Commission to take depositions....................... 40
Issuing execution.................................... 10
Each summons for garnishee 25
Taking examination of garnishee...................... 20
Appeal, with proceedings, bond, and affidavit..... ..... 1 00
Transcript of record, when requested................. 25
Issuing attachment, taking bond, and affidavit.......... 1 50
Each certificate, not otherwise provided for......... ... 25
Taking deposition, each hundred words................ 25
Each affidavit not otherwise provided for.............. 25

Taking proof or acknowledgment of any deed or mortgage concerning real or personal estate, and certificate
thereof, for each party (and the same fees shall be
allowed to all other officers for the same services..)   25
Drawing jury and issuing *venire facias*................   25
Swearing jury and entering verdict...................   25
Advertising an attachment, besides printer's fees........   50

TO NOTARIES PUBLIC.

For protesting bill or note for non-acceptance or non-
payment, and giving notice of same................   2 00
Registering such protest and making record.... ....   1 00
Attesting letters of attorney and seal.................   50
Notarial affidavit to an account, or other writing, and seal   50
Each oath or affirmation and seal   50
Notarial procuration and seal 1 00
Certifying sales at auction and seal   50
Taking proof of debts to be sent abroad..............   50
Protest in insurance cases and seal..................   1 00
Copy of record and affidavit..................... .....   1 00

TO CONSTABLES.

Serving each warrant and summons..............   50
Serving each warrant and summons in criminal cases....   1 00
Serving an attachment...................... ....   1 00
Summoning each witness..........................   25
Executing a mittimus....   75
Taking every bond..............................   50
Levying execution and making the money.............   1 50
Summoning coroner's inquest, to be paid as the coroner's
fees in the same case.. ....   1 00
Conveying a criminal to jail, each mile   10
Attending each trial in justice's court.................   25
Summoning jury...............................   50
Each cause tried by jury..........................   50
For other services the same fees allowed sheriffs for similar
services.

TO COMMISSIONERS AND MASTERS IN CHANCERY.

Taking affidavit................................   25
Summons to attend on reference.....................   50
Report on reference to compute amount due...........   1 00
All other reports, except on taking accounts...........   3 00
Taking an account on reference, for each day actually
occupied......................................   3 00
Taking an examination of a witness, for every hundred
words   20
Certifying each exhibit..........................   20
Copies of reports and such other papers as the parties to a refer-
ence may require, the same fees allowed the clerks for similar ser-
vices.
Executing deed pursuant to decree..................   2 00

Making sale under decree, the same fees allowed sheriffs on sales under execution, and in no event shall the clerk of the chancery court, or other officer, be allowed for taking depositions in any case more than the sum of twenty cents per every hundred words; and in taxing the cost for taking depositions, it shall be the duty of the clerk, or other officer taking the depositions, to state the number of words in each disposition.

TO WITNESSES AND JURY.

Witnesses and jurors, in all cases where they are entitled to compensation, except before justices of the peace in civil cases, shall receive one dollar and fifty cents per day, and also five cents for each mile, going and returning, by the nearest route from their residence to the court house, and also such tolls and ferriages as they may be actually obliged to pay; *provided*, that such mileage, toll and ferriage shall be charged but once at each term.

Witnesses and jurors in civil cases before justices of the peace, shall be allowed one dollar per day, and no more; and the attendance of only one witness to each fact shall be taxed in the cost in cases before justices of the peace.

Jurors on coroner's inquest shall be paid two dollars per day, without mileage, to be paid out of the county treasury.

TO PRINTERS AND PUBLISHERS.

The act of April 15th, 1876, provides: For publishing in a newspaper any advertisement, notice or citation required by law, or the order of any court, to be published, one and a half cent a word for the first insertion, and one-half a cent a word for each subsequent insertion, and no more, to be paid for on proof and delivery of the publication made as now required by law.

Sec. 821, Revised Code 1871, provides: The printer, publisher, clerk, or superintendent making proof shall be allowed the sum of one dollar for making a copy of such publication, and for his attendance with the newspapers to compare and depose to the same; and the officer taking the same shall be allowed fifty cents for administering said oath or affirmation, and certifying to the same.

Sec. 1699, Revised Code 1871, allows publishers for advertising sale of delinquent tax lands, three weeks, fifteen cents for each legal subdivision, which fee shall be charged by the collector in the bill of costs, and collected by him for the use of the publisher.

The Public Printer is allowed, for all advertisements on account of the state, 60 cents per square of ten minion lines, first insertion, and 40 cents per square two additional insertions.

OFFICERS TAKING DEPOSITIONS.

For administering oath and certificate of the same...... 50
Writing or copying the deposition, if required to do so,
    for each hundred words.......................... 20

TO REFEREES.

Referees or auditors, to whom civil causes are referred, shall be shall be allowed three dollars for each day actually occupied in the service, to be ascertained by their report, and taxed in the cost.

TO COUNTY ASSESSORS.

On the aggregate amount of the state taxes as assessed by him and entered upon the assessment rolls of the county, to be paid on the filing of said rolls, three per cent.: upon all other levies predicated on tax assessed by him, state, school tax, or county levies, to be paid when the levy is made, two per centum; but this shall not apply to levies made by the county supervisors to pay installments on interest on any description of bonded debt of the counties, nor upon taxes assessed for levee purposes, upon all of which no commission shall be allowed to the assessor. The allowance for the assessment of the state taxes shall be paid to the assessor by warrant, drawn by the Auditor upon the Treasurer of the state, on receipt of a copy of the rolls, duly certified to by the clerk of the Board of supervisors, as now prescribed by law.

The allowance due assessors upon county levies shall be paid to him by warrant; and drawn in proportional amounts against the respective county funds, by the clerk of the board of supervisors, upon order of the board, when the claim of the assessor has been duly examined and allowed; *provided*, that no assessor shall receive a smaller compensation for completing the assessment than two hundred dollars, nor more than fifteen hundred dollars; and if the assessor's commissions do not amount to two hundred dollars, the deficit shall be paid, one-half out of the state treasury and one-half out of the county treasury.

The Revenue Act 1876, sec. 15, allows the assessor a fee of fifty cents, payable by all persons delinquent in returning tax lists within the time prescribed, subject to the condition in sec. 7, Revenue Act 1877, that the taxpayer make oath that he did not have notice, or was absent, sick, etc.

Sec. 4, p. 37, Acts 1877, requires that the assessors shall, in 1877, and biennially thereafter, enumerate the educable children in their respective counties, and make out two alphabetical lists thereof, giving name, age, sex and color of each educable child, which list shall be verified by the attached oath of the assessor making the same, and file one with the state and the other with the county superintendent by the first day of November of the year in which they are made, and for the services required of him in this section, the said assessor shall receive 1½ cents per capita for the children so enumerated and listed, to be allowed by the board of supervisors and paid out of the school funds of their respective counties.

The Auditor of Public Accounts and the clerks of the boards of supervisors of the several counties of the state are prohibited from drawing their warrants for more than 50 per cent. of the amount of commissions due any assessor for assessing the persons and property in his county, for the year in which such enumeration of the educable children is required to be made, until after such assessor has produced the certificates of the said state and county superintendents, or furnished other satisfactory evidence of the filing with them of the lists provided for as above.

Sec. 5. Be it further enacted, That the fees herein-before mentioned shall be taxed and allowed in the bill of cost in all suits or actions where the services respectively shall have been rendered ; but no more than one copy of any matter shall be allowed in the bill of cost; and if any plaintiff or defendant, his or her attorney, shall take out copies of his or her own declaration or pleadings, or of his or her own paper in any cause, or of any common order made in such cause, the charge of such copies shall not be allowed in the bill of cost, although such party recover.

Sec. 7. Be it further enacted, That none of the fees herein-before mentioned shall be payable by any person until there be produced to the person chargeable with the same, a bill or account, in writing, containing the particulars of such fees, signed by the clerk or officer, in which said bill or account shall be intelligibly expressed every fee for which money shall be demanded ; and if any such fees shall be or have been paid without the production of such bill, the party paying the same shall at all times be entitled to demand and receive from the officer receiving the same, a copy thereof, without charge.

Sec. 8. Be it further enacted, That it shall be lawful for the clerks of the several courts of this state respectively, when suits or causes are determined, and the fees not paid by the party from whom they are due, to make out executions, directed to the sheriff or other proper officer of the county where the party resides ; and the sheriff or other proper officer shall execute and return such execution as in other cases ; and to every execution shall be annexed a copy of the bill of costs, specifying the particular items thereof, in intelligible words and figures ; and all such executions issuing without the copy of the bill of cost as aforesaid, shall be deemed illegal, and no sheriff or other officer shall serve or execute the same.

Sec. 9. Be it further enacted, That on all executions in which any costs are included, a detailed statement of such fees or costs shall be entered in plain and intelligible words and figures, and the sheriff or other officer receiving the same shall add thereto, in like manner, his fees, including all additional fees and costs, and shall make out a fair copy of the same, and deliver it on demand to the person from whom he receives the money, or out of whose property he makes the same.

Sec. 10. Be it further enacted, That if any of said clerks shall neglect or refuse to make out and deliver to the person applying for the same, a certified copy of any paper, record, judgment, decree, or entry, on file, lodged, or remaining in his said office, when the same shall be demanded, he shall be deemed guilty of a high misdemeanor in office, and shall forfeit, for every such neglect or refusal, to the party aggrieved thereby, the sum of five hundred dollars, to be recovered by action of debt, in any of the circuit courts of this state, and shall be liable to indictment for every such neglect or refusal, and upon conviction under such indictment, shall be fined in a sum not exceeding one thousand dollars, and imprisoned for a term not exceeding three months.

SEC. 11. Be it further enacted, That the cost accruing upon suits, in any of the courts of this state, shall not be due until final determination of said suits, and shall then be adjudged to the successful party, and collected by execution ; *Provided,* That the judges shall have power to order and adjudge cost and give decrees and judgments thereon, in the progress of suits, as heretofore practised in said courts.

SEC. 12. Be it further enacted, That it shall be the duty of the judges of the several circuit and chancery courts of this state, to require of the clerks thereof, to combine, in one decree, as many interrogatory or other orders, as can be lawfully and conveniently done, with a view to prevent the increase of cost, and on application of any party, in term time or vacation, to correct any bill of cost as charged and made out by such clerk.

SEC. 13. Be it further enacted, That it shall be the duty of the clerks of the circuit and chancery courts, and of the sheriff of each county, to post, in a conspicuous place in his office, a printed copy of the bill of fees he is entitled to receive under the provisions of this act; and, for a failure to post said bill, as required by this act, shall be deemed guilty of a misdemeanor in office, and liable to indictment by the grand jury of his county.

SEC. 14. Be it further enacted, That if any sheriff, clerk, justice, coroner, constable, assessor, collector, or any other officer, shall, knowingly, demand, take, or receive, under color of his office, any money, fee, or reward, whatever, not authorized by this act, or shall demand and receive, knowingly, any fees not enumerated in this act, such officer, so offending, shall be deemed guilty of extortion, and shall be punished according to law.

THE COURTS.

SUPREME COURT OF MISSISSIPPI.

JUDGES—H. F. Simrall, Chief Justice; H. H. Chalmers, J. A. P. Campbell, Associate Justices.

CLERK—A. W. Little.

Docket of First District taken up 3d Monday in October; Second District, 3d Monday in February; Third District, 1st Monday in January.

FIRST DISTRICT—Warren, Hinds, Rankin, Scott, Newton, Lauderdale, Kemper, Neshoba, Leake, Madison, Yazoo, Issaquena, Washington, Sharkey, Bolivar, Sunflower, Holmes, Attala, Winston, and Noxubee.

SECOND DISTRICT—Claiborne, Copiah, Simpson, Smith, Jasper, Clarke, Wayne, Covington, Jones, Perry, Greene, Pearl, Marion, Hancock, Jackson, Harrison, Adams, Jefferson, Amite, Wilkinson, Lawrence, Pike, Franklin, and Lincoln.

THIRD DISTRICT—Lafayette, Lowndes, Clay, Oktibbeha, Choctaw, Sumner, Carroll, Montgomery, Leflore, Tallahatchie, Calhoun, Yalobusha, Chickasaw, Monroe, Itawamba, Pontotoc, Lee, Panola, Coahoma, Tunica, Quitman, DeSoto, Tate, Marshall, Tippah, Tishomingo, Prentiss, Alcorn, Grenada, Benton, and Union.

FEDERAL COURTS.

UNITED STATES CIRCUIT COURT.

The regular terms are held in Jackson on the first Mondays in May and November.

JUDGE—Robert A. Hill.

CLERK—George T. Swann.

DISTRICT COURT OF THE UNITED STATES.

Session commences for the Northern District, at Oxford, on the first Monday in June and December.

JUDGE—Robert A. Hill.

CLERK—George A. Hill.

Session commences for the Southern District, at Jackson, on the fourth Mondays of June and January.

CLERK—Archie McGehee.

CIRCUIT AND CHANCERY COURTS.

(From Acts of 1876, as amended by Acts of 1877.)

FIRST DISTRICT—Circuit Courts.

Tishomingo—2d Monday January and July—6 days.
Alcorn—3d Monday January and July—12 days.
Prentiss—1st Monday February and August—12 days.
Lee—3d Monday February and August—18 days.
Itawamba—2d Monday March and September—6 days.
Chickasaw, 1st District—3d Monday March and September—12 days.
Chickasaw, 2d District—1st Monday April and October—18 days.
Monroe—2d Monday June and 1st Monday November—24 days.

FIRST DISTRICT—Chancery Courts.

Tishomingo—4th Monday March and September—6 days.
Alcorn—2d Monday April and October—12 days.
Prentiss—1st Monday April and October—6 days.
Lee—1st Monday May and November—12 days.
Itawamba—4th Monday April and October—6 days.
Chickasaw, 1st District—3d Monday May and November—6 days.
Chickasaw, 2d District—4th Monday May and November—12 days.
Monroe—1st Monday March and September—18 days.

SECOND DISTRICT—Circuit Courts.

Pontotoc—1st Monday February and August—12 days.
Union—3d Monday February and August—12 days.
Tippah—1st Monday March and September—12 days.
Benton—3d Monday March and September—12 days.
Marshall—1st Monday April and October—24 days.
Lafayette—1st Monday May and November—12 days.
Yalobusha, 1st District—3d Monday May and November—12 days.
Yalobusha, 2d District—1st Monday June and December—12 days.
Calhoun—3d Monday June and December—12 days.

SECOND DISTRICT—Chancery Courts.

Pontotoc—1st Monday March and September—12 days.
Union—1st Monday May and November—6 days.
Tippah—2d Monday May and November—12 days.
Benton—4th Monday May and November—6 days.
Marshall—4th Monday January and July—18 days.
Lafayette—2d Monday April and October—6 days.
Yalobusha, 1st Dist.—4th Monday March and September—6 days.
Yalobusha, 2d Dist.—1st Monday April and October—6 days.
Calhoun—3d Monday March and September—6 days.

THIRD DISTRICT—Circuit Courts.

Tunica—1st Monday March and September—12 days.

DeSoto—3d Monday March and September—18 days.

Tate—2d Monday after 4th Monday March and September—12 days.

Panola—4th Monday after 4th Monday March and September—18 days.

Tallahatchie—7th Monday after 4th Monday March and September—12 days.

Grenada—9th Monday after 4th Monday March and September—12 days.

Quitman—11th Monday after 4th Monday March and September—6 days.

THIRD DISTRICT—Chancery Courts.

Tunica—1st Monday after 4th Monday March and September—12 days.

DeSoto—3d Monday after 4th Monday March and September—18 days.

Tate—6th Monday after 4th Monday March and September—12 days.

Panola—8th Monday after 4th Monday March and September—18 days.

Tallahatchie—3d Monday March and September—12 days.

Grenada—1st Monday March and September—12 days.

Quitman—12th Monday after the 4th Monday March and September—6 days.

FOURTH DISTRICT—Circuit Court.

Coahoma—2d Monday September and March—12 days.

Washington—2d Monday October and April—24 days.

Bolivar—4th Monday September and March—12 days.

Issaquena—4th Monday November and May—12 days.

Sharkey—3d Monday November and May—6 days.

Sunflower—2d Monday November and May—6 days.

FOURTH DISTRICT—Chancery Courts.

Coahoma—4th Monday October and April—12 days.

Washington—4th Monday November and May—18 days.

Bolivar—2d Monday November and May—12 days.

Issaquena—3d Monday October and April—6 days.

Sharkey—2d Monday October and April—6 days.

Sunflower—1st Monday April and October—6 days.

FIFTH DISTRICT—Circuit Court.

Sumner—3d Monday January and August—12 days.

Choctaw—1st Monday February and September—12 days.

Montgomery—3d Monday February and September—12 days.

Attala—2d Monday March and October—12 days.

Holmes—4th Monday March and October—24 days.

Carroll, 1st Dist.—2d Monday May and November—12 days.

Carroll, 2d Dist.—4th Monday May and November—6 days.

Leflore—2d Monday June and December.—12 days

FIFTH DISTRICT—Chancery Courts.

Sumner—3d Monday March and October—6 days.
Choctaw—4th Mondays March and October—6 days.
Montgomery—2d Monday March and October—6 days.
Attala—3d Monday February and September—12 days.
Holmes—1st Monday February and September—12 days.
Carroll, 1st Dist.—1st Mondays April and November—6 days.
Carroll, 2d Dist.—2d Mondays April and November—6 days.
Leflore—4th Monday January and August—6 days.

SIXTH DISTRICT—Circuit Courts.

Noxubee—3d Monday February and August—24 days.
Clay—3d Monday March and September—24 days.
Lowndes—3d Monday April and October—24 days.
Oktibbeha—3d Monday May and November—18 days.
Winston—3d Monday January and July—12 days.

SIXTH DISTRICT—Chancery Courts.

Noxubee—2d Monday April and October—12 days.
Clay—2d Monday June and December—18 days.
Lowndes—3d Monday May and November—18 days.
Oktibbeha—1st Monday February and August—12 days.
Winston—4th Monday April and October—12 days.

SEVENTH DISTRICT—Circuit Courts.

Lauderdale—2d Monday February and August—18 days.
Kemper—1st Monday March and September—12 days.
Clarke—3d Monday March and September—12 days.
Wayne—1st Monday April and October—6 days.
Greene—2d Monday April and October—6 days.
Jackson—3d Monday April and October—6 days.
Harrison—4th Monday April and October—6 days.
Hancock—1st Monday May and November—6 days.
Pearl—2d Monday May and November—6 days.
Marion—3d Monday May and November—6 days.
Perry—4th Monday May and November—6 days.

SEVENTH DISTRICT—Chancery Courts.

Lauderdale—3d Monday May and November—12 days.
Kemper—2d Monday May and November—6 days.
Clarke—1st Monday May and November—6 days.
Wayne—4th Monday after 4th Monday March and September—
   6 days.
Greene—3d Monday after 4th Monday March and September—
   6 days.
Jackson—1st Monday March and September—6 days.

Harrison--2d Monday March and September--6 days.
Hancock--3d Monday March and November--6 days.
Pearl--4th Monday March and September--6 days.
Marion--1st Monday after the 4th Monday March and September
--6 days.
Perry--2d Monday after 4th Monday March and September--6
days.

EIGHTH DISTRICT—Circuit Court.

Rankin—2d Monday February and August—18 days.
Leake—1st Monday March and September—6 days.
Neshoba—2d Monday March and September—6 days.
Newton--3d Monday March and September--6 days.
Jasper—4th Monday March and September—6 days.
Scott—1st Monday April and October—6 days.
Smith—2d Monday April and October—6 days.
Simpson—3d Monday April and October—6 days.
Covington—1st Monday May and November—6 days.
Jones—2d Monday May and November—6 days.
Lawrence—4th Monday May and November--6 days.

EIGHTH DISTRICT—Circuit Courts.

Rankin--2d Monday March and September—12 days.
Leake—4th Monday May and November--6 days.
Neshoba—3d Monday May and November—6 days.
Newton—2d Monday May and November—6 days.
Jasper--4th Monday April and October—6 days.
Scott—1st Monday May and November—6 days.
Smith--3d Monday April and October—6 days.
Simpson—3d Monday March and September—6 days.
Covington—1st Monday April and October—6 days.
Jones—2d Monday April and October—6 days.
Lawrence--4th Monday March and September--6 days.

NINTH DISTRICT—Circuit Courts.

Hinds, 1st Dist.--4th Monday June and December--30 days.
Hinds, 2d Dist.—3d Monday August and February--24 days.
Copiah—4th Monday April and October--24 days.
Madison—4th Monday March and September—24 days.
Yazoo—4th Monday May and November—24 days.

NINTH DISTRICT--Chancery Courts.

Hinds, 1st Dist.—4th Monday March and September—18 days.
Hinds, 2d Dist.—1st Monday January and July--18 days.
Copiah—1st Monday March and September—18 days.
Madison--4th Monday January and July—24 days.
Yazoo—2d Monday April and October--24 days.

TENTH DISTRICT—Circuit Courts.

Lincoln—4th Monday January and July—18 days.
Pike—3d Monday February and August—18 days.
Amite—2d Monday March and September—12 days.
Franklin—4th Monday March and September—12 days.
Wilkinson—2d Monday after 4th Monday March and September
   —12 days.
Adams—4th Monday after 4th Monday March and September—
   18 days.
Jefferson—7th Monday after 4th Monday March and September
   —12 days.
Claiborne—9th Monday after 4th Monday March and September
   —12 days.

TENTH DISTRICT—Chancery Courts.

Lincoln—4th Monday June and December—12 days.
Pike—2d Monday June and December—12 days.
Amite—3d Monday May and November—12 days.
Franklin—2d Monday May and November—6 days.
Wilkinson—4th Monday April and October—12 days.
Adams—4th Monday March and September—18 days.
Jefferson—2d Monday March and September—12 days.
Claiborne—2d Monday January and July—12 days.

ELEVENTH DISTRICT—Circuit Court.

Warren—1st Monday January, April, October—4 weeks.

ELEVENTH DISTRICT—Chancery Court.

Warren—1st Monday February, May, November—4 weeks.

BONDS OF PUBLIC OFFICERS.

Auditor Public Accounts (Code 1871, § 128).............$30,000
State Treasurer (Code 1871, § 150)......... 80,000
Secretary of State (Code 1871. § 117).................... 3,000
Superintendent Public Education (Code 1871, § 2001)...... 20,000
Superintendent of Penitentiary (Acts 1872, p. 71)......... 30,000
Keeper of the Capitol (Code 1871, § 187)................ 3,000
Public Printer (Code 1871, § 166)...................... 20,000
Clerk Supreme Court (Code 1871, § 427)........ 5,000
Commissioner of Immigration (Acts 1873, p. 103)...... .. 10,000
Commissioner of Swamp Lands (Acts 1877, p. 33)......... 10,000
Lessees Penitentiary.... 100,000
Sheriffs (see Revised Code 1871, § 219).

Coroner (Code 1871, § 241).......................... 2,000
Justice of the Peace (Code 1871, § 1298)............... 2,000
Notaries Public (Acts 1872, p. 147)................... 2,000
Circuit Clerk (Code 1871, § 550)..................... 10,000
Chancery Clerk (Code 1871, § 990), not less than $5.000. nor
    more than.. 10,000
       (To be fixed by Chancellor approving bond.)
County Treasurer (Code 1871, § 261), to be fixed by Super-
    visors, and to cover amount likely to come into his hands
    in any one year.
County Surveyor (Code 1871, § 272)................ 500
Constable (Code 1871, §278).......................... 1,000
Ranger (Code 1871, § 287)........................... 500
County Superintendents Public Education (Acts 1872, § 2),
    not less than $2,000, nor more than $5,000, to be fixed by
    Supervisors.
Supervisors, in a sum equal to one and one-half per cent. on
    all the property assessed and levied upon the county the
    year last preceding their qualification (Acts 1876, p. 46).
State Board of Education—consists of State Superintendent,
    Secretary of State and Attorney-General, and each gives
    a bond of... 20,000

CONGRESSIONAL DISTRICTS.

(As re-organized under Act of March 18, 1876.)

FIRST DISTRICT—Tishomingo, Alcorn, Prentiss, Pontotoc, Lee, Itawamba, Monroe, Chickasaw, Clay, Oktibbeha, Lowndes.

SECOND—Tippah, Union, Benton, Marshall, Lafayette, Yalobusha, DeSoto, Tate, Panola, Tallahatchie.

THIRD—Leflore, Sunflower, Grenada, Carroll, Montgomery, Calhoun, Sumner, Choctaw, Winston, Noxubee, Kemper, Neshoba, Attala.

FOURTH—Holmes, Madison, Yazoo, Leake, Scott, Newton, Lauderdale, Smith, Jasper, Clarke, Wayne, Jones.

FIFTH—Hinds, Rankin, Copiah, Simpson, Covington, Lawrence, Amite, Franklin, Pike, Lincoln, Marion, Pearl, Hancock, Perry, Greene, Harrison, Jackson.

SIXTH—Tunica, Coahoma, Quitman, Bolivar, Washington, Issaquena, Sharkey, Warren, Claiborne, Jefferson, Adams, Wilkinson.

HOUSE OF REPRESENTATIVES.

COUNTIES.	MEMBERS.	COUNTIES.	MEMBERS.
Adams	3	Marshall	4
Alcorn	1	Monroe	3
Amite	1	Montgomery	1
Attala	2	Neshoba	1
Benton	1	Newton	1
Bolivar	2	Noxubee	3
Calhoun	1	Oktibbeha	2
Carroll	2	Panola	3
Chickasaw	2	Perry	1
Choctaw	1	Pike	1
Claiborne	2	Pontotoc	1
Clarke	1	Prentiss	1
Coahoma	1	Rankin	2
Copiah	2	Scott	1
Covington	1	Sharkey	1
Clay	1	Simpson	1
DeSoto	3	Smith	1
Franklin	1	Sumner	1
Greene	1	Sunflower	1
Grenada	1	Tallahatchie	1
Hancock and Pearl	1	Tippah	1
Harrison	1	Tishomingo	1
Hinds	4	Tunica and Quitman	1
Holmes	3	Tate	2
Issaquena	1	Union	1
Itawamba	1	Warren	4
Jackson	1	Washington	2
Jasper	1	Wayne	1
Jefferson	2	Wilkinson	2
Jones	1	Winston	1
Kemper	1	Yalobusha	1
Lafayette	2	Yazoo	3
Lauderdale	2		
Lawrence	1	FLOATERS.	
Leake	1		
Lee	2	Amite and Lincoln	1
Lincoln	1	Alcorn and Prentiss	1
Lowndes	3	Choctaw and Montgomery	1
Leflore	1	Yalobusha and Calhoun	1
Madison	3	Pontotoc and Union	1
Marion	1		

Total..................120

SENATORIAL DISTRICTS.

NO. OF SENATORS.

First District—Hancock, Harrison, Jackson, Greene, Marion, Pearl and Perry.. 1
Second—Wilkinson and Amite................................... 2
Third—Pike, Lincoln and Lawrence............................. 1
Fourth—Adams... 1
Fifth—Jefferson and Franklin................................. 1
Sixth—Copiah and Claiborne................................... 1
Seventh—Warren... 2
Eighth—Wayne, Jones, Covington, Simpson and Smith............ 1
Ninth—Jasper, Scott and Newton............................... 1
Tenth—Clarke and Lauderdale.................................. 1
Eleventh—Rankin and Hinds.................................... 1
Twelfth—Madison.. 1
Thirteenth—Yazoo... 1
Fourteenth—Holmes.. 1
Fifteenth—Leake and Attala................................... 1
Sixteenth—Winston, Choctaw and Sumner........................ 1
Seventeenth—Noxubee, Kemper and Neshoba...................... 2
Eighteenth—Lowndes, Oktibbeha and Clay....................... 1
Nineteenth—Calhoun and Yalobusha............................. 1
Twentieth—Lafayette and Pontotoc............................. 1
Twenty-First—Lee and Itawamba................................ 1
Twenty-Second—Alcorn, Tishomingo and Prentiss................ 1
Twenty-Third—Union, Tippah and Benton........................ 1
Twenty-Fourth—Monroe and Chickasaw........................... 2
Twenty-Fifth—Marshall.. 1
Twenty-Sixth—Panola.. 1
Twenty-Seventh—DeSoto, Tate and Tunica....................... 2
Twenty-Eighth—Coahoma, Bolivar and Quitman................... 1
Twenty-Ninth—Washington, Issaquena and Sharkey............... 1
Thirtieth—Sunflower, Tallahatchie and Grenada................ 1
Thirty-First—Carroll, Leflore and Montgomery................. 1
                                                            —
Total... 36

23

THE VOTE OF MISSISSIPPI-1873-1875-1876.

COUNTIES.	STATE TREAS-URER. 1873.		STATE TREAS-URER. 1875.		PRESIDENTIAL ELECTORS. 1876.	
	Holland, Rep.	Vasser, Dem.	Heming way, Dem.	Buchanan, Rep.	Tilden, Dem.	Hayes, Rep.
Adams........	2066	361	793	2616	1626	2324
Alcorn	397	1423	1806	539	1606	663
Amite............	1080	407	1189	1095	1471	73
Attala................	1130	1249	1840	1210	1972	1071
Benton...............	503	923	1047	293	1150	754
Bolivar...............	813	103	348	1920	1296	2089
Calhoun.............	42	1255	1563	205	1796	166
Carroll.	1082	946	1811	1262	1995	1017
Chickasaw...........	1463	976	1778	887	1892	1005
Choctaw,...........	395	544	778	281	968	153
Claiborne	1880	39	1049	496	1504	423
Clarke..........	1123	582	1289	1225	1451	797
Coahoma.......	1295	294	509	234	789	1446
Copiah..............	1714	1576	2435	1861	2611	1642
Covington...........	229	355	633	308	620	283
Clay.............	1559	41	1737	659	2951	818
DeSoto.	1950	622	2400	1566	2546	1669
Franklin.............	385	513	747	542	919	439
Greene...............	57	80	303	59	381	58
Grenada	1152	543	1230	983	1291	636
Hancock,...........	242	345	492	257	547	309
Harrison.............	312	460	760	290	758	297
Hinds	3489	1184	2836	2321	4502	1475
Holmes..............	2285	578	2291	1254	2614	1151
Issaquena...........	998	45	266	2044	788	969
Itawamba..	....	1073	980	30	1410	41
Jackson..............	322	605	778	312	887	343
Jasper...............	627	468	1163	835	1321	699
Jefferson............	1294	58	678	1547	1547	419
Jones...............	33	156	414	4	342	14
Kemper.............	1229	781	1339	418	1597	904
Lafayette...........	1355	1651	2070	1661	2474	1532
Lauderdale..........	1399	1491	1977	1256	2030	596
Lawrence............	9	57	797	597	847	628
Leake...............	555	688	1182	617	1473	442
Lee,.................	715	1162	2423	183	2731	206
Lincoln	872	488	1317	980	1277	875
Lowndes............	2725	680	2137	2021	2073	2

THE VOTE OF MISSISSIPPI—1873-1875-1876—Continued.

COUNTIES.	STATE TREASURER. 1873.		STATE TREASURER. 1875.		PRESIDENTIAL ELECTORS. 1876.	
	Holland, Rep.	Vasser, Dem.	Hemingway, Dem.	Buchanan, Rep.	Tilden, Dem.	Hayes, Rep.
Leflore	728	216	424	1334	1357	698
Madison	2331	354	1488	2587	1473	13
Marion	216	197	487	214	458	240
Marshall	3126	1998	3186	2856	3278	3050
Monroe	2007	1837	2613	1546	2793	1897
Montgomery	923	940	1291	763	1514	451
Neshoba	108	135	1002	136	1106	119
Newton	232	549	1420	432	1642	302
Noxubee	2378	103	1383	2082	1628	14.9
Oktibbeha	1233	44	736	1598	1373	1023
Panola	2939	1185	2968	2400	2790	2517
Perry	6	48	361	36	332	31
Pike	870	892	1393	1200	1524	875
Pontotoc	474	1292	1442	464	1635	561
Prentiss	248	1202	1857	71	1881	163
Pearl	1	102	133	7	182	11
Rankin	1079	1028	1672	1028	1789	788
Scott	344	723	1138	490	1383	49
Simpson	285	496	737	332	788	341
Sharkey	....	....	....	....	591	92
Smith	25	681	1149	44	1115	10
Sumner	....	....	799	342	987	410
Sunflower	421	299	346	378	529	239
Tallahatchie	812	353	1239	969	1144	1
Tippah	291	1609	1468	262	1559	327
Tishomingo	67	781	1352	12	1282	30
Tunica	720	5	141	1165	229	1398
Tate	1338	1506	1973	1495	1947	1508
Union	481	844	1204	397	1611	398
Warren	1572	1211	3606	2042	2036	623
Washington	1829	473	2013	1638	2901	1598
Wayne	253	245	586	363	622	464
Wilkinson	1497	76	460	1808	1262	1425
Winston	5,4	687	908	377	1173	303
Yalobusha	938	1203	1687	941	1904	861
Yazoo	2427	411	4014	7	3674	2
Total	70,461	47,486	98,715	67,171	109,430	53,234
Majority	22,976	....	Hemingway's maj			31,514
Total vote	117,947	....	Tilden's majority			56,196

VOTE OF MISSISSIPPI, 1876—BY CONGRESSIONAL DISTRICTS.

FIRST DISTRICT.

Counties.	H. L. MULDROW, Dem.	J. W. LEE, Rep.
Alcorn	1605	661
Chickasaw	1894	1005
Clay	1948	816
Itawamba	1396	44
Lee	2724	208
Lowndes	2074	2
Monroe	2765	1915
Oktibbeha	1399	993
Pontotoc	1633	565
Prentiss	1977	181
Tishomingo	1282	30
Totals	20,597	5,420

SECOND CONGRESSIONAL DISTRICT.

Counties.	VAN H. MANNING, Dem.	THOS. WALTON, Rep.
Benton	1147	754
DeSoto	2542	1661
Lafayette	2463	1538
Marshall	3256	3036
Panola	2786	2518
Tallahatchie	1145	1
Tate	1947	1499
Tippah	1554	329
Union	1608	391
Yalobusha	1881	862
Totals	20,329	12,589

THIRD CONGRESSIONAL DISTRICT.

Counties.	H. D. MONEY, Dem.	W. W. CHISHOLM, Rep.
Attala	1977	975
Calhoun	1801	117
Carroll	2008	996
Choctaw	968	155
Grenada	1297	625
Kemper	1573	890
Leflore	1367	696
Montgomery	1545	415
Neshoba	1106	119
Noxubee	1632	1405
Sunflower	523	234
Winston	1177	287
Sumner	989	406
Totals	17,955	7,320

FOURTH CONGRESSIONAL DISTRICT.

Counties.	O. R. Singleton, Dem.	W. M. Hancock, Rep.
Clarke	1443	805
Holmes	2612	1149
Jasper	1314	701
Jones	338	18
Lauderdale	2039	587
Leake	1474	441
Madison	1466	10
Newton	1642	300
Scott	1388	49
Smith	1115	..
Wayne	621	464
Yazoo	3678	2
Totals	19,130	4,529

FIFTH CONGRESSIONAL DISTRICT.

Counties.	C. E. Hooker, Dem.	M. Shaughnessey, Rep.
Amite	1477	73
Copiah	2615	1639
Covington	623	281
Franklin	921	438
Greene	380	58
Hancock	547	304
Harrison	752	301
Hinds	4416	1473
Jackson	890	340
Lawrence	852	621
Lincoln	1280	866
Marion	458	240
Pearl	182	11
Perry	339	24
Pike	1536	862
Rankin	1800	776
Simpson	790	339
Totals	19,858	8,646

SIXTH CONGRESSIONAL DISTRICT.

Counties.	J. R. Chalmers, Dem.	J. R. Lynch, Rep.
Adams	1684	2265
Bolivar	1298	2073
Claiborne	1498	426
Issaquena	938	722
Jefferson	1545	420
Sharkey	591	91
Tunica	958	381
Warren	2043	615
Washington	2905	1591
Wilkinson	1255	1432
Totals	15,988	11,188

ALPHABETICAL LIST OF POST OFFICES IN MISSISSIPPI.

[The names of places in *italic* indicate county sites.]

POST OFFICE.	COUNTY.	POST OFFICE.	COUNTY.
Abbeville	Lafayette.	Black Hawk	Carroll.
Aberdeen	Monroe.	Black Jack	Benton.
Ada	Choctaw.	Blackmonton	Carroll.
Adamsville	Greene.	Blue Mountain	Tippah.
Air Mount	Yalobusha.	Bogue Chitto	Lincoln.
Alexander	Issaquena.	Boland's	Itawamba.
Alexis	Tunica.	Bolton's Depot	Hinds.
Allen's Store	Tishomingo.	*Booneville*	Prentiss.
Allgood's Mill	Noxubee.	Bovina	Warren.
Americus	Jackson.	Bradley	Oktibbeha.
Antioch	Alcorn.	*Brandon*	Rankin.
Appleton	Harrison.	Bridgeport	Simpson.
Areola	Washington.	*Brookhaven*	Lincoln.
Arkabutla	Tate.	Brooks Landing	Claiborne.
Artesia	Lowndes.	Brooksville	Noxubee.
Ash Creek	Oktibbeha.	Brownsville	Hinds.
Ashland	Benton.	Brunswick	Warren.
Atlanta	Chickasaw.	Bucatunna	Wayne.
Auburn	Hinds.	Buck Creek	Greene.
Augusta	Perry.	Buena Vista	Chickasaw.
Austin	Tunica.	Bunckley	Franklin.
Australia	Bolivar.	Bamcombe	Union.
Baldwyn	Lee.	Bunker Hill	Smith.
Baloil	Marshall.	Burnsville	Tishomingo.
Bankston	Choctaw.	Burnt Mills	Tishomingo.
Banner	Calhoun.	Burton's	Tishomingo.
Batesville	Panola.	Burtonton	Copiah.
Bay Saint Louis	Hancock.	Byhalia	Marshall.
Bay Springs	Tishomingo.	Byram	Hinds.
Bear Creek	Hinds.	Cadaretta	Sumner.
Beech Springs	Neshoba.	Caledonia	Lowndes.
Beauregard	Copiah.	Calhoun	Madison.
Bellefontaine	Sumner.	Calvert's Store	Kemper.
Belmont	Tishomingo.	Camden	Madison.
Belan	Quitman.	Campbell Switch	Alcorn.
Benela	Calhoun.	Canaan	Benton.
Benton	Yazoo.	*Canton*	Madison.
Bethlehem	Marshall.	Cardsville	Itawamba.
Beulah	Bolivar.	Carolina	Issaquena.
Bigby Fork	Itawamba.	*Carrollton*	Carroll.
Big Creek	Calhoun.	Carson's Landing	Bolivar.
Big Springs	Clay.	Cartersville	Tishomingo.
Biloxi	Harrison.	*Carthage*	Leake.

Alphabetical List of Post Offices in Mississippi—Continued.

[The names of places in *italic* indicate county sites.]

POST OFFICE.	COUNTY.	POST OFFICE.	COUNTY.
Caseyville	Lincoln.	Conway	Leake.
Caswell	Lafayette.	Coonewar	Lee.
Cato	Rankin.	Coopwood	Winston.
Cayuga	Hinds.	*Corinth*	Alcorn.
Cedar Bluff	Clay.	Cornersville,	Benton.
Cedar Grove	Pontotoc.	Corrona	Lee.
Cedar Tree	Choctaw.	Cotton Gin Port	Monroe.
Center Point	Tallahatchie.	Cotton Plant	Tippah.
Central Academy	Panola.	Cotton Valley	Calhoun.
Centre	Attala.	County Line	Tallahatchie.
Centreville	Amite.	Couparle City	Madison.
Chapel Hill	Hinds.	Courtland	Panola.
Charleston	Tallahatchie.	Crawfordville	Lowndes.
Chastain	Itawamba.	Creswell	Jasper.
Chatawa	Pike.	Crevi	Tallahatchie.
Cherry Creek	Pontotoc.	Cross Roads	Greene.
Cherry Hill	Calhoun.	Crystal Springs	Copiah.
Chester	Choctaw.	Cumberland	Sumner.
Chesterville	Lee.	Cushtusa	Neshoba.
Chewalla Mills	Marshall.	Daleville	Lauderdale.
Chew's Landing	Holmes.	Dallas	Lafayette.
China Grove	Pike.	Damascus	Scott.
Choctaw Agency	Oktibbeha.	Danville	Alcorn.
Chulahoma	Marshall.	Davisville	Jasper.
Chunkey	Newton.	Deasonville	Yazoo.
Church Hill	Jefferson.	Decatur,	Newton.
Claiborne	Jasper.	*DeKalb*	Kemper.
Clarksdale	Coahoma.	DeLay	Lafayette
Clay	Marion.	Delta	Coahoma
Clinton	Hinds.	Denmark	Lafayette.
Cobb Switch	Lowndes.	DeSoto	Clarke.
Cockrum	DeSoto.	De Soto Front	DeSoto.
Coffadeliah	Neshoba.	Dido	Choctaw.
Coffeeville	Yalobusha.	Dixon	Neshoba.
Cold Springs	Wilkinson.	Dobsonville	Smith.
Cold Water	Tate.	Double Springs	Oktibbeha.
Coleman	Marshall.	Dover	Yazoo.
Cole's Creek	Calhoun.	Dowd's Landing	Coahoma.
Columbia	Marion.	Dry Grove	Hinds.
Columbus	Lowndes.	Dry Run	Prentiss.
Commerce	Tunica.	Dublin	Coahoma.
Como Depot	Panola.	Duck Hill	Montgomery.
Conerly's	Pike.	Dumas	Tippah.

Alphabetical List of Post Offices in Mississippi—Continued.

[The names of places in *italic* indicate county sites.]

POST OFFICE.	COUNTY.	POST OFFICE.	COUNTY.
Duncansby	Issaquena.	Georgetown	Copiah.
Durant	Holmes.	Gholson	Noxubee.
Early Grove	Marshall.	Glencoe	Bolivar.
Edinburgh	Leake.	Glenville	Panola.
Edwards' Depot	Hinds.	Good Hope	Leake.
Egg's Point	Washington.	Goodman	Holmes.
Egypt	Chickasaw.	Goshen Springs	Rankin.
Elliott	Grenada.	Grand Gulf	Claiborne.
Elliott's Mills	Panola.	Gray's Mill	Holmes.
Ellistown	Lee.	Graysport	Grenada.
Ellisville	Jones.	Greensborough	Sumner.
Energy	Clarke.	*Greenville*	Washington.
Ennis Store	Oktibbeha.	*Greenwood*	Leflore.
Enon	Perry.	*Grenada*	Grenada.
Enterprise	Clarke.	Gum Grove Landing	Holmes.
Erata	Jones.	Gum Ridge	Jefferson.
Esparanza	Pontotoc.	Guntown	Lee.
Estill	Washington.	Hamilton	Monroe.
Etchehoma	Jasper.	Handsborough	Harrison.
Eucutta	Wayne.	Hardy Station	Grenada.
Eudora	DeSoto.	Harpersville	Scott.
Eureka	Lee.	Harrison Station	Tallahatchie.
Faisonia	Sunflower.	Harrisville	Simpson.
Falkner	Tippah.	Hashuqua	Noxubee.
Fannin	Rankin.	Hays' Landing	Issaquena.
Fayette	Jefferson.	Hazel Dell	Prentiss.
Fearn's Springs	Winston.	*Hazlehurst*	Copiah.
Flint Creek	Harrison.	Hebron	Lawrence.
Flower's Place	Smith.	Herbert	Neshoba.
Fordsville	Marion.	*Hernando*	DeSoto.
Forest	Scott.	Hickory	Newton.
Forest Home	Warren.	Hickory Flat	Benton.
Fort Adams	Wilkinson.	Hickory Plains	Prentiss.
Fort Stephens	Kemper.	High Hill	Leake.
Fredonia	Union.	Highland	Tishomingo.
French Camps	Choctaw.	Hillsborough	Scott.
Friar's Point	Coahoma.	Hillside	Tishomingo.
Friendship	Lincoln.	*Holly Springs*	Marshall.
Fulton	Itawamba.	Holmesville	Pike.
Gainesville	Hancock.	Homewood	Scott.
Gallman	Copiah.	Hopewell	Calhoun.
Garlandville	Jasper.	Horn Lake	DeSoto.
Garner	Yalobusha.	Houlka	Chickasaw.

Alphabetical List of Post Offices in Mississippi—Continued.

[The names of places in *italic* indicate county sites.]

POST OFFICE.	COUNTY.	POST OFFICE.	COUNTY.
Houston	Chickasaw.	Lawrence	Newton.
Hudson	Tunica.	Law's Hill	Marshall.
Hudsonville	Marshall.	Leaf	Greene.
Hulberton	Coahoma.	*Leakesville*	Greene.
Huntsville	Montgomery.	Leota Landing	Washington.
Hurricane	Warren.	Lewisburgh,	DeSoto.
Hurricane Creek	Lauderdale.	*Lexington*	Holmes.
Independence	Tate.	*Liberty.*	Amite.
Indian Bayou	Sunflower.	Line Creek	Sumner.
Ingomar	Issaquena.	Lockhart	Lauderdale.
Iuka	Tishomingo.	Locust Grove	Union.
Jacinto	Alcorn.	Lodi	Montgomery.
JACKSON (capital)	Hinds.	Lone Star	Itawamba.
Jacksonwood	Amite.	Longtown	Panola.
Java	Neshoba.	Looxahoma	Tate.
Jaynesville	Covington.	*Louisville*	Winston.
Jefferiesville	Claiborne.	Love's Station	DeSoto.
Jewell's Hill	Jasper.	Ludlow	Scott.
Johnsonville	Sunflower.	Luxapeliio	Lowndes.
Johnston's Station	Pike.	McCall's Creek.	Franklin.
Jonesborough	Tippah.	McComb City	Pike.
Jonestown	Coahoma.	McDonald's Mills	Perry.
Kellis' Store	Kemper.	McKinneyville	Sharkey.
Kennedy's Store	Itawamba.	McNutt	Leflore.
Kewanee	Lauderdale.	Macedonia	Lee.
Kibbeville	Franklin.	*Macon.*	Noxubee.
Kienstra's Store	Adams.	Madison Station	Madison.
Kilmichael	Montgomery.	*Magnolia*	Pike.
Kingston,	Adams.	Marietta	Prentiss.
Knight's Mills	Jones.	Marion Station	Lauderdale.
Kirkwood	Madison.	Mashulaville	Noxubee.
Knoxville	Franklin.	*Mayerville*	Issaquena.
Kosciusko	Attala.	Mayhew's Station	Lowndes.
Kossuth	Alcorn.	*Meadville*	Franklin.
Lafayette Springs	Lafayette.	*Meridian*	Lauderdale.
Lagrange	Choctaw.	Michigan City	Benton.
Lake	Scott.	Midway	Hinds.
Lake Como	Jasper.	Millville	Madison.
Lake Washington	Washington.	*Mississippi City*	Harrison.
Lamar	Marshall.	Mitchell s Mill	Attala.
Langside	Wilkinson.	Molino	Union.
Lauderdale Station	Lauderdale.	Monroe	Perry.
Laurel Hill	Neshoba.	Monte Vista	Sumner.

Alphabetical List of Post Offices in Mississippi—Continued.

[The names of places in *italic* indicate county sites.]

POST OFFICE.	COUNTY.	POST OFFICE,	COUNTY.
Montgomery	Lincoln.	Osyka	Pike.
Monticello	Lawrence.	Othello	Tunica.
Montpelier	Clay.	*Oxford*	Lafayette.
Montrose	Jasper.	Palmetto Home	Yazoo.
Moore's Mills	Newton.	Palo Alto	Clay.
Mooresville	Lee.	Parmitchie	Alcorn.
Morgan's Fork	Franklin.	Pascagoula	Jackson.
Morton	Scott.	Pass Christian	Harrison.
Moscow	Kemper.	*Paulding*	Jasper.
Moss Point	Jackson.	Peach Creek	Panola.
Mountain Creek	Rankin.	Pearce	Lee.
Mount Carmel	Covington.	Pea Ridge	Kemper.
Mount Hope	Copiah.	Pearlington	Hancock.
Mount Olive	Covington.	Peden	Kemper.
Mount Pleasant	Marshall.	Pelahatchie Depot.	Rankin.
Mount Zion	Simpson.	Percy	Washington.
Mud Creek	Pontotoc.	Perkinsville	Winston.
Muldon	Monroe.	Perth	Jefferson.
Natchez	Adams.	*Philadelphia*	Neshoba.
Neblet's Landing	Bolivar.	Pickens Station	Holmes.
Nesbit's Station	DeSoto.	Pine Bluff	Clay.
New Albany	Union.	Pine Grove	Benton.
New Hope	Yalobusha.	Pine Valley	Yalobusha.
New Ireland	Newton.	Pineville	Smith.
New Port	Attala.	Pinnellville	Jones.
New Prospect	Winston.	*Pittsborough*	Calhoun.
New Site	Prentiss.	Plattsburgh	Winston.
Newtonville	Attala.	Pleasant Grove	Panola.
New Town Landing	Warren.	Pleasant Hill	DeSoto.
Newton	Newton.	Pleasant Mount	Panola.
Noxapater	Winston.	Plum Bluff	Jackson.
Oak Farm	Tishomingo.	Plum Point	DeSoto.
Oakland	Yalobusha.	Polkville	Smith.
Oakohay	Covington.	*Pontotoc*	Pontotoc.
Oak Vale	Lawrence.	Pope's Depot	Panola.
Ocean Springs	Jackson.	Poplar Creek	Montgomery.
Ofahoma	Leake.	Poplar Springs	Pontotoc.
Offutt	Washington.	*Port Gibson*	Claiborne.
Okolona	Chickasaw.	Pott's Camp	Marshall.
Old Hickory	Simpson.	Prairie Point	Noxubee.
Olive Branch	DeSoto.	Prairie Station	Monroe.
O'Neal's	Amite.	Prentiss	Bolivar.
Orizaba	Tippah.	Providence	Grenada.

Alphabetical List of Post Offices in Mississippi—Continued.

[The names of places in *italic* indicate county sites.]

POST OFFICE.	COUNTY.	POST OFFICE.	COUNTY.
Quincy	Monroe.	Shell Mound	Leflore.
Quitman	Clarke.	Sheppardtown	Leflore.
Raleigh	Smith.	Shongalo	Smith.
Randall's Bluff	Winston.	Shubuta	Clarke.
Randolph	Pontotoc.	Shuqualak	Noxubee.
Raymond	Hinds.	Sidon	Leflore.
Red Banks	Marshall.	Siloam	Clay.
Red Land	Pontotoc.	Silver Creek	Lawrence.
Red Lick	Jefferson.	Silver Springs	Alcorn.
Refuge	Washington.	Singleton	Winston.
Riceville	Pearl.	Slate Spring	Calhoun.
Rienzi	Alcorn.	Slayden's Crossing	Marshall.
Rio	Kemper.	Smith's Station	Hinds.
Ripley	Tippah.	Smithville	Monroe.
Riverton	Bolivar.	Sonora	Clay.
Robertsonville	Coahoma.	Sparta	Chickasaw.
Robson's Landing	Coahoma.	Spring Cottage	Marion.
Rock Hill	Benton.	Spring Dale	Lafayette.
Rockport	Copiah.	Springport	Panola.
Rocky Springs	Claiborne.	Spring Valley	Sumner.
Rodney	Jefferson.	*Starkville*	Oktibbeha.
Roebuck	Leflore.	Star Place	Panola.
Rolling Fork	Sharkey.	State Line Station	Greene.
Rome	Winston.	Station Creek	Covington.
Rosedale	Bolivar.	Steen's Creek	Rankin.
Rose Hill	Amite.	Stoneville	Washington.
Ruckersville	Tippah.	Stonewall	Harrison.
Rushing's Store	Lauderdale.	Stormville	Bolivar.
Sabougla	Calhoun.	Strayhorn	Tate.
Saint Elmo	Claiborne.	Sucarnoochee	Kemper.
Salem	Benton.	Sulphur Springs	Madison.
Sallis	Attala.	Summit	Pike.
Saltillo	Lee.	Tacaleeche	Benton.
Santee	Covington.	Tallulah	Issaquena.
Sardis	Panola.	Tamola Station	Kemper.
Sarepta	Calhoun.	Tampico	Clay.
Satartia	Yazoo.	Taylor's Depot	Lafayette.
Scooba	Kemper.	Taylorsville	Smith.
Scranton	Jackson.	Tchula	Holmes.
Senatobia	Tate.	Temperance Hill	Monroe.
Sessumsville	Oktibbeha.	Terrene	Bolivar.
Shady Grove	Jasper.	Terry	Hinds.
Sharon	Madison.	Thomastown	Leake.

Alphabetcal Lst of Post Offices in Mississippi—Continued.

[The names of places in *italic* indicate county sites.]

POST OFFICE.	COUNTY.	POST OFFICE.	COUNTY.
Thyatira	Tate.	*Walthall*	Sumner.
Tibbee Station	Clay.	Walton	Lafayette.
Tillatoba	Yalobusha.	Warrenton	Warren.
Tiplersville	Tippah.	Washington	Adams.
Toccopola	Pontotoc.	Waterford	Marshall.
Toomsuba	Lauderdale.	Water Valley	Yalobusha.
Torrance	Yalobusha.	Watkinsville	Neshoba.
Tougaloo	Hinds.	Watson	Marshall..
Tremont	Itawamba.	Waveland	Hancock.
Trenton	Smith.	*Waynesborough*	Wayne.
Tupelo	Lee.	Webster	Winston.
Turner's	Franklin.	Wesson	Copiah.
Turnerville	Jasper.	Wells	Attala.
Twistwood	Jasper.	West Fork	Lawrence.
Tyro	Tate.	*West Point*	Clay.
Union	Newton.	West's Station	Holmes.
Union Church	Jefferson.	*Westville*	Simpson.
Union Mills	Tippah.	Whitefield	Oktibbeha.
Utica	Hinds.	Why Not	Lauderdale.
Vaiden	Carroll.	Wilkesburg	Covington.
Vaughan	Yazoo.	*Williamsburgh*	Covington.
Vernal	Greene.	Winchester	Wayne.
Vernon	Madison.	*Winona*	Montgomery.
Verona	Lee.	*Woodville*	Wilkinson.
Vicksburg	Warren.	*Yazoo City*	Yazoo.
Wahalak	Kemper.	Yellow Rabbit	Benton.
Wallerville	Union.	Yocony	Itawamba.
Wall Hill	Marshall.	Yorka	Leake.
Walnut	Tippah.	Zion Hill	Amite.
Walnut Grove	Leake.		

COUNTIES AND COUNTY SITES.

COUNTY.	COURTS HELD AT.	COUNTY.	COURTS HELD AT.
Adams	Natchez.	Lowndes	Columbus.
Alcorn	Corinth.	Leflore	Greenwood.
Amite	Liberty.	Madison	Canton.
Attala	Kosciusko.	Marion	Columbia.
Benton	Ashland.	Marshall	Holly Springs.
Bolivar	Floreyville	Monroe	Aberdeen.
Calhoun	Pittsboro.	Montgomery	Winona.
Carroll, {	Carrollton.	Neshoba	Philadelphia.
	Vaiden.	Newton	Decatur.
Chickasaw. {	Houston.	Noxubee	Macon.
	Okolona.	Oktibbeha	Starkville.
Choctaw	Chester.	Panola	Sardis.
Claiborne	Port Gibson.	Perry	Augusta.
Clarke	Enterprise.	Pike	Magnolia.
Coahoma	Friars' Point.	Pontotoc	Pontotoc.
Copiah	Hazlehurst.	Prentiss	Booneville.
Covington	Williamsburg.	Pearl	Riceville.
Clay	West Point.	Quitman	Belan.
DeSoto	Hernando.	Rankin	Brandon.
Franklin	Meadville.	Scott	Forest.
Greene	Leakesville.	Sharkey	Rolling Fork.
Grenada	Grenada.	Simpson	Westville.
Hancock	Shieldsboro.	Smith	Raleigh.
Harrison	Mississippi City.	Sumner	Walthall.
Hinds, {	Raymond.	Sunflower	Johnsonville.
	Jackson.	Tallahatchie	Charleston.
Holmes	Lexington.	Tippah	Ripley.
Issaquena	Mayersville.	Tishomingo	Iuka.
Itawamba	Fulton.	Tunica	Austin.
Jackson	Scranton.	Tate	Senatobia.
Jasper	Paulding.	Union	New Albany.
Jefferson	Fayette.	Warren	Vicksburg.
Jones	Ellisville.	Washington	Greeneville.
Kemper	DeKalb.	Wayne	Waynesboro.
Lafayette	Oxford.	Wilkinson	Woodville.
Lauderdale	Meridian.	Winston	Louisville.
Lawrence	Monticello.	Yalobusha. {	Coffeeville.
Leake	Leakesville.		Water Valley.
Lee	Tupelo.	Yazoo	Yazoo City.
Lincoln	Brookhaven.		

RAILROADS.

NEW ORLEANS, JACKSON AND GREAT NORTHERN RAILROAD.

STATIONS. From New Orleans to	MILES.	STATION. From New Orleans to	MILES.
Sauve	5	Quinn's Station	102
Kenner	10	McComb City	105
Bayou LaBranch	19	Summit	108
Frenier	24	Johnston's	112½
Bayou DeSair	29	Bogue Chitto	118½
Manchac	37	Brookhaven	129
Ponchatoula	48	Montgomery	134
Hammond	52	Wesson	137½
Tickfaw	58	Beauregard	139
Southern Car Works	61	Martinsville	144
Independence	62	Hazlehurst	149
Gullett's	67	Gallman	154
Amite	68	Crystal Springs	158½
Arcola	72	Terry	167
Tangipahoa	78	Byram	174
Kent's Mill and Union Land'g	83	Jackson	183
Osyka	88	Tougaloo	190
Carter's Hill	92	Madison	195
Chatawa	92½	Calhoun	199
Magnolia	98	Canton	206

MISSISSIPPI CENTRAL RAILROAD.

STATIONS. From Canton to	MILES.	STATIONS. From Canton to	MILES.
Way's Bluff	9	Water Valley	117
Vaughan's	14	Springdale	122
Pickens'	20	Taylor's	126
Goodman	27	Oxford	134
Kosciusko Junction	32	Abbeville	144
Durant	35	Waterford	154
West	44	Holly Springs	163
Vaiden	55	Hudsonville	171
62 Mile Siding	62	Lamar	176
Winona	65	Michigan City	182
Duck Hill	76	Grand Junction, Tenn	188
Elliott	80	Hickory Valley	196
Grenada	88	Middleburg	200
Torrance	96	Bolivar	207
Coffeeville	104	Jackson	235
Dickson (flag station)	111	Cairo, Ill	342

KOSCIUSKO BRANCH

OF NEW ORLEANS AND JACKSON RAILROAD.

STATIONS.	MILES.	STATIONS.	MILES.
From Durant to		From Durant to	
Kosciusko Junction	3	Kosciusko	21
Sallis	11		

MISSISSIPPI AND TENNESSEE RAILROAD.

STATIONS.	MILES.	STATIONS.	MILES.
From Grenada to—		From Grenada to—	
Hardy	8	Senatobia	63
Garner	13	Coldwater	69
Oakland	22	Love's	73
Harrison	28	Hernando	78
Pope's	34	Nesbitt's	82
Courtland	36	Horn Lake	88
Batesville	41	Whitehaven	92
Sardis	50	Memphis	100
Como	56		

VICKSBURG AND MERIDIAN RAILROAD.

STATIONS.	MILES.	STATIONS.	MILES.
From Vicksburg to—		From Vicksburg to—	
Bovina	10	Forest	90
Edwards	18	Lake	99
Bolton	27	Lawrence	105
Clinton	35	Newton	109
Jackson	44½	Hickory	116
Brandon	58½	Chunky	122
Pelahatchie	70	Golden Grove	129
Bolers	74½	Meridian	140
Morton	79		

ALABAMA CENTRAL RAILROAD.

(From Meridian to Selma.)

STATIONS.	MILES.	STATIONS.	MILES.
From Meridian to—		From Meridian to—	
Russell's	6	Coatopa	40½
Tocmsuba	13	McDowell's	51½
Cuba	20	Demopolis	57
York	26	Uniontown	77
Bennett's	33	Selma	109
Lee's	37		

MOBILE AND OHIO RAILROAD.

STATIONS.	MILES.	STATIONS.	MILES.
From Mobile to		From Mobile to—	
Toulminville	8	Scooba	176
Whistler	5	Wahalak	182½
Kushla	11	Shuqulak	188¼
Oak Grove	14½	Macon	198
Chunchula	18½	Brooksville	206
Beaver Meadow	25½	Crawford	211
Langdon	29	Artesia	219½
Citronelle	33	Columbus	233
Deer Park	43¾	Mayhew	224
Escatawpa	50¾	Tibbee	227
Brushy Creek, (Alabama)	54½	West Point	232⅓
State Line, (Mississippi)	62¾	Muldon	241
Buckatunna	71	Prairie	245½
Winchester	77½	Egypt	253½
Woynesboro'	82½	Okolona	261½
Red Bluff	93	Shannon	269
Shubuta	96½	Verona	274½
DeSoto	104¼	Tupelo	279
Quitman	109	Saltillo	287½
Enterprise	120	Guntown	292
Okatibbee	129¾	Baldwyn	297
Meridian	134¾	Booneville	308¼
Marion	140	Rienzi	316½
Lockhart	146¾	Corinth	329
Lauderdale	153¼	Jackson, (Tennessee)	386
Tamola	158	Humboldt	403
Gainesville Junction	163½	Union City	446
Sucarnochee	168¾	Columbus, (Kentucky)	472

ABERDEEN BRANCH—Of Mobile and Ohio Railroad.

STATION.	MILES.	STATION.	MILES
From Muldon to—		From Muldon to—	
Sykes	4	Aberdeen	9

COLUMBUS BRANCH—Of Mobile and Ohio Railroad.

STATION.	MILES.	STATION.	MILES.
From Artesia to—		From Artesia to—	
Cobb's	5½	Columbus	8

STARKVILLE BRANCH—Of Mobile and Ohio Railroad.

STATION.	MILES.	STATION.	MILES.
From Artesia to—		From Artesia to—	
Sessums		Starkville	

NEW ORLEANS AND MOBILE RAILROAD.

STATIONS.	MILES.	STATIONS.	MILES.
From New Orleans to—		From New Orleans to—	
Gentilly	5	Scott	63½
Lee	9	Barnes Hotel Station	70½
Michoud	13	Mississippi City	71
Chef Menteur	20	Beauvior	75
Lake Catherine	26	Biloxi	80
Rigolets	31	Ocean Springs	84
Look Out	36	Belle Fontaine	90
Grand Plain	41	West Pascagoula	97
Touline	45	East Pascagoula	100
Montgomery	48½	Murray	107½
Nicholson	50	Grand Bay	115½
Bay St. Louis	52	Saint Elmo	121
West Pass Christian	56½	Fowl River	127
Pass Christian	58	Webb's Landing	132
East Pass Christian	59½	Mobile	141

MEMPHIS AND CHARLESTON RAILROAD.

STATIONS.	MILES.	STATIONS.	MILES.
From Memphis to—		From Memphis to—	
Buntyns	5.5	Pocahontas	74.3
White's	9	Big Hill	78.5
Germantown	14.5	Chewalla	83.7
Bailey	20.3	Corinth	93
Collierville	23.8	Glendale	101
Lafayette	30.9	Burnsville	107.7
Moscow	39	Iuka	115.2
Forty-five mile siding	45.2	Tuscumbia	145.4
LaGrange	48.9	Decatur	188.4
Grand Junction	52	Huntsville	212.8
Saulsbury	57.2	Stevenson	271.8
Sixty-four mile siding	64.1	Chattanooga	310
Middleton	69.1		

NATCHEZ, JACKSON AND COLUMBUS RAILROAD.

STATIONS.	MILES.	STATIONS.	MILES.
From Natchez to		From Natchez to	
Foster's	6	Buie's	4
Brandon's	4	Stampley's	4
Greenwood Church	3	Fayette	5

From Natchez to Fayette, 26 miles. From Natchez to Jackson, by projected route, 96 miles.

WEST FELICIANA RAILROAD.

Woodville to Bayou Sara............................28 miles.

24

GRAND GULF AND PORT GIBSON RAILROAD.

Port Gibson to Grand Gulf.......................... 7 miles.

RIPLEY, KENTUCKY AND SHIP ISLAND RAILROAD.

From Middletown, Tenn. (on Memphis and Charleston Railroad), to Ripley................................. — miles.

MISSISSIPPI RIVER.

DISTANCES FROM VICKSBURG NORTH.

LANDING.	MILES.
To Young's Point, La.	10
Milliken's Bend, La.	21
Tallulab, Miss.	46
Lake Providence, La.	57
Mayersville, Miss.	64
Duncansby, Miss.	68
Carolina, Miss.	79
Leota, Miss.	82
Egg's Point, Miss.	94
Greenville.	111
Bolivar, Miss.	161½
Prentiss, Miss.	182
Napoleon, Ark.	184
Floreyville, Miss.	192
Carson's, Miss.	217
Helena, Ark.	322
Austin, Miss.	339
Memphis.	404
Cairo.	677
St. Louis.	877

FROM VICKSBURG SOUTH.

LANDING.	MILES.
Delta.	4
Davis' Bend.	25
Grand Gulf.	40
St. Joseph.	55
Rodney.	60
Waterproof.	70
Natchez.	100
New Orleans.	400

HOW TO CALCULATE INTEREST.

For finding the interest on any principal for any number of days, the answer in each case being in cents, separate the two right hand figures to express it in dollars and cents.

Four per cent : Multiply the principal by the number of days to run; separate the right hand figure from product and divide by 9.

Five per cent : Multiply by number of days, and divide by 72.

Six per cent : Multiply by number of days, and divide by 6.

Eight per cent : Multiply by number of days, and divide by 45.

Nine per cent : Multiply by number of days, separate right hand figure, and divide by 4.

Ten per cent : Multiply by number of days and divide by 36.

Twelve per cent: Multiply by number of days, separate right hand figure, and divide by 3.

Fifteen per cent : Multiply by number of days, and divide by 24.

Eighteen per cent : Multiply by number of days, separate right hand figure, and divide by 2.

Twenty per cent : Multiply by number of days, and divide by 18.

SECOND METHOD.

Multiply the principal by the number of days, and divide the product, if for 5 per cent., by 7200; if for 6 per cent., by 6000; if for 7 per cent., by 5143; if for 8 per cent., by 4,500; if for 9 per cent, by 4000; if for 10 per cent, by 3600.

EXAMPLE.—What is the interest on $120 for 20 days, at 10 per cent?

```
            120 00   dollars.
Multiply by      20   days.
            ———— ——
Divided by   3600)24000(66.6 cents interest.
```

THIRD METHOD.

Multiply the sum by the number of days, and divide the product by 60 ; the quotient will be the interest in cents.

EXAMPLE.—What is the interest of $330 for 16 days, at 6 per cent.?

```
            330   dollars.
Multiplied by   16   the number of days.
            ————
            1980
            330
            ————
Divided by   60)5280(88 cents interest.
            480
            ———
            480
            480
```

TO CALCULATE INTEREST FOR ANY NUMBER OF MONTHS.

Multiply the sum by half the number of months; the amount will be the interest in cents.

EXAMPLE.—What is the interest of $498 for 6 months, at 6 per cent.?

$$498 \quad \text{dollars.}$$
$$3 \quad \text{half the number of months.}$$

$$1494 \quad \text{cents, or \$14 94.}$$

VARIOUS WEIGHTS AND MEASURES—(GROSS WEIGHT.)

A ton of coal is 2000 pounds.

A legal stone weighs 14 pounds, or the eighth of a hundred, in England, and 17 pounds, in Holland.

A ton of round timber is 40 feet; of squared timber, 45 cubic feet.

A commercial bale of cotton is 400 pounds.

A pack of wool is 240 pounds.

A barrel of flour weighs 220 pounds, gross.

A barrel of pork weighs 350 pounds, gross.

A tierce of rice weighs 600 pounds, gross.

A ferkin of butter weighs 56 pounds, gross.

A barrel of molasses weighs 500 pounds, gross.

A barrel of liquor weighs 400 pounds, gross.

231 cubic inches is one gallon, in liquid measure.

268 4-5 cubic inches is one gallon in dry measure.

2150 2-5 cubic inches is one bushel in dry measure.

A circular measure, 18½ inches in diameter, and 8 inches deep, contains one bushel, dry measure.

A box 16 X 16½ inches, 8 inches deep, contains one bushel.

A box 8 X 8½ inches, 8 inches deep, contains one peck.

A box 4 X 4 inches, 4½ inches deep, contains one half peck.

A box 4 X 4 inches, 4 2-10 inches deep, contains one quart.

The standard bushel of the United States contains 2150.4 cubic inches. The Imperial bushel is about 68 cubic inches. Any box or measure, the contents of which are equal to 2150.4 cubic inches, will hold a bushel of grain. In measuring fruit, vegetables, coal, and other substances, one-fifth must be added. In other words, a peck measure five times even full, makes one bushel. The usual practice is to "heap the measure."

Number of Nails to the pound.—Four-penny, 256; six-penny, 164; eight-penny, 94; ten-penny, 64; twelve-penny, 50.

Glass in a Box.—10 by 8, 90 panes; 10 by 14, 51 panes; 10 by 12, 60 panes; 12 by 14, 43 panes; 12 by 16, 37 panes.

DISTANCES, ETC.

An Irish mile is.. 9240 yards.
    Scotch mile is... 1984 yards.
    English or statute mile is 5280 feet..................... 1760 yards.
    German mile is... 1806 yards.
    Turkish mile is.. 1826 yards.

An acre is 4840 square yards, or 69 yards 1 foot 8½ inches each way. A square mile, 1760 yards each way, contains 640 acres.

A section of Government land is 640 acres (1 mile).

A fathom is six feet; derived from the height of a full grown man.

A league is 3 miles; a cubit, 2 feet; a great cubit, 11 feet; a palm, 3 inches; a span, 10⅗ inches; a pace, 3 feet; a hand, in horse measure, is four inches; 144 square inches, one square foot; 9 square feet, one square yard; 30¼ square yards, one square rod; 40 square rods, one square rood; 4 square roods, one square acre; 640 square acres, one square mile.

To lay off a square acre of ground.—Measure 209 feet on each side, and you will have a square acre, within an inch.

Rule for measuring corn.—Reduce the length, width and height to inches; multiply these amounts together, and divide this sum by 6171, and it will give, within a fraction, the exact number of shelled bushels of corn in the crib.

WEIGHT OF GRAIN AND PRODUCE, PER BUSHEL.

ARTICLES.	POUNDS.	ARTICLES.	POUNDS
Wheat....	60	Dried Peaches	33
Rye	56	Irish Potatoes	60
Corn, shelled.. ..	56	Sweet Potatoes	60
Corn, in the ear	72	Peas (split)	60
Oats	32	Turnips	55
Barley	48	Blue Grass Seed	10
Beans	62	Clover Seed	60
Beans (Castor)	46	Flax Seed	56
Bran	24	Hemp Seed	44
Buckwheat	52	Timothy Seed	45
Corn Meal	44	Coarse Salt	50
Dried Apples	24	Fine Salt	50
Stone Coal	80	Small Hominy	50
Plastering Hair	7	Pindars, or Goobers	24
Barley Malt	34	Unslacked Lime, 3 bushels to bbl.	
Onions	57		

NUMBER OF TREES OR PLANTS SUFFICIENT TO PLANT AN ACRE, AT VA-
RIOUS DISTANCES APART.

1 by 1	43,560	12 by 12	302
2 by 2	10,890	13 by 13	257
3 by 3	4,840	14 by 14	222
4 by 4	2,722	15 by 15	183
5 by 5	1,742	16 by 16	170
6 by 6	1,210	17 by 17	150
7 by 7	888	18 by 18	134
8 by 8	688	19 by 19	120
9 by 9	537	20 by 20	108
10 by 10	435	25 by 25	69
11 by 11	360	30 by 30	18

DISTANCES FOR PLANTING.

Standard Apples.....30 feet apart. Plums and Necta-
Standard Pears......20 "   "   rines..................15 feet apart.
Dwarf Apples and   Blackberries......... 5 "   "
  Pears.................. 8 "   "   Strawberries......... 1 by 1½ feet.
Peaches...... ....15 "   "

Rates of Postage on Domestic Mail Matter.

The weight of any package sent by mail must not exceed four
pounds.

Letters from one office to another in the States or Territories, 3 cents
if not exceeding ½ oz.; 6 cents if exceeding ½ oz. but not exceeding 1
oz., and so on, charging an additional 3 cents for every additional half
ounce or fraction of half an ounce.

At the Post Office where letters brought by steamboats not employed
in carrying the mail, double rates will be charged, collected at the office of delivery, that is, six cents for single weight if mailed, and 4
cents for single weight if delivered at the office. If such letter has
been prepaid by U. S. stamps at such double rates of postage, no extra
charge will be made; if only partly prepaid by stamps, the balance
will be collected on delivery.

RATES OF POSTAGE ON FIRST CLASS MATTER.

On letters, sealed packages, mail matter wholly or partly in writing,
except book manuscript and corrected proofs passing between authors
and publishers, and except local or drop letters or postal cards; all
printed matter that conveys information, outside of original print; all
matter chargeable with letter postage, but which is so wrapped that it
cannot be examined by postmasters without destroying the wrapper or
envelope; all packages containing matter not chargeable with letter

postage, but in which is inclosed or concealed any letter, memorandum or other thing chargeable with letter postage, or upon which is any writing or memorandum; all matter to which no specific rate of postage is assigned, and manuscript for publication in newspapers, &c., 3 cents for each ½ oz. or fraction thereof. On local or drop letters, at offices where free delivery by carriers is not established, 1 cent for each ½ oz. or fraction thereof.

RATES OF POSTAGE ON SECOND CLASS MATTER.

All newspapers, magazines and periodicals, exclusively in print, and regularly issued from a well-known office of publication, and addressed to regular subscribers, without addition of any mark, sign or writing. A regular subscriber is one who has paid for a publication, or for whom such payment has been made or undertaken to be made by some other person. Single rates: On newspapers, one cent each; on periodicals, not exceeding 2 oz., 2 cents each; on circulars, unsealed, 1 cent each.

RATES OF POSTAGE ON THIRD CLASS MATTER.

The third class embraces all circulars, pamphlets, occasional publications, books, book-manuscript and proof sheets, whether corrected or not, maps, prints, engravings, blanks, flexible patterns, samples and sample cards, photographic paper, letter envelopes, postal envelopes or wrappers, cards, paper, &c., 1 cent for each 2 oz. or fraction thereof. Plain or ornamental photographic representations of different types, seeds, cuttings, bulbs, roots and scions, 1 cent each ounce.

ARTICLES THAT ARE UNMAILABLE.

Packages containing liquids, poisons, glass, explosive chemicals, live animals, sharp pointed instruments, sugar, or any matter liable to deface or destroy the contents of the mail, or injure the person of any one connected with the service; all letters upon the envelope of which, or postal card upon which obscene, scurrilous, or abusive epithets have been written or printed, or lottery circulars, gift concerts, or schemes to deceive the public; also, all lewd pamphlets, books, pictures. &c., are unmailable.

DICTIONARY OF LEGAL TERMS.

Compiled and Condensed from Webster's Unabridged, and Bouvier's Law Dictionary. By the Publishers.

Ab Initio—From the beginning ; entirely ; as to all the acts done ; in the inception.

Ad Damnum—In pleading, the technical name of that part of the writ which contains a statement of the amount of the plaintiff's injury.

Ad Interim—In the meantime.

Ad Litem—For the suit.

Ad Quod Damnum—A writ directed to Sheriff, commanding him to enquire, by a jury, what damage it will be to grant a highway, etc.

Ad Valorem—According to the valuation.

Affidavit—A statement or declaration reduced to writing, and sworn or affirmed to before some officer who has authority to administer an oath.

Affirmance—The confirmation of a voidable act by the party acting, who is to be bound thereby.

Alias—Before ; at another time. An *alias* writ is a writ issued where one of the same kind has been issued *before*, in the same cause.

Alibi—Presence in another place than that described.

Alimony—The allowance which a husband, by order of Court, pays to his wife, living separate from him, for her maintenance.

Amende honorable—Satisfactory apology ; reparation.

Amercement – A pecuniary penalty imposed upon an offender, by a judicial tribunal.

Ancillary—Auxiliary ; subordinate.

Animus—The intention with which an act is done.

Appearance—A coming into Court as a party to a suit, whether as plaintiff or defendant. The formal proceeding by which a defendant submits himself to the jurisdiction of the Court.

Arson—The malicious burning of the house of another.

Assumpsit—A promise or understanding founded on a consideration—oral, in writing, express, or implied. An action to recover damages for a breach of such promise or undertaking.

Attachment—The writ commanding seizure by virtue of a legal process.

Averment—A positive statement of facts, as opposed to an argumentative or inferential one.

Bar, to actions—A perpetual destruction of the action of the plaintiff.

Bench Warrant—A process issued by a Court against a person guilty of some contempt, or indicted for some crime.

Bequest—A gift, by will, of personal property.

Bill of Exceptions—A written statement of objections to the decision of the Court, upon a point of law, made by a party to the cause, and properly certified by the Judge or Court who made the decision.

Bond—An obligation in writing, and under seal.

Bonus—A premium paid to a grantor or vendor.

Bribery—The receiving or offering any undue reward by or to any person whomsoever, whose ordinary profession or business relates to the administration of public justice, in order to influence his behavior in office, and to incline him to act contrary to his duty, and to the known rules of honesty and integrity.

Capias—A writ to arrest the person named therein.

Capias ad respondum—A writ for taking and keeping the defendant to answer the plaintiff in action.

Capias ad faciendum—A writ for the taking and keeping the party named until he gives satisfaction to the party by whom it is issued.

Capias profine—A writ which issued against a defendant who had been fined, and did not discharge the fine according to the judgment.

Capitation—A poll tax.

Caption—The heading of a legal instrument, in which is shown when, where, and by what authority it was taken, found, or executed.

Carte Blanche—Signatures in blank, with authority to fill up, by the very person authorized.

Casus Fortuitus—An inevitable accident; a loss happening in spite of all human effort and sagacity.

Caveat—A notice not to do an act, given to some officer, ministerial or judicial, by a party having an interest in the matter.

Certiorari—A writ to call up the records of an inferior court, or remove a cause there depending, in order that the party may have more sure and speedy justice, or that errors and irregularities may be corrected. It is obtained upon complaint of a party that he has not received justice, or that he cannot have an impartial trial in the inferior court.

Cestui que Trust—He for whose benefit another person is seized of lands or tenements, or is possessed of personal property. He who has a right to a beneficial interest in and out of an estate the legal title to which is vested in another.

Chattel Mortgage—A mortgage of personal property.

Chose in action—A right to receive or recover a debt, or money, or damages for breach of contract, or for a tort connected with contract, but which cannot be enforced without action.

Citation—A writ by which a person is summoned or cited.

Cognizance—Acknowledgment; recognition; jurisdiction; judicial power; hearing a matter judicially.

Commutation—The change of a punishment to which a person has been condemned with a less severe one.

Compound Interest—Interest upon interest—when a sum of money due for interest is added to the principal, and then bears interest.

Compounding a Felony—The act of a party immediately aggrieved, who agrees with a thief or other felon that he will not prosecute him, on condition that he return to him the goods stolen, or who takes a reward not to prosecute.

Contra bonos mores—Against sound morals.

Contumacy—The refusal or neglect of a party accused to appear or answer to a charge preferred against him in a court of justice.

Copyright—The exclusive privilege, secured according to certain legal forms, of printing, publishing, and vending copies of writings and drawings.

Corpus Delicti—The body of the offense, the essence of the crime.

Coverture—The condition or state of a married woman. During coverture the civil existence of the wife is, for many purposes, merged in that of her husband.

Crim. Con.—An abbreviation for criminal conversation, denoting adultery; unlawful sexual intercourse with a married woman.

Days of Grace—Certain days allowed to the acceptor of a bill or the maker of a note in which to make payment, in addition to the time contracted for by the bill or note itself.

De bene esse—Formally; conditionally; provisionally. The examination of a witness *de bene esse* takes place where there is danger of losing the testimony of an important witness from death by reason of age or dangerous illness, or where he is the only witness to an important fact.

De facto—Actually; in fact; in deed. An officer *de facto* is one who performs the duties of an office with apparent right, and under claim and color of an appointment, but without being actually qualified in law so to act.

De jure—Rightfully; of right; lawfully; by legal title.

Demurrer—A stop or pause by a party to an action for the judgment of the court on the question, whether, assuming the truth of the matter alleged by the opposite party, it is sufficient in law to sustain the action or defense, and hence whether the party resting is bound to answer or proceed further.

De Novo—Anew; afresh. When a judgment upon an issue in part is reversed on error for some mistake made by the court in the course of the trial, a *venire de novo* is awarded, in order that the case may again be submitted to the jury.

Debit—The left-hand page of ledger, to which are carried all the articles supplied or paid on the subject of an account, or that are charged to that account; also the balance of an account.

Default—The non-performance of a duty, whether arising under a contract or otherwise.

Defeasance—An instrument which defeats the force or operation of some other deed or estate. That which is in the same deed is a condition; and that which is in another deed is a defeasance.

Defunct—A deceased person.

Demise—A conveyance, either in fee for life or for years.

Deponent—One who gives information, on oath or affirmation, respecting some facts known to him, before a magistrate; he who makes a deposition.

Deposition—The testimony of a witness reduced to writing, in due form of law, by virtue of a commission or other authority of a competent tribunal, to be used on the trial of some question of fact in a court of justice.

Detinue—A form of action which lies for the recovery, in specie, of personal chattels from any one who acquired possession of them lawfully, but retains it without right, together with damages for the detention.—Blackstone.

Devastavit—A mismanagement and waste by an executor, administrator or other trustee, of the estate and effects trusted to him as such, by which a loss occurs.

Devise—A gift of real property by a person's last will and testament.

Dictum—An opinion expressed by a court, but which, not being necessarily involved in the case, lacks the force of an adjudication.

Dilatory Plea—One which goes to defeat the particular action brought merely, but which does not answer as to the general right of the plaintiff.

Disaffirmance—The act by which a person who has entered into a voidable contract, as, for example, an infant, disagrees to such contract and declares he will not abide by it.

Distrain—To take as pledge property of another, and keep the same until he performs his obligation, or until the property is replevied.

Distress—The taking of a personal chattel out of the possession of a wrong-doer into the custody of the party injured, to procure satisfaction for the wrong done.—Blackstone. It is generally resorted to for the purpose of enforcing the payment of rent, taxes, or other duties, as well as to exact compensation for such damages as result from the trespasses of cattle.

Distringas—A writ directed to the sheriff, commanding him to distrain a person of his goods and chattels to enforce a compliance with what is required of him.

Domicil—That place where a man has his true, fixed and permanent home and principal establishment, and to which whenever he is absent he has the intention of returning.

Dower—The provision which the law makes for a widow out of the lands or tenements of her husband, for her support and the nurture of her children.

Duress—Personal restraint, or fear of personal injury or imprisonment.

Easement—A right in the owner of one parcel of land, by reason of such ownership, to use the land of another for a special purpose, not inconsistent with a general property in the owner.

Ejectment—A form of action which lies to regain the possession of real property, with damages for the unlawful detention.

Entail—To restrict the inheritance of lands to a particular class of issue.

Escheat—An accidental reverting of lands to the original lord.

Estoppel—The preclusion of a person from asserting a fact by previous conduct inconsistent therewith, or on his own part or of those under whom he claims, or by an adjudication upon his rights, which he cannot be allowed to call in question.

Ex Cathedra—From the Bench, with high authority.

Ex Delicto—Actions which arise in consequence of a crime, misdemeanor, fault, or tort, are said to arise *ex delicto :* such are actions of case, replevin, trespass, trover.

Ex necessitate rei—From the necessity of the thing.

Execution—A writ by which an officer is empowered to carry a judgment into effect ; final process.

Ex-officio—By virtue of his office.

Ex parte—Of the one part. Many things may be done *ex parte*, when the opposite party has had notice. An affidavit or deposition is said to be taken *ex parte* where only one of the parties attends to taking the same.

Ex post facto—After the act.

Fee simple—An estate of inheritance.

Felo de se—A felon of himself ; a self-murderer. To be guilty of this offense, the deceased must have had the will and intention of committing it, or else he committed no crime.

Femme Covert—A married woman.

Fiat—A short order or warrant, commanding that something shall be done.

Fiduciary—In trust, in confidence.

Fieri facias—A writ directing the Sheriff to cause to be made of the goods and chattels' of the judgment debtor, the sum or debt recovered.

Fiscal—Belonging to the fisc, or public treasury.

Feticide—The act by which criminal abortion is produced.

Functus officio—Something which once has had life and power, but which has become of no virtue whatsoever. When an agent has completed the business with which he was entrusted, his agency becomes *functus officio.*

Garnishment—Warning to a person in whose hands the effects of another are attached, not to pay the money or deliver the goods, but to appear in Court and give information as garnishee.

General issue—In pleading, a plea which denies or traverses, at once, the whole indictment or declaration, without offering any special matter to evade it.

Guardian ad litem—A guardian appointed for the purposes of a suit.

Habeas corpus—A writ to bring into Court a party alleged to be unlawfully imprisoned, with a view, by inquiry, to protect the right to personal liberty.

Habere facias possessionem—A writ of execution in the action of ejectment.

Ibidem—The same. The same book or place. The same subject.

Ides—A day in the month from which the computation of days was made.

Impanel—To draw jurors for trial of a cause.

Implead—To sue or prosecute by due course of law.

Imprimis—In the first place ; commonly used to denote the first clause in an instrument, especially in wills, *item* being used to denote the subsequent clauses.

Indemnity—Security to save harmless ; exemption from loss or damage, past or to come.

In propria persona—In his own person ; himself : as, the defendant appeared *in propria persona ;* the plaintiff argued the case *in propria persona.*

In rem—A technical term used to designate proceedings or actions instituted *against the thing,* in contradistinction to personal actions, which are said to be *in personam.*

In statu quo—In the same situation as; in the same condition as.

Injunction—A prohibitory writ.

Inquest—A body of men appointed by law, to inquire into certain matters.

Interim—In the meantime.

Interlocutory—Something which is done between the commencement and the end of a suit or action, which decides some point or matter, which, however, is not a final decision of the matter in issue, as, interlocuthry judgments, or decrees, or orders.

Ipso facto—By the fact itself ; by the mere fact.

Judgment nisi—A judgment entered on the return of the nisi prius record with the postea indorsed, which will become absolute, according to the terms of the "postea," unless the Court, out of which the nisi prius record proceeded, shall, within the first four days of the following term, otherwise order.

Laches—Negligence.

Lex—The law.

Lex Loci—The law of the place.

Lex Talionis—The law of retaliation.

Mala fides—Bad faith ; opposed to *bona fides,* good faith.

Mandamus—A high prerogative writ, usually issued out of the highest court of general jurisdiction in a State, in the name of the sovereignty, directed to any corporation, public officer, or inferior court, requiring them to do some particular thing therein specified, and which appertains to their office or duty.

Mater familias—The mother of a family ; the mistress of a family; a chaste woman, married or single.

Mayhem—The act of unlawfully and violently depriving another of the use of such of his members as may render him less able, in fighting either to defend himself or annoy his adversary.

Mesne profits—The value of the premises recovered in ejectment, during the time that the lessor of the plaintiff has been illegally kept out of the possession of his estate, by the defendant.

Mittimus, (we send)—A writ to send an offender to prison.

Monition—A process in the nature of a summons.

Mulct—A fine imposed on the conviction of an offense.

Mutatis mutandis—The necessary changes. A phrase of frequent practical occurrence, meaning that matters or things are generally the same, but to be altered when necessary, as to names, offices, and the like.

Nisi—Shall take effect at a given time, unless before that time the order or judgment is modified, or something else is done to prevent its taking effect. Continuance *nisi* is a conventional continuance of the case till next term of the Court, unless otherwise disposed of in the meantime.

Nolle prosequi—That plaintiff discontinues his suit, or attorney for the public a prosecution.

Non assumpsit—The plea of a defendant in an action of assumpsit that "he did not undertake and promise, etc."

Non compus mentis—Not in a sound mind.

Non est inventus—I have not found him.

Novation—The substitution of a new obligation for an old one, which is thereby extinguished.

Nulla bona—The return made to a writ of fieri facias, by the sheriff, when he has not found any goods of the defendant on which he could levy.

Noncupative will—An oral will, declared by testator, *in extremis*, before witnesses, and afterwards reduced to writing.

Order nisi—A conditional order, which is to be confirmed, *unless* something be done, which has been required, by a time specified.

Parol evidence—Evidence verbally delivered by witnesses.

Pater familias—One who was *sui juris*—of his own right—and not subject to the paternal power.

Patricide—One guilty of killing his father.

Per capita—By the head or polls.

Per centum—By the hundred.

Per contra—Contrariwise.

Per se—By itself considered.

Petit—A French word signifying little, small—as petit larceny, petit jury, petit treason.

Plaintiff in error—A party who sues out a writ of error ; and this whether in the Court below he was plaintiff or defendant.

Poaching—Unlawful entering land, in night time, armed with intent to destroy game.

Posse comitatus—The power of the county.

Post facto—After the fact.

Posthumus child—One born after the death of its father.

Post mortem—After death.

Prima facie—On the first view.

Process verbal—A written statement.

Pro confesso—As if conceded. A decree taken where the defendant has either never appeared in the suit, or, having appeared, has neglected to answer.

Pro forma—For the sake of form.

Pro rata—In proportion.

Pro renata—For the occasion as it may arise.

Pro tanto—For as much.

Propria persona—In his own person.

Putative—Reputed to be that which is not—as putative father, putative marriage ; putative wife ; putative owner.

Quid pro quo—What for what—one thing for another—an equivalent. A term denoting the consideration of a contract.

Quo animo—The intent; the mind with which a thing has been done.

Quo Warranto—The name of a writ (and also of the whole pleading) by which the government commences an action to recover an office or franchise from the person or corporation in possession of it.

Recognizance—An obligation of record entered into before some court of record, or magistrate duly authorized, with condition to do some particular act, as to appear at the same or some other court, to keep the peace, or pay a debt. A recognizance differs from a bond, being witnessed by the record only, and not by the party's seal.

Rectus in curia—Upright in court; with clean hands. The condition of one who stands at the bar, against whom no one objects any offense or prefers any charge.

Reductio ad absurdum—A position reduced to an absurdity.

Replevy—A writ to get back goods and chattels wrongfully taken or detained, upon giving security to try the right to them in a suit at law, and, if that should be determined against the plaintiff, to return the property replevied.

Replication—In pleading, the plaintiff's answer to the defendant's plea or answer. In equity, the plaintiff's avoidance or denial of the answer or defense.

Res judicata—A legal or equitable issue which has been decided by a court of competent jurisdiction.

Riparian proprietors—Those who own the land bounding upon a water course.

Rule nisi—A rule obtained on motion *ex parte* to show cause against the particular relief sought.

Scire facias—A writ founded upon some record, and requiring the party proceeded against to show cause why the party bringing it should not have advantage of such record.

Semper paratus—Always ready.

Seriatim—In a series; severally; as the judges delivered their opinions *seriatim*.

Sine die—Without a day appointed.

Status quo—The state in which.

Subornation of perjury—The procuring another to commit legal perjury, who, in consequence of the persuasion, takes the oath to which he has been incited.

Subpœna (under penalty)—A writ commanding the attendance in court of the person on whom it is served as a witness. The process by which a defendant in equity is commanded to appear and answer the plaintiff's bill.

Subpœna duces tecum—A writ of the same kind as the *subpœna testificandum*, including a clause requiring the witness to bring with him and produce to the court books, papers, etc., in his hands, tending to elucidate the matter in issue.

Sui juris—Of his own right. Possessing all the rights to which a freeman is entitled.

Summons—A citation or writ to appear in court on a day specified, to answer to the plaintiff, or to testify as a witness.

Supersedeas—That you set aside. The name of a writ containing a command to stay the proceedings at law.

Sub silentio—Under silence; without any notice being given. Sometimes passing a thing *sub silentio* is evidence of consent.

Superficies—Whatever has been erected on the soil.

Testator—One who has made a testament or will.

Tripartite—Consisting of three parts; as a deed *tripartite* between A. of the first, B. of the second, and C. of the third part.

Trover—A form of action which lies to recover damages against one who has, without right, converted to his own use goods or personal chattels in which the plaintiff has a general or special property.

Turpis casua—A base or vile consideration, forbidden by law, which makes the contract void.

Venditioni exponas—That you expose to sale. The name of a writ of execution directed to the sheriff, commanding him to sell goods or chattels, and in some states, lands, which he has taken in execution by virtue of a *fieri facias*, and which remain unsold.

Venire facias—A writ directed to sheriff requiring him to cause a certain number of qualified persons to appear in court at a specified time, to serve as jurors. A writ in the nature of a summons to cause the party indicted on a penal statute to appear.

Verbatim et literatim—Word for word and letter for letter.

Versus—Against; usually abbreviated *v.* or *vs.*

Vi et armis—With force and arms.

Vice versa—On the contrary; on opposite sides.

Virtute officii—By virtue or his office.

Viva voce—By the living voice; verbally; oral testimony.

INDEX TO FORMS.

IN CIVIL ACTIONS.

25

FORMS—AS A CRIMINAL COURT.

MISCELLANEOUS FORMS.

INDEX TO LAW—AS A CIVIL COURT.

INDEX TO LAW—AS A CRIMINAL COURT.

Crimes and Misdemeanors, Punishable by Fines Alone.

Crimes and Misdemeanors, Punishable by Fines or Imprisonment, or Both.

412   *Index to Criminal Law.*

Penal Suits Triable by Justice.

See " Evidence."

INDEX TO LAW—AS A COURT OF INQUIRY.

(The pages under this head refer to Revised Code of 1871.)

INDEX TO APPENDIX.
